Comparative Education

Exploring Issues in International Context

Patricia K. Kubow
Bowling Green State University

Paul R. Fossum
University of Michigan—Dearborn

Merrill
Prentice Hall

Upper Saddle River, New Jersey
Columbus, Ohio

*To all educators, worldwide,
who commit themselves to enhancing the lives of students*

Library of Congress Cataloging-in-Publication Data

Kubow, Patricia K.
    Comparative education: exploring issues in international context / Patricia K. Kubow,
Paul R. Fossum.
       p. cm.
    Includes bibliographical references and index.
    ISBN 0-13-086848-5
    1. Comparative education.   2. Education—Crosscultural studies.   I. Fossum, Paul R. II.
Title.
LB43 .K85 2003
370′.9—dc21   2002027877

Vice President and Publisher: Jeffery W. Johnston
Executive Editor: Debra A. Stollenwerk
Editorial Assistant: Mary Morrill
Production Editor: JoEllen Gohr
Production Coordination: UG / GGS Information Services, Inc.
Design Coordinator: Diane C. Lorenzo
Cover Designer: Ali Mohrman
Cover photo: Corbis Stock Market
Production Manager: Pamela Bennett
Director of Marketing: Ann Castel Davis
Marketing Manager: Krista Groshong
Marketing Coordinator: Tyra Cooper

This book was set in Berkeley by UG / GGS Information Services, Inc. It was printed and
bound by R. R. Donnelley & Sons Company. The cover was printed by Phoenix Color Corp.

Pearson Education Ltd.
Pearson Education Australia Pty. Limited.
Pearson Education Singapore Pte. Ltd.
Pearson Education North Asia Ltd.
Pearson Education Canada, Ltd.
Pearson Educatión de Mexico, S.A. de C.V.
Pearson Education—Japan
Pearson Education Malaysia Pte. Ltd.
Pearson Education, *Upper Saddle River, New Jersey*

10 9 8 7 6 5 4 3 2
ISBN 0-13-086848-5

Preface

A major purpose of this book is to widen the field of comparative education's influence by articulating the relevance of comparative education to include a larger, practitioner-oriented audience. We believe that the comparative study of education fosters depth of reflection that is not only useful but also necessary for all people engaged in the educative task. At present, however, there are few introductory texts available that acquaint students with comparative education and that equip students with the skills of comparative inquiry to enable systematic exploration of key issues affecting educational policies, practices, and reforms at home and abroad.

Over the past 50 years, the field of comparative education has been moving in the direction of examining education-related issues as opposed to educational systems. This focus is a promising direction for the field, because not only does an issues-oriented approach encourage researchers to compare issues that are affecting education worldwide, but it also has relevancy and currency for in-service and preservice educators whose responsibilities are becoming increasingly challenging in light of diverse sociocultural, political, and economic factors shaping the educational landscape at large.

In light of globalization, the educational dilemmas that one society faces are often issues of importance in other nations as well. A primary benefit of comparative inquiry is that it causes educators, as well as their students, to widen their conceptual lenses to see how seemingly similar issues manifest themselves in diverse settings. Comparative perspective taking enables us to see the issues anew in our home contexts for the purpose of informing our decision making on those issues.

THE BOOK'S CONCEPTUAL FRAMEWORK

This book, then, adopts an issues-oriented approach, emphasizing the comparative perspective. The rationale for a comparative examination of educational issues is to broaden students' views of education and the complex interplay of factors that influence it. The four issues explored here are purposes of schooling, educational access and opportunity, educator accountability and authority, and teacher professionalism. These issues continue to be at the center of public scrutiny and educational debate within and outside the United States. We examine each educational issue in the context of two different countries for purposes of comparison and contrast.

The eight countries and regions of study within this text comprise a diverse and broad set but should not be viewed as a representative sampling of all cultures or countries. Rather, the countries and regions selected highlight the complexity and tensions in education and how culture, politics, economics, and social values coalesce to shape ways in which educational issues are interpreted in various settings. A comparative approach, therefore, helps students identify similarities and differences by calling attention to certain aspects of the educational issue within unique national contexts. A benefit of such an approach is that it broadens the scope and context for the examination of education while exposing students to the current comparative literature. These goals are important to students as they sharpen analysis of and reflection on their own professional practice.

ORGANIZATION OF THE TEXT

The text is divided into three parts. Part 1, titled "*Comparative Education and Underlying Assumptions About Education: The Comparative Approach*," consists of two chapters. In Chapter 1, "*Comparative Education*," we introduce students to the field of comparative education and the field's development and usefulness, and in Chapter 2, "*Theory in Comparative Education*," we discuss prevailing theoretical bases that comparative educators have used to interpret educational policies and practices.

In Part 2, titled "*Education in International Context: A Comparative Approach Applied to Contemporary Educational Issues*," we examine the four selected issues, each in relation to two different countries to foster comparative perspective taking. Chapter 3 undertakes the question of how diverse purposes of schooling shape educational curriculum in Hong Kong and Israel. In Chapter 4, we examine challenges to educational access and opportunity in Brazil and South Africa. In Chapter 5 we explore the changing relationship between education and the state and how this affects education accountability and authority in England and Germany. The focus of Chapter 6 is upon different orientations to the issue of teacher professionalism and the ways these perspectives affect teacher autonomy and professional development in Japan and the United States.

Part 3, titled "*Interpreting Educational Issues: Comparison and the Use of Analytic Frameworks*," consists of two chapters. In Chapter 7, "*Applying Frameworks to Analyze Educational Issues*," we encourage students to use frameworks, drawn from diverse disciplines, for systematic investigation and analysis of educational issues. The chapter provides a brief summary of the four frameworks discussed previously in the text. We place the frameworks in graphic organizers with questions to stimulate further thinking. Our purpose in this chapter is to suggest how the frameworks, whose usefulness is demonstrated throughout the entire text, are also effective in helping students consider issues in domestic and localized contexts. Instructors might want to use Chapter 7 earlier in the term to introduce students to each framework prior to their reading of the issue-oriented chapters and/or to generate student assignments. Finally, Chapter 8, "*The Value of Comparative Education*," summarizes benefits of comparative perspective taking and an issues orientation for the field. An innate feature of an issue is that there is a plurality of responses. Because multiple responses are possible for any given question or situation, answers to questions undertaken yield ambiguous responses. Teachers and teacher educators need to be able to recognize these ambiguities and become comfortable enough to move ahead in their practice.

FEATURES OF THE TEXT

To help students view these educational issues in their complexity and to aid in-depth reflection, we use specific **analytic frameworks** to study the educational issues and provide students with a systematic method for examination. The frameworks emerge from diverse disciplines and fields (e.g., political science, educational policy, sociology) and can be applied to other issues of interest to the reader in order to foster critical thinking—the suspension of judgment in order to draw on multiple perspectives. This leads to better understanding of factors affecting the educational issue or phenomenon being studied and to better informed educational reform efforts. The goal is for students to see that education can be better understood when viewed from multiple perspectives and disciplines.

Each chapter includes various pedagogical features, including focusing and closing questions. The "**Focusing Questions**" at the beginning of each chapter serve to identify the particular aspects of the issue to be addressed in the chapter, and the closing statements, termed "**Sustaining Reflection**," that appear at the end of each chapter serve as launching points for further reflection. The book's glossary identifies key terms and definitions that students using a comparative approach should be familiar with and that will aid their understanding of the issues presented.

The text also has a number of special features, including boldface terms and boxed features. In each chapter, key terms appear in boldface with their accompanying definitions. **Biographical sketches** of historical and contemporary comparative educators are featured throughout the text. These help to familiarize students with three international and three American comparative educators who have used international perspectives to guide domestic educational efforts, providing new perspectives on sometimes familiar individuals. "**Points of Convergence**," another boxed feature, appear in the issues chapters within Part 2 and provide readers with side-by-side comparisons of featured countries, with respect to such things as their demographic, geophysical, and sociopolitical factors.

In summary, this text seeks to (1) broaden the scope and context for examining educational issues through an international comparative approach; (2) increase understanding by examining underlying assumptions of education policies, practices, and reforms; (3) encourage multiple perspective taking by viewing educational issues in light of diverse cultural and historical contexts and through interdisciplinary lenses; and (4) employ specific analytic frameworks to "see" educational issues in new ways. The overall goal of these approaches and features is to foster comparative and critical thinking to better inform educational reform efforts.

We hope that professors, teacher practitioners, teacher educators, curriculum developers, and school administrators find that this book stimulates reflection and helps to inform their own personal and professional decision making.

ACKNOWLEDGMENTS

The authors are indebted to a number of people who contributed to this book's creation. For helping ground our thinking in the field of comparative and international education, we are thankful to have benefited from the mentorship and guidance of members of the faculty at the University of Minnesota, especially Drs. John Cogan, Josef Mestenhauser, and R. Michael Paige. Drs. Jane Plihal, Barry Sullivan, and Marion Lundy-Dobbert have also stimulated our thinking about education.

We have also benefited from the able assistance of graduate assistants at Bowling Green State University, namely Mr. Jason Stoots and Dr. Xuelun Liang, for gathering data for this work; and, in particular, Mr. Zhong-Chi Song, for his commitment and efforts to this project over a two-year period. Similarly, discussions in graduate and undergraduate classrooms at Bowling Green State University and University of Michigan–Dearborn— with students too numerous to single out—have similarly stimulated our thinking and direction.

The following reviewers gave us important advice on drafts of our work at various stages, and the text benefits greatly as a result of this input: Carolyn Babione, Indiana University Southeast; Diane L. Brook, University of Georgia; Denise Davis, Ursuline College; James C. Lawlor, Towson University; Elena Lisovskaya, Western Michigan University; Richard R. Renner, University of Florida; Fred J. Rodriguez, California State University, Dominguez Hills; Kim Sebaly, Kent State University; and Robert C. Serow, North Carolina State University. Moreover, Debra A. Stollenwerk, Executive Editor at Merrill/Prentice Hall, has been supportive in creating and sustaining a comfortable environment for our creative work.

Finally, we thank Shirley Kubow; Jennifer, Samuel, and Leah Fossum; Mary Kubow; and Richard and Rosemary Fossum for their support and encouragement in seeing the book to completion.

About the Authors

Dr. Patricia K. Kubow is an Assistant Professor in Educational Foundations and Inquiry at Bowling Green State University in Bowling Green, Ohio. Her scholarship is focused on comparative and international education, democratic citizenship education, teacher education, educational policy, and comparative higher education.

Dr. Paul R. Fossum is an Assistant Professor in the School of Education at the University of Michigan–Dearborn. His scholarship is focused on comparative and international education, teacher education, social aspects of education technology, and institutional cooperation in higher education.

Brief Contents

Contents

Part 2   Education in International Context: A Comparative Approach Applied to Contemporary Educational Issues   59

Comparative Education and Underlying Assumptions about Education: The Comparative Approach

Part I consists of two chapters (chapters 1–2) to introduce students to the field of comparative education and to identify theories guiding comparative educators.

- **Chapter 1: Comparative Education**
  This chapter introduces students to the field of comparative education and the field's development and usefulness.

- **Chapter 2: Theory in Comparative Education**
  This chapter discusses prevailing theoretical bases that comparative educators have used to interpret educational policies and practices.

Comparative Education

Focusing Questions

- What is comparative education? What are the benefits of comparative study?
- What is the function of a discipline? How is an academic discipline different from a field?
- Curiosity or interest in the unknown is an important step in getting people to engage in comparative educational inquiry. What regarding education interests you?
- What are the constraints to pursuing reflection?

INTRODUCTION

Nations have long viewed education as an important factor in both individual and societal development. With growing national concern about how to position one's country for a prominent place on the global stage, schools face increasing demands to meet a number of often conflicting goals. Diverse stakeholders view schooling differently, and this creates tensions over educational content, instruction, structure, and outcomes. The debate encompasses manifold concerns such as the following:

- Egalitarian concern for educational quality and the opening of opportunity for more and more students
- Economic concern for equipping students with appropriate workplace competencies and skills
- Civic concern for educating citizens who can participate effectively in public life in increasingly pluralistic environments
- General humanistic concern for developing the whole person through a process of lifelong education.

Due to the higher stakes within this increasingly globalized world, schools have come under greater national scrutiny regarding the ways they can contribute to or hinder a nation's progress. Calls for greater school accountability and educational reform, both in the United States and abroad, have led to a questioning of the education profession itself. The heightened interest in and concern over education has prompted educators to reexamine, in light of new global realities, the purposes of schooling, the underlying assumptions about the relationship between education and development, and questions about educator professionalism.

Although each successive generation has had to deal with the complex interplay of social, cultural, political, and economic factors and their impact on education, what will distinguish educational debates and reforms in the first part of the 21st century will be how nations will educate students for a global world in light of nation-state allegiances. To illustrate, technology and mass communication are challenging the notion of national boundaries, changing economic relationships, fostering greater interdependence, and challenging citizens to reconsider their loyalties and identities. The question of how technology might affect educational access and opportunity will need to be examined and possible solutions sought in light of local, national, *and* global contexts.

To aid in this critical examination of education, this text offers an issues-oriented approach to examine in international context selected themes of educational importance. This approach emphasizes at least four premises. First, educational issues rather than educational systems become the centerpiece for critical study. Because, as they perform their work, teachers largely take for granted organizational systems and structures, they do not necessarily deal meaningfully with predicaments and decisions that tend to shape the professional world of teaching. Second, the central issues are conceived of as educational dilemmas rather than as problems. This is appropriate because it focuses on the ways teachers need to seek balance and thoughtful responses for which simpler, unidimensional solutions are not available. Third, these issues are examined cross-culturally in order to broaden and deepen understanding of the issues and, in turn, to enable personal improvements of educational practice. Fourth, the text uses analytic frameworks to systematically critique the educational issues.

The enduring, yet contemporary, educational issues that steer the book's organization include differing purposes of schooling, educational access and opportunity, educational accountability and autonomy, and teacher professionalism. These particular issues are and have been at the center of public scrutiny and debate within *and* outside the United States. Because issues connote debate, clearer identification of and focus on issues provides insights into the negotiation that characterizes modern democracy.

The primary rationale, then, for examining educational issues in a comparative manner is to broaden perspective and sharpen the reader's focus. Moreover, the ways in which educators in different countries view these issues and the strategies employed to address them must be understood in light of differing cultural, social, and political contexts in each country. We do not advocate, therefore, the wholesale adoption of one country's strategy by another country. Rather, we take the view that awareness and understanding of the *theoretical and philosophical assumptions* underlying educational issues and educational reform in various nations are necessary for thoughtful, informed *educational practice* in each nation.

The countries examined in this text (Brazil, England, Germany, Hong Kong Special Administrative Region, Israel, Japan, South Africa, and the United States) were chosen as a way to provide diversity and breadth in the exploration of some enduring, important issues in education. The countries selected are not meant to be a representative sampling of all cultures, but rather a way for the reader to consider tensions or dilemmas that surround education and how culture shapes the way in which the educational issue is perceived, understood, and addressed in a particular country. By viewing the educational issue from the perspective of two diverse countries, the reader can identify factors that might be missed when viewing the issue within the context of his or her own country alone.

Specifically, in this text, the reader will learn how diverse purposes of schooling shape education in Hong Kong and Israel, how challenges to educational access and opportunity influence schooling in Brazil and South Africa, how the changing relationship between educators and the state shapes educator accountability and authority in England and Germany, and how different orientations to teacher professionalism in Japan and the United States affect teacher autonomy and professional development. By examining issues in international perspective, readers will begin to recognize that the issues span national boundaries and that people of every nation wrestle with disjunctures between their societal ideals and their educational realities.

It is our desire that this text will help readers explore educational challenges in an in-depth, critical way. Through multiple, cultural perspective taking (i.e., issues across several nations) and analytic frameworks from a variety of disciplines (e.g., political science, sociology, psychology), the text provides an international context as well as tools for opening and widening readers' lenses to enhance their ways of "seeing" education. Each analytic framework is described and applied to an educational issue. The frameworks also serve as freestanding devices that readers can apply to other educational issues. In this way, readers are exposed to numerous frameworks to help them analyze educational issues, as well as being provided with specific examples that demonstrate how the frameworks can be used to systematically critique educational issues.

IDENTIFYING THE FIELD: A HISTORICAL LOOK AT COMPARATIVE EDUCATION

What Is Comparative Education?

In general, "comparative education has developed as a field devoted broadly to the study of education in other countries" (Kelly, Altbach, & Arnove, 1982, p. 505). **Comparative education** draws upon multiple disciplines (e.g., sociology, political science, psychology, anthropology) to examine education in developed and developing countries. Comparative inquiry often leads to an examination of the role that education plays in individual and national development. It also encourages us to question our educational systems and to examine how societal values influence our attitudes about education and how we educate. Questions, such as "Is education a benevolent agent of change?" "Is education a mirror of the larger society, manifesting through its structure, curriculum, and pedagogy inherent inequalities?" "Do educational practices maintain societal status quo?", can help citizens see the disparities between beliefs about the purposes of education and the consequences—intended and unintended—of the education these societies provide. Comparative education and the critical perspective taking that comparative inquiry affords can help bring the interested inquirer into a deeper examination of the tensions among society, development, and education and the role that citizens, either directly or indirectly, play in the educative process.

Comparative education centers on the study of education from cross-cultural, cross-national perspectives. Trethewey (1976) has stated that comparative education "may take the form of a study of responses in other societies to problems that appear very [much] like the ones you recognise in your own educational system" (p. 2). Although comparative education provides an opportunity to explore natural human curiosity about foreign cultures and the education systems those societies support, many have stressed that exploring the value systems of other countries through use of comparative education might provide a refreshed capacity to appraise a person's own culture and educational values. The forces affecting education—and that education, in turn, affects—can be divided into a number of different dimensions: the political, the economic, the sociocultural, and the technological. By focusing on the tenuous relationships between education and these dimensions, comparative study brings greater clarity and insight to educational policies and practices.

As a result of increasing concern over the difficulties nations face internally and externally, education is seen as playing an important role in national progress and globalization. Epstein (1983) suggests that comparative education is not just an academic exercise but has practical utility in the reform of schooling. Thus, not only can comparative education deepen understanding through critical questioning, but a practical benefit can be derived from comparative study as well.

Comparison—a process of studying two or more things to see how they are alike or different—gives attention to certain aspects through the copresence of the other (Eckstein, 1983). Comparative thinking and international perspective taking are essential for citizens to get along in a diverse, global society. Comparison challenges students to suspend judgments of those foreign systems that they might base on their own limited and localized perspectives. Through the development of comparative thinking skills, students should be able to undertake analyses of their home cultures and systems with a more nuanced understanding of the various cultural factors at play.

Comparative education also encourages students and educators to ask, "What kinds of educational policy, planning, and teaching are appropriate for what kind of society?" The field of comparative education focuses our attention on what might be appropriate and inappropriate policy, while fostering awareness of the **ideologies** (defined as systematized bodies of ideas) underlying educational practice. Hence, comparative study can also cultivate a political consciousness.

Broadfoot (1977) and Parkyn (1977) asserted that comparative education is a field, not a discipline. This is an important distinction because, within the specific disciplines, there is a tendency to favor one prescribed method of examination. The word **discipline** itself connotes dedication to a specified set of rules and standards. Any discipline's adherents dedicate themselves to techniques and procedures belonging to that discipline while implicitly or explicitly rejecting methods and techniques of other paths. Along with the rigorous adherence to discipline-specific inquiry comes a tendency to subordinate or dismiss other disciplinary perspectives and thereby limit understanding. Comparative education, however, assumes no such hierarchy; rather, as a **field**, it draws upon a variety of disciplines to better understand the complexity of particular educational phenomena.

Thus, comparative education serves as a device that helps to mediate the relationships among the foundations of education (e.g., history, philosophy, sociology) and challenges students to consider the interplay of philosophical, historical, and sociological factors as they analyze the educational approaches of foreign cultures.

Inherent in human thinking, comparison helps to extend and deepen our understanding of the world; it is a way to advance our total capacity to think (Eckstein, 1983). Thus, comparative thinking is a worthy end in itself. When applied to education, comparison helps students examine particular theories or models put forth to explain educational phenomena and encourages interdisciplinary critique (Klein, 1990, 1996). Comparative education also has practical usefulness in that it helps educators decide what issues are of primary importance and what factors must be considered in order to potentially improve educational practice (Epstein, 1983).

Thus, comparative thinking is an essential skill. It is a useful device for developing the ability to think deeply and comparatively about the political, economic, social, and cultural landscape affecting education, as well as education's influence on that landscape. Although the issues might change in the years ahead, the development of comparative thinking and the ability to use analytic frameworks for critique will remain imperative.

Comparative Education: The Field's Historical Development

Each of several historical stages of the development of comparative education is "characterized by a different motive for comparative study" (Noah & Eckstein, 1998, p. 15). In the first stage of comparative education—which has been called "the period of travelers' tales" (Noah & Eckstein, 1998, p. 15)—curiosity and interest in the unknown prompted exploration of different parts of the world. In the same way that today's tourists share anecdotes regarding their travels, people in this period shared observations about cultural practices and customs that included educational habits.

A second stage of comparative education, associated with the 19th century, featured educational borrowing (Gutek, 1993; Noah & Eckstein, 1998). In this stage, educators traveled to different nations to specifically observe foreign school systems. Their motive was to identify what techniques and practices might be useful in their own countries. These comparative studies examined educational systems, specifically the structure, organization, and method of education in other countries. These visitors—educators and politicians—based their judgments regarding the societal values observed on their own impressions of other cultures. Comparative scholars have suggested that the comparative education literature during this time was primarily descriptive and uncritical of educational systems in other countries.

To illustrate, Horace Mann, American pioneer of the common school movement, visited Germany (then Prussia), in addition to England, France, Holland, Ireland, and Scotland. Prussian education, which was of particular interest to Mann, as a source of ideas for American schools, had in turn been shaped by Humboldt's effort to borrow and develop philosophies and methods of the Swiss educator Johann Heinrich Pestalozzi (Hahn, 1998). Mann's *Seventh Report* (1843) compared the organization and instructional methods of each school observed (Hans, 1967). While acknowledging differences between the political and social makeup of Germany and the United States, Mann felt that significant features of the Prussian system might be helpful in improving American education (Trethewey, 1976). However, Mann provided "limited discussion of cultural contexts in which attractive ideas or practices had developed and into which they would be transplanted" (Trethewey, 1976, p. 17). Although the report might have been "the first attempt at assessing educational values" (Hans, 1967, p. 2), it neither addressed the context in which education occurred nor focused on larger educational issues across these countries. For a biographical sketch of prominent American educator, Horace Mann, see page 9.

Marc-Antoine Jullien de Paris, in contrast to Mann, was meticulous in inventorying his detailed observations of foreign education systems. Although Jullien de Paris is sometimes called "the first scientifically minded comparative educator" (Bereday, 1964, p. 7) because of his more systematic approach, his end product was still descriptive of a foreign education system and was aimed at paving the way for importation of educational practices. With Jullien de Paris, as with other borrowers, "taking educational systems of one country and moving them wholesale to another was thought feasible in the nineteenth century" (Bereday, 1964, p. 7). In sum, educational borrowers had pragmatic purposes in mind: The observations of these borrowers "were *utilitarian* in purpose and also *melioristic*, in the sense that they were based on certain *a priori* values concerning ways of improving education" (Trethewey, 1976, p. 17).

The work of Jullien de Paris foreshadowed a trend toward systematic and scientific methods in comparative education. Noah and Eckstein (1998) asserted that comparative education in the 20th century sought to distinguish the forces shaping foreign educational systems and to employ quantitative methods to explain education–society relationships. At the beginning of the 20th century, Michael Sadler argued "for the acceptance of the principle that each educational system is not readily detachable but is instead intricately connected with the society that supports it" (Bereday, 1964, p. 7). Thus, there was a growing concern that serious sociocultural considerations limited the educational borrowing previously promoted. This realization was often accompanied by a tentativeness to expand analysis beyond Western country comparisons, resulting in comparative educators limiting their purview of study to countries that shared somewhat similar historical and cultural backgrounds and to topics that could be more easily controlled and quantified. For example, over the course of three decades of comparative collaboration, Noah and Eckstein (1998) restricted their study of education primarily to scientific comparisons between Western countries in relation to teacher qualifications and training, business–industry–school linkages, educational achievement measures, national examinations, and educational standards.

The movement toward more control-oriented approaches to comparative education reflected, and to some extent echoed, developments within the social sciences in general. Popkewitz (1994) has pointed out that societal issues in the United States—such as labor conflicts, urbanization, and challenges related to cultural, religious, and ethnic integration—brought with them a press toward sciences of pedagogy that were intended to alleviate these societal strains. There was faith that in overcoming these problems "the social sciences could assure the same material and social progress that had been gained through the natural sciences" (Popkewitz, 1994, p. 5). The societal disruptions of the early 20th-century United States are characteristic of societies worldwide, particularly those in developing

Horace Mann (1796–1859)

Arguably, one of the most prominent figures in American education is Horace Mann, born in Franklin, Massachusetts, at the end of the 18th century. Referred to by many as "the father of the public school," Mann was a key proponent of common schools (or free public elementary schools) in the United States. Mann, and other advocates of the common school movement, argued that schools could provide a way for poor children, children with disabilities, and children of color to raise their social condition, irrespective of birth and socioeconomic background. The common schools, it was reasoned, would serve as the "great social equalizer" with benefits at both the individual and societal level. At the individual level, Mann argued that children from low socioeconomic classes would gain knowledge and skills to foster their **social mobility** (the ability to raise their socioeconomic standing); at the societal level, a skilled labor force would stimulate economic growth and enable citizens to participate in political processes.

The common school movement witnessed tremendous growth between 1820 and 1920, and its proponents viewed the schools as a way to provide American children equal chances for success (Ornstein & Levine, 2000). To business and industry, Mann emphasized that common schools would create a more educated workforce, hence a practical goal of schooling; from a more idealized perspective, common schools would develop the talents of both wealthy and poor children and foster social harmony (Sadker & Sadker, 2000). Thus, the notion of social mobility through the obtainment of a quality education is not a new concept (Ryan & Cooper, 1998).

Known for his oratory skills as a lawyer and as a member of the Massachusetts House of Representatives, Mann used his knowledge of the political system to foster educational reform when, from 1837 to 1848, he served as Secretary to the Massachusetts State Board of Education. Through public lectures, his *Annual Reports*, and the semimonthly *Common School Journal*, Mann advocated new and better-equipped school buildings, the elimination of corporal punishment in schools, and the separation of religion from public schooling. Rather, moral values, such as honesty, were to guide learning and instruction. Mann's belief in the school's centrality in establishing values and the state's role in deciding and inculcating them in children (Tozer, Violas, & Senese, 1998) was shaped, in part, through his travel to Prussia.

The Prussian education system in the 1820s was based on a model purported by Johann Fichte, a German philosopher, during Napoleon's occupation of Prussia (Tozer, Violas, & Senese, 1998). Of most interest to Mann was the Prussian elementary *Volkshule* (people's school). State-financed, universal, and compulsory, the *Volkshule* emphasized basic literacy and the development of patriotic citizens. Moreover, Prussian teachers underwent training at normal schools. The concept of a free, state-controlled school for commoners and teacher training through normal schools were both advocated by Mann. These concepts helped shape the course of public education and teacher training in the United States. In 1823, the first American state-supported normal school was established in Lexington, Massachusetts. The normal school provided elementary teachers two years of training focused more on pedagogical approaches and less on subject content.

Throughout his life, Mann continued to seek the improvement of the individual and national social condition through obtaining public education for all people. In 1852, Mann became president of Antioch College, whose doors were opened to women, all races, and people with diverse religious backgrounds. Some educators who feared that equitable access would bring about the collapse of American higher education criticized Mann for his open door policy.

countries as they have taken on industrialization and nation-building efforts. Accordingly, the same rationale in favor of control-oriented conceptions of social science have characterized their growth and have influenced the field of comparative education.

Although the search for "the best ideas and practices" (Trethewey, 1976, p. 15) is still a preoccupation of comparative education scholars today, it has been tempered with an awareness that what works in one country might not necessarily work in another. Therefore, comparative educators have become more sensitive to indiscriminate borrowing and have come to play a more evaluative role, recognizing that successful implementation of any educational policy and practice depends upon the cultural, historical, and socioeconomic forces operating within and among countries. "The concept of educational systems as organic and dynamic components of society is basic to present day studies and a constant warning against uncritical or piecemeal borrowing" (Trethewey, 1976, p. 19). Wholesale adoption of education is seen to be shortsighted, whereas the process of "interpreting observed practices *in context*, and of judging or predicting whether a particular arrangement or practice could be transplanted successfully in the home environment" (p. 17, italics added) is encouraged.

In the wake of these 20th century developments, one might identify a third and more recent stage in the historical development of comparative education, namely a period of international cooperation, in that comparative education contributes to international peace and understanding (Arnove & Torres, 1999). Such cooperation has been viewed as necessary for world harmony and for the improvement of the quality of citizens' lives. International cooperation has taken the form of sharing of educational knowledge, such as content, pedagogy, structures, processes, and research methods, to expand provision of formal education worldwide. The degree to which there has been a reciprocal relationship of sharing between countries, with each making decisions in light of what is best for development in one's own nation, however, is questionable.

A pressing need in the post-World War I and World War II era has been for education to serve national economic and political development. Isaac Kandel, writing in the first part of the 20th century, emphasized the political dimension and its impact on education. He was especially concerned "with the effects of nationalism and the prospects for internationalism" (Trethewey, 1976, pp. 19–20). Some countries, having received independence from colonizers in recent years, have experienced new forms of imperialism, as evidenced by international aid agreements between developed and developing countries. These **neocolonial** linkages (defined as colonial-like exploitation even after a nation has achieved independence) raise questions regarding the extent to which education might be reflective of policies and practices particular to developed nations, thereby increasing their susceptibility to homogenizing tendencies of Westernization.

Although the classifications of traveler's tales, educational borrowing, and international cooperation help to delineate particular stages in comparative education's development as a field, it is important to recognize that all three of these stages often occur simultaneously as educators study people of other cultures and countries. Curiosity, a concern for practical usefulness of educational concepts "back home," and exchange of information among diverse cultures illustrates the complex dynamics at play when people engage in comparative inquiry.

Conceptualizing Comparative Education: Definitions and Purposes

Major figures in comparative education have conceived of comparative education in different ways. George Bereday, for example, defined comparative education as the analytical examination of education systems in other countries. Bereday (1964) saw comparative education as playing first and foremost an "intellectual purpose" whose aim was "to search for lessons that can be deduced from the variations in educational practice in different societies" (p. xi). In addition to learning about other peoples and cultures, comparative education helps one to know about oneself. As Bereday explained, "It is self-knowledge born of the awareness of others that is the finest lesson comparative education can afford" (Bereday, 1964, p. 6).

Isaac Kandel strove to understand the historical forces within particular nations that might account for the differences between national education; his research centered on elements within school systems, such as school organization, curriculum, and finance (Trethewey, 1976). Kandel (1933), pursuing the notion of national character, treated comparative education "as a branch of politics, using the term in the sense in which it was used by the earliest educational theorists—Plato and Aristotle" (p. xxv). Education, according to Kandel, could not be understood as functional classroom procedures; rather, education must be interpreted "as a part of the activity of humanity, organized into nations, for its own preservation and progress" (p. xxv). Kandel believed that comparative education could lead to a greater appreciation for and understanding of other countries, as well as one's own, and lead ultimately to "the development of an internationalism" (p. xxv). From Kandel's perspective, internationalism was one of comparative education's major contributions.

For Nicholas Hans, the purpose of comparative education was to find solutions to national problems. Historical analysis provided the method by which comparative educators could ascertain such solutions. Hans was concerned with "the role school systems play in contributing to cultural continuity and the maintenance of the nation-state" (Kelly, Altbach, & Arnove, 1982, p. 510). Characteristics, such as unity of race, religion, language, territory, and political sovereignty, formed the nation-state and national character. Extending his analysis further, Hans (1967) argued that national systems, like constitutions and literatures of a nation, formed the "outward expression of national character and as such [represented] the nation in distinction from other nations" (p. 9). Therefore, nations could be comparatively analyzed by examining three factors: natural factors (e.g., race, language, environment), religious factors (e.g., established religious denominations, such as Catholicism, Anglicanism, Puritanism), and secular factors (values reflected such as humanism, nationalism, and socialism).

According to Hans (1967), "only the study of their historical development and their functional role in the social life of a particular nation [could] give a true insight into their values and thus lead to a valid comparison" (p. 8). As a result of Hans's work, "functional analysis of school/society relations become well entrenched in the field" (Kelly, Altbach, & Arnove, 1982, p. 510). In more recent years, the notion of national character accounting for differences in a country's educational practices has been viewed with skepticism by those who favor more positivistic approaches to the study of education. The following comment by Philip Foster (1998) illustrates the more cautionary way in which some researchers have come to view the concept of national character:

> I still believe that the whole question of the degree of symmetry between social structures and personality systems is still important; but [focusing on national character] might raise the eyebrows of hard-nosed sociologists who would regard the conclusions as little more than very plausible hypotheses hardly susceptible to controlled investigation. (p. 5)

As can be ascertained from some of the prominent educators of the 19th and 20th centuries, comparative education has largely centered on comparisons of national educational systems in an attempt to promote international understanding, to improve or reform education at home or abroad, and to determine what accounts for the differences among educational systems (Kelly, Altbach, & Arnove, 1982). As Kelly, Altbach, and Arnove (1982) surmise, "comparison of national educational systems defined the field and it was a definition based on method rather than on the content of study" (p. 509).

During the 1960s and 1970s, Harold Noah and Max Eckstein advocated identifying and perfecting a discrete methodological foundation for the field of comparative education. The **methodology**, understood as the kind of reasoning applied to scientific or philosophical inquiry, they promoted was one that would enable researchers to generalize findings and form law-like principles that governed the relationships between schools and societies. "Comparative education in its most recent phase," claimed Noah and Eckstein (1998), "emerges as the attempt to use cross-national data to test propositions about the relationship between education and society and between teaching practices and learning outcomes" (p. 19). Choosing the scientific method, then, as the appropriate method for the field was viewed as a way to increase comparative education's credibility as a field of study among social scientists and to demonstrate comparative education's relevance and usefulness to educational policy planners, administrators, and funders (Tretheway, 1976).

Noah and Eckstein defined comparative education as the "intersection of the social sciences, education and cross-national study" (Trethewey, 1976, p. 2). However, as Kelly, Altbach, and Arnove (1982) have explained, "not all scholars accepted a definition of the field by its method. Some argued that this was folly, for comparative education was intrinsically a multidisciplinary undertaking that focuses on school/society relations from varying perspectives" (p. 513). Edmund King (1968) argued against law-like generalizations, stating that comparative education was to be concerned with "approximations and contingencies, not laws" (p. 51). King (1968) contended that one cannot dismiss "the human and the socio-cultural element which so often defies predictability" (p. 62). Claiming that schools are social organisms composed of unautomated human interactions, King (1968) proposed that "a forward-looking comparative research" (p. 59) considers both the rationality and half-rationality of those who inhabit schools and those who study them.

By the late 1970s, content (e.g., school outcomes and the relationships between school and society), as opposed to method, "was the thread that held the field together" (Kelly, Altbach, & Arnove, 1982, p. 514). Scholars, such as Michael Apple (1978), devoted greater attention to the internal workings of schools, examining curriculum and pedagogy for ways in which schooling processes maintain inequities and hide particular interests (e.g., interests of an economic or political nature). In an attempt to better understand how schooling privileges and disadvantages particular groups of students, critical inquiry challenges educators to consider who benefits from educational reforms and what kind of knowledge and whose culture is valued in the school. This kind of critical questioning encourages one to consider the underlying assumptions of schooling and to reflect upon the gaps between the stated educational objectives of schools (often asserted in a school's mission statement) and the actual outcomes of schooling. The image of a mirror as a metaphor for education is a powerful one. As Bereday (1964) has explained, how a country educates its citizens might be indicative of the degree to which it values its children.

> Education is a mirror held against the face of a people. Nations may put on blustering shows of strength to conceal political weakness, erect grand facades to conceal shabby backyards, and profess peace while secretly arming for conquest, but how they take care of their children tells us unerringly who they are. (Bereday, 1964, p. 5)

During the 1980s, greater attention was given to the study of educational expansion and reform in different countries and to the equality of educational opportunities and outcomes afforded different groups in various parts of the world. Comparative educators studied such topics as educational reform, society-socioeconomic-school relationships, and ethnic group concerns (Kelly, Altbach, & Arnove, 1982). Likewise, these concerns prevailed in the 1990s. Inquiry into the nation-state, social movements, conceptions of equity, educational control, and centralization-decentralization tendencies continue to receive scholarly attention from those within the field (Arnove & Torres, 1999).

Although a legitimate goal of comparative education is to learn about other countries and their systems of education in their own right, comparative education also contributes to theory building about education-societal relations and to practical application of research to improve education. The ultimate purpose of comparative inquiry for some is to foster "international understanding and cooperation, and the resolution of educational and other problems of an international kind" (Trethewey, 1976, p. 27). Comparative education's contribution is to help one identify and understand the educational ideas, practices, and processes of other countries in an effort to better understand the factors affecting an educational issue in one's own country. "As its final aim, comparative education hopes to relax national pride to permit events and voices from abroad to count in the continued reappraisal and re-examination of schools" (Bereday, 1964, p. 7). The purposes, concerns, and appropriate methods of study in comparative education, however, are matters of continuing debate in the field as a whole (Trethewey, 1976).

TAKING STOCK: A CRITICAL APPRAISAL OF COMPARATIVE EDUCATION

In his historical analysis of the United States during the early 20th century, Popkewitz (1994) noted that the country witnessed growing faith in the idea that human learning and activities could be improved through inquiry rooted in scientific approaches like those from the natural sciences. The so-called hard sciences, after all, had formed a foundation for vast technological innovation during this era, helping people overcome limitations imposed by their physical environment.

Transportation, architecture, and mass communication are all examples of the improvements that this era rendered. Along with the industrial and commercial growth that the technical sciences spurred came a host of pressing social challenges. These included issues such as work readiness in an increasingly industrialized age and coping with the unknowns associated with growing urbanization. In keeping with the *Zeitgeist* of scientifically assisted progress, a prevailing expectation was that the scientific model—if rigorously applied within the disciplines of the emerging social sciences—could help people overcome these societal challenges just as surely as it had assisted technological progress.

The emerging social sciences, as in the natural sciences, stressed the specialized role of the researcher. Thus, the production of the knowledge deemed most useful in social institutions like schools became associated with a relatively constricted circle of academicians and administrators. This had important consequences. It meant, most obviously, that leadership and expertise were placed in the hands of people who were not by and large directly engaged with educational practice. Second, the nature of the pedagogy as defined by this inner circle was suited for evaluation of practice through quantifiable means. Critics, like Popkewitz (1994), have called this orientation "**instrumentalization**" because it favors a stepwise attention to procedural concerns rather than to context-sensitive approaches that many experienced educators characterize as the essence of teaching.

A closer look at the nature of instrumentalization reveals several characteristics that affect the ways in which teaching continues to be conceived and evaluated as a result of history:

- Control orientation: Emphasis is placed on predictability and instructional replicability rather than classroom solutions that often warrant context laden understanding.
- Externality: Recommendations for classroom practice are outputs of a scientific process that relies on specialized expertise, controlled settings, and the consequent exclusion of practitioners.
- Fragmentation: Effectiveness is defined externally and in advance of the contexts practitioners encounter; challenges of practice therefore become failures of practitioners' execution of prescriptions, and devaluing of a more holistic appraisal that accounts for the dynamics of teaching results.

The Constraints of Instrumentalism

What if knowledge pertinent to educational practice had been conceived and validated as something other than a technical science? Jurgen Habermas (1971) has provided some responses to this question by distinguishing among three different motives or interests that people pursue in evaluating their world: the technical, the practical, and the emancipatory. (See Table 1.1.) Empirical research in the natural and social sciences pursues control because of its aim in producing information that is "technically utilizable" (p. 76). From the perspective of technical interest, the prevailing concern is one of managing the "process of both nature and society" (p. 76). This interest in empirically derived knowledge corresponds to the knowledge of "pure reason" that Immanuel Kant described. For Kant, rationalism's "pure reason" and empiricism's insistence upon sensory bases for knowledge arise from a conception of human knowledge that is concerned with explaining external phenomena. In the case of schools in particular, technical interest control is emerging in the administration of standardized tests for students that are often used as measures of teacher and school competence. The empirically oriented specificity with which grade level standards are targeted, for instance, embraces an assumption that stu-

Table 1.1 Habermas's Three Human "Interests"			
"Interest"; Motives	**Bases,** Legitimation	**Knowledge is . . .**	**Consequences,** Implications
"Technical interest"; control-oriented	Empirical tests	Information; facts and principles	Directives, instruments: "What can I know?"
"Practical interest"; emphasizes understanding	Shared meaning	Interpretation; alternative forms of assessment	Teacher reflection: "What ought I do?"
"Emancipatory interest"; social critique and self-analysis	Social change	Critique; transfer of knowledge	Social change agents; educational reform: "What dare I hope?"

dents develop at the same rate. In fact, teachers are continually challenged by the reality that this is not the case.

In attempting to critique the pervasive interest in control within the industrialized West, Habermas (1971) has sought in his work not to discard the power and relevance of this "technical interest"; rather, he has suggested that this motive can be ill-suited in situations that, like teaching, emphasize human interaction in inherently unpredictable circumstances. Habermas—by contrasting technical interest with "emancipatory" and "practical" interest—has provided a means of questioning whether concentrating on technical control is always desirable. With the overvaluation of technically oriented knowledge comes the discrediting of knowledge and understanding derived from sources other than empirical research. In his view, when technical interests dominate human communication, "the result is negative for people" (cited in Coomer, 1984).

Habermas's "emancipatory interest" has roots in Kant's *Critique on Judgment*, both works that are concerned primarily with the liberating power of human thought. In Kant, this power is vested in the free will, which begets human choice and responsibility. A particular peril of technical interest from this standpoint is that the control orientation results in reliance on knowledge that is decided in advance of the situations within which it is used. The prescriptive instrumentalization diminishes thoughtful analysis and reflection-in-action that is characteristic of Habermas's emancipatory interest. Teachers might, for instance, pursue emancipatory interest by examining the factors surrounding policy formation and implementation of standardized testing and by appraising the effects of their own limited role in the creation of this policy.

Habermas's "practical interest" corresponds to the thinking on practical reason within Kant's second critique. Whereas Kant's first critique reveals pure reason's limitations in allowing for human value-directed knowledge, the *Critique on Practical Reason* moves toward explaining cognitive processes like the very act of critiquing in itself (Thompson, 1981). When practical action is separated from interaction in deference to the technical interests of instrumental action, the more authentic communicative experience is "eliminated in favor of repeatable experience" (Habermas, 1971, p. 191). From Habermas's perspective, technical control inhibits communication and interaction and hinders the production of knowledge that emerges from those activities. The infamous difficulty associated with moving from theory to practice is at least partly illuminated by this critique.

Technical interest, seeking to answer with certainty the question "What can I know?" neglects the more normative, more situation-sensitive, and ultimately more "practical" issue of "What ought I do?" Instrumentalized practice diverts our attention to predictability and instructional replicability and away from classroom solutions that often warrant creative and context-laden understanding. Such understanding, Habermas suggested, lies at the heart of practical knowledge.

Instrumentalized focus on technical interest elevates a breed of knowledge that is imposed on the practitioners rather than generated from practitioners themselves. A defining quality of positivism, after all, is its articulation of a position—a hypothesis. In the world of technically oriented positivism, teachers are merely the medium or the instrument through which externally prescribed policies and plans are channeled.

In sum, instrumentalization results when the prevailing recommendations for classroom practice are outputs of a scientific process aimed at generalization. This scientific process tends necessarily to exclude practitioners because of the specialized expertise and controlled settings on which the approach depends. These aims are at odds with the practical world of teachers. Critical analysis suggests that there are alternate sources of knowledge—sources that elevate teachers as capable, reflective, and responsive analysts in their own right. The devaluation of analytical practice in education might also contribute to teachers' limited professional latitude. The elevation of a technically oriented genre of social science corresponded nicely with a growing separation in American schools between administrators who enjoy substantial prerogative in defining their work and teachers who have little such leeway; furthermore, it is perhaps no coincidence that such stratification of the educational workplace created upward mobility primarily for men, as Popkewitz (1994) has maintained.

Instrumentalism and Comparative Education

Habermas's observations enable the conclusion that the same patterns of researcher specialization and practitioner marginalization seem to apply to the field of comparative education. A paradoxical effect of this specialization is that, in spite of the field's cosmopolitanism, comparative education has become localized and insular in significant ways. It is especially ironic that, although major comparative education theories critique high-status knowledge, the field has not opened its arms to mainline educational practitioners—teachers—whose work "in the trenches" has once again apparently relegated practitioner knowledge and perspectives to a lesser status. Knowledge gained within the field has continued to target high policy circles such as governmental bureaucracies and international organizations. Comparative education's potential use as a catalyst for educator reflection and analysis has not yet been realized.

Although one can readily find acknowledgment of the need to extend the field to teachers, literature within comparative education remains predominately unresponsive to a more practitioner-oriented audience. The dearth of material suited to practitioners' study of comparative education is striking given the growing interest outside the field in international, intercultural, and global issues. Although some colleges of education have responded to this general interest by offering comparative courses to preservice teachers in addition to more traditional graduate classes, the field of comparative education has not made a concurrent shift toward a more practical orientation. Therefore, there is need to understand the roots of this unequal attention within the field and to articulate comparative education's relevance to this larger audience.

In 1968, Edmund King challenged comparative educators to consider how comparative education might be used as a teaching and learning activity. He argued that comparative studies of education could provide all educators with "a sense of cultural 'wholeness'" (p. 47). In other words, cross-cultural comparisons of similar educational issues elsewhere could help inform educational decision making in one's own country and classroom. In light of greater globalization, it seems even more important that citizens possess cross-cultural knowledge and skills that provide them with an international vantage point from which to view their local educational endeavors. As Ian Thut and Don Adams (1965, as cited in Tretheway, 1976) contend, "A comparative study of education, properly pursued, should enable [one] to function more intelligently in his [or her] own sphere of responsibility" (p. 28). Thus, it seems important that comparative thinking and comparative perspective taking acquired through comparative education become important features of both preservice and in-service teacher programs in this century.

NEW DIRECTIONS: A PRACTICAL APPROACH TO COMPARATIVE EDUCATION

The meanings and purposes of comparative education have been the subject of debate among comparative educators during the past 30 years. Although the debate has illuminated the differing definitions of comparative education, it has also contributed to comparative education being viewed as "a sprawling and ill-defined field of study" (Tretheway, 1976, p. ix). A further complication, aside from comparative educators talking among comparative educators and lending assistance to the policy-making arena, is that comparative education has remained primarily a domain of academics whose work typically informs policy makers in ministries of education and international development organizations. Much of the research in the field "has been developed with the interests of such groups in mind" because these are the people viewed "as important in applying research, sponsoring studies, and determining the shape of comparative education through their funding of research" (Kelly, Altbach, & Arnove, 1982, p. 508). Kelly, Altbach, and Arnove (1982) have pointed out that comparative knowledge has informed educational reform planning and has helped establish benchmark data to enable comparisons of the proposed effectiveness of certain educational practices, yet this knowledge remains in the hands of administrators and policy planners. Only seldom, however, have the fruits of comparative research been applied to schools; the use of comparative education among teachers themselves is rare.

For the general public, then, and for most education practitioners, the field and the benefits of comparative education remain largely unknown. This problem is exacerbated by the fact that the role of the teacher-educator is not viewed as one of researcher-inquirer or policy-shaper, even though it is well documented that teachers are key to the implementation of educational reforms and to determining how successful those reforms will be (Fullan, 1991). Interestingly, however, comparative education had been one of the standard courses in preservice teacher education during the 1940s and 1950s; but, over the past decades, comparative education has generally been either dropped completely from initial teacher education, incorporated into other courses such as "education in society" or the "social foundations of education," or offered as an elective (Trethewey, 1976, p. 4). Primarily, comparative education is viewed as a specialized field; thus, it is usually only offered at the graduate level and, if available, one of several electives offered in graduate schools of education. Within schools of education, comparative education has become rather isolated, and the "the field [has] increasingly divorced itself from the concerns of educational faculties and teacher trainers" (Kelly, Altbach, & Arnove, 1982, p. 514).

Comparative Education as Foundational in Education

As a result of growing concern over the competency-based movement in education that defines the educator's role in rather narrow and behaviorist terms, the Council of Learned Societies in Education (or CLSE, of which The Comparative and International Education Society is a part) developed particular standards to help define Foundations of Education and to provide rationale to substantiate why foundational inquiry is an important part of educator professionalism. The Council of Learned Societies in Education (1996) identifies comparative education as one of the major academic approaches that defines the character and methods of the Foundations of Education. Accordingly, many comparative education programs are housed within their respective institutions' foundations departments.

Like comparative education, Foundations of Education is a broad educational field that encompasses several disciplines, combinations of disciplines, and studies—among them, history, philosophy, anthropology, political science, economics, comparative and international education, and cultural studies. Because "educators are called upon to exercise sensitive judgments amidst competing cultural and education values and beliefs, they will continue to need studies in the ethical, philosophical, historical, and cultural foundations of education to inform their decisions" (CLSE, 1996, p. 5).

The development of interpretive, normative, and critical perspectives in educators constitutes the primary purpose of the foundations of education. This tripartite purpose provides structure by which educators might address the content and context of issues and dilemmas confronting education today. The **interpretive perspective** focuses on concepts and theories derived from the humanities and social sciences to examine and explain educational phenomena by considering the diverse cultural, philosophical, and historical contexts that affect the meaning and interpretations of that phenomena. The **normative perspective** helps educators to examine and explain education in relation to differing value orientations and assumptions about schooling. Educational policy is examined in light of these differing value positions, and educators are encouraged to develop their own values about education. The **critical perspective** is employed to develop in students the ability to question the contradictions and inconsistencies of educational beliefs, policies, and practices.

Thus, the overall objective of foundational inquiry "is to sharpen students' abilities to examine, understand, and explain educational proposals, arrangements, and practices and to develop a disciplined sense of policy-oriented educational responsibility. Such study develops an awareness of education and schooling in light of their complex relations to the environing culture" (CLSE, 1996, p. 8). Comparative education, as a tool within the foundations, is rarely appropriated to foster such learning on the part of educators and is often a missing course option for students. Without specific courses in comparative education, it is unlikely that many instructors would incorporate the comparative dimension in their existing foundations courses. This argument is supported by the fact that international comparisons and perspectives, when they exist in typical foundations texts, are often relegated to their own chapter or draw upon international comparisons intermittently, leaving the comparative perspective undefined and unintegrated as a conceptual tool for interpreting educational assumptions and practices.

Yet, one of the major challenges confronting instructors of general foundations courses, such as "Schooling in Society," is how to emphasize the usefulness of the foundational perspectives and to demonstrate the connections among those perspectives. In short, comparative education serves as a device that helps to mediate the relationships among the other foundational perspectives. Comparative thinking requires students of education to consider the interplay of philosophical, historical, and sociological factors as they analyze the educational approaches of their home and foreign cultures. Comparative thinking, therefore, provides a way to mediate those perspectives (e.g., sociological, historical, political) and fosters a sense of relevance and connection among the disciplines. Using educational issues as the organizing unit of focus within foundations courses can also enable more regular and structured use of comparison and of the foundational fields as tools for interpreting and understanding current educational dilemmas.

Comparative educators, such as Isaac Kandel and Robert Ulich in America, Nicholas Hans and Joseph Lauwerys in England, Friedrich Schneider and Franz Hilker in Germany, and Pedro Rossello in Switzerland, "all paid much attention to the foundations of education, or the *Triebkräfte*, the *Corrientes*—the social causes behind the pedagogical scene" (Bereday, 1964, pp. 7–8, italics added). Attention to the broader sociocultural influences and policy aspects that affect education is a common feature of contemporary comparative education as well. Because comparative education draws upon a combination of disciplines to study education, it can be argued that, of all the foundations of education, comparative education might be best suited to help develop the interpretive, normative, and critical perspectives in students.

Comparative Education: A Multidisciplinary Field of Inquiry

Comparative education is often described as "a dynamic interdisciplinary field of study" (Kelly, Altbach, & Arnove, 1982, p. 526). Although comparative education draws upon multiple disciplines in an effort to better understand education policies, practices, and issues, it is unlikely that those new to the field will be familiar with all of the terminology and particular lenses employed in the various disciplines. Therefore, in this book we offer disciplinary frames and tools of analysis to aid in examining and understanding a set of selected educational issues. No one discipline alone can answer the complex questions and factors affecting education. Consequently, it is necessary to draw upon the strengths of the various disciplines to help raise questions in order to better understand education and its influencing factors. Comparative education, asserted Bereday (1964), cannot be limited to one particular discipline, such as the philosophy of education or the sociology of education or the history of education. Rather, comparative education draws upon the concerns and methods of the humanities and the social sciences in the study of diverse geographical regions.

> One cannot describe any comparative educational problem in terms of a single discipline. One can, for instance, do a meticulous study of the expansion of educational opportunity in historical terms from the Scottish parish schools to modern American or Russian schools. Such a study would tell us little about questions of social class and education, relation of the schools to man-power problems, definitions and role of intellectual ability and its measurement, or philosophical goals of schooling. Such questions, vital to the full understanding of the problem of educational opportunity, must be treated consecutively by relevant resources of sociology, economics, psychology, and philosophy. In this sense, comparative educators must attempt to utilize the methods of several disciplines. And if they run the risk of being labeled Jacks of all trades and masters of none, they can defend themselves by saying that theirs is a study with a definite limitation of focus—the relevance of education. (Bereday, 1964, p. x)

Various disciplines are drawn upon for the specific purpose of gaining a better understanding of education and schooling, however broadly conceived. Thus, the unifying factor in comparative education is education itself and the disciplines "come within the purview of comparative education only insofar as they are relevant to education and schools" (Bereday, 1964, p. x). Rather than studying education in isolation from other factors that influence it, comparative education "has attempted to bring to bear the contributions of any other fields of human inquiry which will help us interpret the educational phenomena more fully" (Trethewey, 1976, p. 77). Disciplines such as anthropology, sociology, political science, philosophy, economics, history, and psychology have all contributed to a deeper and more complex understanding of education, because the concepts central to each particular discipline can be used to analyze and to help explain educational policies and practices.

To illustrate, the concept of culture is central to anthropological inquiry. Using an anthropological lens to examine education, one might study how the cultural values held by students from diverse ethnic groups mediate against the dominant values within the school, either ameliorating or hindering academic achievement. In sociology, the concepts of group affiliation and subcultures (e.g., student membership in "in" and "out" groups) are used to examine social norms and mores. A sociological analysis of education might entail studying those students who conform to established school norms and those who are the dissenters of such norms in an effort to better understand why some accept or resist school authority and how conformist-nonconformist behavior aids or hinders student acceptance among teachers and peers and, thereby, success in school.

Applying a political science lens, one might study which student groups in the school have power and which ones do not and how resource distribution within the school might further these power divides between students. Politics of education, therefore, can be defined as an arena of conflicting values and limited resources, where those with power make their wants known and have them met, usually in a way that disadvantages another group. Thus, the concepts of power, control, and influence are central to a political analysis of education. Using a philosophical lens to study education, one would direct attention to the philosophical commitment of the school and the society it serves. For example, if schooling is to be a mechanism that develops in students democratic values that enable them to participate in public life, then one would want to investigate the degree to which classroom content and instruction encourages active student participation.

Whereas a philosophical orientation is concerned with what is "the good" for a society, an economic perspective focuses on concepts such as class, market, and human resources. To illustrate, an increasingly globalized economy creates changing relationships among people within and between countries. This, in turn, leads to a greater emphasis given to the kind of education that will best meet the needs of the marketplace. An economic study of education might examine the school curriculum (both content and teaching practices) to see how schools inculcate students with desirable workplace skills that will help them secure jobs that contribute to national economic growth as well as financial benefit to the individual worker.

A historical analysis of education is concerned with interpreting events and periods of the past in an attempt to better understand the character and behavior of peoples and nations at present. Thus, to elaborate upon the preceding example, an educator could examine the influence of the economic dimension in education by studying the arguments and evidence for how schools have changed over time to see whether the claim that the economic perspective is becoming more pervasive in schools is warranted.

Psychology, the discipline primarily concerned with the mind-sets and values people hold individually and as a society, has been called upon to help analyze why people, especially students, act in certain ways. For example, increasing school violence in the United States has led researchers to examine the psychological makeup of those who commit such crimes and to speculate on what the school can do to identify possible perpetrators before such violence occurs. Educators are also looking increasingly at the present practices and policies within schools that might contribute to psychological problems for students.

Trethewey (1976) attributes the perception of comparative education "as being ultimately a loose and general area of study" with "no clear roots in an established discipline" as contributing to its diminished "place in teacher education" if it is found at all (pp. 3–4). However, we believe that the advantage of including comparative education in teacher education is that it helps educators to become more thoughtful and critical about education and to recognize that education does not exist in a vacuum. Rather, by drawing upon multiple disciplines to understand a variety of educational phenomena, one can understand education in its complexity using comparative education.

An Issues-Oriented Approach to Comparative Education

Examining educational issues or dilemmas, as opposed to educational systems themselves, also provides a way to critically evaluate the benefits and drawbacks of educational policies and practices. The most common definition associated with comparative education is that it entails an examination of the similarities and differences of various national education systems and structures. The goal in this book is to depart from the more traditional comparisons of educational systems in an attempt to move toward a more issues-oriented focus for the field. Specifically, we devote attention to issues that are increasingly affecting the work of educator practitioners worldwide.

Globalization has created renewed interest in and a rethinking of the purposes of schooling, issues of opportunity and access, educational accountability, and teacher professionalism. The tensions or dilemmas surrounding these issues are of importance not only in the United States, but in other nations as well. Therefore, a comparative study of issues across a number of selected nations seems to be a worthy pursuit, in that such study can enable educators to better understand the forces and factors that shape these issues and how the issues are perceived and addressed in other countries. Thus, a benefit of comparative education is that the practitioner recognizes that educators in different parts of the world are wrestling with similar issues. Thus, educators not only learn from other educators' struggles and successes, but recognize that they are part of a larger, indeed, global professional community of educators.

Overall, comparative inquiry causes people to widen their conceptual lenses to see how seemingly similar issues manifest themselves in diverse settings. This enables people to see the issues at play in their own societies—to behold educational challenges from new angles for the purpose of informing their decisions. Comparative inquiry can also help educators see how education is connected to development at both national and international levels, and to examine the role education plays in fostering and addressing dilemmas of an economic, political, and sociocultural kind.

To help the reader view a number of selected educational issues in their complexity, we provide specific frameworks or multidisciplinary lenses. We do not advocate dichotomous thinking (e.g., decentralized systems of education are better than centralized systems of education); rather, we seek to have the reader examine the factors that affect how the selected educational issues are understood and addressed in different countries and to realize that there are multiple interpretations of the issues. That is, every educational issue/approach/endeavor reveals a range of particular tendencies that are not static but that fluctuate as a result of competing internal and external forces. For example, professional teacher development within a country can exhibit both decentralizing and centralizing tendencies. Thus, there are multiple factors that affect how educational issues manifest themselves in different countries; hence, one should not rush to judgment in an attempt to create "either/or" categories. Although extreme reactions to educational issues could be placed on opposite ends of a continuum, it is important to realize that there is always a range of responses in any given country and that overall placement on a continuum is not fixed.

Over the past 50 years, the field of comparative education has been moving in the direction of an examination of education-related issues, as opposed to educational systems. Often, though, the issues are articulated as problems—problems that can be analyzed and solved. Kandel (1933) argued that "the greater part of the world thus constitutes today a species of laboratory in which so far as education is concerned, varied types of solution are being attempted for the same general range of *problems*" (p. xx, italics added). Bereday (1964), like his predecessor, believed that "the most fruitful way of studying *problems* is to select those that are living and relevant educational questions in the students' own country"(p. 23, italics added). He continued by stating that "insights into how to solve these disputes can be gained by examining how different areas of the world have solved similar *problems* in similar or different circumstances" (pp. 23–24, italics added). For Bereday, a problem approach to comparative inquiry meant the selection of only one theme or topic and an "examination of its persistence and variability throughout . . . representative educational systems" (1964, p. 23). Questions such as "What is development?" or "What are the methods of teaching languages in a relevant set of countries?" were considered appropriate topics for problem analysis (p. 23).

More recently, Brian Holmes (1981) has taken the work of problem analysis further. He reasons that "problems" do not become problems until the underlying aims and theories of such are contested by others.

> It is because consistency is theoretical and rarely found in practice and because some individuals accept traditional aims and theories while others advance radically different ones that "problems" can be identified. In other words, certain kinds of "problem" can be analysed by studying proposals to change educational aims and to adopt new social scientific theories on the assumption that neither mental states nor human behaviour are necessarily related to stated aims and theories. (Holmes, 1981, p. 120)

Thus, "there is," as Trethewey (1976) has contended, "a growing realisation that many of the major problems confronting nations are, in fact, world problems" (p. 5). There is a sense among comparative educators that educational concerns of one nation are increasingly the concerns of other nations and that this problem-sharing arena provides a natural niche for comparative education.

The problem with problems, however, is that it suggests that something is wrong, that something needs to be fixed, and that something can be fixed once and for all. Education and the dilemmas educators face resurface in new ways with unanticipated consequences, thereby necessitating interpretation and assessment of the dilemmas. Whereas problems are often seen as disruptive to society, dilemmas can be viewed as puzzles to be figured out—conflicts that can encourage reflection, dialogue, and action in order to bring about improvements in education and society. The term *dilemma* seems to accommodate the fluidity, dynamism, and uncertainty that characterize a changing, more global world. The language of dilemmas, as opposed to problems, does not foster a win–lose proposition, but rather a sense of compromise, negotiation, choice, and trade-offs among a host of differing values, philosophies, practices, and alternatives. An examination of dilemmas across countries, therefore, suggests a posture of openness to the exploration of differing national and cultural vantage points and a reluctance to prescribe one recipe, method, or technique for addressing any education issue. Dilemmas, therefore, challenge us to look deeply at what people, worldwide, view to be important, what attributes they believe their citizens should possess, and what kind of education is needed to create the kind of societies desired.

Thus, in Part II (chapters 3–6) of the text, titled "Education in International Context: A Comparative Approach Applied to Contemporary Educational Issues," we address four selected issues and the dilemmas surrounding them. In chapter 3, we examine the diverse purposes of schooling in relation to the shaping of educational curriculum in Hong Kong and Israel. The issue of educational access and opportunity in Brazil and South Africa is the focus of chapter 4, and in chapter 5 we explore the issue of educator accountability and authority in light of the changing relationship between education and the state in England and Germany. Chapter 6 provides an examination of the different orientations to teacher professionalism in Japan and the United States and how these orientations affect teacher autonomy and professional development in each country.

Before turning to these issues, it is important to examine the theoretical bases used by comparative educators to interpret educational phenomena. In chapter 2, "Theory in Comparative Education," we explore prevailing theories in the field of comparative education.

Sustaining Reflection

- Education has been seen as contributing to the improvement of the individual and the national social condition. Do you agree? Disagree? Or both? Why?

- What are the dangers associated with wholesale adoption and importation of one country's educational practices to another country? How does instrumentalization—the concern with procedures over context-sensitive approaches—affect the ways in which teaching is conceived and evaluated?

- George Bereday (1964) explained that "it is self-knowledge born of the awareness of others that is the finest lesson comparative education can afford" (p. 6). What have you learned about yourself through other people? Other cultures? Others' backgrounds?

References

Apple, M. (1978). Ideology, reproduction, and educational reform. *Comparative Education Review*, 28(4), 550–562.

Arnove, R. F., & Torres, C. A. (Eds.). (1999). *Comparative education: The dialectic of the global and the local*. Lanham, MD: Rowman & Littlefield.

Bereday, G. Z. F. (1964). *Comparative method in education*. New York: Holt, Rinehart and Winston.

Broadfoot, T. (1977). The comparative contribution: A research perspective. *Comparative Education*, 13(2), 133–137.

Coomer, D. (1984). Critical science: Approach to vocational education research. *Journal of Vocational Education Research*, 9(4), 34–50.

Council of Learned Societies in Education. (1996). *Standards for academic and professional instruction in foundations of education, educational studies, and educational policy studies* (2nd ed.). San Francisco, CA: Caddo Gap Press.

Eckstein, M. (1983). The comparative mind. *Comparative Education Review*, 27(3), 311–322.

Epstein, E. (1983). Currents left and right: Ideology in comparative education. *Comparative Education Review*, 27(1), 3–29.

Foster, P. (1998). Foreword. In H. J. Noah & M. A. Eckstein. *Doing comparative education: Three decades of collaboration* (pp. 1–8). Hong Kong: Comparative Education Research Centre.

Fullan, M. G., with Stiegelbauer, S. (1991). *The new meaning of educational change* (2nd ed.). New York: Teachers College.

Gutek, G. L. (1993). Defining international education. In *American education in a global society: Internationalizing teacher education* (pp. 18–36). New York: Longman.

Habermas, J. (1971). *Knowledge and human interests*. Boston: Beacon.

Hahn, H. J. (1998). *Education and society in Germany*. Oxford: Berg.

Hans, N. (1967). *Comparative education: A study of educational factors and traditions*. London: Routledge & Kegan Paul.

Holmes, B. (1981). *Comparative education: Some considerations of method*. London: George Allen & Unwin.

Kandel, I. L. (1933). *Comparative education*. Boston: Houghton Mifflin.

Kelly, G. P., Altbach, P. G., & Arnove, R. F. (1982). Trends in Comparative Education: A Critical Analysis. In P. G. Altbach, R. F., Arnove, & G. P. Kelly (Eds.), *Comparative Education* (pp. 505–533). New York: Macmillan.

King, E. J. (1968). *Comparative studies and educational decision*. Indianapolis, IN: Bobbs-Merrill.

Klein, J. T. (1990). *Interdisciplinarity: History, theory, and practice*. Detroit, MI: Wayne State University.

Klein, J. T. (1996). *Crossing boundaries: Knowledge, disciplinarities, and interdisciplinarities*. Charlottesville, VA: University Press of Virginia.

Noah, H. J., & Eckstein, M. A. (1998). *Doing comparative education: Three decades of collaboration*. Hong Kong: Comparative Education Research Centre.

Ornstein, A. C., & Levine, D. U. (2000). *Foundations of education* (7th ed.). Boston: Houghton Mifflin.

Parkyn, G. W. (1977). Comparative education research and development education. *Comparative Education, 13*(2), 87–93.

Popkewitz, T. S. (1994). Professionalization in teaching and teacher education: Some notes on its history, ideology, and potential. *Teaching and Teacher Education, 10*(1), 1–14.

Ryan, K., & Cooper, J. M. (1998). *Those who can, teach* (8th ed.). Boston: Houghton Mifflin.

Sadker, M. P., & Sadker, D. M. (2000). *Teachers, schools, and society* (5th ed.). Boston: McGraw Hill.

Thompson, J. B. (1981). *Critical hermeneutics*. New York: Cambridge University Press.

Tozer, S. E., Violas, P. C., & Senese, G. (1998). *School and society: Historical and contemporary perspectives* (3rd ed.). Boston: McGraw Hill.

Trethewey, A. R. (1976). *Introducing comparative education*. Elmsford, NY: Pergamon Press.

Chapter 2

Theory in Comparative Education

Focusing Questions

- What curricular and instructional elements remained most constant in your own education? What has changed most significantly about schooling emphases in your experience?

- What for you are some signs of societal progress? What is formal education's role in fostering these things?

- In what ways do schools accommodate differences among students? In what ways do schools counteract such differences?

INTRODUCTION

Our work in this chapter of discussing and organizing major theories pertinent to comparative education might be described as a "metatheoretical" effort in that we seek to organize theories in order to bring meaning to them. *Weltanschauung*, translating most literally as "world view," is the German term for "philosophy." And one can liken educational theory in particular to the more general realm of philosophy, because theory is itself a "way of seeing and knowing the world around us" and is "not exclusively the property of academic research" (Okano & Tsuchiya, 1999, p. 1). Just as young teachers are continually pressed to convert their philosophical views and understandings on things as broad as education into practical decisions as specific and everyday as homework, we can also distinguish grand theories that seek to describe broad human and social phenomena from what Merton (1957) called middle-range theories (Ritzer, 1996; Sztompka, 1996). In comparative education, several midrange theories apply broader theoretical assertions, and these theories receive sustained attention here. Theories, in addition, propel more localized and specific attempts to organize thought and action pertaining to particular circumstances (Okano & Tsuchiya, 1999).

The chapter's early focus is first upon the theoretical perspective of structural-functionalism, which was established outside of comparative education and adapted into the field. This grand social theory envisions consensus and equilibrium to be hallmarks of social intercourse and human progress. Next, the Marxist perspective also explores consensus and the maintenance of the societal status quo while taking a view that contrasts sharply with the structural-functionalist perspective by questioning the possibility of true consensus, critiquing the authenticity of apparent consensus, and asserting that conflict rather than stability is the overriding catalyst for social change. Each of these grand social theories makes contrasting claims and promotes different visions about the role of schooling within a society, about ways instruction is designed and delivered, and about the nature of relationships between school and society. Of central importance in comparative education and to this chapter, each of these theories offers a distinct perspective on the matter of international development. These specific models of development might be seen as the midrange theories and as interpretations and adaptations within the field of comparative education of the broader tenets and perspectives of structural-functionalism and Marxism.

In this discussion we explore some of the major differences between structural-functionalist and Marxist theory, reviewing intellectual roots, contrasting their different positions regarding education and national development, and discussing the different models for international development these perspectives promote. We further note several similarities between structural-functionalist and Marxist thinking, noting how these two influential families of theory share a modernist outlook or view of the world. Our discussion then turns to postmodernist and poststructuralist thought, which has helped call into question some of the assumptions of structural-functionalist and Marxist thinking and constitutes a distinct source of theoretical argumentation upon which various and more specific theoretical perspectives in comparative education are linked.

Any book surveying comparative education will include a chapter such as this, describing the theories that dominate the field and explaining the past impact and current status of those theories, and these are functions that we certainly seek to fulfill in this chapter. In pursuing these necessary and seemingly straightforward aims, we introduce and grapple with concepts that are ambiguous, complex, and value laden. This exploration entails different visions of the just society and the fundamental tensions between liberty or freedom on the one hand and equality on the other. We also explore competing interpretations as to the fairest way to resolve these fundamental tensions and the nature of agreement within and across peoples as to the fair distribution of society's energies and resources. Theories about the conduct of formal education—an undertaking that entails huge and visible commitments of human energy and societal resources—provide windows on how people choose to grapple with some of society's most pressing and fundamental philosophical questions.

STRUCTURAL-FUNCTIONALIST PERSPECTIVES IN COMPARATIVE EDUCATION

We can broadly distinguish consensus theories from conflict theories (Clabaugh & Rozycki, 1990) in terms of the fundamental social interactions each set of theories emphasizes in its analysis. Accordingly, the consensus perspective points optimistically to the possibility for societies to seek shared norms and values (Okano & Tsuchiya, 1999, p. 6)—indeed, seeing this tendency as a natural feature of functional social systems. Structural-functionalism's identity as a consensus theory is built upon the conviction that society is unitary and that the building and preservation of agreement is the most powerful and preferred social force. Modernization theory and human capital theory, which will receive more extended attention in a subsequent section, are premised on structural-functionalist assumptions.

Structural-functionalism, and its theoretical impetus, emerged within the discipline of sociology and is especially indebted to the work of Talcott Parsons (e.g., 1937, 1951, 1966) and Robert Merton (e.g., 1957). Dominating sociological theory from the 1940s through the 1970s (Fägerlind & Saha, 1989), structural-functionalism has had broad and enduring influence throughout the social sciences and the allied fields, such as education. And, in spite of its relative decline, structural-functionalism continues to be influential in the contemporary period. Fukuyama's 1999 work, *The Great Disruption: Human Nature and the Reconstitution of Social Order*, for example, emphasizes societies' natural tendency to maintain equilibrium. In particular, Fukuyama argues that in spite of profound forces of social change, new adaptive responses are emerging in businesses, homes, and neighborhoods, helping to forge functional social harmony and stability. Stability and equilibrium, being central within the structural-functionalist analysis, reflect the theory's identity as a consensus perspective.

As Fägerlind and Saha (1989) stressed in their useful historical overview, structural-functionalist theory derives its optimism regarding the stability and coherence of human and social phenomena from Enlightenment antecedents, which celebrated human rationality and ingenuity and stressed the capacity of people guided through these mental abilities to shape circumstances to suit human needs. The Enlightenment intellectual awakening was spurred by the Renaissance—an era in which profound intellectual and geographical growth led to a period of unsurpassed scientific and cultural progress that witnessed, among other things, the preliminary stages of an international economy. Among the major figures and influences during the Enlightenment period, Fägerlind and Saha (1989) have emphasized the contributions of several in particular, including the following:

- Fontenelle, whose characterization of civilization emphasized the possibility of unlimited progress and depicted deterioration as unlikely
- Descartes, who placed prime importance on rational knowledge, stressed the necessity of proof, and therefore affirmed the power of mental faculties as tools by which humankind could foster its own progress
- Leibnitz, who promoted the view that human progress was "continuous, gradual, and cumulative" (Fägerlind & Saha, 1989, p. 9) and that this human progress had momentum
- Kant, who linked civilization's progress with progress in the sphere of human morality

The Enlightenment impulse therefore sees the predictability and control of humans' surroundings as possible, if not virtually inevitable, and promotes scientific explanation as the principal tool for reaching this end. And significantly, although rationalist thought originally exalted the capacity of the individual person as the arbiter of personal destiny, this attribute "was extended to the nation-state level. Each nation state was considered to be sovereign and free to rationally control its progressive development" (Grosfoguel, 2000,

p. 348). This aspect of the structural-functionalist outlook is key because the extent of a country's real freedom and independence becomes a matter of specific skepticism under contrasting Marxist theories of education and educational development.

The term *structural-functionalism* itself, then, reflects the grand social theory's principal assertions. *Structural* underscores the confidence with which the theory views society itself as no arbitrary collection of people but, rather, as an entity having clear purpose and potential. And the term *functional* points to structural-functionalism's philosophical commitments that the relationships among factors affecting humanity can be identified and better understood—just as an if-then formulation in logic is intended to declare causal relationships in terms of functions among various agents.

Structural-functionalism is associated with societal consensus, in that consensus is the vital means toward the end of stability (Okano & Tsuchiya, 1999, p. 6). This underscores the theory's reliance on the notion of equilibrium as a fundamental trait of societies. From the structural-functionalist view, equilibrium is not so much benign as it is a product—almost axiomatically—of the very notion of society. Since a society is broadly defined as a social group whose identity is defined and continually shaped by the values common to its members, structural-functionalism likens society to a biological organism that works toward its own self-preservation. But, as indicated in reviewing the conflict perspective of Marxism, this process of self-preservation—in societal terms, of maintaining stock of values that are perceived as both worthwhile and shared—can be depicted in negative terms as well.

Structural-functionalism involves an aversion to conflict, which, not surprisingly, has been the overriding point of criticism (Fägerlind & Saha, 1989). At face value, political and social dissent are fixtures of everyday life. In politics, witness legislative gridlock within democratic institutions and more specific and persistent issues concerning race relations, and the quandary of developing suitable and equitable strategies for the allocation of societal resources regarding comprehensive health care. And those working within the field of education might also note that discord or lack of consensus about matters both large and small is a fixture of their professional lives. Structural-functionalism's general avoidance of social change constitutes an additional point of criticism. As Fägerlind and Saha (1989) have noted, Parsons later sought to address this weakness, drawing on 19th and early 20th century evolutionary theories, which had described in quasibiological terms society's progress from primitive to advanced forms. This so-called neo-evolutionary theory paved the way for the offshoot of structural-functionalism known as modernization theory.

One might question how a society's educational institutions reflect the view of society that structural-functionalism promotes. Arguably, schools adopt many structures that seem aimed at the maintenance of predictability and stability. To illustrate, students' movement through a sequence of grades mirrors and reinforces notions of functional student performance and behavior (i.e., "normal" promotion through grade levels), at the same time lending a rationale for exceptions (retention), and mechanisms for intercessions (remediation or compensatory instructional practices) also in terms of the desirable, the normal, the stable. For Merton (1957), schools, as socializing institutions, reflected not only **manifest functions** such as their provision of declared curricula and programs of study, but **latent functions** such as less obvious lessons in punctuality and adherence to other social norms and expectations. As we shall see, observers operating from critical neo-Marxist perspectives (e.g., Giroux, 1992) take a much more pessimistic view of the socializing mechanisms of such a "hidden curriculum."

In sum, some of the most important assumptions of structural-functionalist thought are its image of society as:

- Unitary, that is, that society has a clear conceptual boundary, and, moreover, that this unitary entity called society is the principal unit of analysis of interest to the study of human social phenomena
- Coherent, not only as a unit unto itself, but also in terms of the relationships that exist among its various elements
- Stable, working toward harmony and its own self-preservation

Structural-functionalist thought does not itself articulate a model of change, because its proponents view change as a consequence of societal response to imbalances or imperfections—or as adjustments or refinements of existing social conditions—rather than as changes in the social order (Fägerlind & Saha, 1989). However, those promoting the midrange theories known as modernization and human capital formation—more particular to the field of comparative education—apply structural-functionalist perspectives regarding consensus and stability in attempting to explain issues of change and development. We now turn to these two midrange theories.

Modernization Theory

As mentioned, the structural-functionalist framework embraces the notion that change itself is desirable only insofar as it embodies society's impetus toward stability and self-correction. This perspective involves rejecting the notion that change constitutes shifts and differences between one state of affairs and the next, viewing change instead in more linear terms as a matter of natural growth. Change from this perspective is therefore a generally manageable process—one that, with diligence and rationality, can be understood and potentially manipulated to the benefit of humankind.

Modernization theory, which traces its disciplinary lineage primarily to sociology but has been prominent also in social psychology (Fägerlind & Saha, 1989), adopts several assumptions from the grand theory of structural-functionalism. Modernization theory, for instance, involves seeing societies rather than national governments as the appropriate unit of analysis, taking the structural-functionalist view that equilibrium pertains across a spectrum of social institutions including but not restricted to government (Billet, 1993). Further, modernization theorists attribute underdevelopment to shortages in the enablers of growth—low levels of capital in particular (Rostow, 1971), providing a theoretical rationale for economic investment and aid. In addition, however, and of more primary importance regarding the role of education, proponents of modernization theory argue that "modern values" can be nurtured and that human planning and the creation and maintenance of social institutions such as schools are of high importance as venues for socialization (Fägerlind & Saha, 1989). This tenet of modernization theory diverges from the overarching structural-functionalist perspective, then, in that it accommodates the notion of change in ways that structural-functionalism generally does not.

Modernization theory, viewing human nature as a variable rather than a constant in terms of the prospect for change, "attribute[s] the lack of certain behavioral patterns to the 'relativity' of human behavior" and "to the fact that cultural values and beliefs . . . underlie patterns of economic action" (Valenzuela & Valenzuela, 1998, p. 271). This view of human nature as variable, malleable, and therefore subject to refinement is key. Modernization theory ties societal development to the level of the individual person and so provides a rationale for the role of education within societies seeking to modernize. Development from the perspective of modernization, in short, becomes a function of the attainment of modern attitudes at the individual level; society's modernization, that is, becomes a product of the percolation of these attitudes throughout an expanding circle of its individual members. Of further significance is the fact that modernization is defined in the image of the industrialized West and is assumed to be desirable. These are underlying claims that postmodernist theory adherents have criticized.

Modernization theory demonstrates its heredity as Western and rationalist in its depiction of progress as sequential and as possessing momentum. Adopting these aspects and drawing on David McClelland's (1961) assertion that human progress was governed in part by a natural motive toward achievement (Fägerlind & Saha, 1989), Inkeles and Smith (1974) elaborated upon the linear conceptual underpinnings of modernization theory. They offered a model of development that features a chain of functional steps or relationships in which modern institutions beget modern values, which result in modern behaviors; in turn, the modernized society that should emerge spurs economic development (see Figure 2.1). The stepwise nature of the relationship among these stages embodies the structural-functionalist paradigm's faith in strong causal linkages: One discrete event or set of events will produce the next discrete and desirable set of events, and so forth.

There are generally two genres of criticism of modernization theory. The first concerns the ideological and cultural biases inherent in the theory. The endpoint of the mod-

FIGURE 2.1

The Modernization Process

Based on Inkeles and Smith, 1974,
adapted from Fägerlind and Saha, 1989.

Modern institutions
instill in
individuals . . .

modern values
encouraging the
adoption of . . .

modern behaviors
among citizens.
This creates . . .

modern society,
thus paving a
way for . . .

economic development . . .
and natural progress.

ernization process is conceived in the image of the Western countries within which the theory was formulated. Kempner (1998) noted that Western ways of conducting business might not be the most appropriate. "Rather than simply modernizing to emulate the United States," that author noted, education in developing countries might be "better served through policies that are more appropriate to the broader cultural needs of the society" (p. 456). Or, conversely, modern values might not be incompatible with traditional ones (Fägerlind & Saha, 1989), yet the vision for development that modernization theory prescribes tends to treat traditional habits and norms as dysfunctional and therefore promotes the substitution of practices that are unduly disruptive. Seeking in part to address the Western bias in modernization theory and other perspectives of development, scholars have devised methods for measuring societies' relative standing in terms of "quality of life" indicators, for instance.

A second major criticism regarding modernization has centered on the theoretical assumption that the attainment of modern values at the individual level will in fact translate into a societywide phenomenon at levels that are capable of generating and sustaining national development (Portes, 1973). Similarly, because, as mentioned, modernization stresses the importance of strong institutions, modern attitudes alone might not be enough to sow the seeds for change. As Tiryakian (1995) explained, though underdeveloped nations have pursued modernization "the institutional structures and the collective mentalities of many regions were inadequate to the task" (p. 252).

Modernization, in summary, is a midrange adaptation within the field of comparative and international development education of the structural-functionalist perspective, and accordingly involves assuming the existence of strong causal linkages and seeking to describe processes of modernization and national development in a context of general predictability and manageability. Modernization theory, applying and extending structural-functionalism's descriptive foundation, indicates a prescription for change, as education of individuals in the desired values, attitudes, and behaviors of "modern" persons is viewed as necessary to the development of modern institutions and societal progress. Accordingly, modernization's sequential and functional quality is apparent in specific models for change under the theory such as the five steps of Inkeles and Smith's (1974) "process of modernization" (refer to Figure 2.1). Many of the tenets of modernization theory continue to have influence in the articulation of policies aimed at national development and in the generation of research and commentary, although the results of development efforts under the model have been mixed. Not surprisingly, modernization theory's articulation in the West reflects structural-functionalism's embrace of rationalist assumptions about the manageability of progress. In addition, modernization theory's Western heritage has much to do with the modes and forms of development its proponents envision as favorable.

Human Capital Formation Theory

Capital, from which the term *capitalism* stems, is associated with the field of economics. Fittingly enough, then, human capital formation theory, a second major offshoot of structural-functionalist thought within comparative and development education, refers to a theory of development that emerged in the early 1960s from the study of economic growth and progress. The term *capital*—simplified as "ways and means"—pertains to both material and other resources that contribute to the accumulation of wealth by individuals or, as this specific theory of development suggests, societies as well.

Fundamental to the concept of capital is the notion that investments in the acquisition of capital goods will reap returns. Economic historian Walt Rostow (1960) subtitled his *Stages of Economic Growth* as "A Non-Communist Manifesto"—a description that suggests that this author's work was written partly as an antidote to Marxist thinking. Whereas prevailing non-Marxist political ideologies focused on the political apparatus and on processes of decision making within it, Marxism's focus was upon society and was aimed at the elimination of human exploitation and the establishment of a societal order based on mutual prosperity. Although structural-functionalist theory had generated observations and assertions about the favorable environment for social progress, stressing such elements as the need for economic liberalism (see **liberal** in the Glossary, p. 261) and democratic institutions, theories about the more concrete elements of change had been unavailable prior to Rostow. Rostow's work arguably constituted an effort to articulate a vision and theory of a capitalist preferred future and to describe the hallmarks of progress toward this endpoint. He described progress in terms of five stages:

■ In Stage 1, identified as "Traditional Society," agricultural activity dominates and agricultural output is mainly consumed by producers. Limited trade takes the form of barter—exchange of goods for other goods. Production in such agriculture-driven societies is labor intensive, requiring little or no investment.

■ In Stage 2, called the "Transitional Stage," specialization increases and, as a result, surpluses of productive activities become available for trading. And, as transportation becomes necessary to support trade, merchant entrepreneurship emerges. Some trade across societies also begins but concentrates on primary products. The convergence of these conditions creates the necessary environment for what Rostow calls *takeoff*.

■ In Stage 3, the "Takeoff" phase, increased industrialization characterizes a shift from chiefly agricultural to manufacturing activity. Although growth during this phase tends to be concentrated rather than widespread and industrial activity features little diversification, the notion of investment begins to become a significant force. Further, growth in this critical phase becomes self-sustaining because growing income levels enable increasingly significant investment activity.

■ Stage 4, described by Rostow as the "Drive to Maturity," is characterized by economic diversification rather than reliance on one or two major industries. And innovation begets growing opportunities for investment.

■ And in Stage 5, described as a phase of "High Mass Consumption," the production of durable industrial goods flourishes, and economic activity within the service sector becomes dominant.

As Rostow's sequence suggests, the emergence and growth of investment is of critical importance, with progression through the stages providing a fundamental basis for capitalist development. Theodore Schultz (1961), in one of the earliest articulations of human capital theory, maintained that economists had overlooked human propensities to pursue education as an investment and had therefore failed to recognize education's potential as a spur for investments in education at the societal level as well. Education, Schultz (1961) asserted, had untapped potential as a catalyst for the multiplication of both individual and societal wealth. Measurements suggesting high rates of return on investments in both secondary and college level education reinforced Schultz's position (Becker, 1960, cited in Schultz, 1961). These findings and assertions implicated national policy directly, treating "the improvement of the human workforce as a form of capital investment" (Fägerlind & Saha, 1989, p. 18).

Human capital theory, like modernization theory, adopts structural-functionalism's overarching commitments, reflecting a direct and functional relationship between education and development. Human capital theory reflects structural-functionalism's fundamental affinity with economic liberalism as embraced in the progressive democracies of the industrialized West. This contributes to its promotion as a viable strategy for national growth (Fägerlind & Saha, 1989). Further, like the grand theory of structural-functionalism, adherents of the midrange theory of human capital formation view the national society as a discrete and vital level of analysis, attributing economic underdevelopment, for instance, to factors within the society in question. Finally, human capital theorists pursue measurability by seeking to account for all factors that might contribute to economic growth—here again pointing to structural-functionalist dispositions toward causality.

In spite of its continuing influence in policy formulation, critics have questioned the methodological plausibility of its claims regarding measurability in particular. The prospect of even identifying relevant economic growth factors, let alone properly weighing the relative impact of each, is dubious. Further, critics have suggested that raising education levels can actually contribute to disparate income levels across society. Dore (1976) contributed to this argument, describing the effects of a so-called diploma disease: Competition for higher levels of employment leads to the inflation of educational credentials, reducing the relative gains from investments in education. This effect, of course, contradicts human capital formation theory's most fundamental assumption.

In sum, human capital theorists adopt the structural-functionalist tenets in the causal relationship between investment and education that they envision, in their modernist and Westernized vision of progress and development, and in their focus upon the society as the functional and harmonious context for theoretical analysis and policy action. The theory's use has declined with the advent of other modes of economic analysis, although its general appeal persists to many. And domestic policy discourse within the West often reflects ideological and theoretical commitments akin to those of human capital theory, as the United States policy report *America's Choice: High Skills or Low Wages* (Commission on the Skills of the American Workforce, 1990) suggests by the very words of its title. Ironically, however, with respect to the United States, at least, the viewpoint that education should be nurtured and supported through investments is arguably more consistently prescribed as a remedy for developing nations than it is embraced domestically. For instance, a tenor of skepticism about public schools' ability to use funding allocations wisely seems to underlie the American school accountability movement.

MARXIST PERSPECTIVES IN COMPARATIVE EDUCATION

Marxism has an historical identity as a political ideology as well as a theory. Some aspects of Marxism have warranted and received considerable scrutiny and reassessment since the disintegration of many of the world's most prominent Marxist regimes. However, dependency theory and the linked perspective of liberation theory have been hugely influential in comparative education, and understanding the Marxist underpinnings of these theories is therefore essential in any theoretical overview of the field. In addition, however, Marxism retains a life quite independent of the relative decline of Marxist communism worldwide. In particular, Marxism's conflict perspective continues to be an important font of thinking and criticism regarding structures and relations within and between societies. Because of continuing use of the grand theory of Marxism and because of its relationship to the midrange theories of dependency and liberation theory, review of Marxism's roots and major claims is a crucial undertaking in this theoretical overview of the field of comparative education.

Marxist theory is sometimes described as *scientific communism* or as *historical materialism* (e.g., Cohen, 1982). Dismantling the deeper meanings of these terms is a good way to review Marxism's central assertions and to describe the intellectual tools and methods through which Marxist theory derives these claims. The term *material* relates to the object of Marxist analysis, namely the material essentials of food, clothing, and shelter. To Marx, the quest for these material essentials has characterized human existence. Social existence in particular, according to Marx, is defined by social groups' discovery and perfection of methods for dividing not only the labor required to seek or create the material essentials, but, as productive methods become more refined, of dividing and distributing the surpluses that result from these more efficient labors as well. The condition of *communism* is a state within which the concept of ownership is irrelevant and obsolete because of the abundance by which humans produce the material essentials and because of the efficiency and equality by which these abundant material goods are distributed. The endpoint of communism, further, refers to a future social order toward which humans through history have progressed. The notion of progress evident in Marxist thought, together with its faith in causal certainty, points to the tradition's indebtedness to Western Enlightenment thinking. This point of similarity also reflects in large part Marxism's and structural functionalism's shared identity as modernist theories, notwithstanding many key differences between the two perspectives.

Marxist theory is *historical* due to its detailed dialectical analyses of the history of human society. **Dialectics** is the "study of the universal patterns in change and development" (Cohen, 1982, p. 171) and is the philosophical device Marx applied most persistently. Marx viewed change as a dialogue or interaction between two entities—an existing but imperfect condition on the one hand and a possible alternative on the other. Change in human conditions, in this view, is the result of reconciling these two conditions and producing a new status quo that itself will become subject to the continuing dialectic process of change and the perfection of human society. We see here a key difference between the Marxist conflict perspective and the consensus predisposition of structural-functionalist theory: Change in the Marxist model calls for the replacement of one condition of status quo with another social order, whereas structural-functionalists views change as adjustment or refinement—but not replacement—of an existing social order. Further, according to Marx, the process of change is chiefly a product of conflict because of humans' tendency to exploit others in order to increase or preserve their own positions of privilege. For some within a society, that is, changes will be desirable, while for others the same changes will represent infringements upon certain advantages they enjoy. Thus, conditions that are exploitive and oppressive of some people are, for others, the very sources of their positions of greater wealth and higher status within society.

Although Marx saw society as a unit, he emphasized society's substructure of different social classes or social levels, sometimes called *strata*. Bourgeoisie classes, although unengaged in front-line roles as actual producers of goods and services, nonetheless control the productive capacities of those who do occupy these roles as workers. The workers, who together constitute the proletariat class, occupy exploited positions as subjects of bourgeoisie control. This brings to light another key difference between the Marxist and the structural-functionalist positions: Whereas both acknowledge that social institutions and mechanisms do work toward the end of preserving society, the structural-functionalist alone sees this tendency as fundamentally desirable and just. The Marxist, in contrast, views the same arguments in favor of societal stability as a rationale for sanctioning inequity among the substrata of society. Thus, the societal subunits or classes and the latent or overt conflicts among them receive more analytic attention in Marxist theory than does the society at large.

Of particular importance in the capitalist epoch, the Marxist view sees economic activity in capitalism as the vehicle for the concentration of wealth in the possession of relatively few people. Further, adding to the inherent injustice of capitalist society, Marx believed this accumulation of wealth was the result of further injustice in which private parties benefit disproportionately through activities that are not at all private but, rather, social. It is important to understand that Marx viewed work as a social undertaking because labor depends not solely upon the production of goods or services but also upon the distribution of the products to members of society and, thus, to the very valuing of the fruits of the worker's effort. From the Marxist perspective, a particularly regrettable feature of capitalism is the sense of **estrangement** or alienation it can produce for the typical worker in the area of increased industrialization that Marx observed in the late 19th century. For Marx, this sense of **alienation** stemmed especially from peoples' increasing concentration on the process of work and their concurrent distancing from the social context of that work.

In particular, Marx observed the intensifying specialization of the Industrial Revolution, critiquing the ways this specialization reduced people's sense of purpose, especially by undermining their ability to identify themselves with an end product of value to the other members of the communities within which they lived. And significantly, Marx held that this sense of alienation produces in people a sense of powerlessness, instilling in them the impression that there is little they can do to improve their circumstances. At worst, the alienated citizens become so resigned to their condition of powerlessness that they are unable to recognize in the first place that they are subject to unjust conditions that warrant change. Consciousness raising, in this light, is a matter of casting light upon conditions in order to replace feelings of powerlessness with a sense of capacity and agency regarding one's own circumstances. Liberation theory adopts this element of Marxist theory quite overtly, as discussed subsequently.

Because the prospect of social change is undesirable for advantaged members of society, the Marxist conflict perspective maintains that they have no interest in engaging in any discussion regarding peaceful change. Their maintenance of a contradictory and unjust status quo forecloses social intercourse of the sort that might enable peaceful progress and change. Marx contended that this latent conflict between advantaged and disadvantaged classes would inevitably become overt. Thus, Marx's dialectical analysis generally concludes that the history of human experience has exhibited

> a pattern of reckless opposition between those who control the productive forces of society and those who do not, unending conflict between oppressors and oppressed. In every age the resolution of these dialectical conflicts has led to renewed opposition at a higher level, with oppression taking new forms. Marxism explains the successive phases of this continuing struggle, each dominant class replacing its predecessor as it wins control of the material substructure of the society. (Cohen, 1982, p. 171)

Marxism's identification as *scientific* is tied to Marx's methods but even more fundamentally to his methodology—that is, to the ways he identified and evaluated the knowledge he synthesized in his work. Marx, again, focused systematically on historical context. This approach to explaining and describing present conditions in terms of their historical antecedents grew out of a philological intellectual tradition prominent in continental Europe. Marx's output was an interpretation of the meaning of the broad social trends he viewed. This approach to compiling facts and extracting claims differs from the hypothesis building and testing that many associate with the methods and procedures of true science. This interpretive method, then, departs from that of the positivist mainstream, and the extent to which Marx's work is scientific remains questionable from that perspective.

Some thinkers, though (see especially Habermas, 1971), critique the rationalist bias toward a technical view of science and caution against legitimizing as pertinent, valid, and scientific only the knowledge that emerges from the observation of controlled environments and the testing of hypotheses. Such critics note that the impetus toward prediction and control is tied to humans' continuing preoccupation with manipulating environmental conditions so that these conditions might be better appropriated for humanity's material progress. Marx's analysis works from an assumption that not all problems are solved simply by controlling and manipulating the environment alone, and his claims help to clarify and strengthen this position. In particular, Marx maintained that problems relating to the fair distribution of human outputs are addressed by knowledge gained through a science rooted in understanding the nature of human communication and agreement rather than on the prediction and control of natural environments. Given the circumstances he witnessed with respect to rapid and deep social changes during the Industrial Revolution, Marx deemed economic and social issues regarding the fair distribution of material goods to be of overriding importance. This outlook concerning the value and validity of knowledge arising from context-centered analysis is of continuing importance in the field of education in particular. In philosophical and theoretical discussions, epistemology involves giving conscious attention to what genres of knowledge count as knowledge and to the sources and means for verifying such knowledge. The important, but sometimes overlooked, implication of this aspect of philosophy is that there are in fact different sources of knowledge. If science is a methodological strategy for producing knowledge, Marx's science, placing a premium as it did on an epistemology of understanding human patterns of interaction, was arguably a science that was well suited to the circumstances to which he sought to bring new meaning and deeper understanding. For a biographical sketch of Karl Marx, see the Personality Box.

Karl Marx (1818–1883)

Karl Marx, born in the city of Trier in Rhenish Prussia, came from a well-to-do and cultured family and, accordingly, undertook preparation for university level study by completing his secondary education in the local *Gymnasium*. During his time at universities in Bonn, Berlin, and Jena, Marx pursued studies in Latin and Greek, French, history, philosophy, and, ultimately, law with the apparent intention of taking up the profession of his father (Gutek, 1997). During his studies, Marx was particularly energized by the tenets of philosopher Friedrich Hegel, whose ideas regarding both alienation and the dialectic process had enduring influences on Marx's own thinking. Alienation, a concept upon which Marx expanded considerably, was, for Hegel, "a failure to recognize that truth is intimately connected with human thought" (Ozmon & Craver, 1999, p. 319). Dialectics, in the Hegelian scheme, was a mental process that enabled the systematic application of logic, the identification and resolution of contradictions, and the encounter of truth. Unlike Hegel, however, Marx's philosophies focused on the material world of human economic activity rather than on the idealist world of pure ideas.

Following the completion of his doctoral work at Jena, which ended in 1841, Marx returned to Bonn with the intention of taking up a career as an academic. The prevailing reactionary political regime, however, censured the leftist Hegelian thinkers with whom Marx found his closest affinities. Among the intellectuals the political establishment scrutinized most closely was Ludwig Feuerbach, whose treatises on materialism held that history is shaped by material conditions. Marx, adapting Feuerbach's thinking, retained Feuerbach's emphasis on material conditions as the major determinant of humanity and social institutions. Marx's views broke with Feuerbach, though, in that Marx emphasized the role of humans in shaping history through their own interaction with material conditions. Whereas material (chiefly economic) laws formed society's basis, it is people that shape history in Marx's breed of materialist philosophy (Sadovnik, Cookson, & Semmel, 2001), and this conviction lent itself to Marx's later advocacy of proletariat uprising.

In 1841, Marx and a fellow "left Hegelian" Bruno Bauer, became chief contributors to a Cologne newspaper, the *Rheinische Zeitung*. The government censured the periodical due, in large part, to Marx's critical commentary on the political establishment (Gutek, 1997). Marx emigrated to Paris with his young wife, where, for a short time, he was editor of a German language periodical with the evident intent of distributing it widely within Germany—a plan whose logistical challenges evidently accounted in large part for the periodical's early discontinuation. Marx continued to live in exile from Germany during 1847 and 1848, when revolution became widespread in Europe. The prospect of sweeping social change stimulated Marx's contributions to the impetus for such change in the *Communist Manifesto*—a work he completed in 1848 with Friedrich Engels, whom he had befriended while in Paris in 1844.

In spite of the relatively major influence of Marxist thought in comparative education, Marx's philosophical writings did not deal explicitly with education in a sustained fashion. However, Marx's work reveals that he harbored suspicions regarding formal education's capacity to transmit a dominant ideology to the detriment of desirable social movement toward an egalitarian condition. In spite of Marx's skepticism, the *Communist Manifesto* does call for the institution of universal free education. And Marx endorsed the American public schools of his day, whose direct and participatory control at the local level he felt ameliorated the potential for schools' abuse as instruments of indoctrination and, so, for the establishment's maintenance of an unfair status quo. And as part of a rounded, three-prong

(continued)

(continued)

educational program based on mental, physical, and technological training, Marx envisioned exposure to the principles of industrial production as essential "so that ignorance of the inner workings of the economic system would not be used as a way to hold the proletariat in industrial bondage" (Ozmon & Craver, 1999, p. 335) within a continuing classist state.

Marx envisioned the socialist individual as "issue-oriented and dedicated to rational principles rather than showing allegiance to persons or groups" (Ozmon and Craver, 1999, p. 333). But Marx's conviction in this regard was not maintained within Leninist interpretations, which stressed citizens' identification with the collective and the abatement of individual identity and which was a persistent emphasis of schools in the Soviet Union. Marx spent most of his final years living in London and contributing energetically to the cause of the labor movement. Also during this period, Marx studied in a number of languages, including Russian, in his progress on the late work *Capital* (Marx, 1951). This work's ultimate completion was prevented by the philosopher's declining health but its earliest volumes began appearing in 1867.

In terms of its usefulness in furthering comparative interpretations and understandings of education, schooling in Marxist countries can be understood as vehicles for dialectic progress from a capitalist society to the communist society that is deemed more mature. Marx himself supported specialized industrial and technical education as catalysts for human progress, while eschewing forms of education that were too narrow to enable thoughtful appraisals of social circumstances. Marx rejected the use of education for indoctrination and for the creation of a social system dominated by class structures and sanctioned inequity. Marx advocated a curriculum based on the three aims of mental education, physical education, and technological training (Ozmon & Craver, 1999). Adopting a concern that later preoccupied the American educational philosopher John Dewey, Marx was concerned with the relationship between theory and practice, though his primary concern in this realm was to avoid any impetus that would differentiate between physical and intellectual labor (Ozmon & Craver, 1999).

Meanwhile, neo-Marxist adaptations of Marxist philosophies have enriched educational discourse and critique regarding noncommunist countries as well. Samuel Bowles and Herbert Gintis (1976, 1986), for instance, have argued that in the capitalist West, schools are places that institutionalize the very practices that the Marxist vision avoids. Such things as passive compliance with the vertical power structures of authority, strict schedules, and other regimens of school order have counterparts within the modern industrial workplace. Bowles and Gintis's (1976) observations regarding this system of counterparts between schools and workplaces are known collectively as **correspondence theory**. Notably, correspondence theorists critique, in much more pessimistic terms, some aspects that Merton (1957) had noted regarding the manifest and latent functions of school—aspects that Merton's analysis described as stabilizing forces.

Among the limitations and criticisms of Marxist theory is the claim that Marx did not grapple with the issue of underdevelopment (Fägerlind & Saha, 1989). This is probably attributable to the theory's Western bias, focusing as it did upon the history of materialism in the European context. This shortcoming, as discussed in the next section, was partially addressed by the dependency perspective, which emerged in the underdeveloped region of Latin America and employed Marxist tenets to explain the continuing difficulty of development in that region. An additional criticism of Marxist theory is that not all societies reflect the presence of the sorts of class structures Marxist theories describe, although this criticism is not surprising given that Marx's theory was based on an historical analysis, again, of a particular region and not upon positivist generalizations about humankind as a whole.

In sum, adherents of Marxist theory acknowledge the existence of consensus and the appearance of stability but are pessimistic about the degree to which consensus is genuine. Society's function, from the Marxist perspective, is to justify inequitable circumstances, particularly regarding the production and disposition of the material goods of society. Class structures within society only appear to exist in a state of harmony. Social change occurs when latent conflict between exploited working or proletariat classes and capitalist bourgeois classes becomes overt. Especially in the late 1980s and early 1990s, widespread social dissent in various socialist and communistic countries led to the ousting of Marxist regimes within them. Sometimes, Western observers characterize the flaws of Marxist theories as evidence of the bankruptcy of the Marxist analysis on the whole. However, more than an ideological impetus for political enterprises, Marxist theory remains a potent conflict-oriented counterbalance to the prevailing consensus perspectives (Ozmon & Craver, 1999). Dependency theory, to which we now turn, pointedly adapts the Marxist perspective in order to critique dominant patterns of global development and to offer alternative views within a global society of countries.

Dependency Theory

Dependency theory appropriates from the Marxist tradition the belief that capitalism is exploitive, generating and maintaining oppressive conditions that account for considerable human injustice (Frey & Song, 1997). Dependency theory's attention, however, is upon relations between countries in a world system rather than upon class relations within countries, as is the focus in Marxism. In spite of Marxist theory's original focus upon a more localized human context within a country, the theory provides the explanatory tissue on which dependency theory—applied to the broader world—rests. The relationship between Marxist theory and dependency theory is therefore demonstrative of a grand theory's translation to a more particular midrange theory. In particular, dependency theory adapts Marxism's descriptions of class structures, its historical stages as a method for establishing its claims, and its identification of particular mechanisms and methods of exploitation.

In particular, dependency theorists describe patterns of global inequity and uneven development as a North-South phenomenon, in which primarily the North American and European countries enjoy a privileged or upper class position at the expense of underprivileged countries chiefly in Latin America and Africa. Unlike either the Marxist or structural-functionalist perspective, dependency theory originated outside the industrialized West and is indebted in particular to writers such as Henrique Cardoso (1972), Theotonio Dos Santos (1998), and Andre Gunder Frank (1967, 1969, 1972). Marxism's vision of class struggle between privileged bourgeoisie and exploited proletariat working classes, then, is replaced in dependency theory by a parallel, though globalized, pattern of exploitation and oppression. Privileged nations, in the view of dependency theory, constitute a so-called **core** (Galtung, 1971, 1981) or **center** (Wallerstein, 1974, 1979; Valenzuela & Valenzuela, 1998), whereas the underdeveloped nations form the marginalized **periphery** within a global society of nations sometimes called the "capitalist world system" (Wallerstein, 1974) or, more simply, the *world system*. The core or center nations, then, are the counterpart in dependency theory of Marxism's bourgeoisie, and the periphery corresponds to the exploited proletariat.

Dependency theory also adopts from Marxist philosophy an historical methodology in building an explanation of unequal relations among nations. Therefore, also like Marx, dependency theorists have generally described the growth of dependent relationships within the global system in terms of progress through historical stages, as mentioned. Recall that Marx saw capitalism as a stage in the overall process of change regarding the production and distribution of material essentials. In that view, capitalism represented a more mature stage in the material history of humanity and an inevitable step toward even more mature stages, namely socialism and, ultimately, communism (Fägerlind & Saha, 1989). Dependency theory describes the contemporary period of transnational capitalism as a consequence or product of progression in stages from **colonialism** (Valenzuela & Valenzuela, 1998):

■ During a *period of mercantilist colonialism* (spanning from roughly 1500 to 1750), colonizing powers instituted in colonies the production of commodities that were desired but difficult or impossible to produce in the colonizing countries themselves—for instance, sugar, cocoa, or coffee. The productive activities in the colonies therefore created no direct economic competition with the productive activities of the colonizers. This focus upon the production of commodities that were rare and unavailable within the colonizing countries distracted the colonizing countries from establishing economic self-sufficiency within the colonies, sowing the seeds of economic dependency.

■ During the *period of outward growth* (circa 1750–1914) the roles of private elites within the colonies generally declined and the role of an authoritarian colonial bureaucracy generally expanded. This shift formalized the dependent relationship as a state-to-state affair, and, because of the vertical organization of an official bureaucracy, produced a system by which compliance within the periphery could be more easily managed by the privileged nations of the core.

■ A *period of crisis of the liberal model* corresponded with the Depression and the world wars. These events produced "a collapse of external demand" (Valenzuela & Valenzuela, 1998, p. 267) for the dependent nations' products. This ultimately created reliance in the dependent countries upon increased foreign investment and consequently resulted in increased foreign debt. This was a crisis of the liberal model, since, in economic terms, liberalism (connoting literally "freedom") refers not to progressive, left wing politics (as it might mean today) but to the supposed desirability of keeping the market free from manipulation by governmental intercessions—a policy stance normally associated with political conservativism. Thus, a high degree of investment and lending activity was necessary in this period in order to artificially shore up the dependent economies. This situation contradicted economic liberalism's commitments regarding the economy's capacity to mend itself by mechanisms the ideology assumes to be natural and free.

Significant debtorship continues to characterize the contemporary "transnational capitalist" period. And since 1950, the multinational corporation has become more dominant, contributing to increasingly globalized divisions of labor. Dependency is now most overtly apparent in the peripheral countries' provision of cheap labor. Although this activity in one sense does constitute participation in the international economy—a point many free trade supporters emphasize in positive terms—from the perspective of dependency theorists, this labor-oriented economic focus does not provide the majority of people living within the periphery with equitable access to the expensive value-added products produced by the industrialized core countries. The core's membership within the global economy is fundamentally compromised and limited, then, according to dependency theory.

Although the descriptor *dependency* stresses the dependent status of the peripheral nations, dependency theory holds that core members of the world system are in a sense dependent as well, relying upon a mode of international economic relations that justifies the global inequities that exist. Lending credibility to the dependency interpretation as to the core nations' reliance upon the export of low-wage labor, for instance, a United States policy paper titled *America's Choice: High Skills or Low Wages* (Commission on the Skills of the American Workforce, 1990) optimistically predicted that, with proper education, American youths might assume higher-paying positions and avoid lower-paying jobs, such as those in manufacturing trades. This example illustrates, first, functionalist theory in action, with its certainty that educational improvement is a prescription for secure standing within the international economic community. Second, however, the example hints at the continuing relevance of dependency theory's Marxist critique about the ways that the world system seeks, in the name of stability, to sanction the veiled inequities among nations. *America's Choice* does not address the outcome it seeks, by implication, to foster—namely, the performance of essential but low-paying manufacturing work by the peoples in less privileged corners of the globe.

As description of the phases of dependency has suggested, dependency theory also adopts from Marxism a descriptive analysis of various means by which the transfer and control of resources is unfairly manipulated within the capitalist system. In classical Marxism, the bourgeoisie, in its effort to maintain unequal distribution of resources, resorts to collusion, the creation of cartels and monopolies, and, ultimately, to violent means (Cohen, 1982). Similarly, dependency theory describes specific means by which the core nations seek to maintain and nurture the periphery's dependent status in the global society of nations. These strategies include plunder, neocolonial relations, and transnational corporate activity (Fägerlind & Saha, 1989). Outright plunder, which more aptly typified core/peripheral relations in the past, is a core nation's taking of a peripheral country's resources with little pretense of fair remuneration. Kelly and Altbach (1978) have defined **neocolonialism** as "the deliberate policies of the industrialized nations to maintain their domination" through "foreign-aid programs, technical advisors, publishing firms or other means" (p. 30), distinguishing neocolonial activities from classical colonialism's overt "nation-to-nation domination" (p. 1). (For the sake of completeness, but more incidental to dependency theory per se, these authors also describe internal colonialism as the domination of one group by another within the borders of a country.) We have seen that transnational corporate behavior can affect global divisions of labor when corporations headquartered in the core countries export certain tasks to foreign countries where they can be performed more cheaply than they can within the developed core. Transnational corporate intercession within the periphery can easily become more brazen and overt, as it did in Chile in the early 1970s, when the International Telephone and Telegraph Company used both legal and illegal interventions in an effort to prevent Salvador Allende's election as president (Sperro, 1990).

To these more visible and explicit methods for asserting economic domination and exploitation, dependency theoreticians have also noted that overt domination is not essential in maintaining exploitive relations between the core and the peripheral countries. Instead, according to some dependency theorists, as long as elite sectors within the peripheral countries are themselves advantaged by the generally exploitive core/peripheral relationship, these elite elements help sustain inequity in the global system, and they occupy a rung Frank (1972) has dubbed the "Lumpenbourgeoisie." Core and peripheral countries, then, have their own internal core and peripheral structures, as the grand theory of Marxism stressed. Dependency theory describes the behaviors of these internal class structures within a context of global economic relations. The core elements of the peripheral nations, working on their own behalf but to the benefit of the core nations, assert their power and status in ways that preserve inequitable social conditions (Frank, 1972; Galtung, 1981).

Dependency theory is subject to a number of criticisms. First, although the theory offers valuable insights regarding the extent to which external factors can shape the nature of development, dependency theory could focus too completely upon these external factors. Seeking to address this shortcoming, some writers have undertaken to explain more completely the interplay between internal and external factors. Grosfoguel (2000), for instance, has offered an explanation for how elite classes in developing societies (specifically in Latin America) were able to maintain their status by nurturing the appearance of defiance in dealing with the colonial powers, reinforcing perceptions among local working class people that the landowners were kindred spirits unified against European exploitation. Yet, the same elites willingly enough accepted their concurrent role as buffers of conscience for European colonizers themselves.

Dependency theory is further limited by its pessimistic view of the impetus of a society to maintain itself. While, from an anthropological perspective, one might observe with interest or even admiration the ways in which cultural and social ways are passed on from one generation to the next—largely through both formal and informal educational practices—dependency theorists view these efforts with suspicion when viewing the formalized education practices in the industrialized West or in industrializing nations. Marxist theory, in general, critiques this impetus toward consensus in capitalism, yet Marxism's view that centralized rule by a proletarian elite was essential belies some underlying interest in stability—a construct it systematically critiques in capitalist societies. As is apparent in the case of educational reform in the former German Democratic Republic, it is inaccurate to describe the critical theoretical perspective as immune from fostering its own brand of self-preservation.

Dependency theory's Marxist stance has also been criticized on the grounds that its natural bias against capitalism limits the theory's ability to explain relationships among socialist countries that seem quasi-imperial and are in any case exploitive. Similarly, Kreuzmann (1999) emphasized the influence of the East-West dynamic of Cold War bipolarity. In that light, a particular limitation of dependency theory is that its focus on the dynamics between the colonizer and the colony reinforces some inappropriate deemphasis of Cold War economic competition, affecting international relations in profound ways. Fägerlind and Saha (1989) have pointed to additional quandaries regarding dependency theory's critique of capitalism by noting that it is, in itself, a conceptual leap to describe Latin American agrarian production as capitalist, on one hand, while describing the dependent nation as an exploited member of a world "system" on the other, for the economic heritage of Latin America's Portuguese and Spanish colonizers was not capitalist at the dawn of that region's colonial era.

The most persistent criticism of dependency theory, however, emerges from its methodological identity as historical. Dependency theory insists upon concrete historical circumstance, accepting differences from one nation's experience to another's as a natural result of this historical predisposition. Thus, dependency theory "has paid less attention to the formulation of precise theoretical constructs . . . and more attention to historical phases" (Valenzuela & Valenzuela, 1998, p. 267). Accordingly, dependency theory has not provided credible strategies for development. Instead, critics stress, its implicit lessons are to "sever trade relations, . . . refuse international aid . . . [and] nationalize multinational companies" (Fägerlind & Saha, 1989, p. 25). These views, such critics maintain, lack the pragmatism necessary to help members of developing societies to meet their needs and wants. Addressing this shortcoming in part, liberation theory has sought to bring a more affirmative and proactive posture to Marxist and dependency oriented arguments. Adopting Marxist tenets that oppression leads to estrangement and a lack of understanding regarding one's own exploited conditions, for instance, theorists such as Freire have stressed the role of literacy as an essential tool for addressing a similar genre of naive consciousness that oppression instills. In this way and others, liberation theory, our next focus, constitutes a set of approaches that "represent attempts to prescribe specific means to promote certain aspects of [development]" (Fägerlind & Saha, 1989, p. 25).

In sum, dependency theory builds upon Marxism's description of class struggle between privileged bourgeoisie and exploited proletariat working classes in order to describe a parallel but globalized pattern of exploitation and oppression. In this so-called world system, economically less advantaged nations in the periphery are exploited by the advantaged nations of the core or center. Dependency, therefore, is the circumstance in which "the economy of certain countries is conditioned by the development and expansion of another country" (Dos Santos, 1998, p. 252), placing control of the economic capacity and future of the peripheral country in the hands of one or more countries of the economic core. Applying comparative education's lessons to the teaching profession, dependency theory serves as a reminder of ways in which a society's pursuit of its own goals can bring negative consequences in ways that often remain unseen. In a world where continuing economic globalization seems inevitable, the dependency perspective challenges teachers and their students to appraise ways in which prosperity might be a **zero-sum** rather than a **plus-sum** condition.

Liberation Theory

We have seen that an important element of dependency theory derives from the observations of Frank (1972) and Galtung (1981) and describes how elites, within underdeveloped countries, can assert their power to preserve inequalities to their own benefit and to the detriment of less privileged citizens in their countries. Liberation theory, building upon that assumption, takes its name from the proposition that radical change in the economic, political, and cultural structures of the underdeveloped society are necessary to secure progress in the underdeveloped world. The focus of educational efforts toward change, according to the theory, begins and ends with the underdeveloped country's oppressed groups. Because of the theory's emphasis on goals of self-actualization, the success of such an effort is judged not primarily in terms of traditional measures of development, such as the attainment of higher income levels or living standards but rather, in terms of the objectives of participants (Schugurensky, 1998): "Liberation is development" (Fägerlind & Saha, 1989, p. 26). Liberation theory is also distinct from other theories of development by virtue of its aim to establish a dialogical relationship in which "the teacher becomes a facilitator, the traditional class becomes a cultural circle, and the emphasis shifts from lecture to problem-posing strategies" (Schugurensky, 1998, p. 19). Thus, in significant respects, the form of the educational experience liberation theorists envision is at once both a means and an end of education.

Liberation theorists' vision of education as a dialogic process derives from the view that traditional education in itself tends to embody a breed of classism in which the teacher occupies a position of authority—and, thus, of power. This relationship tends therefore to subvert students' progress toward the overarching aim of identifying and pursuing their own visions and goals. The Brazilian educator Paulo Freire, whose life and work is discussed in greater length in Chapter 4, is most prominently tied to liberation theory. Depicting the fundamental problem through imagery, Freire likened traditional authoritarian education to a banking transaction, in which the teacher deposits knowledge into the heads of students. Liberation theory eschews this educational scenario in favor of a liberatory or emancipatory model. The challenge, according to Freire (1984), is "how to teach without imposing to a student our own knowledge" (pp. 520–521) while also taking the equally necessary step of acknowledging to students one's own inevitable predispositions.

Literacy is a key tool in liberation theory's aim of enabling students' progress toward their own goals. This is because of the theory's emphasis on *conscientização*—"concientization" or consciousness raising aimed at arousing students' understandings of their exploited circumstances with an eye on empowerment and action in addressing them. Here, liberation theory draws upon Marxist formulations about the numbing effects of domination and alienation, in which alienated people become unaware of their condition and of their potential to change it. Reading and understanding language is essentially inseparable from the act of understanding and appraising one's circumstances (Schugurensky, 1998). And the cautious responses of some elites within the developing world have tended to validate the theory's claims regarding the importance of literacy in particular and its longer-range goal of consciousness raising. Indeed, when a group of Brazilian peasants acquired functional literacy within a 40-day period, the Brazilian government cancelled their literacy program, forcing their teacher (Freire) into exile.

The reason for the cancellation "was clearly not its inefficiency, but, rather, the military government's fear of its potential political implications" (Schugurensky, 1998, p. 20).

A chief criticism of liberation theory is that it is utopian in its visions both at the level of instruction and in terms of longer-range change (Fägerlind & Saha, 1989). Others have noted that liberation theory might exalt reflection over action toward change and progress, thus undoing the impetus toward change it strives in other ways to fulfill.

In sum, liberation theory involves seeking to enable the self-actualization of participants in a process of joint learning between teacher and student. Its original and primary focus was upon the oppressed and underprivileged sectors within the countries of the developing world. Owing in no small part to the charisma and dedication of Freire, liberation theory has contributed to the expansion of international dialogue on education and its role in social transformation. It's important to note that critical theories, blending Marxist and neo-Marxist traditions with postmodern and poststructural approaches, are contributing to educational research and thinking in the United States in spite of the political scrutiny it endured during and following the McCarthy era (Lincoln, 1995). Critical theory has, as a fundamental purpose, the task of reasserting "the basic aim of the Enlightenment ideal of inquiry," namely, "to improve human existence by viewing knowledge for its emancipatory or repressive potential" (McLaren & Giarelli, 1995, p. 2). The need for such a reassessment is urgent, in that more mainstream scientific and social scientific paradigms undermine the Enlightenment ideals—the freedom and enlightenment of individuals and societies—from which they had derived their impetus (McLaren & Giarelli, 1995). Liberation theory accommodates dependency theory's observation that, without literacy and awareness of oppressive circumstances, self-determination is a goal that will remain unreachable by a majority of people in the developing world.

POSTMODERNISM AND POSTSTRUCTURALISM: THEORETICAL CHALLENGES TO THE MODERN

The preceding parts of this chapter suggest that a preoccupation of many theorists within the social sciences is the question of whether there is or is not agreement across a society. Discussion shows how proponents of the grand consensus theory of structural-functionalism and allied perspectives in comparative education—modernization theory and human capital formation theory—see consensus as a natural and desirable condition that emerges from a social system's tendency to preserve its equilibrium. Meanwhile, conflict theories, such as the grand theory of Marxism and comparative education's subtheories of dependency theory and liberation theory, call for critically questioning the nature of social consensus and considering the ways in which circumstances of apparent accord within a social system might actually be the products of conditions of oppression (i.e., forced agreement rather than genuine consensus). Conflict theorists, therefore, would argue that change and growth within social systems are often the products of struggles or conflicts whose aims are to overthrow privileged groups within an existing social order and, thus, to seek change by replacing, rather than merely revising, existing conditions. As we have seen, these are profoundly different views of social change in many respects.

Although structural-functionalist theories and Marxist conflict theories reach starkly different conclusions about the desirability of consensus and of education's role in preserving it, a crucial point is that both perspectives are an attempt to explain "the maintenance of the status quo in society" (Ballantine, 2001, p. 10). As such, Marxist and structural-functionalist theories, therefore, have additional shared features and foci that postmodernist and poststructuralist thinking have helped to question. We turn now to a description of the roots and implications of poststructuralism and postmodernism, and then to examples of the ways these theoretical developments have influenced comparative education theory.

The Meaning of *Post-* and the Roots of Postmodernism and Poststructuralism

Understanding **poststructuralism** and **postmodernism** requires seeing *post-* as meaning "following" in the sense of "trailing behind and coming in the wake of." Understanding postmodernism and poststructuralism requires a particular mindfulness regarding certain intellectual occurrences that came beforehand. The term *postmodernism* refers to a broad philosophical discussion that presses us to ask, "How is humankind to learn and behave now that it has come to certain realizations about the nature of modernity?" Similarly, the claims and implications that poststructuralism generates are not merely assertions of what we should think "now that structuralism is finished," but rather they require us to ponder more deeply, "What we have learned from the structuralists, and now how can we learn . . . and what should we do?" As Lyon (2000) stated in reference to postmodernism, "the 'post' prefix . . . tantalizes us" in particular because it prompts not only the question of "what is or was the social condition of modernity" but also "how post-modernity might be different" (p. 221).

Having seen, then, that *post-* requires awareness of the continuing influences of prior position, one must be prepared to learn more about the particular significance of **modernity** and of **structuralism**. What are these events or discoveries that poststructuralist and postmodernists would have one bear in mind?

Postmodernism and the Problem of Modernity. At face value, the words *modernization* (discussed in the previous section) and *modernism* (as in *postmodernism*) seem nearly synonymous—an impression that is reinforced by the fact that overt distinctions between these two vastly different perspectives regarding "the modern" are not routinely and systematically explained. The potential for considerable misunderstanding persists, at least in part, due to issues of communication regarding vying perspectives about the essence of modernity. These competing conceptions of "the modern" relate to fundamental differences regarding the ways knowledge is and should be valued. Thus, distinguishing between differing notions of modernity sheds further light on postmodern arguments that influence comparative education's theoretical discourse.

Modernization refers to a particular application of structural-functionalist thought and embodies one predisposition as to the meaning of "the modern." Modernization, from that perspective, is a natural condition to which societies evolve on account of their own tendencies toward growth and self-perfection. From the perspective of modernization, this process can be further spurred by rational and well-conceived plans and policies. An alternative interpretation of the modern condition—and one that receives our attention in this discussion of postmodernism—is more circumspect about the fundamental nature of modernity, describing it as a crisis of certainty.

This crisis is sometimes called the "modern condition" or the "**modern problem**" and found its most important prophecy in the thinking of Friedrich Nietzsche (1844–1900), who described the psychological state of nihilism as the product of humankind's disappointed faith in the morality of truthfulness. The propensity to assign meaning to events is fundamental to the human psychological condition, Nietzsche (1967) stipulated. When confronted with new explanations or patterns of meaningfulness, people respond either by accommodating this explanation into existing schemes of truth and order or by adopting a new scheme. These psychological mechanisms reflect the human need for objective truth—for a master source of explanation to bring meaning and understanding to the world. For Nietzsche, a state of persistent disappointment about the very possibility of an enduring truth epitomized his era. This was a period, after all, in which religious doctrines, a long-standing source of truth and order, were challenged by emerging scientific claims such as the evolutionary theories of Charles Darwin (1809–1882) in particular. Further, the exponential nature of discovery during that period forced humans to adjust psychologically at faster and faster rates. Nietzsche, therefore, described a world in which fundamental notions of truth seemed questionable. When faced with a continuing succession of assertions as to what constitutes truth, the fleeting nature of patterns of truth also becomes evident, and truth is sought more in desperation than for the sake of curiosity and enlightenment.

It is significant that the crisis of certainty that Nietzsche described in the late 19th century persists. Tensions between ethical and scientific imperatives continue to occupy public debate—those regarding a moral course of action regarding human cloning, for example. To the impetus of general doubt that modernity initiates, structuralist realizations about the ways language itself further structures human perceptions of reality and, thus, the truth lend some credence to postmodernism's skepticism.

Structuralist Revelations about Language and Thought. Poststructuralism's principal antecedent is in structuralist linguistics and is most indebted to the work of Ferdinand de Saussure, whose 1913 work *Course in General Linguistics* is an attempt to define the integral object of study in the field of linguistics. Earlier linguists had demonstrated that the sign in human language—that is, the meaningful sound or graphic device—was arbitrary. Thus, they concluded that there exists no intrinsic meaning in signs, but, rather, only the meanings that are assigned to them. Just as a small statue of a horse might to one person be a game piece but a small idol to another person, for instance, the word *die* means one thing in English ("to cease living") and quite another in German ("the"). Saussure concluded, then, that neither the sound or letters, on the one hand, nor the concept these sounds or letters represent, on the other hand, are the true object of interest to the linguist; rather, it was the interface between sounds or letters and the concept they represented that should be the true object of study. This was perplexing, however, because though the interface between sounds or concepts and the things represented obviously enough existed, it was unobservable and inseparable.

Saussure's thinking about the ways signifiers translate to signifieds produced further observations about conceptual value within systems of signs that remain central to poststructuralist thought. Of key importance, for instance, was that linguistic value (e.g., word meaning) is derived from a hidden process of conceptual pairing. One half of such a conceptual valuation is a thing deemed similar with the object valued, and serves as a reference against which comparisons are then possible. The other half is a dissimilar thing against which value can ultimately be determined. This is important because Saussure showed that linguistic value is fixed by concurrence of things lying outside the object valued. Although Saussure further maintained that the realm of language and linguistics is uniquely abstract because it deals with representations of representations, the poststructuralist rejects this assertion about the uniqueness of linguistics. The poststructural argument is that this inseparable nature describes all statements or claims of value. All such claims—not claims as to linguistic value alone—are anchored by the concurrence of things that are supposed to be external but that are actual products of our own conceptions of the external. Paradoxically, these conceptions must be internal, shaped, as they are, by humans' internalized constructions and notions of the things they presume to be external. Thus, all values, the poststructuralist seeks to show—including one's very claims regarding truth and knowledge—can be described as abstractions. Even in the "hardest" of the so-called hard sciences, the poststructuralist concludes, the objects of study assume conceptual functions that are imposed by observer viewpoints.

Poststructuralism and Postmodernism's Allied Argument. Though poststructuralism's roots are distinct from those of postmodernism, the claims of both these *post-s* lend credence to an overall argument that the focus of any study is subjective in nature. A so-called culture war has characterized theoretical debates in and out of comparative education, pitting rationalist views about an ordered and unitary world in which assertions of truth can be objectively verified against postmodernist/poststructuralist claims about truth's subjective nature. It is not surprising that many continue to find the postmodernist and poststructuralist position threatening. For others, postmodernism's and poststructuralism's joint impetus of questioning static and orthodox notions of truth has increased critical evaluation of the knowledge previously accepted without question. From this viewpoint, rather than functioning as a disruptive force in educational theorizing, the postmodernist stance has enriched the field: By calling into question pat formulations of the truth, postmodernist and poststructuralist thought enables contributions from a number of alternative perspectives.

It is in any case not necessary to resolve this debate in order to state that theoretical discourse is no longer characterized solely by formulations purporting objectivity. Taking the growing influence of poststructuralism and postmodernism as a given, objections about these theories often focus on the ways postmodernism and poststructuralism have been haphazardly appropriated such that their most challenging and persistent claims are ultimately ignored. "What we see when the words 'post-modern' and 'poststructural' are thrown around . . . often achieves little more than a sad pastiche of half-digested fragments" (Young, 1997, p. 498) that rarely approach the complexity and depth of postmodernism's and poststructuralism's fundamental argument. For instance, the view that postmodernity is primarily a description of "contemporary social conditions in which communication and information technologies and consumerism have become predominant" (Lyon, 2000, p. 235) seems to neuter the postmodernist and poststructuralist argument by equating the problem of modernity with the "ultra-modern." Such a view would seem to demand only that uncertainties about the relative or subjective nature of truth be interpreted as glitches in a yet-to-be-perfected rationalist view of the world. Further, such a reduction, from the perspective of postmodernism, appears to be "an attempted fashion statement" (Young, 1997) and thus seems to court an aura of complexity while packing postmodernism's more provocative claims about modernity too tightly into more traditional and rational conceptions of the modern. This sort of pragmatic and reflexive reversion to rationalism, in the view of the postmodernist, simply "does not recognize what modern linguistic theories have alerted us to about the inherent ambiguity and relational character of concepts" (Popkewitz, 1999, p. 2).

Postmodernism's Influences in Comparative Education

Neither postmodernism or poststructuralism purports to constitute a theory in the way that either structural-functionalism or Marxism consists of a system or pattern of assumptions and thought. Precisely because poststructuralist and postmodernist are skeptical toward an "all encompassing explanation of the world" (Ballantine, 2001, p. 15), the influences of poststructural and postmodernist thinking are more diffuse and eclectic than is true of the positions of Marxism or structural-functionalism. In general, the major influence of postmodernism and poststructuralism is to provide a rationale for drawing to the **center** human perspectives that have heretofore occupied terrain at the margins—as forgotten, neglected, unexplored, or somehow subverted. As such, postmodernism, according to Ballantine (2001):

- Embraces the diverse and ambiguous nature of human contexts
- Acknowledges and seeks to make explicit the value-laden nature of education but also to explicate the power structures associated with schools' formalization of values and interests (citing Cherryholmes, 1988)
- Stresses local context of theory—the adaptation of theory to context rather than context to theory.

Although neither postmodernists nor poststructuralists hope or pretend that their claims constitute a crystallized theory or system of thought, some of their methods and influences are discrete. As discussed previously, the structuralist linguist argues that linguistic value is derived from a process of appraising an object through a process of dichotomization (see **dichotomy**). In the textual operation known as **deconstruction**, for instance, the poststructural analyst often locates implicit and explicit binary oppositions identifying ways in which one term dominates the other within a **text** (Culler, 1982). This method of critique figures in criticisms of Paulo Freire on the grounds that his arguments often rely on dualistic views of reality, employing pairs of opposites in which, as poststructuralist argumentation maintains,

> one is the preferred position, like banking education and problem-posing education, oppressor and oppressed, culture of silence and dialogue, alienation and solidarity. If each proposition presupposes the opposite, it is asked whether, ontologically, the preferred

polarity actually exists (Schugurensky, 1998, citing Coben, 1997). Moreover, it has been claimed that an opposition between education for domestication and education for liberation is unproductive because education is unproductive.

(Schugurensky, 1998, p. 24)

Similarly, though more generally, poststructuralist thought describes constructs or elements readily accepted by society as occupying a privileged position at the cultural center and, with postmodernism, assists in challenging the presumed superiority of relationships that the center imposes or dictates. This work of decentering an articulation of theory or policy is the intellectual exercise of exposing or making its usually implicit hierarchies explicit. Because poststructuralists hold language to be a principal determinant of human perception, deconstruction is the wider effort within theoretical argumentation in the social sciences to dismantle and question claims and their underlying purposes and presuppositions. Post modernist analyses often take on the work of recentering arguments by reversing hierarchies in order to generate new interpretations of the desirable and thereby to promote new understandings of an entity formerly relegated to an inferior position within the dominant system of assumptions occupying the terrain at the center. Postmodernist argumentation can, for instance, help us question the North-South dichotomy that figures so prominently in both modernization and dependency formulations, showing that its underlying meaning is North/not-North, and substituting a South-centered perspective that illuminates more genuinely the essence of existence in the so-called South. This conscious effort to shift or recenter the operative perspective is further evident, for instance, in descriptions of the colonial experience in terms of "migration, slavery . . . and resistance" (Tikly, 1999, p. 604) rather than in terms of the "deliberate policies of the industrialized nations" (Kelly & Altbach, 1978, p. 30)—a more traditional and modernist summation in that it persists in interpreting the colonized nation in terms of the colonizer's activity.

As mentioned, Marxist and structural-functionalist theories embrace common perspectives as modern visions of society. First, like structural-functionalist theories of modernization and human capital formation, Marxist dependency theory emerged within Western civilization and applies Western values and experiences in pursuing its descriptive and explanatory claims. Both theoretical traditions tend to equate development with social change. Further, although their adherents assert different visions about how change can and should occur, both traditions involve seeing change as inevitable and that the end in view is desirable. Both theoretical traditions—not just structural-functionalism—are structural to the extent that they analyze societies in terms of structure, embracing this structure either as benign, in the case of structural-functionalism, or in more pessimistic terms, in the case of Marxism. Further, each genre of theory is associated with political and economic interests that have a history of competition and hostility. Positions arising from postmodernist and poststructuralist corners have questioned these assumptions, considerably expanding theoretical discourse in comparative education.

Assumptions as to the accuracy of modernist structural-functionalist and Marxist positions on industrial growth "Western-style" are questioned in particular by a postcolonial perspective, which "draws attention to the central role that European colonisation . . . has played in defining the post colonial condition" (Tikly, 1999, p. 606). Specifically, the consensus perspective of structural-functionalist theory promotes a benign view of change as a mechanism of mere realignment. Postcolonialism responds, adopting a postmodern/

poststructural rejection of this Eurocentric reduction that "displaces the 'story' of capitalist modernity from its European centering" (Hall, 1996, p. 250). Meanwhile, Kreuzmann (1998) discusses the Western vantage from which Marx analyzed the process of industrialization in progress and from which he wrote, "The industrially developed country offers the less developed country a picture of its own future. . . . A nation should and can learn from others" (Marx, 1851, cited in Berger, 1996, p. 47). Here, Marx embraces the "modern," promoting its desirability over a way of life he depicts as outdated. The postcolonial response is to reject Western Marxism's view of transition from feudalism to capitalism (Hall, 1996).

The postcolonial argument described here unpacks the Western-centric assumptions of structural-functionalism and Marxism—in particular, those grand theories' embrace of a modernist image of growth. Other postmodern and poststructural perspectives emphasize the modernist view that society at large is an appropriate focus for analysis. Some feminist theorists, for instance, focus on the postmodernist's interest in difference: "The notion that women have been created and defined as the 'other' by men" (Parpart & Marchand, 1995, p. 6) harmonizes with rejections of "male definition of 'woman'," calling on women "to define themselves outside the male/female dyad" (Parpart & Marchand, 1995, p. 6). Regarding specific applications of postmodernist critiques in the developed world, bell hooks argues "for an African-American postmodernism where difference and **otherness** can be used to explore the realities of the black experience in North America" (Parpart & Marchand, 1995, p. 7). Some feminists in the developing world, meanwhile, have charged that feminists in the developed countries could be creating "a colonial/neo-colonial discourse" (Parpart & Marchand, 1995, p. 7) by depicting women in the developing world as consistently poor and powerless (Mohanty, 1991). All of these feminist positions employ postmodernist critical methods to reject the modernist focus on society as a totality, centering their analysis instead on the particular and the local and seeking meaning in these most particular terms.

The postmodernist aim of undoing the notion that society is a discrete entity might be necessary but is not sufficient in defining and delimiting postmodernist from modernist theories. At least two prongs of theoretical discourse falling under the rubric of ecological theories have challenged the notion of society as discrete. Only one can be described as postmodernist, however. The first, which Morrow and Torres (1995) call "ecological world systems theory" blends three elements: direct or indirect attention to population and the underlying theme of competition along neo-Darwinian lines; interplay among governments, formal education, and the work of development under the assumption that each resembles an organism within a single ecology; and the necessity for the construct of a system in order to account for global expansion of education. This genre of ecological theory, with its attention to quantifying the interplay among variables, is arguably functionalist rather than postmodern in its lineage.

A second form of ecological theory, though, does adopt postmodernist critique, extending it even into the so-called hard sciences by calling for a "natural science informed by the sociological imagination" (Dandeneau, 2001, p. 32). Dandeneau argues that science is beginning to question and reject its traditional "positivist self-understanding" (p. 32), which has been characterized by detachment from the social processes of history. He argues further that this cloak of neutrality with respect to human values is becoming increasingly irrelevant, and he noted more optimistically the emergence of calls for a different scientific stance—one that is responsive to imperatives such as historical epoch in addition to the more traditional scientific demands of the subject matter. With a view toward a more sustainable and equitable prosperity, this theory of ecology invites contrasts of mainstream perspectives toward progress (Jenkins, 2000; Williams & Taylor, 1999)—perspectives that are ratified daily in school classrooms—with alternative views toward healthy interaction with the natural world (Kiefer & Kemple, 1999).

There is, then, no single postmodernist/poststructural philosophy precisely because of the circumspection—the "incredulity" (Lyotard, 1988) with which the perspective's adherents view the possibility of a single all-encompassing theory. As a result, there is no single postmodernist list of interpretations about the prevailing mechanisms in schools, nor is there a single set of prescriptions about how they should be. In general, however, "postmodernists hold that the curriculum should not be viewed as discrete subjects and disciplines, but instead should include issues of power, history, personal and group identities, and social criticism leading to collective action" (Ozmon & Craver, 1999, p. 365). Because postmodernism generally suggests that an interplay of many factors shape students' identities, students' own experiences have an enhanced prominence in postmodernist views of instruction—an outlook that echoes that of John Dewey and other educational progressives in some respects. And regarding the role of teachers, postmodernism's lessons about the way language can shape and reinforce patterns of human relation call on teachers to be careful "of their influence over the language process and how it shapes the way students think and conceptualize" (Ozmon & Craver, 1999, p. 370).

As the preceding examples suggest, however, poststructuralist and postmodernist thinking has given rise to a more expansive terrain within the field of comparative education and elsewhere across the social sciences. Michel Foucault, in discussing the paradoxical nature of otherness, pointed to the fundamental unfairness of a world in which difference is prescribed and imposed by the mainstream, yet this imposed status becomes the very basis for exclusion and marginalization. Although the postmodernist and poststructuralist impetus has been dismissed as mischievous or criticized as the root of cultural or moral relativism, its goals, on the contrary, can be considered fundamentally moral: to create "thinking space" (George, 1989) and to make room for understandings of the essence of an experience in its own terms rather than in terms of a dominant other.

Sustaining Reflection

- Think of some instructional practices that you feel reflect education as a benign force. Can you think of any negative effects or by-products in your examples?

- Describe some of the benefits of unassisted (independent) development in underdeveloped regions. Describe benefits of assisted development. Consider whether these two approaches can be reconciled.

- Think of some currently prominent educational practices. What images of culture and society do they promote? How?

References

Ballantine, J. H. (2001). *The sociology of education: A systematic analysis* (5th ed.). Upper Saddle River, NJ: Prentice Hall.

Becker, G. S. (1960). Preliminary draft of study undertaken for National Bureau of Economic Research, New York.

Berger, J. (1996). Was behauptet die Modernizationtheorie wirklich—und was wird ihr bloß unterstellt? *Leviathan, 24* 45–67.

Billet, B. L. (1993). *Modernization theory and economic development: Discontent in the developing world.* Westport, CT: Praeger.

Bowles, S., & Gintis, H. (1976). *Schooling in capitalist America.* New York, NY: Basic Books.

Bowles, S., & Gintis, H. (1986). *Democracy and capitalism.* New York, NY: Basic Books.

Cardoso, F. H. (1972). Dependency and development in Latin America. *New Left Review, 74,* 83–95.

Carnoy, M., & Samoff, J. (1990). *Education and social transition in the Third World.* Princeton, NJ: Princeton Press.

Cherryholmes, C. (1988). *Power and criticism: Poststructural investigations in education.* New York, NY: Teachers College Press.

Clabaugh, G. T., & Rozycki, E. G. (1990). *Understanding schools: The foundations of education.* New York, NY: Harper Row.

Coben, D. (1997). Paulo Freire: Unanswered questions. *Taboo: The Journal of Culture and Education, 2*(2), 144–146.

Cohen, C. (1982). *Four systems.* New York, NY: Random House.

Commission on the Skills of the American Workforce. (1990). *America's choice: High skills or low wages.* Rochester, NY: National Center on Education and the Economy.

Culler, J. (1982). *On deconstruction.* Ithaca, NY: Cornell University Press.

Dandeneau, S. P. (2001). *Taking it big: Developing sociological consciousness in postmodern times.* Thousand Oaks, CA: Pine Forge Press.

Dore, R. P. (1976). *The diploma disease: Education, qualification, and development.* Berkeley, CA: University of California Press.

Dos Santos, T. (1998). The structure of dependence. In M. A. Seligson, & J. T. Passe-Smith (Eds.), *Development and underdevelopment: The political economy of global inequity* (pp. 251–261) Boulder, CO: Lynne Reinner Publishers. [Originally published in 1970, *The American Economic Review, 60*(May), 231–236.]

Fabian, J. (1983). *Time and the other.* New York, NY: Columbia University Press.

Fägerlind, I., & Saha, L. J. (1989). *Education and national development.* Oxford, UK: Pergamon.

Frank, A. G. (1967). *Capitalism and underdevelopment in Latin America.* New York, NY: Monthly Review Press.

Frank, A. G. (1969). *Latin America: Underdevelopment or revolution.* New York, NY: Monthly Review Press.

Frank, A. G. (1972). *Lumpenbourgeoisie and lumpendevelopment.* New York, NY: Monthly Review Press.

Freire, P. (1984). Education, liberation, and the church. *Religious Education, 79*(4), 520–521.

Frey, R. S., & Song, F. (1997). Human well-being in Chinese cities. *Social Indicators Research, 42,* 77–101.

Fukuyama, F. (1999). *The great disruption: Human nature and the reconstitution of social order.* New York, NY: The Free Press.

Galtung, J. (1971). A structural theory of imperialism. *Journal of Peace Research, 8*(2), 81–117.

Galtung, J. (1981). *The true worlds.* New York, NY: The Free Press.

George, J. (1989). International relations and the search for thinking space. *International Studies Quarterly, 33*(3), 269–279.

Giroux, H. A. (1992). *Border crossings: Cultural workers and the politics of education.* New York, NY: Routledge.

Grosfoguel, R. (2000). Developmentalism, modernity, and dependency theory in Latin America. *Nepantla 1*(2), 347–374.

Gutek, G. L. (1997). *Philosophical and ideological perspectives on education.* Boston, MA: Allyn & Bacon.

Habermas, J. (1971). *Knowledge and human interests.* Boston, MA: Beacon Press.

Hall, S. (1996). When was the post-colonial? Thinking at the limit. In I. Chamber, & L. Curti (Eds.), *The post-colonial question: Common skies, divided horizons* (pp. 242–260). London, UK: Routledge.

Inkeles, A., & Smith, D. H. (1974). *Becoming modern*. London, UK: Heinemann Education Books.

Jenkins, T. N. (2000). Putting postmodernity into practice: Endogenous development and the role of traditional cultures in the rural development of marginalized regions. *Ecological Economics, 34*(3), 301–313.

Kelly, G. P., & Altbach, P. G. (1978). Introduction. In P. G. Altbach & G. P. Kelly (Eds.), *Education and colonialism* (pp. 1–49). New York, NY: Longman.

Kempner, K. (1998). Post-modernizing education on the periphery and in the core. *International Review of Education, 44*(5, 6), 441–460.

Kiefer, J., & Kemple, M. (1999). Stories from our common roots: Strategies for building an ecologically sustainable way of learning. In G. A. Smith & D. A. Williams (Eds.), *Ecological education in action* (pp. 21–46). Albany, NY: State University of New York Press.

Kreuzmann, H. (1999). From modernization theory towards the clash of "civilizations": Directions and paradigm shifts in Samuel Huntington's analysis and prognosis of global development. *GeoJournal, 46*(4), 255–265.

Lincoln, Y. S. (1995). Foreword. In P. I. McLaren & J. M. Giarelli (Eds.), *Critical theory and educational research* (pp. vi—ix). Albany, NY; State University of New York Press.

Lyon, D. (2000). Post-modernity. In G. Browning, A. Halcli, & T. Webster (Eds.), *Understanding contemporary society: Theories of the present* (pp. 221–237). Thousand Oaks, CA: SAGE.

Lyotard, J.-F. (1988) An interview with Jean-Francois Lyotard (with Willem van Reijen and Dick Veerman). *Theory, Culture, and Society, 5*(2–3), 277–278.

Marx, K. (1951). *Das Kapital: Kritik der politischen Ökonomie*, Berlin, Germany: Dietz. [First volume of original edition appeared in 1867.]

McClelland, D. (1961). *The achieving society*. New York, NY: The Free Press.

McLaren, P. I., & Giarelli, J. M. (1995). Introduction: Critical theory and educational research. In P. I. McLaren, & J. M. Giarelli (Eds.), *Critical theory and educational research* (pp. 1–22). Albany, NY; State University of New York Press.

Merton, R. K. (1957). *Social theory and social structure*. Glencoe, IL: The Free Press.

Mohanty, C. (1991). Cartographies of struggle: Third World women and the politics of feminism. In C. Mohanty et al (Eds.), *Third World women and the politics of feminism* (p. 1–47). Bloomington, IN: Indiana University Press.

Morrow, R. A., & Torres, C. A. (1995). *Social theory and education: A critique of theories of social and cultural reproduction*. Albany, NY: State University of New York Press.

Nietzsche, F. (1967). *The will to power: Collected works of Friedrich Nietzsche*. New York, NY: Random House.

Okano, K., & Tsuchiya, M. (1999). *Education in contemporary Japan: Inequality and diversity*. Port Chester, NY: Cambridge University Press.

Ozmon, H. A., & Craver, S. M. (1999). *Philosophical foundations of education*. Upper Saddle River, NJ: Prentice Hall.

Parpart, J. L. , & Marchand, M. H. (1995). Exploding the canon: An introduction/conclusion. In M. H. Marchand, & J. L. Parpart (Eds.), *Feminism/postmodernism/development* (pp. 1–21). London, UK: Routledge.

Parsons, T. (1937). *The structure of social action*. New York, NY: McGraw-Hill.

Parsons, T. (1951). *The social system*. Glencoe, IL: The Free Press.

Parsons, T. (1966). *Societies: Evolutionary and comparative perspectives*. Englewood Cliffs, NJ: Prentice Hall.

Popkewitz, T. S. (1999). Introduction: Critical traditions, modernism, and the "posts." In T. S. Popkewitz & L. Fendler (Eds.), *Critical theories in education (social theory, education and cultural change): Changing terrains of knowledge and politics* (pp. 1–13). New York, NY: Routledge.

Portes, A. (1973). Modernity and development: A critique. *Studies in Comparative International Development, 8*(3), 247–279.

Ritzer, G. (1996). *Modern sociological theory*. New York, NY: McGraw-Hill.

Rostow, W. W. (1960). *The stages of economic growth: A non-communist manifesto*. Cambridge, UK: Cambridge University Press.

Rostow, W. W. (1971). *Politics and the stages of growth*. New York, NY: Cambridge University Press.

Sadovnik, A. R., Cookson, P. W., & Semmel, S. F. (2001). *Exploring education: An introduction to the foundations of education*. Boston, MA: Allyn & Bacon.

Schugurensky, D. (1998). The legacy of Paulo Freire: A critical review of his accomplishments. *Convergence, 31*(1–2), 17–29.

Schultz, T. W. (1961). Investment in human capital. *American Economic Review, 51*(March), 639–652.

Sperro, J. E. (1990). *The politics of international economic relations*. New York, NY: St. Martins Press.

Sztompka, P. (Ed.) (1996). *On social structure and science*. Chicago, IL: University of Chicago Press.

Tikly, L. (1999). Post-colonialism and comparative education, *International Review of Education, 45*(5–6), 603–621.

Tiryakian, E. A. (1995). Modernization in a millenarian decade: Lessons for and from Eastern Europe. In B. Grancelli (Ed.), *Social change and modernization* (pp. 249–264). Berlin, Germany: Walter de Gruyter.

Valenzuela, J. S., & Valenzuela, A. (1998). Modernization and dependency: Alternative perspectives in the study of Latin American underdevelopment. In M. A. Seligson & J. T. Passe-Smith (Eds.), *Development and underdevelopment: The political economy of global inequity* (pp. 263–276). Boulder, CO: Lynne Reinner Publishers. (Originally published in 1978, *Comparative Politics, 10*, 543–557.)

Wallerstein, I. (1974). *The modern world system*. New York, NY: Academic Press.

Wallerstein, I. (1979). *The capitalist world economy*. New York: NY: Cambridge University Press.

Williams, D. R., & Taylor, S. M. (1999). From margin to center: Initiation and development of an environmental school from the ground up. In G. A. Smith & D. A. Williams (Eds.), *Ecological education in action* (pp. 79–102). Albany, NY: State University of New York Press.

Young, R. (1997). Comparative method and postmodern relativism. *International Review of Education, 43*(5–6), 497–505.

Education in International Context: A Comparative Approach Applied to Contemporary Educational Issues

Part II consists of four issues-oriented chapters (chapters 3–6).

- **Chapter 3: Purposes of Schooling**
  In this chapter we focus on how diverse purposes of schooling shape educational curriculum in Hong Kong and Israel.

- **Chapter 4: Educational Access and Opportunity**
  In this chapter we explore a number of challenges to educational access and opportunity in Brazil and South Africa.

- **Chapter 5: Education Accountability and Authority**
  In this chapter we examine the ever-changing relationship between education and the state and how this dynamic relationship affects educator accountability and authority in Germany and England.

- **Chapter 6: Teacher Professionalism**
  In this chapter we explore the differing orientations to teacher professionalism and their impact on teacher autonomy and professional development in Japan and the United States.

Chapter 3

Purposes of Schooling

Focusing Questions

- What are the purposes of schooling? How do these schooling purposes represent conflicting societal aims?

- How do schools, through their policies and practices, sort and select students for work in a differentiated labor market?

- What values are represented in the school's curriculum?

INTRODUCTION

There are multiple and often competing purposes of schooling within a given society. Clabaugh & Rozycki (1990), for example, have challenged readers to consider whether schooling should pursue excellence, address the needs of the individual child, or provide equal opportunity for all children. Although educators strive to accomplish a variety of purposes at once, it is not always the case that schools and their respective curricular programs are judged for excellence, individuality, or equity. Rather, schools are often judged by their efficient operation or their maintenance of the established social, political, and economic order. To view schooling as a benevolent or benign institution that enables all students to gain the kinds of skills, attitudes, and knowledge necessary to lead fulfilling lives, at the individual level, and to contribute to a nation's productivity and stability, at the societal level, is to view formal schooling through a structural-functionalist lens. From a structural-functionalist theoretical perspective, the task of schooling is to reinforce the existing social and political structures, thereby maintaining the interests of members of the dominant culture (deMarrais & LeCompte, 1995). The survival of a society—one that favors members of the dominant culture—is dependent upon the transmission of "shared meanings, language, customs, values, ideas and material goods" (Clabaugh & Rozycki, 1990, p. 116). Shared

61

values are central to the concept of **culture** and their transmission is accomplished in part through the schooling of new members (i.e., children or members from other cultures) regarding the society's shared meanings (Clabaugh & Rozycki, 1990).

Hall (1959) has identified three levels at which culture operates: the formal, the technical, and the informal. The *formal level* refers to the explicit rules and understandings of appropriate behavior held by citizens; according to Hall, these overt rules are accepted at face value and seldom questioned. The *technical level*, although explicitly conveyed to citizens, does not invoke a value judgment about appropriate or inappropriate behavior; rather, Hall has pointed out that the concern is for school effectiveness. Educational procedures are developed carefully by outside experts, and the aim is the efficiency of schooling (Clabaugh & Rozycki, 1990). Hall has contended that the *informal level*, including nonverbal communication such as body language and eye contact, provides unconscious messages to citizens about proper and improper behavior. Claubaugh and Rozycki, referring to Hall's work, noted that the informal level is "the least visible level of culture; not because it is deliberately hidden, but because it operates primarily out of our awareness. Only when deviations occur do we notice something 'strange'" (Clabaugh & Rozycki, 1990, p. 129).

These three levels of culture are useful in considering whose culture is represented in a pluralistic society and whose interests are served. It is problematic to assume that all persons benefit equally from the cultural values promoted in schools. Often some students benefit more than others. Those students who benefit the most from schooling often hold views, language, and attitudes that are congruent with the dominant class. In this way, schools serve a reproductive function in that they mirror the society's class stratification: individuals—often divided along class, gender, and ethnic lines—receive differentiated curriculum through the educational practice of ability streaming, tracking, or grouping. Ability grouping refers to an instructional strategy whereby students are segregated via the particular curricular content and pedagogies they are exposed to during their schooling years. **Curriculum**, defined simply as *"what happens to students in school"* (deMarrais & LeCompte, 1995, p. 194), is a term that "refers to the total school experience provided to students, whether planned or unplanned by educators" (pp. 194–195). The planned activities in schooling are associated with the overt curriculum (e.g., textbooks and materials), and the implicit messages students receive about proper values and behaviors (e.g., punctuality, neatness, interaction between teachers and students) is defined as the **hidden curriculum** (Jackson, 1968, cited in deMarrais & LeCompte, 1995).

Through both the school's overt and hidden curriculum, students are exposed to intellectual, economic, political, and social purposes of schooling. From a structural-functionalist perspective, the intellectual purposes consist of students acquiring cognitive inquiry skills and knowledge that will, in turn, prepare them for the world of work (deMarrais & LeCompte, 1995). Thus, schools can be a training ground for students to learn particular work-related attitudes and values that help them assume jobs or positions in the labor force. The economic purposes of schooling, as argued by deMarrais and LeCompte, are manifested in the creation of a meritocracy whereby educators stratify students into classes and programs based on the perceived abilities and backgrounds of students, entitling some students to successful careers and profitable employment upon graduation. These sociologists also contend that schooling serves a number of political purposes, including the development of patriotism in students, obedience to laws, assimilation of immigrants into societal mores to preserve civility, and development of citizens who adhere to the political structure to maintain social order.

In addition to intellectual, economic, and political aims, deMarrais and LeCompte (1995) argue that the social purposes of schooling are accomplished through the development of students' moral and social responsibility whereby the school, in conjunction with other institutions such as churches and civic organizations, equips students with the abilities and skills to address social problems. From a structural-functionalist perspective, problems are viewed as situations to be fixed in order to restore societal balance and cohesion; problems are not seen as societal dilemmas to be questioned or as opportunities to overhaul an entire system (e.g., economic, governmental, social).

Because structural-functionalists value harmony and stability as necessary to a healthy functioning society, the values of efficiency and stability are applied to schooling. Education is seen as a necessary step to enable all students who apply themselves and work hard to climb the social ladder as adults (Okano & Tsuchiya, 1999). It is assumed that a consensus exists among diverse groups that schooling provides children with the requisite knowledge and skills for citizenship and work. The task of schools, therefore, is to identify children's talents and prepare them for specific social roles; unfortunately, as Okano and Tsuchiya have indicated, the matching of talents to positions often results in those categorized as "'talented' being channelled into the most 'important' positions" (p. 8). The researchers extended their analysis further, contending that a structural-functionalist perspective views society as accepting a consensus on social values, roles, and identities, as well as a consensus on who is 'talented' and what positions are 'important' for the talented to hold. From this theoretical perspective, then, the economic purposes of education (e.g., consumer productivity, national economic growth, personal income) override other educational aims (Okano & Tsuchiya, 1999).

In contrast to the structural-functionalist perspective, schooling can also be viewed from a conflict theoretical standpoint. Conflict theorists are concerned about the maintenance of a class structure that serves to privilege some over others and about the school's role in reproducing social class inequities. As deMarrais and LeCompte (1995) have stated, "schools maintain class structure by preparing its members for stratified work roles, giving rewards for use of dominant language, and placing state regulation over most aspects of school life" (p. 13). In other words, messages are conveyed to students that reinforce differences about their abilities and skills and that reinforce class, ethnic, and gender distinctions. The process of **socialization**, whereby a society passes its values and standards to the next generation, can be viewed as one of social transmission (the reproduction of culture) or social transformation (the production of culture) (Weiler, 1988, cited in deMarrais & LeCompte, 1995). Basing their work on Marxist principles of class divisions and class reproduction, conflict theorists claim that a temporary, contrived consensus exists among society's members who have accepted a particular set of values and standards that benefit a small, powerful group as opposed to the majority (Okano & Tsuchiya, 1999, p. 8). This consensus, which Okano and Tsuchiya term *ideology*, "conceals the fact that social relations are based on 'domination' rather than on harmony, and hides from the society's members the real nature of social stability, which exploits, and is contrary to the interests of, the majority" (p. 8).

Hegemony is a term that describes the process by which dominant social groups construct a social consensus—a consensus that is based on the dominant groups' views and that is reinforced and legitimated through positions in the media, government, churches, and schools (deMarrais & LeCompte, 1995). The danger is that the powerful groups that occupy important positions "prevent alternative views from gaining an audience or establishing their legitimacy" (McLaren, 1989, cited in deMarrais & LeCompte, 1995, p. 17). Ideologies are important for those concerned about education to consider because every stakeholder and powerholder embraces particular views of society and the role of schooling in that society. By examining ideologies, educators and others are in a position to better recognize the way ideologies operate in schools and how they might need to be changed to better meet the needs of all students. Schools, through explicit and implicit curriculum, transmit the prominent ideology in a society. For example, selecting youth for advanced classes based on their achievement scores is considered acceptable practice in some societies because schools are viewed as places that provide a level playing field for all students. Oftentimes, however, the students selected for advanced programs are chosen based on other criteria, such as family background, good behavior, or attentiveness to the teacher. deMarrais and LeCompte (1995) have found that "students whose cultural and linguistic competence is congruent with school expectations will be considered academically superior" (p. 16). In this way, "the powerful maintain, and even enhance, their resources and power" (Okano & Tsuchiya, 1999, p. 9).

The goal of exposing educators to consensus and conflict approaches through a sociological lens is to cultivate a broadened and enhanced understanding of the school–society relationship. By analyzing the complex purposes of schooling in an environment where economic, political, and sociocultural interests compete for attention in the school curriculum, the reader should come to better understand how schools are inseparable from the societies of which they are a part. An examination of the purposes of schooling in Hong Kong and Israel should reveal the differing theoretical approaches underlying the role of schools as they carry out their educational missions. Like Okano and Tsuchiya (1999), we describe these different missions in terms of their theoretical premises: (1) that schools, through meritocratic selection, prepare children for life in a society viewed as harmonious and stable (i.e., structural-functionalist, consensus perspectives) and (2) that schools, through curricular choices and educational practices, instill the dominant ideology of a society and cause children to accept that domination (i.e., Marxist, conflict perspectives).

ROLES AND IMAGES OF FORMAL SCHOOLING

Modern schooling assumes at least four roles: the transmission of knowledge, the socialization and acculturation of children, the selection and differentiation among children, and the legitimation of knowledge (Okano & Tsuchiya, 1999). The first role of formal schooling—*transmission of knowledge*—involves viewing schools as dispensers of the kind of knowledge that the society deems desirable and useful. As Okano and Tsuchiya have stated, the acquisition of basic skills in literacy and numeracy are considered essential to helping students reach their potential and fulfill their roles as contributing societal members. Second, schools *socialize and acculturate* students, through the overt and covert curricula. Values and behaviors are instilled through school routines that reflect routines of the work world. In Hong Kong, an examination-based system of entrance to esteemed secondary schools and tertiary institutions is accepted by a society that believes that students' hard work and abilities entitle them to the best schools and workforce positions. In addition to socialization and acculturation, the third role of modern schooling is *selection and differentiation.* According to Okano and Tsuchiya, schools select students for events, classes, and programs based on their academic achievement and other "objective" criteria; these experiences prepare some students to assume leadership positions in the labor market, whereas others are relegated to more subordinate positions. The fourth role of schooling is the *legitimation of knowledge.* That is, "schools legitimate what they teach to students simply by teaching it" (Okano & Tsuchiya, 1999, p. 6). Through the school curriculum, educators transmit a particular body of material for students to learn, thereby legitimating "that version of knowledge as 'true' and 'neutral'" (p. 6). Since all curriculums are value-laden, the school chooses those values that are congruent with the society at large. In time, the particular set of worldviews, values, and behaviors that are legitimated by society can come to be considered by its citizens as universal "and equally valuable for everyone" (p. 6).

The four roles are not mutually exclusive and occur simultaneously. Moreover, these roles can be thought of in divergent ways and contribute to different images of schooling each with its own functions and views of students and educators. Three prominent images of schooling identified by Clabaugh and Rozycki (1990) include school as *temple* or moral community, school as *factory* or production unit, and school as *town meeting.* *School as temple*, according to the researchers, "captures for many the breadth and depth of consensus hard to find in the multiple and shifting associations of our daily lives" (p. 41). Here, Clabaugh and Rozycki contend that schooling is primarily concerned with propriety: forming children's character, procuring their physical and psychological safety, and providing activities and experiences to incite student enjoyment of schooling. *School as factory* is focused on the goal of efficiency. In this conception, students are discouraged from questioning authority and succumb to preordained goals and values; "success is judged by testing outputs [and] infractions are dealt with because they impede production" (Clabaugh & Rozycki, 1990, p. 43). Hence, the principal's role of manager is comparable to that of a factory supervisor, the teacher's role of worker to that of the production-line laborer, and the student's role of raw material to that of a product created from prescribed inputs and procedures. *School as town meeting*, the third image of schooling, is concerned with power. Viewed in political terms, the school is a site in which a host of actors vie for position, power, and control of resources. According to Clabaugh and Rozycki, there is an expectation on the part of the public "that school procedures and processes will be open to negotiation for their sake" (p. 45). As representatives of the various stakeholders (parents, teachers, students, and administrators) vie for their own group's interests, knowledge and negotiation skills are extremely important. A town meeting connotes that there are no passive stakeholders; rather, individuals make sense of the event and act in accordance with their own interests as well as that of the group they represent (Okano & Tsuchiya, 1999).

For Clabaugh and Rozycki (1990), the kind of school image that is embraced is dependent on the benefits desired and the sacrifices made; the dynamic nature of schooling

Table 3.1 Images of Schooling, Roles of Stakeholders, and Benefits and Costs Assumed			
	Image		
Role/Factor	**Temple**	**Factory**	**Town Meeting**
Principal	High priest	Production manager	Negotiator
Teacher	Clergy	Worker	Negotiator
Student	Novice	Raw material	Negotiator
Primary function and basis for decision	Morality	Efficiency	Power
Success	Attaining intrinsic goods	Achieving output quotas	Maintaining power
Infraction	Immorality	Inefficiency	Inapplicable because no right/wrong established
Benefits	■ Clear authority ■ Community ■ Personal contact ■ Role models ■ Sense of unity	■ Established goals ■ Clear measures of progress ■ Impersonal system ■ Employment of technology ■ Disputability of goals	■ Moral equality ■ Changeability ■ Responsiveness
Costs	■ Development of castes (leaders and followers) ■ Domination ■ Suppression of dissent ■ Disguised power	■ Impersonal system ■ Alienation ■ Removed from decision making ■ Avoidance of ethical issues ■ Defined roles (planners and doers)	■ Power dominates ■ Instability ■ Frivolousness

Adapted from Clabaugh & Rozycki, 1990.

is found in the balance struck between the benefits and costs (see Table 3.1). The use of the two predominant theoretical lenses, structural-functionalism and Marxism, enables examination of manifest and latent purposes and aims of schooling.

SCHOOLING AND IDEOLOGY

The purposes of schooling are expressed in both explicit and implicit ways through school curricula and educational practices. Merton (1957) and Clabaugh and Rozycki (1990) have identified these purposes in terms of manifest and latent functions. Manifest functions, according to Clabaugh and Rozycki, are the open, intended purposes or aims of schooling often stated in government documents and school mission statements. Latent functions are more difficult to identify because they are the unintended or unrecognized outcomes of schooling; consequently, "attempts to isolate and highlight them tend to be controversial" (Clabaugh & Rozycki, 1990, p. 119). An example of a latent function is the way in which schools sort and select students for academic programs. An examination of ideology, and how it operates in the schools through both the explicit and implicit curriculum, can bring greater understanding and a more critical analysis to the roles schools play in their respective societies. Ideology refers to the process by which one social group exerts its own views and beliefs onto other social groups; thus, the dominated groups come to understand and accept this distorted view as reality (Cheung, 1997).

This process of the dominant social group exerting its own forms of consciousness and meaning onto dominated groups, as explicated by Cheung, is referred to by Easton (1965) as the **mobilization of bias**. Schools play a role in mobilizing bias through the organization and structure of the school curriculum. That is, the ideology of the dominant social group is transmitted to students through the kind of knowledge and values to which they are exposed. Even if students are exposed to the same curriculum, though this is often not the case, they experience the curriculum differently due to their own diverse backgrounds and abilities, and their interactions with peers, teachers, and school officials. In this way, "individuals attach varying meanings to schools as institutions and to the education that they provide" (Okano & Tsuchiya, 1999, p. xii).

AIMS OF SCHOOLING

The aims of schooling, according to Holmes (1981), are often expressed in general terms in order to induce widespread public appeal. Aims such as the holistic development of children and the acquisition of skills and knowledge deemed desirable for societal well-being are often palatable to a variety of stakeholders, including governments, businesses, parents, educators, and students (Holmes, 1981). Thus, the intentions of education, as Holmes has argued, are often described in terms of their intrinsic value (knowledge for knowledge's sake), their social value (process of initiation into acceptable social standards), and their intended outcomes (all-around individual development). The aims of schooling, therefore, represent a society's idealized hopes and visions for its citizens:

> In so far as aims are statements of what "ought to be the case" and represent man's hopes and aspirations not only for himself but for future generations, they are part of our socially constructed world and can be accepted or rejected according to taste. (p. 114)

The aims of education not only identify an intrinsic good, but also serve an instrumental function. "Intrinsic aims," according to Holmes (1981), "imply that certain educational activities, moral, aesthetic, intellectual and physical, are worthwhile in themselves and need no further justification" (p. 115). However, intrinsic aims only become meaningful when citizens understand how the aims are tied to demonstrable personal and societal outcomes. For example, the instrumental focus of formal education was apparent during the Middle Ages, when education was viewed as providing individuals with a vocation.

Toward this end, selected individuals were educated in three professions (clergy, medicine, and law), with the majority of citizens often trained through apprenticeships to fulfill less prestigious jobs and positions (King, 1968). Thus, as King has contended, formal education has always been restricted, in some form or fashion, to a narrowly defined group of people, as evidenced in the extensive formal training that was granted to males over females. From this analysis, one can infer that formal education has been "intended for recognisably restricted purposes" (King, 1968, p. 72).

Even though the opportunity for formal education has been extended to more and more people, the restricted nature of schooling is still manifested in the kind of knowledge that is validated, the ways students are stratified for purposes of learning, and the interests served by the implemented curriculum. The restricted nature of schooling is an area that concerns critical theorists such as Michael Apple, Samuel Bowles, and Herbert Gintis. The work of critical theorists has challenged educators and others to consider how schooling, disguised as a neutral and fair credentialing process, actually reproduces economic and social inequalities. Because curriculum inculcates students with particular social awareness, values, and behaviors, it can be said that the curriculum assumes a social and political role. Examining curriculum as social practice, therefore, can yield insights about the ways it privileges some citizens at the expense of others.

CURRICULUM: A MECHANISM OF SOCIAL AND CULTURAL REPRODUCTION

deMarrais and LeCompte (1995) have defined **cultural reproduction** as a process by which class-based differences, cultural and linguistic practices, and politics are embedded in the school's formal curriculum. A primary responsibility of the school, then, is to transmit those values, ideas, attitudes, and language (i.e., culture) deemed important by a society (Postiglione, 1997). According to Bowles and Gintis (1976), education is used to reproduce the kind of society favored by those in dominant or powerful positions. Schools in capitalist societies, therefore, are mechanisms for the social and cultural reproduction of a capitalist society. This reproduction, for Bowles and Gintis, is accomplished as schools (1) sort and select students for work in a differentiated labor market, (2) develop in students certain attitudes and views about their place in that work structure, and (3) legitimate social stratification through meritocratic ideology which espouses rule by a small elite.

Education, as a social process, exists for some particular purposes or ends (Kandel, 1933). These purposes or ends of schooling can be referred to in terms of their contributions to different aspects of human growth and national development. Thomas (1990) has identified a number of purposes that schools, in their respective societies, seek to cultivate in students. Generally, society has grouped these purposes into four areas, constituting particular curricular agendas for schools. First, schools seek to develop "good people" and "faithful supporters of the society" (Thomas, 1990, p. 26) through moral, social, and citizenship education. Second, schools seek to cultivate "skilled communicators" who are well-informed and who understand how the social and physical world operates (p. 26). According to Thomas, these skills and knowledge bases are cultivated through basic and liberal education programs. Third, schools seek to promote the physical and mental health of students in order that they might realize their dreams and experience personal fulfillment (Thomas, 1990). Finally, schools strive to develop "efficient workers" through vocational education (p. 26).

Whereas these general purposes of schooling could be considered the manifest functions of the curriculum, the ways in which curriculum is legitimated, stratified, and used to protect certain people's interests constitute the more latent functions of the curriculum. **Legitimate knowledge** is associated with the ideological dominance by powerful groups over less powerful groups in a society and how these ideological messages are communicated through the educational curriculum and practices. Michael Apple (1990) has challenged educators to consider what knowledge is of a high-status and low-status nature in schools. In other words, "What constitutes valid knowledge?" and "Whose purposes are served by that knowledge?" Apple, focusing his work on the ideological functions of school curriculum, proposes that the latent intention of the curriculum is to preserve the status quo. The goal of those in power is to safeguard their power; this is accomplished as power holders exert their ideological influence regarding the appropriate relationship of the individual to his or her society through school curriculum. In this way, knowledge can be understood as a commodity valued "not for itself, but as an instrument to something else" (Clabaugh & Rozycki, 1990, p. 508). The social, political, or ideological influence of curriculum, then, must "be situated within the trend of capital accumulation" (Cheung, 1997, p. 121). Thus, it is important to examine how the vocational or economic purpose of schooling "becomes the logic of curriculum" (p. 121). For a brief biographical sketch of critical educator Michael Apple see page 70.

According to Cheung (1997), schooling is often viewed "as the road to the promotion of the general welfare and interests of society" (p. 117). As such, the organization, structure, and content of schooling is rarely questioned; even when people do propose ways to improve education, their proposals are often "rejected in principle" (Cheung, 1997, p. 117). Thus, ideological dominance toward the economic purpose of schooling is evidenced in its stratified nature. A **stratified curriculum** constitutes another latent function of the schooling process. Clabaugh and Rozycki (1990) have found that curriculum is usually ordered in a logical fashion, whereby students progress from simple to more complex materials and skills. Moreover, as these sociologists have observed, educators are thought to have used sound pedagogy when theories (often based on how one cultural group learns) are applied to the curriculum. At the institutional level, schooling is thought to be efficiently managed when practices that minimize teacher workload and that maximize student learning are employed. The result is a curriculum that is stratified under the pretense of efficiency, while actually serving to categorize students based on their socioeconomic backgrounds and to lower the expectations underachievers hold for themselves.

In addition to legitimate knowledge and stratified curriculum, one must examine interests served by the curriculum. Clabaugh and Rozycki (1990) have identified three curricular interests that shape schooling: vocational interests, social control interests, and status interests. Vocational interests, according to these educators, are apparent in the kinds of skills to be derived from students' exposure to certain curriculum. Whereas vocational interests (e.g., reading, writing, and mathematics) are manifest functions of schooling, the other curricular interests, namely social control and status, operate in more latent ways. For example, Clabaugh and Rozycki have argued that social control interests, embedded in the curriculum, serve to protect the values and interests of the dominant cultural group

Michael Apple

Arguably, one of the more prominent contemporary American scholars interpreting U.S. education–society relationships through a neo-Marxist lens is Michael Apple. From a working class, inner city family himself, Apple's scholarship has embraced concepts of oppression and struggle, and his work reflects an ongoing concern for how citizens' material conditions can limit or privilege their voices in the public sphere. Viewing the state as an arena of struggle, Apple has contended that citizens vie for resources, with some people benefiting more than others. The involvement of his father and mother in political activism and his own background as a teacher and vice-president and president of the teacher union in New Jersey (1964–1966) have contributed to his political awareness and interest in the policy realm.

Upon receiving his doctorate in Curriculum Studies from Columbia University in 1970, Apple assumed an academic position at the University of Wisconsin-Madison. In his role as teacher–researcher, he has examined how the dominant majority culture is constructed and reconstructed in society through schooling. Apple, in his seminal work, *Ideology and Curriculum* (1990), argued that culture is transmitted through the official knowledge and socialization processes in American schools. Although school knowledge is often disguised as neutral and fair, students are selected and sorted through practices such as standardized testing and ability grouping that expose some students over others to high- or low-status knowledge. Because school curriculum inculcates students with particular social awareness, values, and behaviors, it can be said that the curriculum assumes a social and political role.

Apple has contended that the purposes served through differential exposure to high- and low-status knowledge is to preserve the existing inequalities mirrored in the society at large. To preserve the status quo and to safeguard power, the power holders in society exert their ideological influence through such differentiated curriculum. An example of curricular control is evident in the explicit and implicit messages in school texts and the economics associated with textbook publishing. For example, Texas has the second largest textbook market in the United States. The State Board of Education in Texas oversees the process of textbook adoption by ensuring that the texts promote values such as citizenship, patriotism, and free market enterprise. Moreover, a private citizen commission ensures that the guidelines for textbook adoption are followed, with the content of textbooks espousing the values of the dominant Texan majority (cited in Tozer, Violas, & Senese, 1998). This illustration provides but one example of the kind of critical analyses Apple has employed to reveal how the dominant culture is transmitted and the status quo is preserved at the state and national levels.

In 1991, Apple was awarded a distinguished professorship as John Bascom Professor of Curriculum and Instruction and Educational Policy Studies in the School of Education at the University of Wisconsin-Madison. At present, Apple continues to teach courses in curriculum theory and research and in the sociology of curriculum. His research interests are focused on the relationship between culture and power in education. Representative publications include *Education and Power* (1995) and *Cultural Politics and Education* (1996). The latter book is focused on the politics of national curriculum and testing wherein Apple analyzes the conservative agenda. In an interview with Carlos Alberto Torres, Michael Apple stated the twofold purpose of his book: " 'to interrogate critically the conservative restoration in education and the larger society; and to help make public the daily struggles to form an education in which democracy, caring, and social justice are not simply empty slogans' "(Torres, 1998, p. 44). Apple's recent scholarship has centered on the limits and possibilities of critical educational policy and practice within a nationally conservative political climate.

while suppressing the voices of less dominant groups. Status interests, according to these sociologists, are reflected in a curriculum that not only favors the dominant group's values (i.e., education for economic progress) but also enhances the dominant group's status (e.g., personal income) over that of other groups.

Consequently, one must consider whose interests are served by the formal curriculum. For example, Arnove, Kelly, and Altbach (1982) have argued that "teachers do not always represent the goals of those who set policy but mediate knowledge in ways that are favorable to their own class, cultural, and social interests" (p. 7). French and Raven (1959) have distinguished various forms of power that a person or group exerts according to the base of that power. Expert power, according to French and Raven, derives from specialized knowledge; referent power springs from trust; legitimate power is linked to title or position; reward power stems from the ability to provide something desirable to others; and coercive power is associated with the ability to invoke punishment. We argue that the most powerful connection between power and authority lies in **legitimate power**, whereby a dominant group exerts influence through a set of values that have been internalized by the dominated groups. In this way, culture can be reproduced to the benefit of the dominant group because those without power have come to believe in the values as well. Legitimate knowledge, stratified curriculum, and interests served, therefore, constitute a powerful framework to examine the purposes of schooling in any society.

THE HISTORICAL AND CULTURAL CONTEXT OF EDUCATION IN HONG KONG

The economic prominence of Hong Kong on the world's stage is astounding and warrants examination. Between the 1950s and 1996, Hong Kong transformed itself from a manufacturer of goods to the eighth largest trading entity in the world. Research conducted by the Heritage Foundation revealed that "Hong Kong has grown from a small fishing village to the world's freest economy out of 140 economies studied" (Cheung, 1999, p. 25). Formerly a British colony, Hong Kong's official status, as of July 1, 1997, has been that of a Special Administrative Region (SAR) of China, agreed upon in the Sino-British Declaration in 1984. Bray (1997) has described Hong Kong's process of reintegration with China as a prominent feature that distinguishes it from other colonial relationships. Because Hong Kong has not moved toward independence, researchers like Scott (1995) have argued that the situation is just another kind of dependency, a recolonization with external control being exerted by China rather than Britain. The motto "one country, two systems" is found in many documents detailing Hong Kong's transition. "One country" refers to Hong Kong's integration with China, and "two systems" describes the coexistence of two economic and political systems, namely the capitalist system of the SAR and the socialist system of the People's Republic of China (PRC). According to Bray (1997), "many constitutions permit diversity in the ideology of subnational governments, but no other country in the world has [a] formal provision which quite matches this arrangement" (p. 159).

In terms of citizenship identity, Hong Kong residents have been affected by traditional Chinese culture, British colonization, rapid modernization, and reunification with China

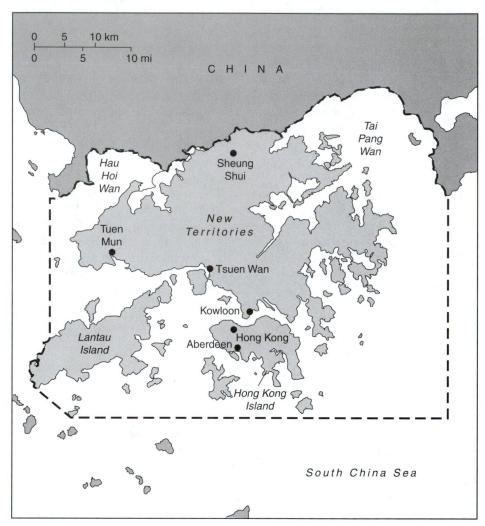

Hong Kong

*Source: The World Factbook. (2001). Hong Kong. Washington, DC: The Central Intelligence Agency,
U.S. Government. http://www.odci.gov/cia/publications/factbook/geos/hk.html*

(Friederichs, 1991). A feature common in Asian societies is that citizens hold a deep respect
for education. Hong Kong is no exception. Its education system emphasizes student effort
and discipline over inherited ability. Discipline is considered essential to the moral development of children. According to Cheng (1997), "traditional Chinese education accommodates moral, intellectual and physical education as its major ingredients" (p. 39), and discipline is part of this holistic vision of providing students with important life skills. In the
West, however, discipline is viewed in pragmatic terms—a necessary technique to curb
undesirable student behavior in order that teaching might proceed effectively. From a
Chinese perspective, then, discipline is part of moral education, and the role of schools is to

impart this shared value of Hong Kong society. For a comparison of sociopolitical factors shaping education in Hong Kong and Israel, see the Points of Convergence box (Figure 3.1).

Schooling in Hong Kong is structured in terms of primary, junior secondary, and senior secondary education. Since 1978, nine years of schooling has been mandated, and students must attend formal schooling until they reach age 15 or Form 3 (Cheng, 1997). The nine years of schooling is divided into six years of primary education and three years of secondary education. In Hong Kong, primary and junior secondary schooling is referred to as basic education. As Cheng has explained, "junior secondary education is part of a five-year secondary education provided by secondary schools. In most of the secondary

FIGURE 3.1

Points of Convergence

HONG KONG	Sociopolitical factors and educational consequences	ISRAEL
Aspect: In 1841, Hong Kong was occupied by the United Kingdom. One year later, however, Hong Kong was formally ceded by China. Based on the agreement signed by China and the U.K. in December 1984, Hong Kong became the Hong Kong Special Administrative Region (SAR) of China on July 1, 1997.		**Aspect:** After the Second World War, Britain withdrew from Palestine, and the United Nations partitioned Palestine into separate Jewish and Arab states—an arrangement that was unsatisfactory to the Arabs (*World Factbook*, 2001).
Response: Referred to as "one country, two systems," the agreement promises that China's socialist economic system will not be practiced during the next 50 years. Rather, Hong Kong SAR will maintain its capitalist economic system and enjoy autonomy in domestic matters, except for foreign and defense affairs (*World Factbook*, 2001).	How have unique sociopolitical factors shaped education?	**Response:** The Israelis and Arabs engaged in a series of wars that only deepened existing tensions. Since the Madrid Conference in October 1991, bilateral negotiations between Israel and Palestine have ensued. Israel withdrew from the Sinai region in April 1982 and from southern Lebanon in May 2000. However, the tensions between Israel and Arabs continue to this day.
Consequence: One year before the change of sovereignty, the state directed attention to the formation of a national, civic identity. The focus in civic education was to produce "good" Hong Kong citizens who recognize their membership to a larger entity, the People's Republic of China (PRC). One of the most apparent changes has been the revision of syllabi and textbooks that give more attention to the PRC and that depict China in a more positive light (Tan, 1997).		**Consequence:** In an attempt to facilitate a peace process between Israelis and Arabs, Israel adopted a new civics curriculum in 1994 that was to focus on human rights and universal democratic principles (Sprinzak, Bar, & Levi-Mazloum, 1994). A review of history and civics textbooks (Firer, 1998), however, revealed that human rights violations and controversies faced by minorities were often missing from Israeli texts and that only one text, used as optional reading, presented students with information on the Arab–Israeli conflict.

schools, there is an additional two-year pre-university sector comprising Form 6 and 7, sometimes known as the sixth forms, preparing students for entrance to higher education institutions" (p. 26). The major subjects studied by students in junior secondary education include mathematics, Chinese language, and English language. In senior secondary classes (i.e., Form 4 and 5), students learn science, arts, commerce, or other general education streams. According to Cheng (1997), students enrolled in pre-university courses (i.e., Form 6) are exposed to a narrowly defined curriculum encompassing about three to six subjects based primarily on tertiary entrance requirements.

There are three types of schools in Hong Kong: government, aided, and private schools. Governmental schools are managed and financed by the central Education Department in Hong Kong. Although financed through public funds, aided or sponsored schools are managed by charitable organizations, churches, fraternities, and voluntary agencies. Private schools, managed independently, are funded by school fees. In general, the average class size at secondary government and aided schools is 40; by Form 6, this number is reduced to 30 (Cheng, 1997). The student–teacher ratio is lower at private schools, some of which are international schools.

Due to a traditional high regard for education in general, people in Hong Kong strive to obtain as much education and as many levels of education as possible (Cheng, 1997). Moreover, "parents regard education as the proper and almost unique route for upward social mobility" (Cheng, 1997, p. 37). Thus, competition for entrance to the best secondary schools, tertiary institutions, and workforce positions is accepted. The Secondary School Places Allocation scheme is based on a meritocratic system whereby secondary schools are assessed and rated from high to low based on students' aptitude tests. Despite some randomization and some concern for geographic distribution, the end result is that the best students attend the best schools (Cheng, 1997). According to Cheng, approximately one third of the student population is selected for pre-university study (i.e., Forms 6 and 7) based on their Hong Kong Certificate of Education Examination (HKCEE) scores. "Because of the recognized screening function of the HKCEE, the examination syllabuses have virtually governed teaching and learning in secondary schools, especially in senior secondary classes" (Cheng, 1997, pp. 32–33). After Form 7, students take the Hong Kong Advanced Level Examination (HKALE); approximately 50%–60% of students score high enough to secure their entrance into higher education institutions (Cheng, 1997).

Although access to higher education has been expanding in Hong Kong, Cheng believes that tertiary entrance "will remain a fairly competitive system as long as society gives differential rewards to people with different educational experiences" (Cheng, 1997, p. 34). Because higher education does make a difference in a person's income over time, there is incentive at the individual level to compete for entrance to top-notch higher education institutions. Psacharopoulos (1985), in comparing the costs and benefits of higher education in several countries, found that Hong Kong experiences some of the highest return rates. Thus, although higher education costs are exorbitant and benefit a few, Hong Kong officials rationalize these large expenditures on the premise that such higher education results in economic benefits at the societal level. In this way, the principle of efficiency continues to be favored over equity, and primary and secondary schools experience its adverse effects. For instance, Cheng has found that primary and lower secondary schools are forced to make the most use of existing space, using "floating classes" to accommodate more classes with the same number of rooms, and employing nongraduate as opposed to graduate teachers. Opting for efficiency over equity results in the creation of schools that do not play a social transformative role. Students are not educated to critically question the examination-driven system. Rather, the schools and the students are more inclined to maintain the status quo, thereby legitimizing the present political and economic systems and reproducing a class-oriented, stratified society (Postiglione & Lee, 1997). Although schools had become tools of social transformation during China's Cultural Revolution for instance, only rarely are schools so overtly used as mechanisms of social change (Postiglione & Lee, 1997).

A tendency toward conformity and intense competition is evidenced in Hong Kong's school curriculum—a curriculum that reinforces an examination-driven system and the stratification and selection of a relatively small portion of students for higher education. Often, the needs of individual learners and alternative types of education take a back seat to what has been described by Cheng (1997) as a "monolithic education system" (p. 38). Although experts from different countries consider Hong Kong to have the most up-to-date techniques and well-equipped facilities, only 5% of the population is attracted to vocational and technical education (Cheng, 1997). Cheng has found that most citizens, who favor an examination-intensive curriculum with little diversification, consider educational options, such as vocational education, irrelevant. The hierarchical placement of subjects is apparent in the way students, teachers, and parents perceive the utility of science and the arts: Each is viewed as a different curricular stream in the secondary schools, with science being the higher status subject. Unlike many Western countries, concepts such as a life-oriented curriculum and student-centered teaching have not generally been incorporated into schooling in Hong Kong. This reluctance toward individual-based educational approaches is a result, in part, of Chinese values that emphasize classroom organization, competition, and social relations. "Peer pressure, which often has negative connotations in the West, is traditionally used in Chinese classrooms for positive motivation" (Cheng, 1997, p. 39). Because competition and pressure are viewed as favorable elements in education, it is not uncommon to rank students based on examination scores or to report the results to the media. As Cheng has explained, "the notion that students should not be competing with others is simply unacceptable in the community" (p. 39).

Hofstede (1986) has contributed to a deeper understanding of the cultural differences exhibited by various societies in relation to work-oriented values. These values are helpful in examining the complex relationship between Hong Kong society and its schools. Hofstede's model consists of four dimensions: power distance, uncertainty avoidance, social principledness, and locus of control (see Table 3.2).

The first dimension, *power distance*, is the degree to which citizens tolerate social inequalities. Power distance can be described as a situation in which those with less power

Table 3.2 Hofstede's Framework			
Power Distance	**Uncertainty Avoidance**	**Social Principledness**	**Locus of Control**
Citizens' toleration of social inequalities	Discomfort with unknowns	Acquiescing to authority and accepting conventional norms	Beliefs about the degree to which an individual controls outcomes

accept power imbalances and view them as a normal part of society (cited in Friederichs, 1991). On this dimension, Hofstede found that the citizens of Hong Kong scored high, which suggests that they are more likely than other cultural groups to accept social inequalities in power distribution.

Hofstede's second dimension, *uncertainty avoidance*, is the degree to which a cultural group becomes nervous about unpredictable and complex situations and tries to avoid them through the maintenance of strict behavior codes and faith in absolute truths (cited in Friederichs). According to this measure, the people of Hong Kong were viewed as being unlikely to assert aggression "when confronted with personal risks in new situations" (Friederichs, 1991, p. 203). Friederichs has postulated that it is Hong Kong's exposure to Western values and culture that has resulted in their reluctance to challenge existing power imbalances.

The third dimension of Hofstede's model, *social principledness*, is associated with a strong inclination on the part of a culture to acquiesce, without question, to authority, thereby accepting the conventional values and norms of that society (Bond, 1986, cited in Friederichs, 1991). On this dimension, Hong Kong citizens scored very low, which Hofstede interpreted as a strong orientation on the part of residents to not question authority and to accept existing social standards.

Locus of control, the fourth dimension of Hofstede's model, refers to "a set of generalized beliefs or expectancies about how positive and negative reinforcements are obtained" (Friederichs, 1991, p. 203). Conceptualizing the locus of control dimension as a continuum, one end of the continuum can be labeled internality and the other, externality. Internality is the belief that a person receives rewards and avoids punishments through his or her own skills, efforts, and personal responsibility, whereas externality is the belief that positive outcomes depend on circumstances outside one's control, such as luck, chance, and the actions of powerful others (Friederichs, 1991). On this dimension, Hofstede found that Hong Kong residents strongly believed in externality, the notion that positive outcomes are due to the actions of powerful groups (Friederichs, 1991). Hence, less powerful individuals' circumstances are dependent upon the behavior of those with more power.

Of the four dimensions, Hofstede's *power distance* and *social principledness* are the most salient concepts in helping one understand how ideology and social privilege are embedded in a country's school content and practices. We now examine the stated and implied functions of schooling in both Hong Kong and Israel.

The Manifest and Latent Functions of Schooling in Hong Kong

The manifest functions of schooling in Hong Kong are expressed in a generalized statement in the Education Commission's 2000 Report:

> To enable every person to attain all-round development in the domains of ethics, physique, social skills and aesthetics according to his/her own attributes so that he/she is capable of life-long learning, critical and exploratory thinking, innovating and adapting to change; filled with self-confidence and a team spirit; willing to put forward continuing effort for the prosperity, progress, freedom and democracy of their society, and contribute to the future well-being of the nation and the world at large. (p. 4)

Schooling in Hong Kong, like other societies, is viewed as a necessary vehicle to bring about individual fulfillment and national prosperity. For Hong Kong to realize its social vision, particular aims or objectives have been identified to guide schooling in the 21st century. As clearly outlined in the Education Commission's report, the first aim of schooling is to build lifelong learners—citizens who possess a willingness to learn and who have access to a host of learning opportunities. The second aim is to raise the quality of students. It is believed that the overall quality of Hong Kong's society will improve if the abilities, dispositions, and knowledge of citizens are upgraded. This upgrading of skills requires that schools continue to give attention to the vocational interests of the curriculum.

To create a diverse school system by injecting into the curriculum an ideology centered on student choice and the development of students' varied talents is the third aim of schooling in Hong Kong. The Education Commission (2000) intends to accomplish educational diversity through its fourth aim of schooling: the creation of an inspirational learning atmosphere "conducive to the creative and exploratory spirit" (p. 5). This does not mean, however, that moral education is ignored as individuals pursue diverse paths. Rather, structured learning experiences are viewed as integral to moral development, which constitutes the fifth aim of schooling in Hong Kong. Moral education, including spiritual and emotional areas, is viewed as necessary in helping Hong Kong maintain its Confucian heritage while also continuing to embrace Western principles of capitalism, individualism, and democracy. Hence, the sixth aim of schooling in Hong Kong is to develop a cosmopolitan yet tradition-rich education system, one that develops in students "an international outlook so that they can learn, work and live in different cultural environments" (Education Commission, 2000, p. 5).

It is evident that a structural-functionalist understanding of education and its role in national development tends to support the overt aims of schooling in Hong Kong. This structural-functionalist viewpoint is revealed in the government's depiction of the educated citizen as one who holds balanced Eastern and Western perspectives, for this balance is considered necessary to creating and maintaining a harmonious society. Postiglione and Lee (1997) have asserted that schooling in Hong Kong embraces a Durkheimian (1969) perspective in that education plays a significant role in integrating and ordering social institutions. In Hong Kong, a concern for an individual's relationship with his or her society—a philosophy centered in Chinese traditions of schooling—has melded with Western principles of laissez-faire economics. Whereas mainland China has used schooling to shape a collectivist–socialist vision of society where individualism is demoted and patriotism and egalitarianism are encouraged (Jiang, Wang, Zhang, Jiang, & Xu, 1993; Jin & Ouyang, 1992; Teng & Zhang, 1992), researchers, such as Cheung and Kwok (1998) and Lau and Kuan (1988), have argued that schooling in Hong Kong has promoted an individualistic spirit and encouraged citizens to pursue self-interests. Durkheim's conception of a society that is held together through the social division of social labor is discernible in Hong Kong's education system (Postiglione & Lee, 1997). A class-based ideology is most apparent in the school curriculum that reflects the values and beliefs of the dominant group or power holders in the society.

From a Marxist perspective, then, the school curriculum is an arena where "the conflict between antagonistic social forces" (Postiglione & Lee, 1997, p. 16) is played out. The knowledge that students are exposed to in schools serves to maintain and promote unequal relationships between the resource-rich bourgeois and the resource-poor proletariat. This inequality is observed in schooling when students from lower class backgrounds experience school failure and are made to believe that it is due to their own shortcomings or lack of skills (Cheung, 1997). In Hong Kong, an elitist system that caters to children of the privileged is maintained through a particular ideology called "the myth of merit." Through school processes such as educational streaming and grouping based on perceived student abilities, members of the lower class come to understand that their educational failure is a result of their own lack of effort or individual deficiencies. Rather than viewing education as a system that has failed them, the principle of meritocracy causes underprivileged students in Hong Kong to view education as "a good discriminator of the elite"; in this way, education preserves the status interests and class positions of the dominant group (Cheung, 1997, p. 120).

Hofstede's (1986) model examining social distance and the development of work-related attitudes can be extended to the school setting. Two of the four dimensions, namely *power distance* and *social principledness*, are especially reinforced through schooling processes in the Hong Kong context. The toleration of social inequalities, referred to as *power distance*, is maintained because students come to accept that they play particular roles in society. The education system in Hong Kong, like other countries, serves a social selection function. This occurs when students who score high on academic examinations are rewarded with exposure to high-status curriculum through classes that acquaint them with the knowledge and skills to obtain high-paying positions in society. For example, students who have opportunities to gain English proficiency are often those who come from upper class backgrounds, whose parents are more likely to associate with English speakers as a result of their own social positions. Proficiency in English, in turn, bolsters self-confidence, thereby decreasing the social distance with English speakers and increasing the social distance between Hong Kong peers from lower class backgrounds (Postiglione & Lee, 1997). Consequently, students' access to the language of power through schooling serves to position them for even greater socioeconomic opportunities upon graduation.

To accomplish this social stratification, schools target students for particular roles, defined as "culturally prescribed behaviors relating to social position" (Clabaugh & Rozycki, 1990, p. 116). In this way, schools create what Atkinson (1985) has termed "symbolic boundaries" (p. 27). Through the organization and structure of schooling, particular "domains of knowledge and experience are kept separate" (p. 27), with certain groups of students being introduced to differentiated curriculum according to the roles they are expected to play in society. Social stratification, according to Postiglione and Lee (1997), can be viewed in at least two ways. First, society acknowledges stratification as a natural, equitable social process by which citizens "get what society seems to say they deserve" (Postiglione & Lee, 1997, p. 17). The second view rejects the notion that an equitable relationship exists between achievements and rewards; rather, as Postiglione and Lee have explained, rewards are distributed in fundamentally unequal ways based on people's class backgrounds, providing students from the upper classes with greater chances for academic achievement and greater social rewards than those from the lower classes. Thus, through the ideology of merit and the practice of social stratification, schooling in Hong Kong contributes to students' toleration of social inequalities.

Much of the toleration for social inequalities—the ranking of positions based on perceived importance and the transmission of advantage to some over others (Postiglione, 1997)—is due to an assumption that causal linkages exist between examination scores, academic achievement, and economic performance. LeTendre (1999) questions the premise that high test scores represent a nation with better schools that cultivate students who perform better in the global market. In his view, high stakes tests are not adequate measures of academic achievement; rather, they are the means by which societies rationalize investment in selected students (i.e., human capital) to stimulate economic progress and to reinforce economically motivated schooling purposes. Although schools are expected to increase people's life chances by providing equal opportunities for all, the situation in Hong Kong is such that schools aid the social advancement of upper class children and socialize the lower class children to accept blame for their own social stagnation (Postiglione, 1997). According to Postiglione (1997), "growing numbers of people are beginning to believe that complete personal responsibility for success in school is largely a myth that acts, intentionally and unintentionally, to justify the never-ending striving of students" (p. 139). Some people in Hong Kong are beginning to see that school failure "is socially rather than individually determined" (p. 139). Moreover, educational attainment is not only stratified by social status in Hong Kong, but also by gender, for men are predominately the power holders in society, assuming prestigious positions in the political and business sectors (Postiglione, 1997).

Class and gender differences can be found in the curriculum content and schooling practices, namely through the kind of knowledge portrayed in textbooks and the practice of ability grouping and educational streaming. The curriculum, as a form of social practice, does foster a kind of social principledness in Hong Kong. Social principledness, understood by Hofstede (1986) as citizens' reluctance to question central authority and to acquiesce to conventional values and norms, is manifested in both the content and process of schooling in Hong Kong. The notion of the curriculum affording students differentiated school experiences has been a central topic for gender researchers, whose work has focused, thus far, on the stereotyped images of gender conveyed to students through text (Cheung, 1997). In 1992, Au found an unbalanced and disproportionate representation of male versus female characters in school textbooks. Au's analysis revealed that male characters were represented more than females (1.9:1) in textbooks, which was an inaccurate reflection of the male–female ratio (1.038:1) of Hong Kong's population the year before. Au also found that 70% of the male textbook characters were engaged in labor activities; this was significantly higher than the actual percentage of males (62%) in Hong Kong's workforce. Cheung (1997), commenting on the research conducted by Au, expressed concern that stereotyped gender roles were being conveyed to students, with males depicted as dominant and holding many types of jobs and females portrayed as subordinate and assuming more limited social roles. Moreover, the quotes of famous Hong Kong figures provided in the textbooks were those of males; voices of world-prominent female figures were rarely found (Cheung, 1997).

Reducing the school curriculum to students' mastery of competencies and skills (Cheung, 1997) also limits discussion about other purposes of schooling and tends to minimize conflicts surrounding the values and images represented in the curriculum (Clabaugh & Rozycki, 1990). In this way, curriculum becomes more "a technical matter—a 'curriculum decision'" (p. 131)—that serves to silence disagreements, stifle people's emotions, and promulgate the official curriculum. It has been argued, by Cheung (1997) and others, that school knowledge produces "certain types of consciousness in pupils' minds," prepares them for particular work roles, and reduces student achievement to outcomes that "can be marked, monitored and assessed" (p. 123).

The practice of ability grouping in schools is another way social stratification occurs. Ability grouping, often based on reading or math scores, is utilized in schools as a method of categorizing students according to their abilities for efficiency of instruction. Studies have shown, however, that placing students in low, medium, and high ability groupings have negative effects on students. That is, the groups to which students are assigned influence the way in which students respond to learning. Postiglione (1997) has found that "students in low ability groups become stereotyped as low achievers, which in turn diminishes their chances of moving into a higher group" (p. 150). Criterion such as family socioeconomic background is proven to be a key characteristic in ability grouping placement. According to Postiglione, "student cultures develop within each [academic] stream, and may perpetuate attitudes and behaviors which reproduce social class" (p. 150).

In addition to ability grouping within schools, students in Hong Kong also experience a hierarchy among schools. Since a correlation exists between family background and students' educational attainment, students from upper class backgrounds in Hong Kong are more inclined to be educated in the best schools with the most resources and exposure to the right kinds of knowledge (Postiglione & Lee, 1997). In addition to qualified teachers and school resources, the Llewellyn Commission, in 1982, found that the composition of the school body affects student achievement; evidently, students who "attend school with the children of Hong Kong's elite families" are more likely to "attain a higher level of achievement" than if they attended schools with students from lower socioeconomic backgrounds (Postiglione, 1997, p. 148). Because schools are arenas wherein social status is passed to subsequent generations, parents have a vested interest in using their influence to obtain a quality education for their children (Postiglione, 1997). The narrower the stratification system becomes, the more schooling plays a key role in social mobility (Tsang, 1993).

Social mobility, as defined by Postiglione (1997), refers to citizens' movement, either upward or downward, in relation to their social positions over the course of a lifetime or between subsequent generations. The kind of curriculum to which students are exposed, therefore, becomes an important issue when linked with the prospect of social mobility. Oftentimes, debates over curriculum are centered on the degree to which a vocational or classical academic curriculum is useful to society and to the individual. The argument by educational planners that vocational or technical training is necessary to the fulfillment of much-needed social roles is often not a compelling reason for students to desire and enroll in such programs. This is because in many societies, such as Hong Kong, vocational training does not significantly improve a person's class (wealth), status (prestige), and party (power). These overlapping variables, identified by German sociologist Max Weber (1978), have contributed to a deeper understanding of social stratification (cited in Postiglione, 1997) and help to answer why students are reluctant to embrace vocational options. In general, vocational routes have not been popular with Hong Kong students compared with the prestigious government schools and higher education institutions, despite prevocational schools at the secondary levels, craft certification options at technical centers, and practical subject training at technical schools (Cheng, 1997). For a comparison of geophysical and economic factors influencing education in Hong Kong and Israel, see the Points of Convergence box (Figure 3.2).

Extending Weber's analysis further, Scimecca (1980) has suggested that occupation, class, status, and power do stratify individuals. Thus, if one's vocational occupation does not generate as much income as a position in the civil service sector, for instance, then one's status—the degree of deference the society accords that occupation—diminishes. To the extent that the source and amount of one's income affects one's chances to realize other goals (class) or to exert one's will (power), vocational training will be viewed as a lesser curriculum promoted for the lower segments of society by power holders who personally

FIGURE 3.2

Points of Convergence

HONG KONG		ISRAEL
Aspect: Located in Eastern Asia, Hong Kong borders the South China Sea and China. Because natural resources are limited, much food and raw materials are imported (*World Factbook*, 2001). Hong Kong's exports include clothing, textiles, electronics, watches and clocks, and footwear. According to the *World Factbook*, the per capita gross domestic product in Hong Kong is $181 billion, similar to that of four large Western European countries.	**Geography and educational consequences**	**Aspect:** The Middle Eastern country of Israel is located between Egypt and Lebanon and borders the Mediterranean Sea. Despite its limited natural resources, Israel is largely self-sufficient in food production, aside from grains. During the past 20 years, Israel has developed its industrial and agricultural sectors; primary exports include cut diamonds, high-tech equipment, and fruits and vegetables (*World Factbook*, 2001).
Response: Regarding occupations, 31.5% of the labor force is involved in wholesale and retail trade/hotels/restaurants; 24% in community and social services; and 14.5% in financing/insurance/real estate; and 11.6%, 7.7%, and 2.6% are employed in transport/communications, manufacturing, and construction, respectively (*World Factbook*, 2001).	How have geophysical realities influenced education?	**Response:** Israel's labor force assumes various occupations, with 31.2% in public services; 20.2% in manufacturing; 13.1% in finance/business; 12.8% in commerce; 7.5% in construction; 6.4% in personal services; 6.2% in transport/communications; and 2.6% in agriculture, forestry, and fishing (*World Factbook*, 2001).
Consequence: Despite state-of-the-art vocational facilities, vocational education, considered an undesirable career path, does not generate as much personal income or status as positions in the civil or business sectors. In school, students gravitate toward curriculum that will help them obtain more tangible social rewards.		**Consequence:** Vocational education has resulted in the tracking of Eastern Jews and those from low socioeconomic backgrounds into vocational education, leaving them reduced opportunities to cycle into other educational paths. In this way, the academic track is reserved for Western Jews and students from higher socioeconomic backgrounds.

shun such education for their own children (Postiglione, 1997). In this way, students learn about the latent functions of curriculum—that curriculum serves to stratify individuals in order that necessary, but less desirable, social tasks will be accomplished by those categorized by society and schools as low achievers. Although vocational and technical education has remained "a rather subsidiary system in Hong Kong" (Postiglione & Lee, 1997, p. 12), the recent exodus of highly educated residents and an influx of at least 2 million Chinese from the mainland are providing an impetus for Hong Kong to reform its curriculum to accommodate more diverse and flexible educational paths (Lumby, 2000). Yet one can assume that upper class students will continue to gravitate toward a curriculum that will provide them with the knowledge and skills that enable them to obtain more tangible rewards, such as opportunities to obtain desirable occupations, housing accommodations, a decent monthly income, language ability, travel, overseas investments, and influence or leverage to enhance opportunities for family and friends (Postiglione, 1997).

To be sure, curriculum is not "a socially neutral recipe for the transmission of knowledge" (Cheung, 1997, p. 130). Rather, curriculum perpetuates social stratification according to socioeconomic class and gender through schooling ideology, power distance and social principledness, curricular texts, ability groupings and categorizations, and vocational and academic tracks. Thus, both manifest and latent functions of schooling must be considered in any examination of the purposes and aims of education.

Language: The Medium of Instruction

An area that is of great concern and that has received significant attention in Hong Kong is the debate about what language should serve as the medium of instruction in schools. Because language is central to people's construction of their social reality, social institutions rely on language for their successful functioning (Lee, 1997). As Berger and Berger (1976) have pointed out, education—like the economy and the state—are dependent on linguistic concepts and classifications to spur individual action; in other words, these systems depend on a set of meanings constructed and sustained through language (cited in Lee, 1997). In Hong Kong, Cantonese is the mother tongue spoken by 98% of the 6.3 million population. Cantonese, the Chinese language of daily life, is the language of instruction in primary schools. English is the language of trade and international business, spoken by only 2% of Hong Kong's population. At the secondary level, students attend either English-medium or Chinese-medium schools. At English-medium schools, all subjects are taught in English, aside from Chinese language and literature and Chinese history. In Chinese-medium schools, every subject is taught in Chinese, except for English. Lee (1997) has found that English-medium schools have gained in popularity over the past 30 years. To illustrate, only 57.9% of secondary schools in 1960 were English-medium schools; by 1990, over 91.7% were categorized as such (Lee, 1997).

English, as the medium of instruction, can be characterized in terms of its ebbs and flows. Although the English language was unknown in Hong Kong prior to Britain's arrival, familiarity with the English language become more important as the British amassed their colonial government (Tung, Lam, & Tsang, 1997). During the period between World War I and World War II, China's influence was manifested in Hong Kong's decreased use of English; however, as Tung, Lam, and Tsang found, "the rapid surge of

English as a medium of instruction in the latter half of [the 20th] century in Hong Kong has been the result of replacing China's influence with that of the West" (p. 458). Despite Hong Kong having returned to Chinese sovereignty in July 1997, the language of the former colonizer has been viewed by the people of Hong Kong as a way to improve their own social status, income, job prospects, and mobility. A survey conducted by the British Council on the "Use of English in Hong Kong" showed a clear linkage between English language proficiency and increased income. Gibbons (1982) found that the survey respondents who were proficient in English belonged to the highest income group (i.e., HK$5000 or more per month) and those who were not proficient belonged to the lowest income group (i.e., below HK$500 per month) (cited in Lee, 1997).

Because the most prestigious positions in Hong Kong are held by foreigners who are proficient in English, the citizens of Hong Kong have come to accept that English language mastery is important to achieving success. Friederichs (1991) has interpreted this concern for English language acquisition in terms of the colonized–colonizer relationship. In this case, the people of Hong Kong, according to Friederichs, accept and learn the language of the colonizer to improve their own life chances; employment, therefore, is dependent on obtaining a "European style education" (p. 204). For Guy (1988), social power has always been vested in the "linguistic elite, who spoke a language unrelated to those of the indigenous peoples" (p. 46). Those considered disadvantaged in society were deficient in the colonizer's language. And even after the colonial presence was physically removed from a region, the indigenous elite still maintained the language of the colonizer, which they viewed as indispensable to the organization and governance of the region. Lack of language proficiency on the part of the working class, then, resulted in limited access to political sites and power (Guy, 1988).

Analyses by Wong and Lui (1992) have revealed several social class distinctions in Hong Kong: upper service class, intermediate class, and working class. The upper service class consists of high and low level professionals, managers, administrators, and technicians; the nonmanual employees, petty bourgeoisie, and lower-grade supervisors and technicians form the intermediate class; and the skilled manual laborers and semi- and unskilled laborers comprise the working class. These class divisions are helpful in understanding the social distance and target language acquisition model proposed by Schumann and developed by Gibbons. For Schumann, "the more socially distant a target language group is from a putative language learner, the more difficult it becomes to learn the target language [e.g., English]" (cited in Lee, 1997, p. 167). Schumann's model is based on eight elements that affect social distance in language acquisition: (1) dominance, (2) integration, (3) enclosure, (4) cohesion, (5) size, (6) congruence, (7) attitudes, and (8) residence.

Dominance refers to the unequal power relationships that exist between groups and that accentuate the distance experienced by the groups. *Integration* suggests that "social distance between the language learning group and the target language group will be increased without an intention of acculturation, assimilation or integration" (Lee, 1997, p. 167). *Enclosure* is associated with the isolation of social groups from one another (e.g., restrictions on intermarriage or interaction in clubs or churches). *Cohesion* describes the internal structure of the language learning group; "the more internally cohesive the language learning group, the greater the social distance" (Lee, 1997, p. 167). *Size* is a factor in that the larger the group, the greater the social distance. *Congruence* refers to how similar the cultural groups are to one another; more similarities result in less social distance. *Attitudes* can be positive or negative; the greater the negativity toward other groups, the greater the social distance. *Residence* is the term Schumann used to describe the amount of time the learning group plans to reside in the target learning area; the less time the learners intend to stay, the greater the social distance experienced. In his analysis, Gibbons found particular differences in social distance between the upper classes (Chinese elite) and the Chinese working class in relation to social distance with English speakers (the Western elite). Specifically, the Chinese elite perceive the Western elite "as political and social equals;" consequently, they are more inclined to integrate and less likely to experience enclosure (Lee, 1997, p. 167). Because the working class feels inferior to and has limited contact with English speakers, both groups experience a greater social distance. Thus, Gibbons has reasoned that integration and direct social contact are powerful indicators for English language acquisition (cited in Lee, 1997).

Just as language creates power divisions in the society at large, the medium of instruction to which students are exposed in schools serves to stratify them. As Postiglione and Lee (1997) have contended, the language of instruction in classrooms has a social function: to differentiate students. Drawing upon the work of Bernstein (1971), the authors have described two language codes associated with different social class backgrounds: the restricted code of the working class family and the elaborated code of the middle class family. The language code of lower class families consists of parental commands with little opportunity for children to discuss with or receive explanation from their parents, whereas the language code of middle class families provides children with opportunities "for more discussion and individual expression of experience and emotion" (p. 19). Extending this analysis to the school, Postiglione and Lee have argued that the medium of instruction in schools often reinforces the language habits of middle class children, giving middle class children greater opportunities to master school knowledge. Thus, "English proficiency is unequally distributed among students in Hong Kong according to their class origins" (Tsang, 1991, cited in Lee, 1997, p. 168). Lack of English acquisition on the part of working class children has an impact on their academic achievement. A study by Siu (1988) revealed that most students from lower class backgrounds do not see an urgent need to acquire English, which is a prerequisite for higher education; without English, working class children have fewer opportunities to attend prestigious schools that have higher quality programs (cited in Lee, 1997).

In a comparative study of language experience and cognition in Alberta, Canada, and Hong Kong, researchers Yu and Bain (1985) found that rich learning experiences enable students to better accomplish conceptual tasks. Thus, school programs and family backgrounds are linked to cognitive outcomes. As Lee (1997) has surmised, students who lack English proficiency are disadvantaged when "competing with their upper-middle-class counterparts on the educational path" (p. 171). Tsang (1991) has also argued that the language of the colonizer is associated with both social class and opportunities for educational success. The work of Pierre Bourdieu (1977), a French sociologist, has been particularly helpful in illuminating how language and knowledge act as a kind of currency that enables some students to perform better in school. The term **cultural capital**, coined by Bourdieu, describes how educators assume that students have the cultural knowledge of the dominant class. Understood as "high culture" by Bourdieu, educators come to expect that students have the kind of knowledge, learning styles, and language of the upper and middle classes (Postiglione, 1997). Consequently, language is a form of cultural capital and functions to differentiate the treatment of schoolchildren. Even Hong Kong's Education Commission, a state apparatus, has acknowledged the importance attached to English language learning. In its 1995 report, the Education Commission, which establishes objectives, formulates policy, and makes recommendations, stated the urgency of equipping Form 6 students with English proficiency in order that some might enter higher education institutions and other school leaders might obtain work in the public and business sectors (cited in Tung, Lam, & Tsang, 1997).

Despite Hong Kong's return to Chinese sovereignty, the English language has been retained—not for the purpose of national unification, but rather for personal and societal economic gain. Friederichs (1991) has contended that the citizens of Hong Kong have internalized, and are motivated by, principles of the marketplace rather than the political realm. Bray (1997), however, has argued that due to Hong Kong's reintegration with the People's Republic of China (PRC), there is greater opportunity for the Chinese language to rival English as the medium of instruction in schools. The movement toward Chinese-medium schooling, though, has favored Cantonese as opposed to Putonghua, the national language of the PRC. This move, according to Bray, "symbolises a form of continued self-determination and distinctiveness for Hong Kong within the new national framework" (p. 164). The debate over medium of instruction reinforces the importance of language as a transmitter of a society's cultural identity. Despite greater attention to Chinese language as a medium of instruction, educational curriculum has not, to a large extent, been linked to local culture (Friederichs, 1991). A primary reason is that parents desire English as the medium of instruction in Hong Kong's schools (Postiglione & Lee, 1997).

Recently, Tung et al. (1997) conducted a large-scale study to gather the preferences of students, teachers, and parents regarding the medium of instruction in schools in Hong Kong. The study involved more than 5,000 first-year secondary students from 24 schools, 700 of their teachers, and more than 4,600 parents. The researchers found that, although students reported Chinese as being an efficient and effective language for learning, the students viewed English proficiency as indispensable to their careers. Toward this end, students suggested that they study texts in English and Chinese simultaneously. According to Tung et al.'s findings, teachers believed that Chinese instruction enhanced student learning, allowing for depth of coverage and increased student interest in the material. The study revealed, however, that teachers lack resources for Chinese instruction as well as Chinese equivalents for certain English terms; limited resources, in their opinion, necessitated governmental support if the mother tongue is to be taught. Tung et al. also found that teachers favor the controversial policy of educational streaming, whereby the high academic performers are educated in English and the academically average are taught in Chinese. A study by Tung (1990) showed that teachers chose English as a more manageable medium of instruction due to their training in English and their difficulties with written Chinese. In general, teachers are expected to teach in English at the upper secondary levels in Anglo-Chinese schools (Brown, 1997).

The study by Tung et al. (1997) also reinforced earlier findings by So (1992) that parents want their children to learn English. Strong parental preference for English-medium schools, especially for students in the senior grades, reveals attitudes aligned with the market-driven ideology prevalent in Hong Kong (Lin, 1997, cited in Tung et al., 1997). In Tung et al.'s study, the parents perceived Chinese instruction in the subjects of history and geography to be acceptable. This suggests that history and geography are not important to the passage of examinations, which reinforces the belief that the more high-profile subjects are mathematics, English, and Chinese and that these should remain prominent in the curriculum. Although students, teachers, and parents agreed that Chinese can promote student learning, parents and students contended that instruction in English fostered a better standard of English necessary for tertiary placement and career advancement (Tung et al., 1997). Unlike the students and parents, the teachers in Tung et al.'s study were uncertain as to whether Chinese instruction would adversely affect the degree of English proficiency attained by students. Surveys conducted by Tung (1990) and So (1992) have indicated that a person's own role (student, teacher, or parent) impacts his/her views regarding preferred medium of instruction in schools (Tung et al. 1997). Thus, Tung et al. (1997) have concluded that "as long as English remains dominant in government, businesses, and higher education, it will be preferred by teachers and students as a medium of instruction" (p. 458).

There have been problems associated with using the English language as a medium of instruction. Many students have experienced difficulty learning when English is used; thus, a significant number of schools thought to teach in English actually teach in mixed code or Cantonese (Bray, 1997). Yu and Atkinson (1988) found that students in the poorly funded private schools, which have a larger proportion of students from lower socioeconomic backgrounds, have had difficulty learning English compared with students in the prestigious public schools. Despite these hardships, students have consciously opted for English-medium schools, hoping "they will be the few who will succeed in the face of the hurdle imposed by the unfamiliar English language" (Tung et al., 1997, p. 458).

Further complicating the medium of instruction debate is whether the use of Putonghua or Cantonese should be encouraged. Certainly mainland China has a stake in promoting its national language in the Hong Kong SAR. As early as the 1980s, students have been encouraged to study Putonghua at the primary and secondary levels (Tan, 1997). In 1994–1995, Kwok (1996) found that almost 40% of secondary and primary schools offered Putonghua as an optional school subject. Although steps have been made "to bring Chinese language teaching closer in line with that in the mainland" (Tan, 1997, pp. 308–309), English is still associated with status and mobility, and Cantonese is associated with a unique Hong Kong identity. Since there is provision in Article 9 of Hong Kong's Basic Law that English can remain the language of government, the demand will continue for English-medium instruction. "The continuing demand for English-language qualifications," as Bray (1997) has asserted, "is perhaps the most obvious manifestation of the ways in which large segments of the population continue to see the education system, with all its imported attributes, as a vehicle for achieving higher social status and economic reward" (p. 165).

Citizenship Education and National Identity in Hong Kong

An enduring issue in education is the relationship of the individual to his or her society. That is to say that individuals are connected in different ways to the overall economic and political structures in their societies. Within this complex landscape, schools assume particular responsibilities for developing individuals in ways that are linked to the fulfillment of society's needs. The school, therefore, is an institution wherein the "formalized statuses, roles, and norms" of a society are taught (Clabaugh & Rozycki, 1990, p. 117). One of the overarching purposes of schooling is to develop citizens who not only are loyal to their country, but carry out their social roles in ways that contribute to the stable functioning of their society. *Citizenship education* is a term used to describe this overarching school mission. The kind of citizenship development promoted in schools can be understood through an examination of questions such as patriotism and nationalism, curricular content and methods of instruction, and freedom of thought and indoctrination (Kandel, 1933, pp. xx–xxi). Kandel has argued that a democratic spirit is cultivated not only in terms of the mechanics of government but with all of the particular aspects of life—political, economic, and social—that individuals relate to and interact with in their society. Nationalism, defined as "a condition of mind or loyalty to ideals based on a national state," is manifested in schooling through the kinds of ideas, emotions, and moral and intellectual outlook that are considered important to national development (Kandel, 1933, p. 10). Thus, a particular portrayal of the state (the society's political apparatus) is legitimated through the citizenship education messages students receive in school.

In Hong Kong, the state has attempted to play a role in the formation of a national, civic identity. The focus has been on using schools to produce good Hong Kong citizens who recognize their membership to a larger geopolitical entity, the PRC. The 2000 Report of the Education Commission states that schools should continue to enhance students' understanding of Chinese history and culture and to develop students' sense of commitment and belonging to the PRC. However, what constitutes a "good" citizen is dependent upon what kind of society its power holders envision. For example, from a classical Greek interpretation of citizenship, character formation and the quest for freedom were considered essential citizen traits, whereas the Spartan conception of warrior-citizen meant commitment to a military state (Morris, 1997, p. 108). In Hong Kong, a mixture of both Western and Eastern values have coalesced to create a complex citizen identity, as evidenced by Hong Kong's tendency to keep features of traditional Chinese culture alongside Western features of modernity and individualism (Bond, 1993, cited in Morris, 1997). This combination of pioneer spirit and communal values was articulated in the government's 1993 booklet, *School Education in Hong Kong: A Statement of Aims.* According to this document, the primary goal of education is "to develop . . . independent-minded and socially-aware adults, equipped with the knowledge, skills and attitudes which help them lead a full life as individuals and play a positive role in the life of the community" (cited in Education Commission, 1997).

Distinguishing between different conceptions of citizenship education—loyalty to the state, on the one hand, and civic participation in public affairs, on the other hand—is central to the analysis of citizenship development or civic education in schools (Morris, 1997). Although generalizations of national systems can be restrictive, they do provide an opportunity to identify how particular political values are manifested in schooling. Kandel (1933) has contended that more autocratic or centrally organized governments are inclined to emphasize social conformity in schools, as evidenced in "standardized culture, good form and conventions" (pp. 20–21). Decentralized governments, for Kandel, are more inclined to respond to public demands, emphasizing initiative and individuality in their schools. An examination of civic education in Hong Kong, then, provides a concrete way to observe how the relationship between the individual citizen to his or her society is portrayed to children.

Morris (1997) has examined the role of civic education in Hong Kong in relation to three historical time periods. From 1945 to 1965, the state assumed a coercive role in its promulgation of a particular kind of knowledge that catered to British colonial interests; any attempts to question the curriculum were seen as a threat to the colonial government's legitimacy (Morris, 1997). During the period 1965–1984, the official knowledge conveyed in schools was influenced by market values with care taken on the part of the state "to avoid offending the sensitivities of the People's Republic of China" (Morris, 1997, p. 109). In the 1980s and to the present time, school knowledge has been defined in terms of market principles but has also been cognizant of Hong Kong's transition from British colonialism to Chinese sovereignty (Morris, 1997).

One year before the change of sovereignty, greater policy attention was directed to civic education in order that schooling in Hong Kong might contribute to the peaceful transition of power and the continued improvement of society. In the *1996 Guidelines for Civic Education*, the Education Department viewed the purpose of civic education as inculcating students with a new political and cultural identity—an identity influenced by the Chinese community, British colonialism, and its status as a Special Administrative Region (cited in Bray, 1997). Thus, "the changing nature of civic education within the formal curriculum in Hong Kong is in effect a portrayal of the shifting images of society portrayed by the state" (Morris, 1997, p. 109). One of the most apparent changes has been the revisions to syllabi and textbooks to give more attention to the PRC and depict China in a more positive light (Tan, 1997). Despite greater coverage of China in the formal curriculum, the critical study of controversial issues is discouraged at the classroom level. For example, students are not encouraged to discuss or make judgments about the Chinese government's actions in the 1989 Tiananmen Square incident, when demonstrators were killed for protesting government brutality and for supporting democratic ideas. According to Morris (1997), textbook publishers also faced pressure from the Director of Education, who advised them to either avoid controversial topics altogether or to treat controversies in an uncritical fashion. Although the civic guidelines and other education documents instruct schools to develop students' decision making, critical thinking, and reflective skills, teachers recognize the real intent of the curriculum: to promulgate an official, abstract knowledge devoid of controversy. Hence, educators have come to understand that the more critical aims of schooling are "at best rhetorical" (Morris, 1997, p. 122).

Curricular Change as Symbolic Action

Both social studies and civic education have had a limited impact on students at the school level, partly because curriculum reform is more a symbolic action on the part of the government than an opportunity to change instruction to more critical, participatory modes. For Cuban (1992), **symbolic action** is a means by which the government expresses "concern for the perennial problems of schooling" as opposed to actually changing the way curriculum is implemented (Morris & Chan, 1997, p. 247). The guidelines, as Leung (1995) has argued, served to trivialize civic education in Hong Kong rather than to bring about substantial change. Although schools have been primarily assigned the responsibility for civic education reform, educators are reluctant to put their efforts in that direction due its low status and the government's protection of the existing political establishment.

Social studies, a part of the official curriculum, "is offered in less than 20 per cent of schools" (Morris, 1997, p. 113). Consequently, the way in which most students have access to civic learning is through civic education as a cross-curricular theme rather than civic education being treated as a separate subject in its own right. Although educators understand the importance of civic education, they have not been convinced that it is a high priority, partly because the government has provided minimal financial and personal assistance to a civic education agenda at the level of implementation (Morris & Chan, 1997). Moreover, if schools were to embrace civic education, this would come at the expense of losing the best students who enroll at schools in Hong Kong where curricular priorities are given to high-status examination subjects (Morris & Chan, 1997). Government officials' encouragement of a market atmosphere, in which schools compete for the best pupils, seems to have superseded official concern for patriotism. In effect, the government in "its traditional laissez-faire role" (Morris, 1997, p. 113) has legitimated the kind of knowledge reflected on examinations, leaving little incentive for teachers, students, or schools to target their efforts toward a more active conception of civic education.

The relationship of the individual to his or her society, therefore, seems to be influenced the most by market principles of individual competitiveness and preparation for work-related roles. Students have come to accept "the school treadmill" and are too preoccupied with examinations to become actively involved in political activities or social action (Friederichs, 1991). Martin Carnoy (1974) has examined this preference for marketplace interests over other interests. He has argued that citizens' preference for the values of the colonizer prepares them, in turn, for a world of limited roles that actually suit the interests of the colonizer. In Hong Kong, Western influences introduced by British colonialists have motivated Hong Kong citizens to attain the kinds of positions and rewards of their former colonizers. Hence, students' acceptance of an intense, examination-driven system and the schools' acceptance of an image of itself as an arena for competition reveals the extent to which individualistic, laissez-faire principles of the marketplace have pervaded education in Hong Kong. The internalization of market principles over political ones (Leung, 1986) has led Friederichs (1991) to conclude that public demand for curricular changes might increase if the changes were viewed "as having a market value" (p. 206).

Despite arguments, such as the one advanced by Kandel (1933), that economics is only one of many factors influencing education, it has been difficult in Hong Kong to convince citizens of the need for a civic education that extends conceptions of citizenship beyond individual interests and work-related competencies to that of rights and responsibilities within a larger collectivity. The notion that senior secondary education curriculum is designed to help students develop their strengths and aptitudes in order that they might obtain future employment is perhaps best captured in the following statement by the Education Commission (2000) in Hong Kong:

> Compared with basic education, senior secondary education should provide students with more work-related experiences, enhance their knowledge about the working life, help them develop a positive attitude towards work, and help them explore their own aptitudes and abilities to prepare them for future employment. (pp. 99–100)

Statements such as these reveal that the state gives highest priority to workplace readiness. The state, therefore, conveys a message to schools that the high status subjects, namely mathematics, English, and Chinese, are the core or taken-for-granted portion of the curriculum. Because almost 70% of students' time is devoted to these high status subjects, educational efforts in support of cross-curricular themes are considered extraneous to a teacher's primary mission of preparing students to compete well on the high-status subject examinations (Morris, 1997).

Although curriculum in Hong Kong has been criticized for its examination emphasis, Cheung (1999) has also admonished parents for allowing their own material interests to override their concern for schools that equip children with the kinds of skills that help them cope with their society. As Cheung has reasoned, "even if schools become vehicles for pupils to obtain better qualifications and better jobs, there is no guarantee pupils will become better people after graduation" (p. 24). Although Cheung has argued for Personal and Social Education to be introduced into Hong Kong's secondary curriculum, it is unlikely that it will be viewed as an integral school subject without an agency or group assigned responsibility for overseeing its implementation (Morris, 1997). Attempts to implement a participatory citizenship education—one in which students learn how to live meaningful lives as independent individuals and who cooperate with others for the sake of the community (Cheung, 1999)—will require more than the state's rhetorical promotion of an ideal citizen. For civic or social education to truly take hold in Hong Kong, teachers must come to view themselves as change agents (cultural transformers) as opposed to pre-servers of the status quo (cultural transmitters) (Morris & Williamson, 1998). Because decisions are made at the local school level regarding which subjects are to be studied and how much time is to be allocated to each (Morris, 1997), educators have an important part to play in enhancing the status of civic education in the curriculum. Yet, "their power to change the curriculum is severely constrained by the need to survive within a market within which schools compete for pupils" (Morris, 1997, p. 123).

At present, the heavy emphasis on academic results sends students a powerful message that academic performance for eventual economic leverage is the most important purpose of schooling, despite schools' claims to a host of educational aims and outcomes. A vivid demonstration of academic results overriding moral and social concerns is the practice of school banding. Schools in Hong Kong are divided into five bands, with a Band 1 school admitting the best students perceived by teachers as being well-disciplined and motivated to learn, while students enrolled in a Band 5 school are often perceived as stupid and disruptive (Cheung, 1999). To change the situation, Cheung has found that a school's administrators will try to incrementally strive to increase its status from Band 5 to 4 and so on, with the ultimate goal of achieving Band 1. This means that school administrators use their time and resources in the pursuit of raising academic performance rather than addressing other educational aims, such as students' civic development (Cheung, 1999).

It is interesting that students' exposure to civic education could be the very vehicle by which they could problematize the purposes of schooling in Hong Kong and challenge the practices of school stratification, thereby giving a sincere effort to the development of the five learning experiences considered "essential" by the state: "moral and civic education, social service, intellectual development, physical development, aesthetic development as well as work-related experiences" (Education Commission, 2000, p. 15). However, as

Arnove et al. (1982) conclude, debates over the purposes of schooling are a reflection of shifting economic, political, and social alignments in conjunction with national and international forces. In Hong Kong, the economic purposes of schooling overshadow even new political arrangements and confound citizenship education efforts. Similar themes, in relation to the purposes of schooling, are addressed in the next section on education in Israel.

THE HISTORICAL AND CULTURAL CONTEXT OF EDUCATION IN ISRAEL

The state of Israel, founded in 1948, has experienced successive waves of immigration and now has a population representing more than 70 countries. Educational documents published by the State of Israel divide the main immigration movements by decades. In the 1950s, people came to Israel primarily from Arab countries and Europe, whereas Jews from North Africa constituted the largest influx of immigrants during the 1960s. In the 1970s, Israel witnessed the arrival of Soviet Jews, and by the early 1990s, approximately 800,000 Jews from the former Soviet Union had made their home in Israel. Moreover, in two movements, almost the entire Jewish community in Ethiopia relocated to Israel in 1984 and 1991. Hence, the social integration of immigrants into Israeli society has been of central concern to the state that has aggressively sought to absorb immigrant children into a Jewish, Zionist identity. Education, as a particularly important state apparatus, was considered essential in facilitating some kind of homogenous unit in light of its rapidly increasing multiculturalism. The purpose of schooling in Israel, therefore, has focused on creating an exclusive Jewish identity (Dahan & Levy, 2000). For a comparison of how demographic attributes of the population affect education in Israel and Hong Kong, see the "Points of Convergence" box (Figure 3.3).

The education system in Israel is composed of pre-primary, primary, and secondary education. Secondary schooling consists of both a lower secondary (grades 7–9) and an upper secondary (grades 10–12). The intent of 11 years of compulsory education is to provide students with the kinds of experiences and opportunities that will enable them to achieve personal fulfillment (Sprinzak, Bar, & Levi-Mazloum, 1994). Personal fulfillment, an underlying assumption of education, is to be met through students' attendance at one of four kinds of schools: state schools, state religious schools, Arab and Druze schools, and private schools. The majority of students in Israel attend state schools, but some attend state religious schools that emphasize Jewish studies and traditions (The State of Israel, 1999). In addition to Arab and Druze schools, which give special attention to Arab and Druze history, culture, and religion, a host of private schools "operate under various religious and international auspices" (The State of Israel, 1999, p. 1). The Israeli government finances 72% of educational expenses, with the remaining amount funded through local educational authorities and other sources.

Curricular Subjects and Differentiation

There are at least three ways, according to Ayalon (1994), that curricular subjects are stratified in Israeli schooling: (1) based on their academic nature versus their more utilitarian purposes; (2) between scientific and nonscientific subjects; and (3) in relation to those who

Israel

Source: The World Factbook. (2001). Israel. Washington, DC: The Central Intelligence Agency, U.S. Government. http://www.odci.gov/cia/publications/factbook/geos/is.html

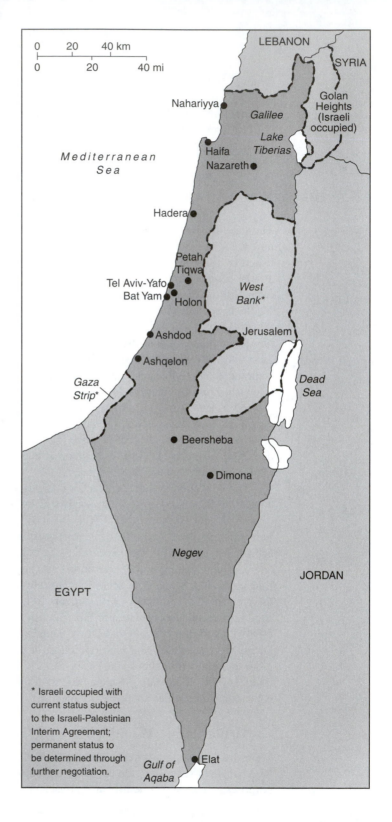

FIGURE 3.3

Points of Convergence

HONG KONG	Demography and educational consequences	ISRAEL
Aspect: Of the 7,210,505 people in Hong Kong, 95% are Chinese and 5% are of other ethnic backgrounds (*World Factbook*, 2001). **Response:** Educated citizens who hold balanced Eastern and Western perspectives are considered necessary to the creation of a harmonious society. Whereas mainland China has used schooling to shape a collectivist-socialist vision of society, schooling in Hong Kong promotes an individualistic spirit and has encouraged citizens to pursue self-interests (Cheung & Kwok, 1998; Lau & Kuan, 1988). **Consequence:** A class-based ideology is most apparent in Hong Kong's schools. Social inequalities are tolerated because students accept that they play particular roles in society. An elitist system that caters to children of the privileged is maintained through "the myth of merit." Through practices such as streaming and ability grouping, students from lower social class backgrounds come to believe that their educational failure is a result of their own lack of effort or individual deficiencies. Meritocracy, therefore, preserves the class positions of the dominant upper class group (Cheung, 1997).	**Demography and educational consequences** How have attributes of the population affected education?	**Aspect:** Founded in 1948, Israel has experienced successive waves of immigration, with its 5,938,083 population representing more than 70 countries. Approximately 80.1% of the population are Jewish (32.1% Europe/America-born; 20.8% Israel-born; 14.6% Africa-born; 12.6% Asia-born), and 19.9% are non-Jewish and mostly Arab (*World Factbook*, 2001). **Response:** The integration of immigrants into Israeli society has been an aim of the state, which has aggressively sought to absorb immigrant children into a Jewish, Zionist identity. **Consequence:** This "ingathering of the exiles" rhetoric has promoted segregation of immigrants, especially those from Arab countries, through social policies that have caused them to settle in rural areas and to create their own schools (Dahan & Levy, 2000). For immigrant children in urban areas with veteran Israeli residents, Dahan and Levy found that *Mizrahi* children (Eastern or Oriental Jews) are tracked into different courses, exposed to ill-equipped facilities, and receive less resources than *Ashkenazi* children (Western Jews).

are exposed to arts and humanities, considered "high culture," and those who are not exposed to cultural capital subjects. According to Bernstein (1971), knowledge is organized through school subjects. In turn, societies identify some kinds of knowledge as superior to others and decide which social groups will have access to that knowledge (Eggleston, 1977; Labaree, 1988; Young, 1971). Hence, differential curriculum offerings are a way in which dominant groups amass social power and preserve that power by deciding who will have access to higher-status knowledge (Apple, 1990; Ayalon, 1994). Most of the research on educational inequality, within the Israeli context, is centered on the different educational experiences of two major Jewish ethnic groups, namely Jews of European or American origin (Western Jews) and Jews of Asian or North African origin (Eastern Jews). Research conducted by Shavit (1990), Yogev (1981), and Yogev and Ayalon (1986) reinforces the notion that school curriculum is differentiated by ethnic composition, with the disadvantaged Eastern Jews experiencing lower levels of academic achievement, higher levels of representation in vocational education, and lower numbers obtaining the matriculation diploma necessary for postsecondary enrollment.

One way that school subjects contribute to student stratification is by their categorization as either academic or utilitarian (Ayalon, 1994). In schools, this is manifested in an educational practice called *tracking*, whereby students are grouped into the classical, academic track or the vocational track. According to Adler and Sever (1994), only 20% of secondary students in Israel were enrolled in vocational schools, with the majority of students attending academic high schools based on the European conception of the grammar school or gymnasium. By the late 1980s, however, the authors found that vocational education had expanded from only 2,000 students at 25 schools to 90,000 pupils at 300 schools. More recent figures reveal that 57% of students in upper secondary schools in Israel are enrolled in the general, academic track, and 43% of students are in the technological, vocational track (Sprinzak, Bar, & Levi-Mazloum, 1994). As an educational response to the country's rapid immigration, state officials viewed vocational education as a way to help the nation meet its economic needs (Adler & Sever, 1994). The result of this approach is that Eastern Jews and those from low socioeconomic backgrounds have been tracked into vocational education, with little opportunity to cycle into other educational paths. In this way, the academic track was reserved for educating Western Jews and students coming from higher social class backgrounds.

In the pre-independence era, vocational education was more a political than economic endeavor, as the state needed workers to produce weapons as a defense against Arab military threats (Gelbart, 1987). Therefore, vocational programs, from their inception, were "more supply than demand oriented" (p. 64) and served as an educational mechanism to absorb immigrants. To illustrate, Gelbart (1987) found that the immigration of people from industrialized Islamic countries, along with their higher birth rates compared to the pre-independence population, actually doubled Israel's population between 1948 and 1951. In 1984, Shavit studied the educational paths taken by 2,000 immigrants to Israel in 1954. Despite the state's goal of integrating immigrants into Israeli society, Shavit found that a large portion had been products of vocational tracking, an exclusionary practice, that did not open opportunities for ethnic immigrants, but rather decreased their chances of obtaining a matriculation diploma to enter higher education (cited in Gelbart, 1987).

According to Adler and Sever (1994), Israeli education actually sorted primary school graduates "perceived as unable to cope with academic curricular components and sophisticated thought processes" (p. 57) into vocational tracks. The view that new immigrant children lacked the cognitive skills to do well in academic tracks is associated with the cognitive-deficit school of thought, which says that the difficulties immigrant children encountered in school were due to cultural differences that deprived them of the intellectual functioning necessary for academic achievement and the attitudes and motivation necessary for success in a modern society (Adler & Sever, 1994). According to this theoretical approach, it was cultural differences that prevented immigrant children from competing with more academically able students. As a result of this approach, social gaps emerged between those whom educators assumed could handle adult roles and those whom the school considered unable to master the basic skills of citizenship (Adler & Sever, 1994).

In the Israeli context, Carl Frankenstein (1970), a prominent figure of the cognitive deficit approach, has argued that children who grow up in impoverished, preliterate cultural situations are cognitively impaired. The cognitive deficit theory proffered by Frankenstein has been challenged by Klinov (1991), who was concerned that lower class students and students of disadvantaged ethnic origins were being viewed as incapable of learning academically oriented curriculum. In a study of mathematics and reading achievement tests completed by all individuals 17 years of age who reported for military duty, Klinov found that the "test scores of the higher achieving half of vocational school graduates were only slightly lower than those of academic high-school graduates" (Adler & Sever, 1994, p. 62). Thus, the claim that students in vocational programs are somehow less able to do well in regular academic programs appears questionable.

Moreover, the notion that students in vocational school tracks are provided with a second chance at social mobility and participation in the larger society has been contested by Sever and Inbar (1990) and Willis (1981). For Willis, schools indoctrinate students into what he has termed "the mass ideological conviction of the voluntary industrial army" (p. 1). Accordingly, some students—through schooling curriculum and practices—learn that they are unfit for the rigor of more academically oriented schooling; they settle, therefore, for a vocational education in which they reap inferior rewards and obtain the "undesirable social definition" of manual laborers (p. 1). For Sever and Inbar, vocational education does not represent a reopening of future opportunities for vocationally tracked students; rather, it is an alternative, inferior route taken by ethnic minorities and those of lesser socioeconomic backgrounds who are not selected to academic secondary schools.

The work of Willis (1981) and Sever and Inbar (1990) is based on a neo-Marxist theoretical approach in which academic and vocational tracking is understood in terms of ethnic class discrimination as opposed to cultural deficiencies in intellectual functioning. For neo-Marxists, race or ethnic relations are analyzed in relation to competition for economic resources (Adler & Sever, 1994). Arguing from this perspective, Swirsky (1981) has contended that many of the Eastern Jews who fled to Israel from European countries as a result of Jewish persecution had actually traded one form of oppression for another. The settlement of Eastern Jews in Israel has resulted in their being stratified by ethnicity and relegated to proletariat status, with even less social prestige than they had witnessed under the British and French colonizers they had left (Adler & Sever, 1994). As Adler and Sever (1994) have argued, this disadvantaged position of Eastern Jews will persist if the ethnic class divisions in the Western-oriented Israeli society are not confronted. The differing theoretical bases, namely the cultural deficit approach and neo-Marxism, applied to the Israeli context have shaped the way in which immigrant socialization has been interpreted. Moreover, it has shaped the ways in which people view the purposes of schooling and the role of curricular subjects in Israel. In summary, to straddle educational models of equality and excellence, the Israeli elite developed "a vocational school track that catered to nonacademic bound students, without foregoing the chance of educating a professional and intellectual elite in the academic high schools" (Adler & Sever, 1994, p. 59).

Moving from the stratification of subjects based on their academic or utilitarian character, Ayalon (1994) has identified a second kind of curricular stratification, one between scientific and nonscientific subjects. In Israel, the study of inequitable secondary education has centered on the academic–vocational debate but has not focused on school subjects as sources of inequality among students (Ayalon, 1994). Scientific subjects, such as biology, chemistry, physics, mathematics, and computer sciences, are accorded higher status than the humanities. Ayalon cites two possible reasons for the prestige and status associated with the sciences. First, the more traditional explanation is that technology is vital to the creation of modern economies; thus, those who possess scientific knowledge obtain socially desirable positions (Ayalon, 1994). The second explanation, based on Apple's (1990) application of a neo-Marxist perspective, is that the high status scientific subjects are readily testable, making them useful stratification tools for schools to select students and to foster a type of social engineering. In addition to within-school tracking, Ayalon has argued that between-school differentiation also stratifies students based on the subjects they are offered within the same educational track. The author hypothesized that, in Israel, college-track students in higher status schools with higher proportions of Western Jews have more access to socially valued knowledge than college-bound students in lower status schools with higher proportions of Eastern Jews.

Based on the cultural deficit model, Eastern Jews have been stereotyped as being less likely to succeed in scientific subjects and assumed to be less interested in these subjects (Ayalon, 1994). Consequently, "the availability of different school subjects in Israeli high schools . . . are differentiated by their ethnic composition" (Ayalon, 1994, p. 266). Results from Ayalon's study of 208 Jewish schools showed that Eastern Jews had less access to scientific subjects and cultural capital subjects such as literature, French, and art than Western Jews. In fact, students of Eastern origins were exposed to fewer high status subjects in all areas except religious studies (Ayalon, 1994). Thus, as Ayalon has asserted, "curricular decisions that are based on the matching of subjects with the assumed capacities and interests of the students seem to end in the monopolization of highly valued knowledge by privileged social groups" (p. 264). This monopolization of superior knowledge by the most powerful groups at the expense of the less powerful groups is evidenced by the concentration of Eastern Jews in smaller schools, their overrepresentation in religious studies, and teachers' distorted views about their abilities and interests (Ayalon, 1994).

Like Hong Kong, the schools in Israel are experiencing greater pressure to increase the number of students who receive their diplomas. The local media in Israel, as in Hong Kong, report the percentage of students who pass examinations, thereby providing a means of ranking schools and their principals (Ayalon, 1994). Because students who take particular subjects at the same level are required to take the same examination, schools find ways to control the results. For instance, Ayalon found that schools "encourage less-able students to drop out, place academically weaker students in nonacademic programs, and permit less-able students to take examinations only in lower-level courses within subjects" (pp. 268–269). Ironically, because educators at the local level have autonomy to shape the curriculum, this actually increases students' inequitable access to high-status knowledge in Israel's centralized education system (Ayalon, 1994). Ayalon tentatively concluded that tighter supervision of curricular decisions on the part of the state would aid educational equity.

Research conducted by Stevenson and Baker (1991) supports this conclusion. In their 15-country comparative study, the authors found that the implemented curriculum in countries with centrally controlled educational systems is less dependent on student characteristics (i.e., ethnicity, gender, and socioeconomic class) than locally controlled educational systems. Ayalon, in her study of Israeli high schools, found that scientific subjects were offered more than other subjects, thereby supporting others' findings (Kliebard, 1992; Labaree, 1988; Stray, 1985) that humanities and arts are allotted less time in the curriculum than sciences. There is also differentiation within scientific subjects, with physics and computer sciences considered more "masculine" than the more "feminine" subjects of biology and chemistry (Ayalon, 1994). Moreover, the gender makeup of Israeli high schools also affects which subjects are available, as Ayalon found that humanities are more likely to be offered in high schools in which more females are enrolled.

Although the sciences have higher status in the school curriculum than do the humanities, the arts and humanities do serve a social selective role in that they enable some students to acquire what Bourdieu (1977) has termed "cultural capital." Subject stratification between those students who are exposed to arts and humanities (high culture) and those who are not constitutes, for Ayalon (1994), a third way in which curriculum is differentiated in schools. An examination of this differentiation between instrumental subjects and high culture subjects, conducted by Eggleston (1977), revealed that the humanities and arts are a means of social exclusion among diverse cultural groups.

Although cultural capital subjects have been explored in relation to class-based differences; Ayalon (1994) has extended her analysis to explore how ethnicity in Israel is a factor in deciding which students are exposed to high culture. According to Ayalon, "the Western nature of the knowledge defined as high culture facilitates the image of this knowledge as irrelevant to youngsters who originate from Africa or the Middle East" (p. 269). Her research confirmed that cultural capital subjects were offered less often to Eastern Jews than to Western Jews. Because students are not required to take any higher-level subjects to obtain their matriculation diploma, schools "can settle for a curriculum composed solely of lower-level subjects" (p. 269), such as geography, Arabic, and the Bible. Even when students obtain knowledge to assume high-status positions, Ayalon found that they are often asked to prove their "familiarity with high culture" (p. 265), which serves as a legitimating device for those selected to elite professions (DiMaggio & Useem, 1982). A study of prestigious American boarding schools, conducted by Cookson and Persell (1985), revealed a vast array of cultural capital offerings for students. Their work reinforces the view that the acquisition of high culture helps to prepare students for socially desirable positions upon graduation.

Citizenship Education and National Identity in Israel

"The Israeli space," according to Gur-ze'ev (2000), "is an arena where the relevance, vitality, and productivity of conflicting philosophies of education are manifested in a unique clarity" (p. 363). This uniqueness is manifested in the way education has been used to proffer competing images of citizenship in a premodern, modern, and postmodern society. In large part, nation-building efforts in Israel have been based on the metaphorical notion of the "melting pot," whereby immigrants are exposed to a "common" Jewish culture, despite their diverse linguistic, historical, and cultural backgrounds (Dahan & Levy, 2000). Hegemony, the process by which dominant social groups create a social consensus that favors their own views and positions, has been cultivated in Israel through a national,

Zionist ideology that emphasizes social integration for purposes of national unification. This "ingathering of the exiles" rhetoric, though, has promoted the segregation of immigrants, especially those from Arab countries, through social policies that caused them to settle in rural areas and to create their own schools (Dahan & Levy, 2000). For immigrant children in urban areas with veteran Israeli residents, Dahan and Levy found that *Mizrahi* children (i.e., Eastern or Oriental Jews) were tracked into different courses, exposed to ill-equipped facilities, and were provided with less adequate resources than *Ashkenazi* children (i.e., Western Jews). Schooling has played a key role in the socialization of young *Mizrahi* children, exposing them to cultural-deficit understandings of their home and cultural backgrounds as unsuitable for life in a modern society. "In this context, 'modernizing' the immigrants meant that they had to be secularized and adapted into an economy undergoing a process of industrialization" (Dahan & Levy, 2000, p. 425). According to Dahan and Levy, "nationhood implied modernity" (p. 425), and the role of the school, through its curriculum and instructional practices, was to create modern citizens.

Toward this end, citizenship education is a vehicle for students to learn the particular attitudes and skills to enable their competent participation as social members (Turner, 1993). The State of Israel has proffered the following linkage between citizenship and schooling:

> The educational system aims to prepare children to become responsible members of a democratic, pluralistic society in which people from different ethnic, religious, cultural and political backgrounds coexist. It is based on Jewish values, love of the land and the principles of liberty and tolerance. It seeks to impart a high level of knowledge, with an emphasis on scientific and technological skills essential for the country's continued development. (The State of Israel, 1999, p. 1)

According to Alexander (2000), a primary purpose of schooling in Israel is the promotion of various religious, cultural, labor, and political ideologies. Through its sponsorship of schools that proffer these particular ideologies, the state has fostered indoctrination and inhibited the development of a common, inclusive social vision (Alexander, 2000). **Indoctrination** has been defined by Snook (1972) as the intent "to deny students relevant and developmentally appropriate information or choices by teaching *content* known to be false or using instructional *methods* that disrespect students, such as inappropriate rewards and punishments" (Alexander, 2000, p. 497). For Alexander, the Zionist rhetoric accompanied by segregationist educational practice has "succeeded in part because it took full advantage of the ecological connection between school, community, and home, especially in elite kibbutzim, religious Zionist communities, and where peer led youth movements received strong parental support" (p. 491). This intent on the part of the state to promote ideology through schooling has contributed to social divisiveness, wherein non-Jewish identities are excluded from educational discourse and teaching caters to uncritical assumptions about how different ethnic and religious groups learn (Alexander, 2000).

The exclusion of non-Jewish identities and an uncritical stance toward social controversies is apparent in Israeli textbooks. Textbooks, according to Firer (1998), represent the legitimate knowledge of a society and can be considered "reliable mirrors of the political culture of societies" (p. 196). In other words, textbooks are tools through which the state establishes a particular view of citizenship and fosters its idealized national ideology.

Moreover, the state has a captive audience, as teachers employ textbooks as their primary means of instruction. Gal (1981), in a survey of 13,000 American teachers spanning kindergarten through college, found that interaction with textbooks and other printed matter constituted 90%–95% of a students' time in school (cited in Firer, 1998). Thus, the kind of material students are exposed to shapes the ways they view themselves as citizens. Consequently, one must consider whose interests are served in the official texts that students study. Because textbooks are the prominent medium by which students are exposed to "the norms, the values, and the 'formal truth' of the state and its adult society" (Firer, 1998, p. 196), an examination of history and civics materials can uncover ideologies that reflect a country's political and social values.

In an attempt to make "the peace process between Israel and the Arab states and the Palestinian people" a central part of the school curriculum, Israel adopted, in 1994, a new civics studies curriculum focused on human rights and universal democratic principles (Sprinzak, Bar, & Levi-Mazloum, 1994, p. 50). To analyze how Israeli–Arab relations are portrayed to students, Firer (1998) reviewed 44 history and 23 civics textbooks, as well as five 'peace' manuals, previously and presently used in Jewish religious and nonreligious secondary, intermediate, and comprehensive schools. Her analysis centered on the presentation of conflicts and value dilemmas during the past 50 years, the implicit meanings of these events, the curriculum missing from texts, and the degree of tolerance or intolerance reflected therein.

The treatment of human rights in the texts revealed that the state's attempt to substantiate a new civics curriculum is more a symbolic act of reform than real reform. For example, Firer (1998) found that human rights violations and controversies faced by minorities were often missing from Israeli textbooks, that dry, objective language was used to declare human freedoms, and that students were not encouraged to question or critique Israeli society. Every textbook that Firer examined emphasized Israel's desire for peace with Arabs but claimed that, until recently, Arabs have rejected peaceful resolution to Israeli–Arab tensions. Moreover, only one text, titled *Arab Citizens of the State of Israel* published in 1982, presented students with information on the Arab–Israeli conflict; however, the text is only optional reading for students and focuses on internal challenges of Arabs in Israel as opposed to external politics and foreign relations (Firer, 1998). Firer concluded, therefore, that the intent of civics textbooks was to present students with the state's image of the good citizen and to refrain from placing citizenship in a larger, more global context. Although the state contends that schooling has been a vehicle for cultural tolerance and antidiscrimination (Sprinzak et al., 1994, p. 50), Firer's analysis has shown that little has been done at the official level to prepare citizens for the Arab–Israeli peace process, much less to address the internal tensions between Western and Eastern Jews.

Multicultural Responses to State Rhetoric and Social Exclusion

Since the early 1950s, when Israel absorbed approximately one million Jewish refugees, social integration among European or Western Jews (*Ashkenazi*) and Oriental or Eastern Jews (*Mizrahi*) has been fraught with problems (Firer, 1998). Although large in number, the *Mizrahi* hold minority status in terms of socioeconomic, cultural, and political clout and are discriminated against by the *Ashkenazi* who hold positions of power (Firer, 1998).

Despite the claim that all Jewish immigrants are entitled to citizenship (Iram & Schmida, 1998), integration has not paved the way for *Mizrahim* political participation, nor has assimilation of the main attributes of the Israeli nation resulted in their acquisition of cultural knowledge to obtain desirable social positions. Rather, as Adler and Sever (1994) have contended, the state has expected the *Mizrahi* to relinquish their indigenous values and cultural mores in order that they might be absorbed into the dominant culture of the *Ashkenazi*. Thus, "citizenship appears as a central and highly controversial issue whenever social order and solidarity in (post)modern societies is debated" (Fogiel-Bijaoui & Berl, 1999, p. 159).

Israel's process of integrating *Mizrahi* into a narrow, Israeli–Jewish identity has been challenged by *Mizrahi,* who seek multicultural educational policies and practices. As in other industrialized modern states, the impetus for multiculturalism in Israel has stemmed from a reaction by those of the dominated or minority group, in this case the *Mizrahi,* who have been systematically relegated to lower social positions and whose cultural identity has been dismissed in state curricula (Dahan & Levy, 2000). Specifically, two kinds of multicultural responses have emerged within the non-European Jewish communities. The first, according to Parekh (1997), is a "critical multiculturalism" based on a social-democratic philosophy; the second is an "autonomist multiculturalism" that caters to fundamentalist interests (p. 184).

To examine these multicultural responses, we apply Hofstede's dimensions of *power distance* and *social principledness*, as utilized in the Hong Kong section, to the Israeli context in order to better understand ethnic minority reaction to the state's ideology as manifested in schooling. Recall that *power distance* is the degree to which citizens tolerate social inequalities and accept these power imbalances as normal. Whereas lower class residents in Hong Kong, in large part, accepted their dominated state, the Islamic Jews in Israel have come to reject segregative, ethnic-biased educational practices and have pushed for change through two distinctive responses: *Kedma* and *Shas*. Each represent *Mizrahi* reactions to the discrimination they have experienced. Both movements attest to the state's failed attempts to foster a national, Zionist citizen identity (Dahan & Levy, 2000).

Established in 1993, *Kedma*, an educational reform movement based on principles of equity and democratic empowerment, established academic secondary schools in disadvantaged neighborhoods (Dahan & Levy, 2000). Advocates of *Kedma* asserted that *Mizrahi* marginalization was due to the state's exclusionary practices that erased non-European Jewish history and culture from Israeli society. Through a more critical approach, advocates reasoned that multiculturalism would not only raise students' academic performance but also help them view their culture as valuable. The task of *Kedma*, as Dahan and Levy have asserted, was to add *Mizrahi* literature and history to the curriculum and to encourage students to complete multicultural projects designed to bolster their self-esteem. Through its open admission policy and tutoring programs, *Kedma* created opportunities for students to take and pass matriculation examinations irrespective of their past academic performance (Dahan & Levy, 2000). Moreover, history textbooks were modified to include the contributions of *Mizrahi* Jews that had been purposefully omitted from the official curriculum, and multicultural projects, such as "My History," were incorporated to increase students' familiarity with and interest in their own families and histories (Dahan & Levy, 2000). Thus, *Kedma* is an example of what Parekh (1997) has termed "critical multiculturalism" (p. 184).

Whereas the *Kedma* Association's approach to addressing past inequities was to critically question the educational system and modify it to accurately reflect *Mizrahi* social contributions, the intention of *Shas* was "to garner political power by establishing itself as a mass-based popular movement with its own, autonomous educational system" (Dahan & Levy, 2000, p. 430). Established in 1984, *Shas*, the third largest political party in Israel, created separate, independent schools composed primarily of, but not restricted to, *Mizrahi* children. Located in disadvantaged communities and characterized by their "highly politicized" curriculum, *Shas* schools continue to draw upon Israeli social dissension to bolster its ultra-Orthodox message as the "sole and true representative" of the *Mizrahi* people (Dahan & Levy, 2000, p. 433). A 1994 study, reviewed by Dahan and Levy, revealed that approximately 60%–75% of students' time in *Shas* schools was devoted to religious studies, text recitation, and socialization into its religious society. Hence, the intent of *Shas* schooling is to advance its own political agenda rather than to raise student achievement or increase social mobility. *Shas*, therefore, represents what Parekh (1997) has termed an "autonomist multiculturalism" (p. 184).

Social principledness, another dimension of Hofstede's model, refers to the degree to which a culture will acquiesce, without question, to authority and accept that authority's values and norms as conventional social standards. Unlike Hong Kong's lower class, the Islamic Jews in Israel have seriously questioned the state's narrow definition of Jewish citizenship; their critical response represents a strong reaction against and rejection of the kind of citizenship portrayed in the official school curriculum. Like nation-building efforts elsewhere, the state of Israel used its educational system to promote *mamlakhtiut*, a term that describes the specific citizenship ideology that legitimated segregative schooling and that stigmatized *Mizrahim* as "nonmodern" (Dahan & Levy, 2000, p. 437). As a result, the *Mizrahi* were relegated to vocational tracks, special classes, and different schools, while the intent of the state was to inculcate students with a Zionist, homogenous ideology of citizen identity (Dahan & Levy, 2000). The processes of privatization and liberalization that characterized economics in the 1980s further alienated non-Western Jews, as deregulation policies and educational decision making at local levels provided an environment where the *Ashkenazi* could leverage even greater opportunities for their children (Dahan & Levy, 2000). These practices increased the ethnic and class divides and caused the *Mizrahi* to question the state's claim of universal, egalitarian education. Hence, non-Western Jews protested the state's "monoethnic curriculum" that emphasized Western values (Iram & Schmida, 1998) and exposed the state's intent to erase what the dominant group viewed as an inferior, primitive *Mizrahi* identity (Dahan & Levy, 2000). Thus, both *Kedma* and *Shas*, in their own distinctive ways, strove to enhance *Mizrahi* status and to advance *Mizrahi* cultural values and views.

Although opportunities for formal education have been extended to more and more people, the restricted nature of schooling is still manifested in the kind of knowledge that is validated, in the ways that students are selected and stratified for learning, and in the ways that particular groups' interests are served. The ideology—whether economic, political, cultural, or social—conveyed in schools plays a powerful role in transmitting different messages to students about their backgrounds, abilities, skills, and aspirations. Although the overt aims of schooling speak to education's role in developing students' competencies in order that they might find personal and social fulfillment, it seems that those who benefit the most from schooling are those whose values, views, language, and attitudes match the dominant culture.

An analysis of the latent functions of schooling in Hong Kong and Israel reveal how school curriculum, through both its content and practices, reproduce the ethnic, class, and gender divisions in their societies at large. In Hong Kong, individualism and market principles create a competitive environment where students strive to enter prestigious secondary schools and higher education, believing that schooling provides a level playing field wherein all can benefit if they apply themselves. The economic purposes of schooling in Hong Kong, then, overshadow even new political arrangements and confound other schooling aims, such as civic development. In Israel, ethnic discrimination occurs alongside a Zionist ideology of national unification and social integration. Schooling, here, serves to protect the intellectual, economic, political, and cultural interests of Western Jews at the expense of Eastern Jews. Thus, a comparative, sociological analysis of schooling exposes the disparities in relation to who receives what kind of education and for what purposes. In the next chapter, we address educational disparity by examining the issue of equal opportunity and access as manifested in the schooling processes in Brazil and South Africa.

Sustaining Reflection

■ The "myth of merit" describes how students from lower socioeconomic backgrounds come to understand that their educational failure is a result of their own lack of effort or individual deficiencies rather than due to systemic and school inequities. What is your view on this?

■ How is the restricted nature of schooling manifested in your educational environment?

■ What kind of knowledge is validated at your educational institution? In what ways are particular groups' interests served?

References

Adler, C., & Sever, R. (1994). *Beyond the dead-end alley of mass education.* Boulder, CO: Westview Press.

Alexander, H. A. (2000). Education in the Jewish state. *Studies in Philosophy and Education, 19* (5–6), 491–507.

Apple, M. W. (1990). *Ideology and curriculum* (2nd ed.). New York, NY: Routledge.

Apple, M. W. (1995). *Education and power.* New York, NY: Routledge.

Apple, M. W. (1996). *Cultural politics and education.* New York, NY: Teachers College Press.

Arnove, R. F., Kelly, G. P., & Altbach, P. G. (1982). Approaches and perspectives. In P. G. Altbach, R. F. Arnove, & G. P. Kelly (Eds.), *Comparative education* (pp. 3–11). New York, NY: Macmillan.

Atkinson, P. (1985). *Language, structure and reproductions: An introduction to the sociology of Basil Bernstein.* London, UK: Methuen.

Au, K. (1992). *A study of gender roles as defined in primary school textbooks in Hong Kong.* Hong Kong: Hong Kong Institute of Asia-Pacific Studies (Chinese).

Ayalon, H. (1994, Oct.). Monopolizing knowledge? The ethnic composition and curriculum of Israeli high schools. *Sociology of Education, 67*(4), 264–278.

Berger, P. L., & Berger, B. (1976). *Sociology: The biographical approach* (revised ed.). Harmondsworth, NY: Penguin.

Bernstein, B. (1971). On the classification and framing of knowledge. In M. F. D. Young (Ed.),

Knowledge and control (pp. 47–69). London, UK: Cassell & Collier Macmillan.

Bond, M. H., ed. (1986). *The psychology of the Chinese people*. Hong Kong: Oxford University Press.

Bourdieu, P. (1977). Cultural reproduction and social reproduction. In J. Karabel & A. H. Halsey (Eds.), *Power and ideology in education* (pp. 487–511). London, UK: Oxford University Press.

Bowles, S., & Gintis, H. (1976). *Schooling in capitalist America*. New York, NY: Basic Books.

Bray, M. (1997). Education and colonial transition: The Hong Kong experience in comparative perspective. *Comparative Education*, *33*(2), 157–169.

Brown, H. O. (1997). Teachers and teaching. In G. A. Postiglione & W. O. Lee (Eds.), *Schooling in Hong Kong: Organization, teaching, and social context* (pp. 95–116). Hong Kong: Hong Kong University Press.

Carnoy, M. (1974). *Education as cultural imperialism*. New York, NY: David McKay, Inc.

Cheng, K. M. (1997). The education system. In G. A. Postiglione & W. O. Lee (Eds.), *Schooling in Hong Kong: Organization, teaching, and social context* (pp. 25–41). Hong Kong: Hong Kong University Press.

Cheung, C. (1999, June). The introduction of personal and social education in secondary schools in Hong Kong. *Pastoral Care*, 23–26.

Cheung, C., & Kwok, S. (1998). Social studies and ideological beliefs in mainland China and Hong Kong. *Social Psychology of Education*, *2*(2), 217–236.

Cheung, K. W. (1997). Curriculum as a form of social practice. In G. A. Postiglione & W. O. Lee (Eds.), *Schooling in Hong Kong: Organization, teaching, and social context* (pp. 117–134). Hong Kong: Hong Kong University Press.

Clabaugh, G. K., & Rozycki, E. G. (1990). *Understanding schools: The foundations of education*. New York, NY: Harper & Row.

Cookson, P. W., & Persell, C. H. (1985). *Preparing for power: American elite boarding schools*. New York, NY: Basic Books.

Cuban, L. (1992). Curriculum stability and change. In P. Jackson (Ed.), *Handbook of research on curriculum* (pp. 216–247). New York, NY: Macmillan.

Dahan, Y. & Levy, G. (2000). Multicultural education in the Zionist state—The Mizrahi challenge. *Studies in Philosophy and Education*, *19*(5–6), 423–444.

deMarrais, K. B., & LeCompte, M. D. (1995). *The way schools work: A sociological analysis of education* (2nd ed.). White Plains, NY: Longman.

DiMaggio, P., & Useem, M. (1982). The arts in class reproduction. In M. W. Apple (Ed.), *Cultural and economic reproduction in education* (pp. 181–201). London, UK: Routledge & Kegan Paul.

Durkheim, E. (1969). *The evolution of social thought*. London, UK: Routledge & Kegan Paul.

Easton, D. (1965). *A systems analysis of political life*. New York, NY: Wiley.

Education Commission. (1995). *Education Commission Report No. 6: Part 1* (Main Report). Hong Kong: Government Printer.

Education Commission. (1997, September). *Education Commission Report No. 7: Consultation papers and reports*. Hong Kong: Government Printer. (Hong Kong government Web site: *http://www.info.gov.hk/emb/eng/public/no7_0.html*).

Education Commission. (2000, September). *Learning for life, learning through life: Reform proposals for the education system in Hong Kong. Education blueprint for the 21st century*. Hong Kong Special Administrative Region of the People's Republic of China: Government Printer. (Hong Kong Web site: *http://www.e-c.edu.hk/eng/aims/report.html*).

Education Department. (1996). *1996 Guidelines on civic education in schools*. Hong Kong: Government of Hong Kong, Education Department.

Eggleston, J. (1977). *The sociology of the school curriculum*. London, UK: Routledge & Kegan Paul.

Firer, R. (1998). Human rights in history and civics textbooks: The case of Israel. *Curriculum Inquiry*, *28*(2), 195–208.

Fogiel-Bijaoui, S., & Berl, B. (1999). Women in Israel: The social construction of citizenship as a non-issue. In G. Brauer, P. Fenn, A. Hofmann, I. Schnell, & G. Stephan (Eds.), *Nationality-identity-education* (pp. 159–192). Hamburg, Germany: Verlag Dr. Kovac.

Frankenstein, C. F. (1970). *Impaired intelligence: Pathology and rehabilitation*. New York, NY: Gordon & Breach.

French, J. R. P., & Raven, B. (1959). The bases of social power. In D. Cartwright (Ed.), *Studies in social power* (pp. 150–167). Ann Arbor, MI: The University of Michigan.

Friederichs, J. O. (1991). Whose responsibility? The impact of imminent socio-political change on Hong Kong education. *International Review of Education, 37*(2), 193–209.

Gal, M. D. (1981). *Handbook of evaluation and selecting curriculum materials*. Washington, DC: Allyn & Bacon.

Gelbart, R. (1987). *School-based vocational education and industrial schools*. Unpublished doctoral dissertation, Brandeis University. Ann Arbor, MI: Dissertation Information Service.

Gibbons, J. (1982). The issue of the language of instruction in the lower forms of Hong Kong secondary schools. *Journal of Multilingual and Multicultural Development, 3*(2), 117–128.

Gibbons, J. (1984, June). Interpreting the English Proficiency Profile in Hong Kong. *RELC Journal, 15*(1), 64–74.

Gur-ze'ev, I. (2000). Introduction. *Studies in Philosophy and Education, 19*(5–6), 363–367.

Guy, G. R. (1988). Language and social class. In F. J. Newmeyer (Ed.), *Language: The socio-cultural context*. Cambridge, UK: Cambridge University Press.

Hall, E. T. (1959). *The silent language*. Greenwich, CT: Fawcett.

Hofstede, G. (1986). Cultural differences in teaching and learning. *International Journal of Intercultural Relations, 10*, 301–320.

Holmes, B. (1981). *Comparative education: Some considerations of method*. London, NY: George Allen & Unwin.

Iram, Y., & Schmida, M. (1998). *The educational system of Israel*. Westport, CT: Greenwood Press.

Jackson, P. (1968). *Life in classrooms*. Chicago, IL: University of Chicago Press.

Jiang, B., Wang, K., Zhang, H., Jiang, Z., & Xu, K. (1993). *Introduction to spiritual civilization*. Shanghai, China: Shanghai People's Press.

Jin, Y., & Ouyang, B. (1992). *Study of Deng Xiaoping's thought on the construction of socialist spiritual civilization*. Shenyang, China: Liaoning People's Press.

Kandel, I. L. (1933). *Comparative education*. Boston, MA: Houghton Mifflin.

King, E. J. (1968). *Comparative studies and educational decision*. Indianapolis, IN: Bobbs-Merrill.

Kliebard, H. M. (1992). The decline of humanistic studies in the American school curriculum. In H. M. Kliebard (Ed.), *Forging the American curriculum: Essays in curriculum history and theory* (pp. 3–26). New York, NY: Routledge.

Klinov, R. (1991). *Priorities in the allocation of public resources to education*. Jerusalem, Israel: The Center for Social Policy Studies in Israel (Hebrew).

Kwok, S. (1996, April 23). Pioneering Putonghua. *South China Morning Post*, 5.

Labaree, D. F. (1988). *The making of an American high school*. New Haven, CT: Yale University Press.

Lau, S. & Kuan, H. (1988). *The ethos of the Hong Kong Chinese*. Hong Kong: The Chinese University Press.

Lee, W. O. (1997). Social class, language and achievement. In G. A. Postiglione & W. O. Lee (Eds.), *Schooling in Hong Kong: Organization, teaching, and social context* (pp. 155–174). Hong Kong: Hong Kong University Press.

LeTendre, G. K. (1999). International achievement studies and myths of Japan. In G. K. LeTendre (Ed.), *Competitor or ally? Japan's role in American educational debates* (pp. 3–24). New York, NY: Falmer.

Leung, S. (1986). *Perception of political authority by the Hong Kong Chinese* (Occasional Papers No. 17). Hong Kong: Centre for Hong Kong Studies, Institute of Social Studies, CUHK.

Lin, A. M. Y. (1997). Analyzing the "language problem" discourses in Hong Kong: How official, academic, and media discourses construct and perpetuate dominant models of language, learning, and education. *Journal of Pragmatics, 28* (4), 427–440.

Llewellyn Commission. (1982). *A perspective on education in Hong Kong*. Hong Kong: Government Printer.

Lumby, J. (2000). Restructuring vocational education in Hong Kong. *The International Journal of Educational Management, 14*(1), 16–22.

McLaren, P. (1989). *Life in schools*. New York, NY: Longman.

Merton, R. (1957). *Social theory and social structure*. Glencoe, IL: The Free Press.

Morris, P. (1997). Civics and citizenship education in Hong Kong. In K. Kennedy (Ed.), *Citizenship education and the modern state* (pp. 107–125). London: Falmer.

Morris, P. & Chan, K. K. (1997). The Hong Kong school curriculum and the political transition: Politicisation, contextualisation and symbolic action. *Comparative Education, 33*(2), 247–264.

Morris, P. & Williamson, J. (1998). Teacher education in the Asia Pacific Region: A comparative analysis. *Asia-Pacific Journal of Teacher Education and Development, 1*(1), 17–27.

National People's Congress of the People's Republic of China. (1990). *The Basic Law of the Hong Kong Special Administrative Region of the People's Republic of China.* Hong Kong: The Consulative Committee for the Basic Law of the Hong Kong Special Administrative Region of the People's Republic of China.

Okano, K., & Tsuchiya, M. (Eds.). (1999). *Education in contemporary Japan: Inequality and diversity.* Cambridge, UK: Cambridge University Press.

Parekh, B. (1997). National culture and multiculturalism. In K. Thompson (Ed.), *Media and cultural regulation* (p. 184). London, UK: Sage Publications and The Open University.

Postiglione, G. A. (1997). Schooling and social stratification. In G. A. Postiglione & W. O. Lee (Eds.), *Schooling in Hong Kong: Organization, teaching, and social context* (pp. 137–153). Hong Kong: Hong Kong University Press.

Postiglione, G. A., & Lee, W. O. (Eds.) (1997). *Schooling in Hong Kong: Organization, teaching, and social context.* Hong Kong: Hong Kong University Press.

Psacharopoulos, G. (1985). Returns to investment in education: A global update. *World Development, 22*(9), 1325–1343.

Schumann, J. H. (1976, June). Social distance as a factor in second language acquisition. *Language Learning, 26*(1), 135–143.

Scimecca, J. (1980). *Education and society.* New York, NY: Holt, Rinehart & Winston.

Scott, I. (1989). *Political change and the crisis of legitimacy in Hong Kong.* Hong Kong: Oxford University Press.

Scott, I. (1995). Political transformation in Hong Kong: From colony to colony. In R. Y. W. Kwok & A. Y. So (Eds.), *The Hong Kong-Guangdong link: Partnership in flux* (pp. 189–223). Hong Kong: Hong Kong University Press.

Sever, R., & Inbar, D. E. (1990). Evaluating second-chance educational programs. In D. E. Inbar (Ed.), *Second chance in education* (pp. 287–300). London, UK: Falmer.

Shavit, Y. (1990). Arab and Jewish minorities in Israeli education. *American Sociological Review, 55,* 115–126.

Siu, Y. M. (1988). Bilingual education and social class: Some speculative observations in the Hong Kong context. *Comparative Education, 24*(2), 217–227.

So, D. W. (1992). Language-based bifurcation of secondary schools in Hong Kong: Past, present and future. In K. K. Luke (Ed.), *Into the twenty first century: Issues of language in education in Hong Kong* (pp. 69–95). Hong Kong: Linguistic Society of Hong Kong.

Snook, I. A. (1972). *Concepts of indoctrination.* London, NY: Routledge & Kegan Paul.

Sprinzak, D., Bar, E., & Levi-Mazloum, D. (Eds.). (1994). *Facts and figures about education and culture in Israel.* Jerusalem, Israel: State of Israel, Ministry of Education, Culture and Sport.

The State of Israel. (1999). *Facts about Israel: Education.* Jerusalem: The State of Israel, Ministry of Education, Culture and Sport.

Stevenson, D. L., & Baker, D. P. (1991). State control of the curriculum and classroom instruction. *Sociology of Education, 64*(1), 1–10.

Stray, C. A. (1985). From monopoly to marginality: Classics in English education since 1800. In I. F. Goodson (Ed.), *Social histories of the secondary curriculum: Subjects for study* (pp. 19–51). London, UK: Falmer.

Swirsky, S. (1981). Orientals and *Ashkenazim* in Israel: The ethnic division of labor. *Mahbarot Lemehkar Velebikoret, 6,* 27–44 (Hebrew).

Tan, J. (1997). Education and colonial transition in Singapore and Hong Kong: Comparisons and contrasts. *Comparative Education, 33*(2), 303–312.

Teng, C., & Zhang, Z. (1992). *Study of Deng Xiaoping's thought on education.* Shenyang, China: Liaoning People's Press.

Thomas, R. M. (1990). The goals of education: How do different societies compare in their intended educational outcomes? In R. M. Thomas (Ed.), *International comparative education: Practices, issues, and prospects* (pp. 25–56). New York, NY: Pergamon Press.

Torres, C. A. (1998). *Education, power, and personal biography: Dialogues with critical educators.* New York, NY: Routledge.

Tozer, S. E., Violas, P. C., & Senese, G. (1998). *School and society: Historical and contemporary perspectives* (3rd ed.). Boston, MA: McGraw Hill.

Tsang, W. (1991, November 23–24). *English proficiency as cultural capital in the colonial schooling system of Hong Kong.* Paper presented at the Hong Kong Educational Research Association Eighth Annual Conference, Hong Kong Baptist College.

Tsang, W. (1993). *Education and early socioeconomic status.* Hong Kong: Hong Kong Institute of Asia-Pacific Studies.

Tung, P. C. (1990). Why changing the medium of instruction in Hong Kong could be difficult. *Journal of Multilingual and Multicultural Development, 11*, 523–534.

Tung, P., Lam, R., & Tsang, W. (1997). English as a medium of instruction in post-1997 Hong Kong: What students, teachers, and parents think. *Journal of Pragmatics, 28*(4), 441–459.

Turner, B. S. (1993). Outline of a theory of human rights. In B. S. Turner (Ed.), *Citizenship and social theory* (pp. 162–190). London, UK: Sage.

Weber, M. (1978). Economy and society. In G. Roth & C. Wittich (Eds.), *Economy and society: An outline of interpretive sociology.* Translators Ephraim Fishoff et al. Berkeley, CA: University of California Press.

Weiler, K. (1988). *Women teaching for change.* South Hadley, MA: Bergin & Garvey.

Willis, P. (1981). *Learning to labor: How working class kids get working class jobs* (Morning-side ed.). New York, NY: Columbia University Press.

Wong, T. W. P., & Lui, T. L. (1992). *Reinstating class: A structural and developmental study of Hong Kong society.* Hong Kong: Social Sciences Research Centre with Department of Sociology, The University of Hong Kong.

World Factbook. (2001). Washington, DC: Central Intelligence Agency, U.S. Government. Retrieved: February 18, 2002, from http://www.odci.gov/cia/publications/factbook/geos/is.html

Yogev, A. (1981). Determinants of early educational career in Israel: Further evidence for the sponsorship thesis. *Sociology of Education, 54*, 181–195.

Yogev, A., & Ayalon, H. (1986). High school attendance in a sponsored multi-ethnic system: The case of Israel. In A. C. Kerckhoff (Ed.), *Research in sociology of education and socialization*, Vol. 6 (pp. 45–78). Greenwich, CT: JAI Press.

Young, M. F. D. (1971). An approach to the study of curricula as a socially organized knowledge. In M. F. D. Young (Ed.), *Knowledge and control* (pp. 19–46). London, UK: Cassell & Collier Macmillan.

Yu, A., & Bain, B. (1985). *Language, social class and cognitive style: A comparative study of unilingual and bilingual education in Hong Kong and Alberta.* Hong Kong: Hong Kong Teachers' Association.

Yu, V. W. S., & Atkinson, P. A. (1988). An investigation of the language difficulties experienced by Hong Kong secondary school students in English-medium schools: II some causal factors. *Journal of Multilingual and Multicultural Development, 9*(4), 307–322.

Chapter 4

Educational Access and Opportunity

Focusing Questions

- What reasons might a teacher have for differentiating instruction? What rules should guide this practice? How might differences in educational experiences among a society's members be beneficial? How can it be harmful?

- In what ways was your education similar to and different from others you know? What accounts for these differences and similarities?

- Can you think of a time that you felt excluded from an experience? What accounted for this exclusion? Have you ever excluded yourself from a school experience that you knew might have profited you? What accounted for your decision?

INTRODUCTION

Which is preferable—an excellent education for some members of a society, or something less than excellent for every member? For most of us, perhaps, it is natural to object to this question on the grounds that no such choice should be necessary—that an excellent education can and should be available to everyone. Further consideration of the question, as discussed in this chapter, suggests that in some ways the very notion of educational excellence might rely on the maintenance of inequitable educational opportunity—depending precisely upon differentiation among a society's educational experiences, curricula, and settings. The question posed here as to whether education *is* uniform in form and scope within a society is often less revealing than the question of how a society *does* make distinctions in apportioning education to its members. What spoken or unspoken rationale does a society embrace in reconciling the problems of availing equitable learning opportunities to its members? What societal rules determine differences in educational access and opportunity? To what extent, in short, does education reflect a society's justification for social difference—and how?

The focus in this chapter is on two countries typically called "developing": Brazil and South Africa. Yet, even countries whose identities as industrialized, or developed, are not exempt from the problems associated with educational access and opportunity. Core principles that transcend modernizing societies and that appear central to the democratic ideal are sometimes contradictory. **Liberty** and equality, for instance, are not policies or directives for action but instead are slogans that are difficult, if not impossible, to bring alive in reality without compromise. To what extent can a society foster **equality** without limiting the extent to which the society also responds to the democratic imperative of liberty? Doesn't the self-determination that liberty implies lead inextricably to differences among people? These inherent tensions between such apparently essential values often remain ignored. This chapter explores some of those tensions.

EDUCATIONAL ACCESS AND OPPORTUNITY AS A FUNDAMENTAL SOCIETAL ISSUE

The larger contradictions between liberty and equality underlie more specific compromises regarding educational access and opportunity. The ways societies allocate schools, teachers, and other educational resources—that is, the ways societies distribute education to students—reflect efforts to reconcile natural tensions between values like equality and liberty. Differences among students can become significant in terms of educational opportunities afforded them. When differences among students are apparent, societies sometimes interpret these differences as signs of their system's educational outputs and at other times as attributable to innate differences to which schools should react. Analysis of different countries' education systems in light of such questions, then, demonstrates the compromises that cultures make as they confront larger value driven issues.

Questions of educational access and opportunity mirror tensions between overarching democratic values. Yet the tendency to keep the related issues of access and opportunity tightly linked seems sometimes to result in the view that the terms are interchangeable. Reducing the issues of access and opportunity too completely in this way can preempt analysis of some contradictions between the two. Resolving the often-conflicting aspects of educational access and opportunity constitutes one of the most basic challenges for any society and one of the most revealing windows into unfamiliar cultures. Study of these aspects provides a means of reassessing one's own culture and the ways a familiar education system reflects compromises in reconciling issues of access and opportunity.

Why Focus on South Africa and Brazil?

South Africa and Brazil are comparable in noteworthy ways. Both have been subject to colonization by European powers, yielding some similar experiences and outcomes. Both countries have a large stake in extractive industries such as mining, creating circumstances in which politically powerful sectors in populated parts of each country place pressure on remote regions—often with severe consequences for the inhabitants of those hinterlands.

Both South Africa and Brazil, further, have indigenous populations whose worlds have been changed by the economic, political, and cultural forces that the countries' colonizers have introduced. Thus, the South African and Brazilian societies face particular challenges of educational access and opportunity due to sociocultural complexities of race and ethnicity. And population displacement along rural and urban lines has affected policies regarding the distribution of education in both Brazil and South Africa.

Still, in spite of these points of comparison, the differences between Brazil and South Africa are remarkable. As was true of South Africa under its past ideology of **apartheid**, the ways in which race results in differences of educational opportunity is sometimes blatant and overt. The Brazilian example, however, demonstrates that race-based disparities in educational access can be less obvious. Because of its higher degree of racial integration, differences in educational opportunities among racial groups are in some ways more illusive, having been dictated by cultural forces that some claim are especially entrenched precisely because of the peculiarities of Brazilian notions of race. Pursuing understanding of the factors that account for these differences is, therefore, a further purpose in this chapter.

But, in addition to the comparisons and contrasts between Brazil and South Africa, both countries invite some comparisons with other countries. Significantly, South Africa is comparable to the United States in that both countries have regions and pockets of uneven development. In this way, a country's identity can be at once both **developed** and developing. The country's economic growth linked it strongly with commerce in the homelands of its Dutch and English colonizers. Although to this extent, South Africa's colonial identity was comparable to that of Brazil's relationship with its Portuguese colonizers, the country's earlier industrial development has contributed to South Africa's fuller and more long-standing integration with global commercial hubs in Europe and North America. Yet the country still features significant underdevelopment, a face of South Africa that clashes with the country's identity as relatively industrialized and modernized. If modern development relies in part on proportional participation in the project of development, South Africa's dual economic and social identity is, in the end, comparable to circumstances in a more fully modern state, such as the United States, where increasing income disparity points to fractures in the ideal of proportional participation in economic progress. Samoff (1999) noted that the "extremism of *apartheid* and South African politics more generally [was] reflected in the extremism of its education" (p. 423), but that, though striking, "South Africa was never as unique as was commonly thought. The use of education to structure economic, political, and social roles . . . is common throughout the world" (p. 423). Our use of South Africa in this chapter, therefore, enables critique and commentary about the contemporary developed world.

Brazil, for its part, also invites comparison with developed nations such as the United States. Brazil, like the early United States, was a slave society. Though African slavery in each country has given way to the significant Africanization of the cultures of both the United States and Brazil, each society manifests African influences uniquely. Brazilian society, even more so than the United States, has been malleable to various ethnic, religious, and cultural influences (Neuhouser, 1999). Further, Brazil's geographical vastness and the presence within its borders of plentiful natural resources is analogous with circumstances in the United States. Expansion has encroached, east to west, into the homelands of each country's indigenous population. The quest for discovery and settlement of territory resulted in an attitude of domination toward native peoples.

A non-Brazilian's stereotypical impression of Brazil may rest on assumptions that the country's economy is driven by agriculture. Although this perception has some basis in the country's past reliance on agricultural production—particularly sugar—the notion that Brazil is an "industrializing" nation is partly challenged by the reality that industrial goods already constitute three quarters of the country's exports (Neuhouser, 1999). In spite of its large and growing role in global industrial trade, however, a relatively small proportion of working Brazilians—about 20%—are involved in the industrial arena (Gomes, Capanema, & Camara, 2000). With a large proportion of the Brazilian population engaged in agriculture and with subsistence farming a way of life for many of the country's citizens, particularly in northwestern Brazil, inequality in the distribution of wealth characterizes Brazilian society to a pronounced degree (Stromquist, 1997).

Although it is accurate that Brazil's income inequity stems in part from unequal rates of industrial development across this vast country, it is improper to view disparities in the distribution of wealth as a problem solely of societies typically known as developing. The dynamics of rapid economic globalization and technological change have already helped widen income gaps in the so-called developed world—a phenomenon that is bound to become more pronounced. In a sense, then, due to these changes and unknowns, all nations are in a sense developing. For a comparison of how demographic attributes of the population affect education in Brazil and South Africa, see the Points of Convergence box (Figure 4.1).

In terms of education access and opportunity—our focus in this chapter—the Brazilian and South African examples are informative. As is true elsewhere in the world, with disturbing predictability across societies, cultural variables such as race, ethnicity, gender roles, and poverty mediate against the equitable distribution of resources in both Brazil and South Africa. These resources include education. Still, this occurs in ways that differ from one society to the next. Under apartheid, South Africa's inequities in educational access and opportunity have been neither covert nor even a matter of mere doctrine; instead, under apartheid, discrimination became codified in the country's laws and instituted in its schools and governance structures, as we shall see. To a substantial degree, the South African case in the aftermath of apartheid finds parallels in American Jim Crow laws and the overt pursuit of "separate but equal" policy from the United States' still-recent past. These examples offer lessons about the tenaciousness of discrimination—a societal mind-set that persists well beyond the disappearance of the express policies that have sanctioned it and the formal institutions that have reflected and reinforced it (Nkomo, 1990). In Brazil, meanwhile, in spite of growing evidence as to the severity of differential access due to race, a tendency—even among the country's lower status racial groups—is to deny that the structural differences that account for this discrimination constitute racism (Neuhouser, 1999). The Brazilian example, therefore, provides a vivid reminder of the extent to which race is a social construct that will have various meanings in various societies. As the concept of racism itself becomes a social construct—one subject to variation within different societies—discrimination due to race and other perceived physical differences can become even more invisible to those living within the culture and, thus, becomes all the more pernicious.

FIGURE 4.1

Points of Convergence

BRAZIL		SOUTH AFRICA
Aspect: Three main ethnic groups have influenced Brazilian culture: the indigenous peoples or "Indians," the Portuguese Europeans, and the Africans, owing to Brazil's former use of slaves especially in coastal plantations.	**Demography and educational consequences**	**Aspect:** Around three fourths of the South African population is of African descent, and 10.9% are of European descent (chiefly British or Dutch), 8.9% of mixed descent, and 2.6% are Asian, primarily Indian (*The Europa World Year Book*, 1999).
Response: Centuries of intermarriage and racial and cultural mixing have shaped the Brazilian population. A more unified and distinctly Brazilian "race" has emerged as a result (Gomes, 1995). In spite of the fact that few Brazilians have ancestry strictly of one particular group, over half of the Brazilian population describes itself as white.		**Response:** The doctrine of racial separation became particularly pronounced beginning with the apartheid-minded Nationalist rise to power in 1948, the 1953 creation of a system of "Bantu education," and, later, a school system for mixed race or "colored people" in 1963 and for Indian people in 1965.
Consequence: Though evidence points to limitations in the educational opportunities of less privileged races, since most Brazilians claim the identity of the dominant or high-status race, there has been a general lack of acceptance that racism is a pronounced problem and a lack of recognition for its negative effects in terms of differentiated educational access (Neuhouser, 1999).	How have attributes of the population affected education?	**Consequence:** Apartheid's formal system of separation within these four distinct school systems adopted differential access and opportunity into its most fundamental formal structures until dissent, mounting in the 1970s and 1980s, led to the dismantling of the system and Nelson Mandela's election in 1994 as the first South African president from the racial majority.

BRAZIL, SOUTH AFRICA, AND FACTORS OF EDUCATIONAL ACCESS AND OPPORTUNITY IN PERSPECTIVE

As late as 1983, amendments to the South African Constitution—reflecting South Africa's institutionalization of racial difference and separation—declared that each of the four (racial) populations was in charge of its "own affairs." The formal education system in South Africa provides preprimary, primary, secondary, and tertiary education. Language and cultural differences continue to characterize education at all levels, in general, in spite of the disappearance of apartheid as an official regime and policy. The language of instruction has traditionally been in the mother tongue of students, though instruction in English and Afrikaans are taught to all, unless the student selects an African language as an alternative to these two European languages (Bondesio & Berkhout, 1995).

Brazil

Source: The World Factbook. (2001). Brazil. Washington, DC: The Central Intelligence Agency,
U.S. Government. http://www.odci.gov/cia/publications/factbook/geos/br.html

Early in their six total years of primary education, South African students' curricular focus is on reading, writing, and arithmetic. Primary instruction is later augmented by other subjects such as health education, mathematics, environmental studies, science, music, arts and crafts, physical training, and languages. Secondary education, meanwhile, is intended to provide a more flexible curriculum in order to broaden the general knowledge of the various academic subjects and to prepare students for their choice of career or further study. Several streams of instruction at this level provide for concentration in

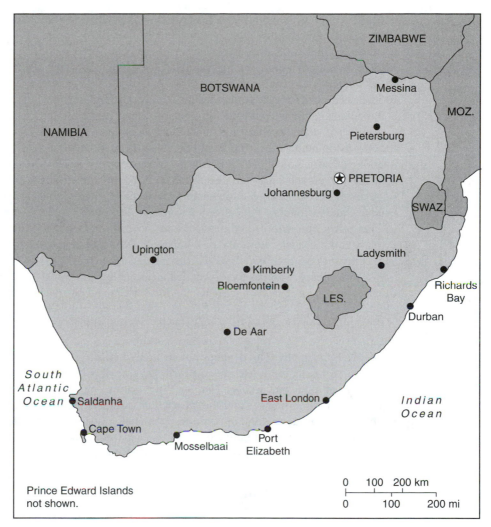

South Africa

Source: The World Factbook. (2001). South Africa. Washington, DC: The Central Intelligence Agency,
U.S. Government. http://www.odci.gov/cia/publications/factbook/geos/sf.html

various areas, including general and commercial education, natural and social science, technical studies, art, agriculture, and domestic science (Bondesio & Berkhout, 1995). South African higher education occurs in a total of 21 universities and more than 150 additional specialized post-secondary institutions and technical schools, nearly all of which were formally intended for a single one of the country's separate racial groups in the apartheid era (Gilmour, Soudien, & Donald, 2000).

The Brazilian education system has four levels or cycles: primary, middle, higher, and advanced. Primary education consists of eight grades corresponding roughly to elementary education in the United States, for instance. Middle education of three or four years corresponds most directly to secondary education in the United States, although in Brazil this often occurs in schools called "colleges." Primary education is both compulsory and free. Middle education is also free in Brazil and is open to graduates of the primary schools. Middle education is characterized by a two-tier structure of academic and vocational/professional schools, with the former preparing students generally for university-level studies and the latter equipping students for more immediate entry into the Brazilian workforce.

In Brazil, public primary and middle schools are operated by either the state or municipal/township authorities. The Brazilian Ministry of Education and Sports implements overall education policy, which is devised by an advisory panel of recognized educators. The council sets standards and makes curricular recommendations. "The states have their secretariats of education, with planning and executive roles in connection with preschool, primary, and secondary education" (Gomes, 1995, p. 131). These state agencies also inspect private preschools and primary and secondary schools" (Gomes, 1995, p. 131). Primary and secondary curricula are composed of common and diversified areas of study: The common core area is defined by the Federal Board of Education and is mandatory across the country, whereas the diversified areas are defined by the state boards of education and by schools based on regional and local needs and on student differences (Gomes, 1995).

As discussed subsequently, a number of elements affect the distribution of education across a society. These things can include circumstances that are relatively intrinsic, such as physical geography. The dynamics of societal interaction with physical place is in fact significant for both South Africa and Brazil. Patterns of density and settlement and of ethnic and racial difference across a "national" population could be affected, in turn, by geography. Historical influences and the legacies of various social traditions and preferences affect educational access and opportunity. A crucial lesson of this chapter is that issues of access and opportunity are political. Education's distribution—or its withholding—is tied to the motives and capacities of the members of the society.

Demographic Challenges

Conditions of widespread poverty characterize both South African and Brazilian societies. In these countries, as elsewhere, conditions of poverty have severe implications for equalizing educational access and opportunity. A look first at some of the roots of these unequal circumstances is appropriate. In both Brazil and South Africa, dynamics of rural and urban population distribution can play a prominent role in questions related to the distribution of education to members of a society. We explore here some of the causes for disparities in educational opportunity in Brazilian and South African cities and countrysides.

In South Africa, disparities in income distribution are a prominent legacy of the apartheid regime. From the middle of the 20th century until 1994, apartheid dictated social conditions for the country's racial groups as a matter of formal policy—not merely due to de facto circumstance. The policy of apartheid ultimately resulted in the massive redistribution of nonwhite racial groups into "homelands," generally in areas that were least promising in terms of their potential for economic development. "The homelands were human dumping grounds where people were literally forcibly resettled from 'white' areas"

(Gilmour et al., 2000, p. 342). One consequence of this population redistribution is that an intensified disparity in the distribution of wealth in South Africa is not strictly racial in nature. Statistics suggest considerable decline in the size of the South African white population relative to the total (Riordan, 1993), and the white population's dominance in the urban areas of the country is also shrinking. Yet, results of South Africa's past policy of race-based relocation are evident. Rural schools are far behind those in South Africa's cities. With the nonurban schools constituting nearly three quarters of all South African schools, inequitable expenditure is an urgent problem.

Brazil's own geography and topography, together with historical, economic, and cultural factors, have created significant regional identities affecting educational access and opportunity for Brazilians. Beginning in the 16th century, Portuguese settlers, recognizing commercial potential of Brazil's northeastern coastal area, extracted exotic products from the coastal forests. A system of "captaincy" placed large land parcels into the hands of a relatively few Portuguese settling families who served as custodians against Portugal's competitors. This practice concentrated wealth in the hands of a relatively few elites (Stromquist, 1997). A marked class structure, in which wealth, land ownership, and political power are often synonymous, is a legacy of this practice that preserves an elite class in modern Brazilian society. Reforms in the use and distribution of land—fairly direct attempts to rectify income disparity—have been difficult to enact due to the degree to which this pattern of power and privilege has become intractable. The social stratification that characterizes Brazilian society continues to foster inequalities in educational access and opportunity. In spite of recent progress and policies aimed at universalizing education and at eradicating illiteracy (Gomes et al., 2000), many poorer Brazilian citizens continue to have limited access to schools, and when schooling is available, severely inequitable educational experiences.

A variety of factors have contributed to severe population displacement in Brazil. Massive relocation has generally implicated declines in the size of Brazil's rural population and an explosion in the size of the country's urban areas. A steady influx of Brazilians into urban regions has contributed to substantial urban poverty—a situation that contrasts with South Africa's relatively well-off cities—and many of Brazil's biggest problems related to educational access stem from the phenomenon of urban poverty (Stromquist, 1997). What accounts for this population explosion in Brazilian cities? Hardships in the rural areas, in part. Inland from the fertile areas occupying the northeastern coastal regions themselves, for instance, an arid and seemingly uninviting region called the *sertao* affords its residents a modest agricultural livelihood in good years. But severe droughts periodically force waves of the *sertao*'s residents into Brazil's cities (Neuhouser, 1999). The exodus from the *sertao* has contributed to rapid urban growth, especially in northeastern cities such as Recife and Salvador, but also in more distant urban areas in the southern coastal area, such as Sao Paulo. Because the cities are ill-prepared to accommodate influxes of the magnitudes they have experienced, those arriving are often relegated to life in *favelas*—underdeveloped areas generally in the most unusable or most undesirable metropolitan areas.

In other cases, modernization itself has contributed to Brazil's population displacement problem. Agricultural production—still a central part of the Brazilian economy and culture—is most robust in the fertile heartland of Brazil's inland south. But, seeking to take advantage of the heartland's potential, *fazendieros*—holders of large tracts of agricultural land—have turned increasingly to mechanization of farming practices. Because mechanization requires fewer farm workers, this practice has left many of the region's former farm workers unemployed, and their flight to urban areas accounts for additional stress on Brazil's cities.

Yet, although poverty is widespread among those relocating to Brazilian cities, conditions of poverty are also striking also in rural Brazil, and this contributes to severely compromised educational circumstances throughout much of rural Brazil. The average subsistence farmer choosing to persist in the face of the relatively barren *sertao*'s climatic unpredictability, for example, faces a feudal lifestyle, in which access to land and water come in return for their loyalty and manpower to the elite *fazendiero*s. These landowners' tracts of land, typically vast, have often been family assets dating from the colonial system of captaincy. Those staying in the agricultural heartland—even those who have employment—fare little better.

Further, Brazilian policy aimed at alleviating the population explotion in metropolian areas has contributed to the emergence of new underserved rural populations. In an effort to ease the problem of urban growth, the Brazilian government has attempted to stem the influx to urban areas by encouraging settlement of the immense northwestern regions. Due to its sparse population, the Amazon region seems, after all, to be better able to accommodate the waves of displaced people overcrowding Brazil's cities. Agricultural subsistence in this area is problematic; the abundant vegetation of the rainforest that dominates the area belies spectacularly low levels of nutrients. Slash-and-burn practices produce a short-term prosperity as the ash temporarily nourishes the soil and sustains a few seasons' crops. Though indigenous peoples have successfully applied this practice on small scales for centuries, "modern, large-scale attempts at permanent farming in the Amazon generally have produced disastrous results. Production is low and risks desertification, as clear-cutting, burning, and erosion overwhelm the fragile ecosystem" (Neuhouser, 1999, p. 13). To some extent, then, Brazil's policy to encourage relocation to the northwest does resemble South Africa's apartheid-era forced relocation: The quality of the land to which relocation has been encouraged is so low that impoverished circumstances naturally result.

In sum, Brazil's huge population displacement has not come as a result of forced relocation as occured in South Africa. Brazil's challenges with regional disparities are, therefore, not fully analogous to South Africa's relocation effort. But Brazil's problems regarding equitable distribution of education are severe as in South Africa. Further, problems of education's distribution implicate dynamics of rural and urban settlement in both countries. More so than in South Africa, a major challenge in Brazil revolves around the rapid growth of the country's urban centers; since around 1950, Brazil has changed from a largely rural society to an urban society. Industrialization, which has helped propel this displacement, has contributed to severe disparities in income distribution within some urban settings, such as Sao Paulo and Rio de Janeiro, whose impoverished *favela*s provide sharp contrasts between educationally advantaged and disadvantaged groups (Stromquist, 1997; Swift, 1997; Neuhouser, 1999). Poverty in other Brazilian cities, meanwhile, is even more endemic and widespread. Fifty percent of the population of the northeast Brazilian city of Recife, for instance, lives below the government's defined poverty-level (Neuhouser, 1999).

In rural Brazil, limited educational participation in school is abetted by the shortage of schools—a condition that is akin to the situation in rural South Africa. As is also true of conditions of poverty in South Africa, a shortage of school spaces limits participation for the poorer members of Brazilian society. Regional differences are marked in Brazil—with disparities between the poor northwest and the richer southeast even more pronounced now than in 1940 (Stromquist, 1997). And although population displacement from rural to urban areas might be less prominent in South Africa than in Brazil, both the Brazilian and the South African cases reflect ways in which changes associated with modernization can affect equitable educational experiences in pronounced ways. For a comparison of geophysical and economic factors influencing education in Brazil and South Africa, see the "Points of Convergence" box (Figure 4.2).

FIGURE 4.2

Points of Convergence

BRAZIL	Geography and educational consequences	SOUTH AFRICA
Aspect: With the world's fifth largest land area, Brazil's 3,000-mile Atlantic coastline in the east has affected population distribution throughout history due to its influence on settlement and commerce. Around 90% of Brazilians live within 200 miles of the Atlantic—a population skew toward the coastal zone that continues to climb in spite of efforts to develop the interior.		**Aspect:** South Africa's considerable natural resources include gold, gem quality diamonds, and a number of other minerals of commercial value. As a result, mining has been a mainstay of the South African economy, requiring the involvement of significant proportions of the South African population.
Response: Population shifts and imbalances are tied primarily to the country's history of economic development, and thus to Brazilian citizens' continuing interaction with their country's geography. Providing education due to these shifts is a major challenge. Brazilians attempting to settle the interior find little infrastructure—including schools—to support them. And tides of Brazilians leaving unfavorable inland conditions return to the already crowded coast.	How have geophysical realities influenced education?	**Response:** Not coincidentally, the parts of South Africa that were designated homelands for the black racial majority do not contain the richest mineral deposits. Yet mining operations require the participation of the homelands' residents, and employment in the mines draws many of the male residents away for extended periods. This leaves the maintenance of the homelands' households and communities primarily in the hands of women.
Consequence: Overwhelming rates of urban growth make equitable provision of educational opportunity difficult to achieve in both accessible coastal regions and in the more remote parts of Brazil.		**Consequence:** As a result, their sense of domestic obligation makes many women feel unable to participate in their own educational advancement. And girls often also adopt domestic roles at early ages, shaping their impressions of women's roles in society, and interfering with their involvement in education.

Consequences of Poverty

Poverty can disrupt access to education in several ways, and the degree to which school is valued or even perceived as viable among a society's poor is often implicated (Birdsall, Bruns, & Sabot, 1996). Though lack of motivation is sometimes noted as an inhibitor to the involvement of people in literacy programs, "motivation" as a descriptor is of limited usefulness unless it is used primarily to account for the ways that logistical challenges contribute to poor people's unwillingness to take advantage of available educational opportunities. To describe the anatomy of motivation more specifically, Stromquist (1997) observed literacy education efforts among the Brazilian poor, noting that "logistic and situational problems" (p. 10) impose demands on the poor, making both their participation and their use of learned skills tenuous. Education often seems simply to compete too directly "with other time demands and priorities in the lives of low income social groups" (Stromquist, 1997, p. 10).

As in Brazil, conditions of underdevelopment make everyday life challenging for South Africa's poor, as well. Fifty-three percent of all South African families currently live below the poverty line (Fuller & Liang, 1999), and for a majority of South Africans mundane tasks like obtaining food and water consumes much of the time that might otherwise be dedicated to education. These chores fall to children and adults alike—limiting children's participation in basic education and stifling adult participation in training and education programs.

Epitomized by hunger in particular, poverty can disrupt demand for education in that poor families are often forced to depend on the immediate monetary benefits they can reap by sending their school-aged children to work (Birdsall et al., 1996). In playwright Berthold Brecht's *Three Penny Opera*, Macheath justifies his suspect priorities with the remark, "First comes nourishment, then comes morality." And Abraham Maslow brought Brecht's point more directly to bear in the fields of human psychology and education. He contended that people are unlikely to aspire to goals like personal actualization—through education in part—until more basic needs are first satisfied. Both South Africa and Brazil reflect these observations about poverty. Similarly, when work in and out of the house takes both father and mother away from home, as is typical among the poor in rural South Africa (Nadeau, 1996) and in Brazil (Stromquist, 1997), children who might otherwise be in school are expected to help with child rearing and other domestic chores.

In addition to its negative impact on the demand for education, poverty has additional implications related to the physical and mental capacities of poor children to succeed in school. Poverty and poor health go hand in hand, and the environmental conditions of the impoverished interfere "with all aspects of the child's development, that is, physical, mental, and social" (Nkabinde, 1997, p. 79)—consequences that can be either temporary or lifelong. Lack of education tends to produce children's very ineducability, making the cycle of poverty more intractable in developing countries such as Brazil and South Africa. Inadequate nutrition and health care education among impoverished parents, for instance, increases the likelihood that children will have learning disabilities or other congenital problems that impair their ability to learn (Asbury, Maholmes, & Walker, 1993; Nkabinde, 1997).

Poverty can reduce demand for education because the poor may actually be uninformed about the benefits of education and remain unaware of the ways education can improve personal prosperity (Birdsall et al., 1996). This observation describes Brazilian circumstances more fully than it does those in South Africa, however, for reasons that are worth noting and that provide a bridge to discussion of racial issues. In Brazil, a core part of the work of Paulo Freire (see page 120) was to raise Brazilian poor people's consciousness about their conditions, their unequal position within Brazilian society, and the benefits of education—of literacy in particular—as a means of confronting these circumstances. In South Africa, on the other hand, poverty follows racial lines so markedly, and inequitable conditions among black South Africans were so blatantly institutionalized, that disparities in educational opportunity became a particular point of contention among the black majority. The separatist policies of apartheid therefore "bred a spirit of defiance and resistance among people of color and produced what came to be known as *the struggle* for equal rights and democracy" (Gilmour et al., 2000. p. 342).

Race and Its Influence on Educational Access and Opportunity

Contrary to popular fables that Brazil is a racial democracy—that is, that the country is relatively free from racial biases—growing evidence points to the degrees to which race influences daily life and social position in Brazilian society: darker skinned Brazilians have less access to education, proper health care, and equitable employment opportunities (Lovell & Wood, 1998). In spite of this evidence, though, and because of the marked cultural and racial melange that characterizes Brazilian society, there is less overt racial conflict in Brazil than in other multicultural societies. This mediates in favor of a "discourse of equality" in Brazil and against the sort of antiracism popular movement (Neuhouser, 1999, p. 22) that has characterized South African society. Like South Africa and the United States, Brazil's entrenched racial stereotypes and the educational disparities that spring from them are attributable to the country's participation in the black slave trade, which marked Brazilian culture from the early colonial era beginning in 1538 until nearly the end of the 19th century (Neuhouser, 1999).

The Brazilian construct of "race" is itself complex, making redress of race-based disparities especially difficult. Discrimination along lines of social class is far more pronounced in Brazil than is race-based discrimination, and this tends to further obscure the problem of racism. In addition, beyond skin color alone—for which there is a finely differentiated classification system in Brazil—Neuhouser (1999) has enumerated several other factors that can influence Brazilian perceptions regarding race:

- People having the same skin color can be categorized differently based on other physical characteristics.
- Social standing affects racial designation as well, with people of higher social status being perceived as "whiter."
- Social familiarity—the degree to which a person is already known and familiar—further increases one's likelihood of being perceived as "whiter."

Neuhouser (1999) further distinguished Brazilian racism from the racism occurring in the United States: In the United States, a child is socially assigned "to the race of the parent with the lower social status" (p. 21)—a social norm that largely does not exist in Brazil. But there is a fundamental similarity between racial differentiation as practiced in those two countries—or in South Africa, to be sure—in that "white is higher status than black" (p. 21).

Paulo Freire (1921–1997)

Many would argue that Paulo Reglus Neves Freire was the 20th century's most influential educator. Although throughout his life Freire's professional work retained a strong focus on improving educational conditions within his native Brazil, his identity as an educational philosopher and activist was international. Among those whose work Freire profoundly influenced are Michael Apple, Stanley Aronowitz, Henry Giroux, Jonathan Kozol, Donald Macedo, Peter McLaren, Ira Shor, and Carlos Alberto Torres. By 1968, when the English translation of Freire's most famous tract, titled *Pedagogy of the Oppressed*, was released, the work had been widely influential in Latin America (Britton, 1994). In addition to the philosophies of education that Freire expounded in that book and in many other works, his global renown became even larger on account of his worldwide demand as a lecturer and on his engaging style in that role.

Freire grew up in Recife, in Brazil's northeastern region, during the global economic depression of the 1920s. Freire's lifelong dedication to the cause of relieving the hunger and exploitation of the poor was inspired by his family's own poverty during his formative years. Because illiteracy was endemic in the Brazilian northeast when Freire began his work there—nearly three quarters of the population being unable to read or write at that time (Donohue, 1994)—confronting the problem of illiteracy was at the center of Freire's work throughout his life. Brazil's impoverished citizens were a particular focus of *Pedagogy of the Oppressed* and of much of Freire's continuing professional attention. Though a large part of his most prominent work was among adults, Freire's theories and ideas apply readily to—and have been exhaustively extended to—education at all levels.

Among Freire's major intellectual contributions was to the corpus of liberation theory. Criticism of dependency theory—upon which liberation theory is built—has generally stressed that, although dependency theory might provide plausible if not potent descriptions of inequitable relationships, it generally presents little means of addressing the circumstances it describes (Hlatshwayo, 2000). Freire adapted Marxist thought and extended dependency theory's tenets in ways that enabled progress beyond mere critique of an inequitable status quo, instead creating a template for the empowerment of dominated peoples. From Marxist theory, Freire adapted the notion that literacy was a key enabler for consciousness raising. According to Freire, facilitating a special level of consciousness (*concientizacao*)—merging self-awareness and social awareness—is a necessary step toward helping poor and exploited peoples understand their own roles not only as submissive toward, but even as accomplices in, their own subjugation and powerlessness. Arriving at this self-realization opens the door for empowerment and self-determination.

Freire's position was revolutionary, then: Brazil's marginalized poor should awaken to their oppressed conditions and should confront those who maintained inequitable social structures at their expense. Not surprisingly, this stance was offensive to Brazil's military and political elites, and, when a reactionary government assumed power in 1964, Freire was jailed for activities deemed subversive. After over two months in prison, Freire was exiled to Chile, where, for the next five years within the more sympathetic Chilean political climate, he continued his cause of education for literacy among the poor. Freire later worked at both Harvard University and the Office of Education of the World Council of Churches in Geneva. Finally, after political changes enabled Freire's return to Brazil, the locus of much of his work was among the urban poor in Sao Paulo. He was appointed Secretary of Education in 1988 after the socialist Workers' Party, with which he had long been affiliated, won municipal elections (Torres, 1998).

Racial discrimination, of course, accounts for disparate access to education and uneven distribution of societal resources as noted previously: Brazil's intricate system of racial distinction has produced circumstances within which black Brazilians' access to education is, on the whole, far more constrained than that of whites. Although illiteracy, for instance, is well documented in many parts of Brazil and is a problem that extends across racial boundaries, the illiteracy rates of blacks in Brazil is around twice that of whites (Margolis, 1992). And poverty, which has profound consequences for education participation and attainment, as just discussed, is far more prevalent among black Brazilians than among whites (Page, 1995).

South Africa's discriminatory education practices, in contrast, existed well before the onset of apartheid with the earliest colonization of the territory now known as South Africa (Hlatshwayo, 2000; Nkabinde, 1997). Black inhabitants of present-day South Africa were first exposed to Western education when, in 1658, schools were opened to instruct slaves of Dutch settlers in the Dutch language and in the fundamentals of Christianity. A further purpose of these schools was to encourage pupils to be compliant workers (Hlatshwayo, 2000)—thus providing an early precedent for later education.

Distinctions between formal and nonformal education have been common within Western observers' descriptions of traditional African education. Although traditional education continues to shape customs among indigenous African peoples and to influence their views toward education, in the views of some, the description of indigenous education as chiefly informal diminishes and debases traditional education's processes and aims: "African customary education was a true education" whose aims were achieved "long before the European brought to Africa the view that education necessarily involved the skills of writing and reading books" (Castle, 1966, p. 29). "The process of schooling within the Western world is characterized by the separation of schools from the . . . community of the students," whereas the education traditional to indigenous Africa fostered a "close link between education and the material aspects of life" (Hlatshwayo, 200, p. 27). From the African perspective, then, the formal/informal dichotomy is exemplary of a stilted distinction between education and daily life.

In the contemporary era, within the first few years following the 1976 Soweto uprising and partly in response to the growing unrest that this uprising embodied, the South African government commissioned and funded an independent study known as the "de Lange Committee Report on Education in South Africa." It was named after J. P. de Lange, who spearheaded the effort; he was then Rector of the Rand Afrikaans University and later served as president of the Afrikaner Broederbond. The focus of the report that emerged from the de Lange study was "equality of educational quality," and its aim was to identify and document inequalities in order, ostensibly, to correct them. Simultaneous with its 1981 release of the de Lange Report, the South African government issued its response to the report, expressing a series of "points of departure" and "reservations." Although approving in principle to freedom of choice with respect to education and career, the government maintained, most notably, that this must occur "within the framework of the constitution" (de Lange Report, excerpted in Marcum, 1982, p. 134).

Observers critical of the de Lange process (e.g., Hlatshwayo, 2000) have questioned the government's motives for establishing the de Lange Commission in the first place. This perspective stresses that the report was certainly not intended to respond to moral imperatives nor even primarily to political pressure and civil unrest. The primary motive in this view, instead, was the country's realization regarding its shrinking capacity for industrial growth. This, in turn, was due especially to mounting shortages of skilled workers—a need that the white majority was unable to meet by maintaining its monopoly on all occupational rungs above the most menial (Nkabinde, 1997). Further, the white population could not realistically address the problem by encouraging further immigration (Chisholm, 1984). These factors, according to critical historians, provided some means of legitimizing new workplace roles for black South Africans, and the task of legitimization was the true motive of the de Lange Commission's work. But, while acknowledging these limitations, others have pointed out that the de Lange Report did constitute the most in-depth investigation of South African education disparity to date (Buckland, 1984; Nasson, 1990). This fact, together with the comments of some directly associated with the de Lange Commission, justify a more moderate assessment of the de Lange Report's intentions, perhaps. One member of the Commission, noting that the governmental response contradicted the spirit of the de Lange Report, stated that the response "in fact, reestablishes *apartheid* education and places us back where we started" (Frankiln Sonn, cited in Marcum, 1982, p. 130, from *Rand Daily Mail*, October 9, 1981).

Regardless of alternate interpretations of the de Lange Report and of the Commission's motives, the South African response to the report warrants more attention than historians have generally accorded it. The response claimed, in short, that each racial population should have its own schools and its own school authorities and departments. It, therefore, reasserted institutions and practices in ways that were reminiscent of the Eiselen Report, which the Nationalist Party had commissioned soon after its rise to power in 1948 (Hlatshwayo, 2000). That report, released in 1951, had served as the blueprint for the 1954 establishment of a "Bantu education" system and for separate systems also for the country's "blacks" (nonwhites), for "colored people" (those of mixed race) in 1963, and, in 1965, for the country's significant Indian population. The comments of one past Minister of Native Affairs regarding the Bantu education system leave little unsaid about the intents of apartheid policy, the increasing formalization and institutionalization that characterized South African education for most of the 20th century:

> There is no place for [black South Africans] in the European community above the level of certain forms of labor. . . . For that reason it is of no avail for him to receive training which has as its aims absorption in the European community while he cannot and will not be absorbed there. (cited in Nkabinde, 1997, p. 7)

Gender Norms and Biases

Divisions of labor along gender lines tend to disadvantage females, as is well documented cross-culturally, and these disadvantages certainly affect the educational participation of women and girls in both South Africa and Brazil. Population displacement and the relative inequalities in circumstances between rural and urban settings interact with gender roles to make problems of educational opportunity for women and girls even more pronounced in developing countries such as Brazil and South Africa.

A number of factors that are especially pronounced in the developing world restrict the ability and willingness of females (both women and girls) to participate in education: the press of domestic work, the fact that men might be away from the home, which increases women's already heavy domestic demands, and gender norms that discourage women from advancing their education. Although these factors are especially evident among those living in less developed rural areas or in conditions of poverty, the fact that many of these factors cross income and rural/urban boundaries makes it apparent that gender roles and norms can be a strong mediating factor in the distribution of societal resources. Additional factors often serve to compound females' exclusion from equitable educational experiences.

In rural areas of developing countries, daily rigors can include walking over long distances to collect water and performing chores associated with small-scale subsistence farming for their families (Stromquist, 1997). Further, pregnancies and health issues particular to women add to a day-to-day existence that is generally far more demanding for women than for men (Nadeau, 1996). As these gender-based practices regarding the distribution of work are passed from one generation to the next, girls come to expect that they await a life of domestic labor. Their incentive to participate in basic education wanes.

Not only is it often imperative for women and girls to perform domestic work in the developing world, but poverty also decreases the amount of time men are available to contribute to family work. Because of the modernity of South Africa's cities and industrial sites (especially mining operations), as mentioned, and given the relatively underdeveloped circumstances in the country's rural areas, work opportunities often draw South African men away from their rural homes. Men returning home from work view rural areas as preserves of "traditional" life, viewing their rural homes as a place in which they command respect and a sense of status that their work in the city does not provide (von Kotze, 1996). Whereas rural life represents liberation and validation for men, it often represents oppression and subjugation for women—a place "where men come home to drink and lord it over women, only to leave them again, penniless and pregnant with another child" (von Kotze, 1996, p. 157).

Brazilian men might be threatened by women's participation in education on the grounds that the women could eclipse them in productivity or social status (Rockhill, 1987). Reflecting the submissiveness scripted by society's ingrained roles, Brazilian women sometimes acquiesce through their own exclusion from educational opportunities. Once in school, classrooms in Brazil and South Africa—as in the developed world—reinforce sex roles through textbook depictions of women performing culturally sanctioned tasks, through teachers' treatment of students, which is typically differentiated along gender lines, and through differences in the curricula prescribed or encouraged for male and female students.

It is worth noting that gender-based social norms can sometimes mediate against male participation in education, and that gender roles' effects are therefore not strictly a zero-sum game pitting males against females. In South Africa, for example, statistics demonstrating higher educational attainment among females 9 to 12 years of age (Archer and Moll, 1992) appear to be at least partially related to the tendency of South African boys' to forego basic education and to seek work at earlier ages. Gender roles, therefore, compound the effects of poverty. Economic necessity requires early entrance into the world of work, accounting for males' withdrawal from school at relatively early ages, just as domestic roles often account for females' exclusion from education. Yet, in spite of gender roles that subordinate women in important ways, sex norms could paradoxically inhibit male attainment relative to girls in some respects. Black South African women, for instance, often pursue fields (as social workers or nurses, for example) for which a higher level of education is required. Black men in South Africa—especially due to their apartheid-era exclusion from skilled and profes-sional positions—have typically worked manual jobs that require little education (Archer and Moll, 1992).

Traditional Brazilian society reflects sex roles that can contribute to differential participation in education, as discussed previously, and as in South Africa, gender norms can inhibit Brazilian males' educational participation and attainment. The strength and persistence of the traditional Brazilian conception of the male as assertive and powerful can sometimes leave them less able than women to deviate from their prescribed sex roles. Social expectations, which further depict ideal Brazilian men as income providers, can reduce male participation in education when high rates of unemployment make it difficult for Brazilian men to embody their primary cultural roles as breadwinners. The relatively circuitous route toward reemployment that further education or training implies may be a relatively less acceptable means of demonstrating manhood (Neuhouser, 2000), and other less productive, but more culturally validating behaviors, might constitute a more opportune alternative. There is little question that gender roles disadvantage females in both Brazil and South Africa relative to their male peers. Thus, gender-based differences are even more confounding to address. For a comparison of sociopolitical factors shaping education in Brazil and South Africa, see the Points of Convergence box (Figure 4.3).

FIGURE 4.3

Points of Convergence

BRAZIL	Sociopolitical factors and educational consequences	SOUTH AFRICA
Aspect: Brazil is perhaps the most developed of the Latin American countries. Its increasing industrialization has made emphasis on economic and social policies favoring broader participation in world trade. This has made the expansion of existing industrial operations a priority and has contributed to the development of new industries and the expansion of existing commercial activities.		**Aspect:** South Africa's efforts to address the lingering effects of decades of racial separation under apartheid have included policies and incentives aimed at redistributing teaching expertise. The goal has been to move some of the skilled and highly qualified teachers from the more prosperous urban areas to the more disadvantaged rural and inland areas.
Response: Mining operations in the more remote regions of the country are expanding, for instance, contributing to general population displacement and to environmental disruption.	How have unique sociopolitical factors shaped education?	**Response:** To be fair to the skilled teachers not wishing to relocate, policies have provided a means of opting out of the relocation through retirement from the teaching profession.
Consequence: A "boom town" effect results, in which significant numbers of people move into areas that have little capacity to address peoples' everyday needs. Adequate schools, instructional materials, and teaching expertise are in even shorter supply.		**Consequence:** Large numbers of the country's most qualified teachers have left the teaching field even though in sum, there is an increasing need for teachers. The country's effort to improve access and equalize opportunity has therefore yielded new challenges with respect to those very problems.

What Is Quality Education? Considering the Means and Ends of Education

Education planning and reforms—within South Africa and Brazil as elsewhere—are undertaken in the name of improvement with an eye on higher quality education. Overt use of the term *quality* is in fact widespread in the policy discourse of industrialized nations (e.g., Tobias & Miller, 1999), within developing countries (e.g., Guimaraces de Castro, 1999; Soto, 1997), and in international comparative tracts (e.g., Rosenberg, 1998). Even when expressions of quality are less explicit, the tacit goal of educational policy is generally the pursuit of higher quality education.

In spite of the prominence of quality as an impetus for education planning and reform, the meanings and implications of the term are rarely clarified. Brazilian philosopher Paulo Freire (1998), when asked to provide opening remarks at a convention on education and quality, challenged those in attendance to ponder the assumptions underlying the relatively abstract and imprecise notion of quality by assessing the political underpinnings of the term's usage: "Precisely because there isn't a substantive quality whose profile you can find universally produced and available . . . we must think about the concept and determine the nature of the quality we are talking about" (p. 42). Although it might be safe to assume that pressure for educational change mounts as negative perceptions regarding educational quality grow, it is far more hazardous to assume that broad consensus regarding the meaning of quality exists in the first place. With invocations of quality in the abstract, much is presumed about the desirability of various educational aims and the kinds of educational approaches promoted. This kind of detached use of the term risks foreclosing productive discourse about the specific societal needs that education might address and about schools' needs if they are to fulfill their end of the social contract by meeting societal expectations.

Noting the need for more precision if quality is to be communicative and useful as a basis for education policy making, Lee Harvey (1995) identified five discrete conceptions of education quality:

- *Education quality as exceptionality*: education upholding a "gold standard" and promoting the pursuit of educational excellence in terms of the strengths of a school or system relative to others
- *Education quality as consistency*: education providing for equivalent educational experiences for all implicated
- *Education quality as fitness-for-purpose*: education refining participants' abilities for performance in targeted roles
- *Education quality as value for money*: education reflecting reasonable correspondence to the individual and societal investments it entails
- *Education quality as transformative potential*: education propelling change and enabling movement toward different and preferred futures

The implication of this perspective is not that "good" education should necessarily address all of these multiple conceptions. Each of these conceptions of education quality has its rationale; each stands as a plausible justification for educational change (see Table 4.1). Nor are these views of educational quality mutually exclusive, as the alternative definitions sometimes harmonize and at other times conflict (as Table 4.1 suggests). But due

Table 4.1   Harvey's Alternative Conceptions of Educational Quality

Conception of Education Quality	As Exceptionality	As Consistency	As Fitness-for-Purpose	As Transformative Potential
Vision, or associated term	Excellence	Equality	Refinement and perfection	Social or personal change
Normative position	■ "Quality education is that which is exemplary. Some education is simply distinguishable as better or best." ■ "Schools should maximize pursuit of the highest potential, recognizing that results vary just as potential varies."	■ "Quality education ensures equitable experiences." ■ "Schools should be consistent across students, classrooms, schools, and regions."	■ "Quality education shapes students for specific roles." ■ "Schools should maximize attention to aims shaped by roles school leavers will play, and should deemphasize unimportant aims to enable this progress toward perfection."	■ "Quality education is a catalyst for positive changes in individual and societal conditions." ■ "Schools should replace uncertainty with purpose, and ignorance with insight, and should provide for articulation and pursuit of desirable futures."
Examples	■ Identification of "higher and "highest" performance ("valedictorian") ■ Norm referenced tests ■ "Traditional" (bell curved) grading ■ Rhetoric applying superlatives	■ Comprehensive high schools (U.S.) ■ "Minimum" standards; criterion referenced tests ■ Rhetoric promoting opportunities "for all"	■ Instructional specialization ■ Career and vocational tracks, workplace readiness, college prep ■ Rhetoric favoring competency	■ Education for social change ■ Preservation of options; favors flexibility ■ Rhetoric emphasizing social mobility
Tensions and interactions across the conceptions	Conflicts directly with consistency: Differentiated instruction demands participation and opportunities that are dissimilar (unequal). Some harmony with fitness-for-purpose is evident.	Conflicts directly with exceptionality: Exceptionality and consistency might be reconciled, but this demands compromises; without recognition that compromise is implicit, simultaneous pressure toward both produces diluted policy and practice.	Conflicts with transformation: differentiation could foreclose flexibility and optimal social mobility. Instructional differentiation to tailor instruction to suit express and finite aims is supported by this conception, reflecting harmony with exceptionality.	Conflicts with fitness-for-purpose and exceptionality: its bias toward flexibility favors instructional open-endedness, not refinement (through targeted instruction, specialization) of existing condition or of particular aptitudes or capacities.

Adapted from L. Harvey, 1995

to competition among values that typifies democracy within a globalizing economy—between liberty or equality, individualism or collectivism, economic purpose and direction or flexibility, for instance—these differing visions of quality clamor simultaneously for attention. This coexistence of competing visions of quality necessitates compromises. Yet, too often, public discourse fails to acknowledge the necessity for compromise. It is politically expedient to focus upon the things that public policy can do rather than what it cannot. Among the compromises subsumed within these alternative visions of education quality, issues of educational access and opportunity are heavily implicated.

In short, closer consideration of alternative visions of quality makes it fairly clear that widespread support for educational improvement, in general, does not by any means ensure agreement about the desirability of various structures and practices or about the focus and direction that educational change should take. On the contrary, in spite of the merit at face value of many contrasting conceptions of education quality, tensions and conflicts are inescapable. Thus, as the impetus to assess, reform, and improve education rises, so too does the need to reconcile the implicit conflicts and trade-offs. Although this imperative pertains not only when reform and improvement seeks directly to address issues of equitable access, two dilemmas of particular interest to education distribution are illustrated in Table 4.1 and Table 4.2 and will guide our analysis of circumstances in Brazil and South Africa.

The *value for money* conception of education quality is readily aligned with typical arguments for school accountability and, therefore, has important implications for education. But the following analysis employs Harvey's four other conceptions of education quality—*exceptionality*, *consistency*, *fitness-for-purpose*, and *transformative* potential. This approach, in addition to providing a means for exploring access and opportunity within South Africa and Brazil, demonstrates the special bearing that these interpretations of quality have upon issues of education's distribution across a society.

Table 4.2	Conflict Between Harvey's Differing Conceptions of Educational Quality			
Conflict Between the Fitness-for-Purpose and Transformation Conceptions of Educational Quality				
Normative Conception of Quality	Assumption; contribution to conflict		Assumption; contribution to conflict	Normative Conception of Quality
fitness-for-purpose	The pragmatism of this view predisposes it to favor refinements of present circumstances and indifference to or ignorance of preferable futures.	⟷	Bias toward change and against refinement of existing condition leads to rejection of progress deemed too incremental.	**transformation**

Since formal education in any country embodies policy—planned and intentional action toward goals presumed to be favorable—the distinctions Harvey has identified are useful as a tool for description and analysis of issues in foreign context. Furthermore, the tensions inherent between various conceptions of quality might be universal to modern democracies and reflective of a culture's more basic compromises—between individualism and collectivism, between the relative roles of effort and aptitude in learning, and between academic and vocational educational aims, for instance. The following analysis adapts and applies Harvey's framework by exploring two tensions in particular:

- Educational quality as *transformation* as opposed to *fitness-for-purpose*
- Educational quality as *exceptionality* as opposed to *consistency*

The purpose of this effort is to augment understanding of the overarching dilemmas regarding educational access and opportunity in South Africa and Brazil and to refresh readers' perspectives regarding their own cultures.

Fitness-for-Purpose Versus Transformation: Competing Views of Education's Aims

The transformation perspective, as Table 4.1 indicates, typically focuses on students' social mobility as a means for addressing societal inequities that could arguably leave certain members of society locked in conditions that they seem to be unable to escape—conditions that education's structures and practices reinforce and preserve (Bowles & Gintes, 1976; Oakes, 1985). Impediments to access and equal opportunity have characterized education in Brazil and South Africa, and, as we have seen, are systemic in scope. But the consequences of these social structures have real-world consequences for individuals, "shap[ing] people's lives and their place in the material world" (Carnoy, 1997, p. 16). Thus, social mobility tends to function as an indicator at the student level of societal structures to which the transformation view is ultimately sensitive.

The fitness-for-purpose conception of education quality values education that molds existing circumstances to suit specific and certain aims—providing a suitable rationale for vocational specialization, for instance, because of the finite set of skills and the steps toward attainment of those skills that vocationalism implies. But, to a striking degree, different callings command different levels of status and respect. Where vocational educational aims connote lower status careers, the merits of this sort of specialization can be discredited as being at odds with goals of social mobility.

These conceptions of educational quality are allied, in part, with existing theories of education and development. The fitness-for-purpose notion, for instance, bears considerable ideological harmony with human capital theory in particular. Policies for economic growth within developing economies have commonly viewed schooling as a mechanism for building a stock of human capital. In this view, national progress depends on an educated pool of labor just as surely as it does on other means of production—ready supplies of natural resources, endowments of machinery and equipment, and viable infrastructures. If workforce skills and knowledge are requisite to larger goals of national progress and development, this perspective holds schooling to be a chief instrument for transmitting the training and knowledge that builds the workforce.

This blueprint for education and its role in contributing to national progress has tended to be especially prominent in developing economies such as Brazil and South Africa for at least two reasons. First, the ideology of human capital formation emphasizes that expenditures on education promise greater returns than do investments on physical capital, often making monetary aid and other forms of support contingent upon progress defined in those terms. Embracing this perspective, the developed world, in order to encourage international development, has prescribed investments in education rather than physical capital. Second, and similarly, the task of nurturing industrial development toward maturation puts a premium on labor rather than on managerial, administrative, or professional expertise (Hlatshwayo, 2000). Development from this perspective, then, depends on broadened societal participation in economic activities considered desirable for economic progress. Enhancing productivity and capacity implicates new roles for individuals within modernizing societies according to this development perspective, and an important part of education is tailoring a suitable fit between people and desirable roles—fitting them for specified purposes, in Harvey's (1995) vernacular.

But this view of education as a tool for building a labor pool has implications that competing theoretical perspectives have noted are suspect, particularly on the grounds that such an education tends to emphasize lower levels of educational attainment. Social reproduction theory, for instance, has sought to illuminate the negative implications of education's role in shaping a workforce, seeing the human capital perspective of education as overly optimistic. This critical perspective, which has been most exhaustively applied in describing the dynamics of fully developed economies, is telling also in the cases of maturing economies such as Brazil and South Africa.

Of particular concern within social reproduction theory are the ways in which workforce creation competes with aims such as individual self-determination and social mobility. Most prominently, Bowles and Gintis (1976) have explicated this most clearly (and most famously) by describing the so-called correspondence principle. This theoretical element has become a central element in the social reproduction perspective, holding that formal education reflects workplaces—and corresponds to them as follows:

- Social relationships in schools—between educators and students and among students themselves—mimic the hierarchic organization of workplaces.
- The social experience of schooling therefore prepares students for future social roles as workers, rewarding compliance and encouraging passive acceptance of duties.
- Schooling produces attitudes that are requisite to the workplace but also affirms or legitimates those roles, whose continuing existence depends on compliant attitudes.

In sum, rather than a catalyst for democratization through enhanced social mobility and preparation for political participation, education in the light of social reproduction theory is a means of reproducing inequalities that characterize modern—and modernizing—capitalist economies (Carnoy & Levin, 1985).

To improve conditions of educational access and opportunity in South Africa and Brazil—as elsewhere in the developing world—the view that quality education reflects fitness-for-purpose has a practical orientation that tends to generate stepwise plans for progress. As long as education planning is "framed explicitly in relation to political and economic strategies" (Wolpe, 1992, p. 1), even incremental progress toward such explicit goals is worthwhile. From this perspective, further, goals of transformation in the abstract, like those characteristic of South Africa's ideologically charged transition out of *apartheid*, can have an imprecise and "ad hoc" nature (Wolpe, 1992, p. 1). Without translation into more specific terms, the goal of transformation in and of itself falls short of realistic progress toward equalizing educational access. The South African Freedom Charter, in particular, provided an invaluable impetus for change, articulating a vision for a more equitable society and serving as a source of inspiration and a mobilizer of support for that just end. Once real progress toward freedom was achieved, though, the Charter provided few tangible policies and plans.

In an effort to make specific steps and to provide needed direction in South Africa, policy makers have promoted a number of strategic responses. As abstract visions become translated into specific plans, however, they often meet with resistance, resting precisely on the argument that proposed policies are not "transformative" enough in their scope. Regarding issues of how schools might best elevate black South African's participation in the country's workplaces, for example, those proposing strategies have sought to respond to the fact that, under apartheid, black South Africans had been systematically excluded from skilled occupations and relegated instead to the most menial positions in the work force. For those embracing a fitness-for-purpose perspective, this reality implicates education programs aimed specifically at equipping as many of the black majority as possible— and as quickly as possible—for productive roles in higher skill positions (Wolpe, 1992). But these specific strategies imply narrowness and inflexibility, both of which veer from transformative views about quality education. For those advocating pragmatic policies oriented toward fitness-for-purpose, in short, desirable transformation per se only seems truly possible when educational plans are responsive to existing conditions, are systematic, and are manifestly attainable. From this viewpoint, South African blacks' "virtual exclusion" [under *apartheid*], . . . from skilled occupations makes [post-*apartheid*] access to those occupations more urgent than the status distinctions entailed in the vocational or academic differentiation" (Wolpe, 1992, p. 11).

But for those judging the merits of vocationalist policies in more transformative terms, the fitness-for-purpose perspective threatens genuine transformation. Teaching for specific vocational competencies withholds access to academically grounded educational opportunities. From this perspective, the narrow, incremental, and practical steps toward equity sound like more of the same: educational opportunities that by their nature fall well short of equity—the very problem that policy is supposed to remedy. This reaction echoes critics of the de Lange Report, who claimed the report was a cloaked response to the demands of industrial growth and an effort to legitimize new workplace roles for black South Africans. Such "technocratic" views of policy making "relegate significant mass constituencies to the status of mass observers" (Badat, 1992, p. 25). From the transformation view, further, those seeing quality education in terms of fitness-for-purpose seem too comfortable with their purported neutrality and pragmatism and overlook their own ideological moorings as a consequence. As a result, they fail to see that "select groups and social classes benefit or suffer" (Prunty, 1982, p. 135, cited in Badat, 1992, p. 25) due to continuing incrementalist policies.

In Brazil, meanwhile, a similar tension characterizes governmental policies aimed at educational opportunity and equity. Although Brazilian President Fernando Cardoso had established his identity as a progressive thinker, having been among the first to develop dependency theory, his policies adopted a tone that—in its pragmatism—forsakes his revolutionary and transformative credentials. "Cardoso believes that Brazil first needs to grow more confident of its economic future" even if this means the adoption of a less transformative stance that "delays equalization" (Carnoy, 1997, p. 14). Participation in education is growing in Brazil as a partial result of these policies, despite the skepticism of the country's more transformative thinkers.

From the standpoint of transformation, policies and judgments in terms of fitness-for-purpose might be falsely and unadvisedly precise in the purposes they purport to target. And as the rate of social change accelerates—a circumstance that envelopes the entire world and not just developing countries like Brazil and South Africa, of course—the risks associated with refining education to suit futures that are difficult to forecast are arguably increasingly pronounced. Noting a strength of the transformative perspective within a global environment of uncertainty and change, Samoff (1999) has observed that as the world economic environment becomes more competitive, the imperatives of change and flexibility require at least some workers who "reject old ways of doing things, insist on looking for better alternatives, and are willing to run the risks associated with criticism and innovation" (p. 421). Thus, the face of education's purposes—and of implications regarding quality educational opportunities as a consequence—has changed. The need within developing economies for education that can "enhance its citizenry's capacity to criticize, analyze, and create . . . in other words, to solve problems" (Marcum, 1982, p. 13) underscores this tension regarding differing conceptions of school quality.

A competitive global economy, then, favors at one turn educational quality in terms of its transformative potential, requiring critical and nimble thinking, an eye on the future, and tolerance for uncertainty. Yet, critical minds could, in the end, threaten a status quo that education, valued in terms of its fitness-for-purpose, seeks at other turns to build: "Critique and innovation have a momentum of their own" (Samoff, 1999, p. 421). Thus, although the human capital theory for economic development continues to serve as a primary rationale among many encouraging growth and modernization, countries that focus too completely on tenets of human capital and on fitting students for particular economic purposes could in the end be undermining progress toward other goals that are important—even if uncomfortably imprecise.

Exceptionality Versus Consistency:
Competing Views of Education's Results

South Africa's 1981 de Lange Report, as mentioned, was the product of an effort to document inequalities in educational opportunities in apartheid-era South Africa. Its writers made considerable effort to point out the difficulties that de Lange's team had in operationalizing the concept of equality due to the inherent differences between equality of attainment and equality of opportunity. Educational difference, the team acknowledged, is partly attributable to factors such as aptitude, mental ability, effort, and ambition. Equalization of these things would, in the view of those submitting the report, be undesirable, unethical, and impossible in any event (the de Lange Report, excerpted in Marcum, 1982). The Commission's observations draw attention to one of the quandaries regarding issues of equality of education. To what extent does a society attribute differences in educational outputs, such as student achievement, to factors whose manipulation may be difficult? The de Lange Report was relatively candid in its criticism of apartheid policy in South Africa and made significant recommendations favoring equalization of education for the various racial groups in the country. It concluded ultimately that, in a society that strives to be just and equitable, the focus of equalization should be on factors whose control *is* within reach, making it clear that assumptions about other factors was inappropriate. Societies differ, though, in the extent to which they attribute successes to factors other than those directly within the control of schools and the structures that support them.

As shown in Table 4.3, quality in terms of exceptionality connotes tolerance for difference. *Exceptional* means "different from the rest" or "distinguished." Without a supply of lower performing students or schools, such distinctions are, of course, impossible. Yet those who are eager to identify "the best" schools are seldom willing to acknowledge the distasteful implication that "nonbest" schools are "worse." Because of these unpalatable implications, deeper issues of parity in terms of inputs—a generally level playing field— are rarely untangled from issues of outputs such as student attainment. Tolerance for educational difference in the abstract could in the end rationalize differentiated instruction toward that end.

Consistency, in contrast to exceptionality, implies emphasis on equality. Equalization of opportunity is valued. Generalized intolerance for inequality in any form (e.g., of attainment) may result. In addition, innate differences among students could be ignored, even where its acknowledgment might be instructionally beneficial.

Analysis of some tensions between the fitness-for-purpose and transformation viewpoints suggested that short-term policies could undo long term intentions. The impetus toward goals of both consistency and exceptionality, too, could create short-term inequities. This can result in confusion in educational policies regarding equity or in societal confusion regarding the fairness and propriety of those policies.

Table 4.3   Additional Conflict Between Harvey's Differing Conceptions of Educational Quality

Conflict Between the Exceptionality and Consistency Conceptions of Education Quality

Normative Conception of Quality	Assumption; contribution to conflict		Assumption; contribution to conflict	Normative Conception of Quality
Exceptionality	Educational differentiation in pursuit of exceptional (distinguished) attainment is at odds with consistent educational experiences.	⟷	Consistency connotes equalization of opportunity, leading also to the leveling of educational experience— inimical to exceptionality.	**Consistency**

South African policy illustrates this problem. Fiscal allocations for schools in South Africa have disproportionately favored urban areas such as Durban and Cape Town (Gilmour et al., 2000). In an effort to alleviate the urban/rural inequities that apartheid fostered, policies evolving since 1994 have involved attempts to redistribute allocations to South Africa's schools. In addition, years of neglect in rural South Africa are not reflected merely in terms of material investments but in terms of the relative strength of the teaching force as well. Discrepancies between the country's urban/rural teachers are both qualitative and quantitative in nature: In addition to their severely undereducated teaching force (Arnott & Chabane, 1995), rural regions of South Africa are severely challenged by teacher shortages.

Emerging South African policy has, therefore, sought to address this problem. A particular thrust of the government's effort to address the legacies of *apartheid* focuses on redistribution of teachers (Gilmour et al., 2000). South African policy has focused on encouraging the relocation of qualified teachers from urban locations to rural areas. In implementing these plans, however, the government's responsiveness to issues of individual fairness and equity has, at times, competed with the targeted goal of creating a more equitable education system. This has blunted real progress toward a more equitable system.

For instance, the government might have required teacher relocations—just as relocations of nonwhite racial groups occurred in *apartheid*-era South Africa—but the prospect of implementing authoritarian and mandated relocations was unpalatable, particularly for a government otherwise attempting to pursue democracy and fairness in its policies. Teachers in overstaffed regions have, therefore, had the alternative of a severance or "retrenchment" package. And because many implicated teachers have, in fact, opted for this buyout in favor of relocation, the South African teaching force as a whole has been reduced at a time when a net increase is needed. Further, because the teachers who opted to accept the severance alternative have typically been among the most experienced, the loss is a matter of more than numbers alone. The cumulative decline in the expertise of the overall teaching force has been significant (Gilmour et al., 2000).

A further irony of South Africa's relocation effort is that teachers' unions maintained—and equity in the short term demanded—that policies regarding the retrenchment option should be applied similarly to all. As a result, the government was obliged to make options for severance uniformly available rather than limiting more targeted options to the specific communities where teacher redistribution was most necessary. All teachers—including those in already disadvantaged schools—therefore became candidates for voluntary departure. Because many teachers from rural areas have elected to leave the teaching force (Gilmour et al., 2000), the drain of talent resulting from teacher retirement has extended to areas in which teachers were already in short supply. In this way as well, then, the South African government's efforts to correct the inequitable distribution of teaching expertise have failed to yield hoped-for results. And in this case, again, sensitivity to matters of equity in the short term seems to have hamstrung intended progress.

Although Brazil, in contrast, was relatively late in ending its import of African slaves and its abolition of slavery in 1888 (Neuhouser, 1999), the modern Brazilian constitution envisions a country based on egalitarian tenets of freedom, justice, mutually cooperative society, and individual rights, and aimed at the reduction of inequality (Gomes et al.,

2000). A number of aspects of Brazilian education reflect the country's attention to principles of equality—compulsory schooling for Brazilians 7 to 14 years of age and the inclusion within regular classrooms of students with special learning needs, for instance. Growing recognition that severe income disparities persist and require resolution is itself a sign of progress and commitment to egalitarian ideas. Yet, issues of population displacement continue to contribute to the inequitable educational experiences across Brazilian society, and urban and rural dynamics contribute to this disparity.

LESSONS FROM BRAZILIAN AND SOUTH AFRICAN EXPERIENCE

Exploration of Brazil and South Africa—especially in the context of quality—demonstrates the difficulty of distributing education in ways that respond to all democratic values at once. Policy goals that might be unassailable at moral levels are difficult to operationalize to the satisfaction of all sectors of a society. South African policy dilemmas associated with its redress of apartheid, for example, bear some comparison with the United States' efforts to undo centuries of institutionalized discrimination (in the form of Jim Crow laws and doctrine of "separate but equal") against its own black population. Notably, though, the political stances of the principal parties in each country seem reversed. American affirmative action is incrementalist and pragmatic in nature, and those questioning the policy's continued usefulness seem in a sense to be more idealistically driven and abstract in their claims regarding the justice of the system. Affirmative action, for them, embodies a prima facie stance toward equity that cannot be justified through short-term breaches of equity in the form of hiring quotas, incentives, and so forth. This turns the current South African situation somewhat on its head, since in that country a more incrementalist and pragmatic position (akin to affirmative action in its endorsement of stepwise progress toward change) has characterized strategies associated with conservative views. The more revolutionary stance of South Africa's blacks seems in its idealism to parallel the stance of against affirmative action opponents in the United States (e.g., Steele, 1990), who tend to reject such incrementalist policy as morally untenable. Justice for both parties, that is, seems an all-or-nothing proposition.

The earlier analysis has shown other ways in which the purported beneficiaries of policies do not always perceive such programs as beneficial or equitable. One aspect not explored previously, but deserving mention here, concerns the issue of language of instruction, which, in ethnically heterogeneous countries such as Brazil and South Africa, provide another window into this paradox. In South Africa, where *apartheid* policies required instruction in the mother tongue at least for young students, the black South African population tends very strongly to see knowledge of English as essential (Marcum, 1982). Thus, in another unexpected way, the South African situation parallels circumstances in the United States—yet, as mentioned previously, with some unexpected twists. Specifically, bilingual education has met with mixed degrees of acceptance among United States' speakers of languages other than English. This instructional program has generally tapped the same ideological and moral wells as have supporters of multiculturalism. Both bilingual linguists and multiculturalists generally seek to elevate the cultural equality of all of the country's diverse nationalities and races. Yet bilingual instruction has not always enjoyed consistent support among populations targeted by the policy. Most prominently, of course, Californians in the United States—due in part to the Latino population's skepticism about the program—voted to curtail bilingual education. In this respect at least, their views align with those of observers like E. D. Hirsch, whose calls for "cultural literacy" have been widely derided as an affront to multiculturalism. Hirsch's views, in turn, seem to dovetail with those of black South Africans: Dismissing questions of justice and propriety as irrelevant, both Hirsch and the black South African population tend to see knowledge of the dominant language as a stepping stone to power and meaningful participation in society.

Other observations that are generally pertinent in different countries, and that our look at South Africa and Brazil has permitted, revolve around the rhetoric of school accountability, the age-old debate regarding academic versus vocational aims of education, the implications of growing income inequality even in the developed world, and the propriety of "standards" in light of the elusiveness of defining the aims of education. These themes receive more extended treatment in the next sections.

Accountability and the Equalization of Educational Indicators

South Africa's 1981 de Lange Commission had ultimately noted that "the reduction and elimination of demonstrable inequality in the provision of education available to members of different population groups" was impeded in South Africa by certain inequalities that could in fact be "clearly defined and documented as concrete, empirically determinable facts on the basis of several specific indicators" (from report excerpted in Marcum, 1982, p. 121). Such demonstrable educational inequities, according to the de Lange Report, implicate the following:

- General accessibility, in particular, freedom of choice in determining paths of study, for instance
- Curriculum content, including aspects such as curricular alternatives available, textbooks, and syllabi
- Expectations, for example regarding rules governing general compulsory education
- Teachers and the level of their training, and numbers relative to pupils
- Physical educational facilities and their comparative condition
- Financial resources and their relative parity in terms of per capita expenditure (from de Lange Report, excerpted in Marcum, 1982).

The de Lange Report has been criticized for the persistence of racial stereotypes it reflects (Marcum, 1982) and for the authoritarian and technocratic policies it ultimately spurred, as noted (Badat, 1991; Buckland, 1984; Chisholm, 1984; Hlatshwayo, 2000). Yet, the report's comments regarding "demonstrable inequalities" reveal the difficulty inherent in untangling factors related to differences in students.

But the report also points out, significantly, that certain factors that are bound to affect student performance are in fact measurable. The effects of the various "empirically determinable indicators" that the de Lange process identified remain difficult to pinpoint in spite of decades of research. But this continuing problem, as the de Lange Report has further underscored, is no excuse for presuming those indicators are inconsequential when it is politically expedient and fiscally thrifty to do so. Whether in spite of itself or not, the de Lange Report enumerated educational inputs whose equalization is, from a policy standpoint, inexcusable.

The de Lange Report's inventory of the factors contributing to differences across students and schools might, then, be informative for contemporary debates regarding "accountability" in countries such as the United States. Tests of school and teacher performance, which accountability proponents generally favor, implicate comparisons of districts, schools, and teachers, while paying little attention to other factors that contribute to the differences that such comparisons yield. The contemporary accountability movement, as the de Lange group reminds us, emphasizes a single factor—teacher preparation and performance—when many other relevant and measurable factors have an important role. Within societies in which accountability debates are most heated, some schools are better equipped, boast better facilities, have larger budgets, and so forth. The de Lange Commission in a sense argued that, precisely because the many factors accounting for student and school performance remain ill understood, the society favoring equitable opportunities must see the equalization of every factor *within* human control as the just and rational course.

Societies, as they accommodate "excellence" and "distinction" in response to the imperatives of education as exceptionality, will necessarily reflect some level of tolerance for educational inequities of educational outcomes. No matter how complicated the exact relationships between educational inputs and outcomes might be, there is considerable evidence of widespread faith in these factors' contributions to educational effectiveness. This is sometimes reflected, for instance, in the contradictory acceptance of conditions of inequitable distribution of resources, on the one hand, together with efforts to distinguish better schools from their lesser counterparts, on the other.

The society that pursues relatively one-dimensional assessments of accountability might in fact be pursuing a justification for inequitable distribution of human and material resources to schools. From the more objective viewpoint that our international explorations have provided, though, the most generous interpretation of these accountability debates is societal ignorance—embodied in calls for further study until the relationships between educational expenditures and school effectiveness are better understood. Our discussion of Brazil and South Africa has afforded a less optimistic but perhaps more plausible explanation, however. The typical accountability movement reflects some failure to acknowledge that the task of reconciling freedom and equity necessitates compromise. Willingness by proponents of the accountability movement to evaluate education simplistically seem to point to some contempt for the democratic principle of equality.

Classism and the Academic versus Vocational Education Debate

Is it possible to structure equal educational experiences for all people when the societal and economic imperatives seem to dictate differentiation? In spite of the value of general and readily transferable skills promoting flexibility (critical thinking and problem solving, for instance), work deemed high status derives its status, in large part, from the degree to which societies perceive their work to be specialized.

One status distinction has long favored academic education over vocational education—embodied, for instance, in the medieval distinction between the liberal (arts or disciplines of free people) and the servile arts (formerly referring to the disciplines of the servant classes). The academic/vocational distinction has contributed to disagreements in developed and developing capitalist countries regarding how education can most appropriately foster social progress. In South Africa, as we have seen, some education policy proposals have sought to move blacks from the ranks of unskilled labor—the racial majority's traditional role under *apartheid*—and into the skilled labor pool that had traditionally been substantially out of reach (Kubow, 2001). This suggests a prominent role for vocational education. Those favoring vocationalism see it as a necessary strategy toward building the black population's more widespread participation in higher education and, eventually, augmenting their representation in the professional sector. Others see the idea as a barrier to blacks' more equitable access to academic education (Wolpe, 1992).

This scenario is analogous in other societies, epitomizing the United States' "school-to-work" debate, for instance. Alternative historical interpretations see school-to-work's conception in the late 1980s as either the private sector's blatant attempt to manipulate public education so that the curriculum might be tailored to meet industry's needs or as a rational policy response to the fact that a large proportion of America's youths were not destined for college but that secondary education served a primarily college-preparatory role. Opponents of early school-to-work plans often saw them as repugnant precisely because they threatened aspirations toward higher education. And the fact that some of the most heavily implicated populations were economically disadvantaged or members of racial minorities contributed to political resistance to the school-to-work idea. The 1994 School-to-Work Opportunities Act that ultimately emerged focused on providing "work-based learning" opportunities to all students (Fossum, 1996) rather than the more specific "forgotten half" that early proponents maintained were of greatest concern (Parnell, 1985).

In spite of the differences, one factor that seems to have aligned both the typical academic and the vocationalist position is the faith with which each camp links education of some form with economic roles and economic and social status. Education, for both academics and vocationalists, ultimately embraces the goal of social mobility at some level. For opponents of the school-to-work vision, higher education provides superior economic potential and, so, fosters the greatest potential for the highest possible social standing. Proponents of education that is overtly vocational, in contrast, see such educational approaches as an important means for social mobility.

But a darker side of the assumptions fueling the academic versus vocational education debate flows from this common concern for social mobility. Namely, whether the means toward better pay and higher potential is vocational or academic, both subscribe to the ultimately classist notion that there are "higher" and "lower" occupations. True, those favoring vocational education see such approaches as the necessary step toward attainment of a targeted and in-demand skill, and, so, as a means toward economic security. But in a similar vein, those who exalt academic knowledge typically envision college as the natural end point of the educational path toward "high callings" in professional or leadership positions, and, so, as a means for advancement from lower to higher social roles. Each view, therefore, has a stake in the maintenance of social distinction.

The point is not that disparities should be accepted as inevitable, regardless of whether these matters of educational access and opportunity follow racial lines or any other means of social distinction. But a glaring question remains: Are so-called unskilled labor roles essential to society or are they not? If they are, the most pernicious form of discrimination and disparity, likely, does not revolve around race, or gender, or ability, either. Until a society's people recognize and dignify the importance of all kinds of contributors to society, mutual respect—the moral imperative that propels us to undo discrimination where we find it—will remain a fleeting hope, to be dreamt of but never reached.

Standards and the Illusive Nature of Quality

The Harvey framework, with its consideration of education in terms of various conceptions of education quality, suggests that it is misguided to assume that standards in and of themselves can somehow clarify schools' sense of direction. Although this chapter's discussion focuses partly on the contradictions between the imperatives of educational consistency and exceptionality, the point is not to show that these tensions are absolutely irreconcilable but, instead, to show that these tensions are common within modern democracies. Different societies reflect different solutions to these contradictions—different ways of accommodating competing aims. Discourse surrounding educational standards reflects these fundamental tensions. Although performance standards might be indicative of fitness for some specific purpose, other sorts of standards are based on different visions of quality—sometimes confirming attainment of acceptable minimums (consistency), at others, distinguished achievement (exceptionality).

In this light, polemics favoring stronger educational standards in the abstract merely sidestep fundamental questions about the purposes and aims of school. Simultaneous pressure toward both consistency and exceptionality conceptions of education is bound to require some resolution, and not all solutions are fully coherent in terms of the policies and practices they imply. In the United States, for instance, "grade inflation"— widely held to be a major problem in the United States—is more fully understood as a partial product of this fundamental tension between imperatives of consistency and exceptionality. Consistency mediates in favor of the equalization not only of educational inputs, such as facilities and resources, whose improvement has been a predominant project in both Brazil and South Africa. Outcomes, though, are sometimes used as measures of relative equity, producing a justification that an equitable system will necessarily produce leveled results. At the same time, traditional grading schemes (e.g., the United States' A–F system) were generally conceived to compare and communicate differences in performances among students—that is, to distinguish the more exceptional students from the less exceptional. This perception persists in spite of the imperative of equality, which, as discussed previously, mediates against such distinction. This is an imperative that, with good reason, has grown in prominence in the wake of the civil rights movement and with rising international attention to human rights, in general. But the impetus toward equality has not been fully reconciled with that of achievement. American schizophrenia regarding the meaning of "traditional" grading reflects this quandary:

American society favors success for all at one turn yet pines for the time when "an A was an A" at another.

Neither the consistency conception nor the exceptionality conception of education quality is wrong. Both the egalitarian impulse of consistency and exceptionality's push to distinguish various educational performance are justifiable. Further, to varying degrees, societies are apt to favor both kinds, and, with compromise, both kinds of judgments can be accommodated: Societies can and perhaps should explicate the things their members feel all school children should know, and this need not preclude some effort to distinguish among students. But one sort of standard or judgment cannot at a single stroke serve both of these purposes. Ultimately, societies must reach conclusions about the factors that contribute to differential student and school attainment.

As indicated in our discussion of poverty in developing countries such as Brazil and South Africa, income disparity can be very intractable, making educational access and opportunity difficult to achieve. Research comparing Brazil with other developing countries suggests a relationship between income inequality and national willingness to invest in education. The nature of this relationship has some implications that the world's more industrialized and developed nations might find disturbing. Most notably, in countries that feature high levels of income inequality across their populations, willingness to invest in education is more limited than in countries featuring lower levels of income inequality (Birdsall et al., 1996). Thus, because a nation's relative income disparity could in part diminish its citizens' willingness to invest in education, income inequalities could be exacerbated within countries in which such disparities are more pronounced in the first place. Countries with more moderate income inequality, in contrast, have been better able to alleviate income disparity and poverty through investments in education. Accordingly, both South Africa and Brazil have encountered considerable difficulty in overcoming entrenched income stratification.

Although the factors linking income disparity and societal attitudes about educational investment are complex, an unsettling implication for any country is that increasing rates of income inequality could introduce a spiraling of disparity that is difficult to overcome. Income disparity, which is apt to rise with continuing economic globalization and the maturation of the information age (Fukuyama, 1999), could usher in declines in popular support for education. Universal availability of education as a device for individual growth and opportunity could consequently wane, contributing in turn to further stratification along income lines. It is not whimsical, in fact, to speculate that proposals in the United States for vouchers and other alternatives to traditional public education might be tied to growing income inequality. Classism—social differentiation chiefly along income lines—provides a means (one among many, as discussed previously) by which people distinguish themselves as different from others in society. With this impulse toward sectorization, a society's sense of shared norms, values, and experiences might decline. And this declining social capital makes group consensus harder to achieve, in turn contributing to differences that become even more pronounced.

In the next chapter we examine the ever-changing relationship between education and the state and how this relationship affects education accountability and authority in England and Germany.

Sustaining Reflection

- Locate a reference to "educational quality" in the popular press or elsewhere from public discussion of education. What seems to be the meaning of the term as used? For what purpose is the reference to quality made?

- Think of a school you consider "good." What characteristics of the school contribute to your positive impressions of the school's quality? Do you think the same traits can be achieved by all schools? Why or why not?

- We have learned that Paulo Freire dedicated much of his energy to the cause of literacy. Technology critic Neil Postman, among others, has contended that it is easier to be manipulated through nonprint forms of information such as television than with information that you read. In what ways might this claim be true?

References

Archer, S., & Moll, P. (1992). Education and economic growth. In I. Abejan, & B. Standish (Eds.), *Economic growth in South Africa: Selected policy issues* (pp. 147–186). Cape Town, South Africa: Oxford University Press.

Arnott, A., & Chabane, S. (1995). *Teacher demand, supply, utilisation and costs: Report for the National Teacher Education Audit*. Craighall, South Africa: Edusource.

Asbury, C. A., Maholmes, V., & Walker, S. (1993). Is there a relationship between disability and education? *The Negro Education Review, 44* (1–2), 3–11.

Badat, S. (1992). Democratising education policy research for social transformation. In E. Unterhalter, H. Wolpe, & T. Botha (Eds.). *Education in a future South Africa* (pp. 17–38). Trenton, NJ: Africa World Press.

Birdsall, N., Bruns, B., & Sabot, R. H. (1996). Education in Brazil: Playing a bad hand badly. In N. Birdsall, & Richard H. Sabot (Eds.), *Opportunity foregone: Education in Brazil* (pp. 7–48). Washington, DC: Inter-American Development Bank.

Bondesio, M. J., & Berkhout, S. J. (1995). South Africa. In T. N. Postlethwaite (Ed.), *International encyclopedia of national systems of education* (pp. 891–900). Oxford, UK: Elsevier Science Ltd.

Bowles, S., & Gintis, H. (1976). *Schooling in capitalist America: Educational reform and the contradictions of economic life*. New York, NY: Basic Books.

Britton, J. A. (Ed.). (1994). *Molding the hearts and minds: Education, communications, and social change in Latin America*. Wilmington, DE: Jaguar/Scholarly Resources.

Buckland, P. (1984). Technicism and de Lange: Reflections on the process of the HSRC investigation. In P. Kallaway (Ed.), *Apartheid and education* (pp. 371–386). Johannesburg, South Africa: Ravan Press.

Carnoy, M. (1997). Foreword. In P. Freire, *Pedagogy of the heart*. New York, NY: Continuum.

Carnoy, M., & Levin, H. M. (1985). *Schooling and work in the democratic state*. Stanford, CA: Stanford University Press.

Castle, B. E. (1966). *Growing up in East Africa*. London, U.K.: Oxford University Press.

Chisholm, L. (1984). Redefining skills: Black education in South Africa in the 1980s. In P. Kallaway (Ed.), *Apartheid and education* (pp. 387–410). Johannesburg, South Africa: Ravan Press.

Donohue, J. W. (1994). Paulo Freire: Philosopher of adult education. In J. A. Britton (Ed.), *Molding the hearts and minds: Education, communications, and social change in Latin America* (pp. 177–185). Wilmington, DE: Jaguar/Scholarly Resources.

The Europa World Year Book. (1999). London: Europa Publications Ltd.

Fossum, P. R. (1996). Implementing school-to-work reform policy: Three case studies in youth apprenticeship. *Dissertation Abstracts International, 57* 11A (University Microfilm No. 9711407).

Freire, P. (1998). *Politics and education* (P. L. Wong, Trans.). Los Angeles, CA: UCLA Latin American Center Publications.

Fukuyama, F. (1999). *The great disruption: Human nature and the reconstitution of social order.* New York, NY: Free Press.

Fuller, B., & Liang, X. (1999). Which girls stay in school? The influence of family economy, social demands, and ethnicity in South Africa. In C. H. Bledsoe, J. B. Saterline, J. A. Johnson-Kuhn, & J. G. Haaga (Eds.), *Critical perspectives on schooling and fertility in the developing world* (pp. 181–215). Washington, DC: National Academy Press.

Gilmour, D., Soudien, C., & Donald, D. (2000). Post-apartheid policy and practice: Educational reform in South Africa. In K. Mazurek, M. A., Winzer, & C. Majorek (Eds.), *Education in a global society: A comparative perspective* (pp. 341–350). Boston, MA: Allyn & Bacon.

Gomes, C. A. C. (1995). Brazil. In T. N. Postlethwaite (Ed.), *International encyclopedia of national systems of education* (pp. 127–134). Oxford, UK: Elsevier Science Ltd.

Gomes, C., Capanema, C., & Camara, J. (2000). Brazil: Overcoming five centuries of undereducation. In K. Mazurek, M. A. Winzer, & C. Majorek (Eds.), *Education in a global society: A comparative perspective* (pp. 35–51). Boston, MA: Allyn & Bacon.

Guimaraes de Castro, M. H. (1999, April 28–30). Education for the 21st Century: The challenge of quality and equity. Paper presented at the symposium on Brazilian Science and the Transition to Sustainability, organized by the Brazilian Academy of Sciences, Rio de Janeiro, Brazil (ERIC Document Reproduction Service No. ED439147).

Harvey, L. (1995). Editorial [prefatory introduction for inaugural issue]. *Quality in Higher Education, 1* (1), 5–12.

Hlatshwayo, S. A. (2000). *Education and independence: Education in South Africa, 1658–1988.* Westport, CT: Greenwood Press.

Kubow, P. K. (2000, March). *Preparing educational leaders for a global society: A comparative study of higher education in South Africa and the United States.* Paper presented at the Globalisation and Higher Education: Views from the South Conference. Cape Town, South Africa.

Lovell, P. A., & Wood, C. H. (1998). Skin color, racial identity, and life chances in Brazil. *Latin American Perspectives, 25* (3), 90–109.

Marcum, J. A. (1982). *Education, race, and change in South Africa.* Berkeley, CA: University of California Press.

Margolis, M. (1992, Summer). The invisible issue: Race in Brazil. *Ford Foundation Report,* 3–7.

Nadeau, D. (1996). Embodying feminist popular education under global restructuring. In S. Walters & L. Manicom (Eds.), *Gender in popular education: Methods for empowerment* (pp. 44–60). Atlantic Highlands, NJ: Zed Books.

Nasson, B. (1990). Modernization as legitimation: Education reform and the state in the 1980s. In M. Nkomo (Ed.), *Pedagogy of domination: Toward a democratic education in South Africa* (pp. 147–178). Trenton, NJ: Africa World Press.

Neuhouser, K. (1999). *Modern Brazil.* Boston, MA: McGraw-Hill.

Nkabinde, Z. P. (1997). *An analysis of the educational challenges in the new South Africa.* Lanham, MD: University Press of America.

Nkomo, M. (1990). Introduction. In M. Nkomo (Ed.), *Pedagogy of domination: Toward a democratic education in South Africa* (pp. 1–15). Trenton, NJ: Africa World Press.

Oakes, J. (1985). *Keeping track: How schools structure inequality.* New Haven, CT: Yale University Press.

Page, J. A. (1995). *The Brazilians.* Reading, MA: Addison Wesley.

Parnell, D. (1985). *The neglected majority.* Washington, DC: The Community College Press.

Prunty, J. J. (1985). Signposts for critical educational policy analysis. *Australian Journal of Education, 29* (2), 133–140.

Riordan, R. (1992). South Africa: The state of its political transition. In A. M. Micou & B. Lindsnaes (Eds.), *The role of voluntary organizations in emerging democracies: Experience and strategies in Eastern and Central Europe and in South Africa* (pp. 38–48). Skive, Denmark: The Danish Centre for Human Rights. [Report of a

June 21–24, 1992 satellite meeting of the United Nations Conference on Human Rights.]

Rockhill, K. (1987). Gender, language and the politics of literacy. *British Journal of Sociology and Education, 8*(2), 153–167.

Rosenberg, D. (Ed.). (1998). Getting books to school pupils in Africa: Case studies from Ghana and Tanzania, Mali, South Africa, Mozambique, and Kenya. (ERIC Document Reproduction Service No. ED439074)

Samoff, J. (1999). No teacher guide, no textbooks, no chairs. In R. F. Arnove, & C. A. Torres (Eds.), *Comparative education: The dialectic of the global and the local* (pp. 393–431). Boulder, CO: Rowman & Littlefield.

Soto, L. D. (1997). *Language, culture, and power: Bilingual families and the struggle for quality education.* New York, NY: State University of New York Press.

Steele, S. (1990). *The content of our character: A new vision of race in America.* New York, NY: St. Martin's Press.

Stromquist, N. P. (1997). *Literacy for citizenship: Gender and grassroots dynamics in Brazil.* Albany, NY: State University of New York Press.

Swift, A. (1997). *Children for social change: Education for citizenship of street and working children in Brazil.* Sandiacre, England: Educational Heretics Press.

Tobias, R., & Miller, R. (1999, April 19–23). The relationship between accountability, measurement scale, and grade inflation in school quality review ratings. Paper presented at the Annual Meeting of the American Educational Research Association, Montreal, Canada (ERIC Document Reproduction Service No. ED439140).

Torres, C. A. (1998). Introduction: The political-pedagogy of Paulo Freire. In P. Freire, *Politics and education.* Los Angeles, CA: UCLA Latin American Center Publications.

von Kotze, A. (1996) "The Creaking of the word": A feminist model? In S. Walters & L. Manicom (Eds.), *Gender in popular education: Methods for empowerment* (pp. 149–168). Atlantic Highlands, NJ: Zed Books.

Wolpe, H. (1992). Education and social transformation: Problems and dilemmas. In E. Unterhalter, H. Wolpe, & T. Botha (Eds.). *Education in a future South Africa* (pp. 1–16). Trenton, NJ: Africa World Press.

World Factbook. (2001). Brazil. Retrieved on February 18, 2002, from http://www.odci.gov/cia/publications/factbook/br.html.

Chapter 5

Education Accountability and Authority

Focusing Questions

- In what ways are the relative importance of teaching and schools reflected in your society? To what degree is teacher authority evident or absent?

- What is teaching? Compose a list of tasks that you associate with the work of teachers. How are these tasks and responsibilities assessed or supervised?

- What school and teaching reform and improvements can you identify? What are their intended results and their specific strategies? What are teachers' roles in planning and carrying out these strategies and in judging their success?

INTRODUCTION

Accountability is a loaded term within the school improvement and reform movements of several countries, including the United States. Efforts to introduce educational standards, to enact school **choice**, and to require more rigorous forms of teacher preparation are largely attributable to the popular impression that teachers and schools should become more answerable to their publics. Substantially less visible in the public discourse on teacher accountability is some systematic attention to other complex social factors with which accountability might be intertwined. Also relatively absent is consideration of the ways in which heightened public scrutiny of schools and teachers might interact with these factors. A particular point of tension related to building teacher accountability is the problem of doing so in a way that maintains teachers' **authority**. The intense scrutiny implicit in accountability-related policies appears to have a stultifying effect on teachers' willingness and capacity to perform their work. Tension between authority and accountability is especially pertinent in the modern postindustrial world because social contexts are complex and can converge in unintended and unpredictable ways (Albornoz, 1991). Elements of balance and reciprocation complicate the authority–accountability issue: Just as educators might be justified in advocating their own authority, it is not capricious for a society's members to expect its servants—teachers among them—to accept public scrutiny. Often, practitioners seem unwilling to accept legitimate responsibility for education when they contribute their perspectives regarding the limitations of simplistic definitions of accountability. Because the accountability movement is a politicized arena, teachers' skepticism is often dismissed as defensive, self-serving, and politically rather than pedagogically oriented.

Simey (1985) has observed that "accountability is not a mechanism or routine but a principle . . . a principle which serves a purpose" (p. 20). This claim draws out two hazards regarding accountability's use as a tool for education reform. First, accountability, when viewed as a mechanism, tends to instrumentalize the performance of teachers in order to pave the way for more systematic observations and judgments regarding their work. Instrumentalism can be troublesome in that effective engagement in complex social environments does not lend itself to such reduction. Judgments about teachers, if they are to be fair and replicable at face value, require detail and focus. But in pursuing focus and detail with an eye on routinized summative judgment, teaching itself tends to be reduced to a routine. In short, instrumentalized scrutiny of teachers and schools may excuse teachers from prioritizing behaviors that, while harder to define, are nonetheless imperative. Accountability has, from that perspective, become an overly reduced recipe for a cure—a routine.

A second limitation of accountability-based school reform is that a principle should itself be more than a simple rule of practice. Instead, like a social norm, it should logically extend to all of society's members. One can, therefore, question whether excessive focus on the roles of schools and teachers in today's challenging educational environments might at some level be intended to relieve other actors of their own obligations.

PROBLEMATIZING ACCOUNTABILITY

In this chapter, we consider some of the philosophical dimensions of accountability. The first philosophical perspective involves questioning the assumption that the work of teaching is discrete enough to stand up to measurements and checks that are widely assumed to be valid. A second philosophical perspective revisits some of the underpinnings of democracy and raises questions about the propriety of using accountability as a concrete process rather than an abstract principle. Education reforms in England and Germany are then examined in light of these dimensions.

What Teachers Do: Philosophical Insights on Accountability

A crucial part of being effective in any profession is decisiveness—a sense of certainty and purpose in moving ahead with an informed course of action. With teaching, this includes conveying to students a certain body of knowledge. But the successful teacher also makes the most of observed strengths in students and classes, seizes opportunities that arise in daily instruction, and recognizes and responds to problems and challenges. There is, in short, a broad range of skills that teachers must apply in performing effectively and a range of domains within which teachers must exercise these skills.

But these responsibilities of teachers are not clearly aligned with common conceptions of accountability. Societal expectations of teachers include not only tasks that are identifiable and measurable but also duties that are less clearly defined. Pincoffs (1973) has referred to the more easily measured tasks as "determinate," describing the less measurable tasks as "indeterminate" (p. 14). Whether or not they are defined as standards—and regardless of the governance level at which any such standard might be articulated—societies generally maintain certain curricular expectations. And in general, these goals are measurable. In the United States, for instance, college-bound high school graduates are expected to know algebra—an expectation that college admission procedures have reinforced without significant objection although there has been no formalized uniform standard. Students demonstrate their algebraic skills through their performance of various operations, their understanding of key terms, and their grasp of a specific set of concepts. The relatively bounded nature of this area of learning is correspondingly clear for the teacher and is part of an algebra teacher's determinate work.

But societies expect their students to achieve other harder-to-define competencies. In addition to the determinate work described previously, the algebra teacher is probably expected to nurture student progress in other ways. Maybe the teacher runs a "home room" during which someone—perhaps an aspiring young radio announcer—reads announcements deemed important enough to the life of the school and its students to warrant that expenditure of time. Though some (e.g., Stevenson, 1998) have questioned the extent of these kinds of infringements on the school day and have asserted that educators should strive to limit unnecessary interruptions, few argue that the social ends they serve are totally without merit. Further, the algebra teacher in our example is more and more commonly expected to inculcate in students a sense of how and where they might use their algebra skills in everyday life. Neither of these typical indeterminate goals is easily measured. Moreover, to the extent that these tasks might be assessed, such judgments do not readily yield comparisons.

The tendency of many educational reformers to focus on teachers' determinate work produces a self-contradictory and ironic result. Because they have some duties that are clearly defined along with others that are less specific, teachers are responsible for a good deal more than the typical accountability based assessment reflects. A negative by-product of the justifiable desire to ensure teacher competency is that the focus is on tasks that yield results deemed easiest to validate, replicate, compare, and interpret. Linking teacher performance to students' performances on standardized tests, though, renders validity far more tenuous, and it absorbs considerable administrative time and energy. This might encourage teachers to constrict their own conceptions of the parameters of their work. In this light, "teaching to the test" embodies a teacher's effort to attend to the more measurable aspects of curricula and student performance. Educators' harder-to-measure roles and functions can fall by the wayside. Contrary to its intentions, the accountability movement could threaten school quality.

Accountability and Democratic Theory: Responsibility as Authority

Across virtually all cultures, education is considered important enough to warrant the attention of citizens, politicians, and other members of society. And few credible observers dispute the importance of teachers in the crucial enterprise of education. Given its importance, education benefits from widespread participation—the involvement of not only teachers but also other members of society such as parents, whose children provide the reason for the school's existence. And precisely because effective pluralistic democracy is characterized by broad participation, the prerogative of teachers working within a democracy is not absolute. A consequence of the shared responsibility implicit in education is that teachers' work is open to scrutiny in ways that are not true of other professions.

Democracy is premised on a system of both rights and responsibilities. In terms of rights, careful reconciliation of several forms and sources of authority are involved. Strike (1990) has argued that legitimate administrative authority tends to establish a hierarchy in which elected school boards followed by district superintendents and building principals embody core principles of participatory democracy in that their work is legitimized on account of their authorization by an electorate. But if other necessary ends, such as educator autonomy and professionalism, are to thrive, other forms of authority are necessary in functioning societies, and each of a plurality of participants justifies its pursuit of different rights in terms of different forms of authority. Government—representing a society's shared will and culture—exercises its legitimate authority through administration oversight. But teachers claim expert authority in exercising professional judgment to implement curriculum. And citizens, further, pursue their right to educate their children via the authority of their positions as parents (Mintrop, 1996). Although the precise nature of the relationships among these parties and the rights that each claims will shift across time—and will vary from one society to the next—if schools are to embody and nurture democracy, it is important "that one domain not rule to the exclusion of the others" (Mintrop, 1996, p. 358).

The notion of accountability is useful because it not only helps outline the rights of various groups, but also because the term connotes reciprocity. Accountability "provides the basis for a relationship between society and its members, between those who govern and those who consent to be governed" (Simey, 1985, p. 20). The idea of consent here must not be trivialized in a vital democracy because it implies "the striking of a bargain or the drawing up of a contract between people who are partners in some joint enterprise" (Simey, 1985, p. 20). In short, just as the various players in a democracy have rights associated with various and interdependent forms of authority, the very notion of a contract serves as a reminder that privileges necessarily come at some expense to each participant. A contract, in short, obligates all involved.

And in schooling, many are involved. Burgess (1992) has defined the web of obligation surrounding education by identifying seven forms of stakeholder accountability, with each form implicating different parties in different ways:

- *Political* accountability in education applies most directly to the relationship of elected education officials to teachers serving under them.

- Through *professional* accountability, teachers are bound to their peers, because a teacher's acumen and integrity sustains the public perception of the essential nature of teaching and, therefore, helps preserve teacher authority.
- *Financial* accountability obligates schools' financial managers to their institutional managers, who, in turn, are similarly accountable to government regarding school expenditures.
- Institutional managers are further obligated to governing bodies with regard to their *managerial* accountability.
- *Contractual* accountability speaks to teachers' formally negotiated commitments to employers—for instance, regarding certain basic working conditions, days and times of service, and other specified duties.
- *Legal* accountability, pursuant to compulsory education laws, also holds parents responsible for their children's education. And notwithstanding the contemporary erosion of the traditional principle of *in loco parents*, American teachers continue to assume legal accountability for student safety.
- Finally—and sometimes particularly overlooked—parents and students are accountable to society through their *personal* responsibility. Societies, for example, have a stake in the security, nurturance, and encouragement that parents can extend to their children at home. Recognizing the importance of this form of support, in fact, governments in some societies subsidize several months of paid maternity leave—and in some cases, paternity leave as well. And it is personal accountability that obligates students—in reciprocation for society's investments—to commit the levels of initiative and effort necessary to reach their fullest potential.

These examples do more than suggest the nature of the specific obligations underlying education. And although this list does not exhaust the examples of mutual reliance that characterizes schooling, it does reinforce the point that both obligations and rights sustain pluralistic democracy and its formal institutions.

The 1980s and 1990s have witnessed shifts in the political environments of many countries and corresponding changes in policy-making processes. In general, the trend has been away from a proactive stance and toward an overtly politicized and reactive mode (Macpherson, 1998). This has had negative consequences in the way teachers view the accountability movement and their responsibility in light of this movement. When public policy formation is less politicized and more proactive, it is regularly very slow. The chief advantage of this slow pace is that it affords broad input toward consensus and the investment of those affected. But slow deliberate policy making has decided disadvantages where there is public impatience for change. Conversely, reactive policy gives the impression that changes are being made quickly. Such policies often gain political legitimacy because of public perceptions that they are responsive. But for those left to implement resulting policies, reactive policy making can be less than ideal. Teachers question the legitimacy of policies that emerge in this reactive environment. The accountability thrust constitutes one such reactive policy.

Teachers, on the whole, have become circumspect about educational reform in general. Thus, skepticism among teachers regarding the potential of accountability as a specific reform device is reinforced by their observation that none of the veritable tide of reforms in recent decades has been successful on a large scale. Skepticism toward educational reform can stem from the centralizing and decentralizing tendencies that are often built into the plans for change. Movement or change in the locus of governance produces uncertainty and hesitation as the people involved reclarify roles—their own roles and those of others. Relationships shift and principles such as mutual trust, reciprocity, and obligation, upon which the relationships are based, tend to be destabilized. And when reforms involve equivocation in mixing strategies that centralize educational control at higher levels with localizing, decentralizing strategies, the destabilizing effects can be more pronounced. Notions of accountability can vary with historical and social circumstance. Strained society–educator relationships are readily apparent in England and Germany, although their lineage is different.

ACCOUNTABILITY AS INSTRUMENTALIZED EDUCATION REFORM: ENGLAND'S EDUCATION REFORM ACT

Tensions between centralized state control, regulated markets, and teacher autonomy and professionalism are reflected in England's recent experience with an educational accountability movement. The primary legislation responsible for changes in the provision of education and for a redefinition of educators' work lives and roles was the Education Reform Act (ERA) of 1988. With the passage of the ERA, British lawmakers enacted four broad sets of changes in the country's educational system:

- A restructuring of school governance roles and duties
- A call for parental choice in determining their children's schools
- The adoption of a national curriculum
- The establishment of national student assessment guidelines

The ERA's sweeping changes constituted the United Kingdom's effort, through large-scale educational innovation, to revive its flagging economic fortune since its gradual post–World War II decline. To grasp the intentions and the impact of the ERA, it is necessary to understand also the process of educational restructuring and experimentation that preceded the ERA from 1979 to 1986.

Educational Restructuring Prior to ERA: Historical Antecedents

Educational accountability in England set a broad agenda for educational reform and gained momentum for a number of historical, political, economic, and social reasons. Historically, the United Kingdom's ideological stance has focused on development of commerce and empire. Because the United Kingdom was the first industrial power, an ideology among intellectuals and politicians was established, proclaiming the United Kingdom as "a world power within a liberal world economy" (Miller & Ginsburg, 1991, p. 51). Economically, the global oil crisis emerging in the 1970s, and the lack of money for public expenditures it created, promoted a privatization of education and instilled the notion that inequities were inevitable. Politically, liberals struggled to move British education from its elitist past to a more **egalitarian** present and future, whereas conservatives stressed traditional subjects and technical competencies and encouraged business funding of elitist institutions. Socially, conservatives played on the dissensions and confusions among more progressive groups. By emphasizing falling reading and writing standards, the Conservative Party, along with the media, appealed to the public on the basis that teachers and progressive curricula (e.g., peace studies, racial awareness, multicultural education) were contributing to the nation's economic and moral decline. Hence, due to a combination of historical ideologies, economic crises, and social factions and to their own political prominence, the Conservatives were able to embark on a restructuring plan in which progressive agendas were denounced, the role of the state was redefined, and teacher autonomy was severely restricted. An "emboldened centralizing pattern" (Miller & Ginsburg, 1991, p. 61) pervaded the country, with the country's political conservatives exercising in some respects a regulatory role more often associated with progressive political doctrines.

Using their political position and rhetoric, the Conservative Party initiated educational reform policies that limited governmental financial allocation to education, extended governmental control over teacher education and curriculum, and restricted autonomy for its educational workers. The educational accountability reform, reflecting its conceptual mooring in human capital theory, called on education "to be the efficient servant of a corporately managed economy" (Miller & Ginsburg, 1991, p. 57). Conservatives assumed that with greater governmental control of education in England, the human workforce would be improved, providing needed skills and positions in a stratified society and resulting in industrial development and economic growth. Restructuring the state and education was a tactic in an overall plan to revitalize the United Kingdom's position in the world economy (Miller & Ginsburg, 1991).

There were many expected outcomes of the highly centralized accountability reform. First, advocates of the ERA thought that by reducing governmental expenditures, the reform would force tertiary institutions to create linkages with businesses and become more entrepreneurial. Second, because the ERA established a national teacher education curriculum, in which teachers would be required to study two years in each academic subject, advocates believed this would limit progressive curricula and usher in a more traditional and ordered society. Third, by limiting teachers' collective power and effectively managing teachers and their salaries, government officials anticipated that they would be able to push forward with more traditional reforms. Overall, conservatives expected the administratively–oriented accountability reform to eradicate liberal ideas that some viewed as contributing to a misguided country. For many, the conservative agenda was a way to create a orderly, monetaristic society.

The 1988 Education Reform Act

The declared purpose of the ERA (1988) and subsequent legislation has been to improve "educational standards through support for, and pressure from, the educational marketplace" (Ouston, Fidler, & Early, 1998, p. 108). The 1988 ERA is, like the reform effort preceding it, partially a response to the perceived need in the United Kingdom to reassert influence following approximately 50 years of relative decline in its international stature. The United Kingdom had been the premier world power at least through World War I and arguably until the United States—which had maintained a stance of isolationism in the global community—entered World War II. The United Kingdom's global preeminence is recent enough to remain vivid in collective memory of the British, and efforts to maintain the country's international economic and political stature have fueled reform efforts across many aspects of British life (McAdams, 1993).

A complex and contradictory national spirit underlies England's sweeping educational reforms specifically and English society more generally. On the one hand, England continues to retain a deeply ingrained sense of social class tied, among other things, to the country's identity as the world's last great monarchy. Maintaining the aristocratic class system that underpins monarchic rule is therefore a means of preserving a link to its past. On the other hand, English society has consistently demonstrated its considerable investment in the notion that government could and should intervene against the effects of social class. Thus, the United Kingdom developed "one of the most extensive welfare systems in the industrialized world" (McAdams, 1993, p. 155). Accordingly, in the realm of education, the British government developed a system of comprehensive secondary schools to serve all classes of students and to tend to the issue of educating its considerable immigrant population, although various **elite** structures were established and maintained as well. The country's more current pursuit of parent choice and accountability in education has revealed this latent psychosocial conflict and has forced the question of whether British citizens do indeed want an egalitarian school system. For a comparison of how demographic attributes of the population affect education in England and Germany, see the Points of Convergence box (Figure 5.1).

The ERA is also a direct response to almost 20 years of public criticism aimed specifically at education and mounting in the years leading up to the ERA's 1988 enactment (Miller & Ginsburg, 1991). The voices of teachers and students, and of politicians and social critics alike, contributed to the widespread clamor for educational change. English secondary teachers, for instance—pointing to the child-centered, self-paced, low-stress teaching approach of elementary teachers—complained that students were underchallenged and generally unfamiliar with academic rigors when they came to the comprehensive schools (McAdams, 1993). And the British population demonstrated its own dissatisfaction with the system. Chubb and Moe (1992) have have noted, for example, that a large portion of England's students quit school before completing high school. Large numbers of British students assume that they are destined for working-class niches in society (Willis, 1977) and that "academic effort will not translate into a good job" (McAdams, 1993, p. 157). Business and industry interests, meanwhile, have claimed that English schools "failed to equip the economy with skilled workers who can be flexible, innovative, and productive" (Chubb & Moe, 1992, p. 3). The rhetoric in the halls of Parliament, unsurprisingly, has echoed this broad dissatisfaction: Said one lawmaker, "[British education] has become producer-dominated. It has not proved sensitive to the demands for change that have become ever more urgent over the past ten years" (Hughes, Wikeley, & Nash, 1994, p. 9). The 1988 ERA, that politician declared, would "raise standards, extend choice, and produce a better educated Britain" (p. 9).

FIGURE 5.1

Points of Convergence

ENGLAND	Demography and educational consequences	GERMANY
Aspect: England's regions and peoples are distinct because of geographic features and their impact on the course of civilization there. Scotland, for instance, was remote and inhospitable for Romans exploring what we now call the British Isles. Scotland, and some other outlying regions, retained this identity as hostile after the monarchy was established in England. And even after hinterlands came under the crown's reach, significant latitude was granted to local populations in steering public affairs. **Response:** Culture and its institutions have taken alternate courses in each of the member "nations" of the United Kingdom—England (the focus in this chapter), Northern Ireland, Scotland, and Wales—although substantial similarity also exists (Raffe, 2000). **Consequence:** The various school systems within the United Kingdom are typified by this blend of mutual difference and similarity (Raffe, 2000); Wales, for instance, has the same architecture of Local Education Authorities—though it is much smaller because of region's relatively sparse population (Gorard, 2000).	How have attributes of the population affected education?	**Aspect:** The Rhein River is significant to Germany's economic activity in terms of shipping and certain industrial activity. But its economic significance is not coincidental, and the Rhein has had additional effects on culture, settlement patterns, and so forth (Tenbrock, 1979). **Response:** Once breaching the Alps, Romans exploring Germany progressed north following the Rhein. Early civilization was therefore concentrated in the Rhein region, and that pattern continued into the Christian era. Catholicism continues to dominate in Germany's south and along the Rhein, whereas Protestantism flourishes in the North (Tenbrock, 1979). **Consequence:** The most highly populated areas in Germany are along the Rhein River, accounting for a substantial portion of Germany's 82 million citizens. Large parts of the country are sparsely settled, and maintaining a level of instruction that is comparable to that of the German city presents challenges in Germany as in any country (Führ, 1997).

In the years prior to the ERA, offices known as Local Educational Authorities (LEAs) exercised supervisory clout over English head teachers, the English counterparts to American principals. The LEAs had selected head teachers for local schools, for instance, without significant input from the affected parents or teachers and directed day-to-day administration of England's schools. Under the new system established by the ERA, in contrast, a head teacher is far more directly influenced by the wishes of a school's board of governors and, in turn, by the wishes of the parents that those boards serve. The 1988 reform also stipulates that head teachers are responsible for regularly evaluating the work

United Kingdom

Source: The World Factbook. (2001). United Kingdom. Washington, DC: The Central Intelligence Agency, U.S. Government.
http://www.odci.gov/cia/publications/factbook/geos/uk.html

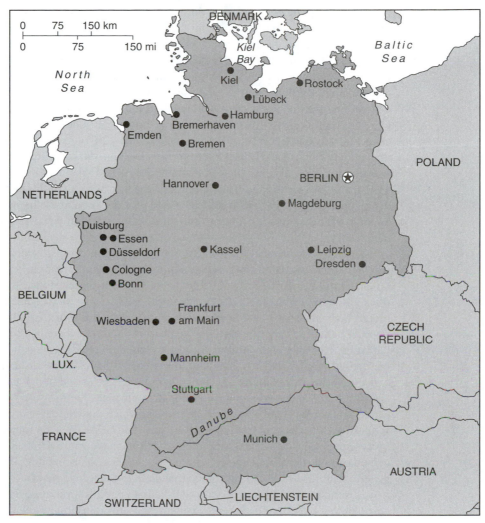

Germany

Source: The World Factbook. (2001). Germany. Washington, DC: The Central Intelligence Agency, U.S. Government. http://www.odci.gov/cia/publications/factbook/geos/gm.html

of the teachers in their schools. Contrary to the literal meaning that their title would imply, then, the LEAs have traditionally been "local" only relative to the most centralized offices in London: LEAs were in fact national field offices overseeing schools in many regions. In contrast, although each school has long had its own board of governors, these bodies have, until the ERA, had little authority over either their school's head teacher or the pertinent LEA. The 1988 reform reverses the traditional power structure that had been in place by diminishing the national role in school governance and concurrently augmenting the role of governing boards.

Among the further revamped duties of the governing boards is the task of ensuring that a school's children are receiving the national curriculum as the ERA mandates. The 1988 law prescribes the curriculum for all of England's schools—public and private—and requires students to study nine foundational subjects: English, math, science, technology, history, geography, art, music, and physical education. A 10th foundation area, modern foreign language study, starts at about 11 years of age. The curriculum includes time allocations for specified topics in each area, and the government further prescribes detailed learning requirements for each subject. According to one government document, the expectation is that teachers will spend no less than 70% of available instructional time on the national curriculum (Education Reform in Britain, 1989). In line with the national curriculum, the ERA also established that students would take nationally devised tests at 7, 11, 14, and 16 years of age. The purposes of the tests were twofold. First, the assessments were supposed to help ensure student mastery of the content of the national curriculum. Second, the tests provided a means for determining the relative success of schools across the country.

The purported reason for collecting information on comparative school success is to supply parents with a means for determining which school their child should attend. And this impetus toward choice is arguably the most potent aspect of the ERA. Employing theories of the marketplace, school choice in England, as in several other countries, uses the linked mechanisms of customer decision and competition in the faith that these forces improve schools. Under England's system prior to reforms, there had been no flexibility in the practice of assigning children to schools based on residence location. That traditional method, of course, remains dominant in the United States, notwithstanding the country's expanding experimentation with choice-based reform. An additional aspect of the ERA in terms of parental choice and local prerogative, involves the measure's creation of the so-called grant-maintained school. Such schools, which are comparable to the U.S. **charter schools**, are independent from the jurisdiction of an LEA. They are founded as the result of successful petitioning of the government and through the approval of a majority of the concerned parents. Grant-maintained schools receive their financing directly from the national government rather than through an intermediate level of government.

In sum, the 1988 ERA features substantial centralization, especially in terms of the curriculum it prescribes and the assessment measures it institutes. Yet, there are simultaneous moves toward decentralization in terms of its structures for local oversight and governance and of parental choice (Lawton, 1993).

Applying a Critical Framework to Understand Educational Restructuring in England

Frank (1972) used three elements—*theoretical adequacy, policy effectiveness,* and *empirical validity*—as tools for the critical evaluation of educational reform. Table 5.1 shows questions that emerge from each of Frank's three evaluative constructs and that lend themselves to structured critique. The ability to critically evaluate educational reforms and other policies is important for all educators—teachers applying new ideas in a classroom as well as administrators dealing with resource allocation issues (Paige, 1995). If undertaken solely by policy makers and planners and by researchers evaluating the reform policy, a

Table 5.1 Framework for Critique of Educational Reforms		
Theoretical Adequacy	**Policy Effectiveness**	**Empirical Validity**
Is there a theoretical foundation for the proposed reform?	Is there support for this reform (e.g., public, governmental)?	Is there any empirical evidence regarding the reform?
What is the hypothesized relationship of the reform to its stated outcomes?	Will there be threatened interest groups that will attempt to sabotage it?	Is research available elsewhere regarding the successes of similar programs?
Are the claims being made in favor of the reform theoretically sound? plausible?	What are the resource allocation, teacher training, and cost requirements of the reform?	If research was conducted, how satisfactory was the research design?
What other factors might theoretically account for the observed outcomes?	Is it financially feasible? cost-effective?	What kind of claims and interpretations are being made of the research findings?
Is the reform program taking those factors into consideration?	How long will it take to implement it, and is enough time being given to adequately assess it?	Are the research findings unequivocal or ambiguous? What else might account for these findings?

Adapted from Frank (1972) and Paige (1995).

likely result of policy assessment is the institutionalized externalization of educational theory and practice. The discussion that follows demonstrates the usefulness of Frank's critical constructs as tools for thinking about the 1988 ERA and its broader implications.

The ERA's Theoretical Adequacy. Various sources agree that, upon conception, the 1988 reform was major in scope (Chubb & Moe, 1992; McAdams, 1993). The law's implementation and revision has proceeded at a dramatic rate since its enactment (Feintuck, 1994). But many observers (Chitty, 1989; Hughes et al., 1994; Lawton, 1993; McLean, 1993) show the changes that the ERA instituted were far more the result of politics than of pedagogical theorizing.

ERA's proponents sought through the policy to reverse England's economic decline, maximize human resources, and stimulate social progress. The motives behind the ERA are clearly related to the theory of human capital formation, which rests on the assumption that national economic improvement is strongly linked with educational improvement (Fägerlind & Saha, 1989). There is apparent harmony, then, between the theoretical tenets of human capital formation and the capitalist ideology dominating Britain's economy and government.

The more specific theoretical cast of the ERA is evident in both its application of accountability strategies and its introduction of market forces. In pursuit of the educational improvement it promises, the ERA adopts two guiding assertions. First accountability—through clearer management roles and the administration of a prescribed curriculum with regular assessments—purports to hold educators and educational leaders responsible "for the authority they have exercised on behalf of the public" (Feintuck, 1994, p. 39). And second, the ERA's injection of market forces is evident in its use of increased parental choice and localized control as vehicles for positive change. Parents are to choose schools for their children, and because school funding is tied to numbers of pupils, schools must raise their standards in order to attract the positive attention of their potential clients. Schools not responding face the prospect of closing for lack of interested student-customers. "The introduction of market forces in this way, according to the theory, will lead directly to higher standards in education" (Hughes et al., 1994, p. 79). The element of choice introduces a consequence for failure and, to that extent, is a forceful device to make schools and educators responsive. Further, the policy's choice element reduces teachers' autonomy by increasing their interest in parental preferences and aligning instructional practice accordingly.

The express objectives and purposes of the ERA are difficult to pinpoint precisely because the reform program is the result of political rather than educator-driven processes. In the abstract, though, the popular impression was that the schools were hampered by a lack of rigor. Therefore, one broad aim of the ERA was to address a lack of standards. In response, the government adopted a highly detailed national curriculum and articulated its expectation that schools will "bring 80 to 90 percent of all pupils at least to the level of pupils of average ability in individual subjects" (Education Reform in Britain, 1989, p. 5). A second broad ERA goal was to extend to a greater cross-section of the society the instructional rigor long available to the English elite. The program's theoretical soundness with respect to this entitlement issue is equivocal. On the one hand, the nationalized curriculum and assessment measures have the potential to promote greater homogeneity in schools throughout the system. Consequently, British parents have generally perceived the system as being fairer to students (Hughes et al., 1994). Yet, valid concerns that popular schools could eventually become "able to choose their parents, rather than parents choosing popular schools" (Hughes et al., 1994, p. 79) point to one way the policy could reinforce difference from school to school rather than a more homogenized or standard educational experience.

Proponents of the ERA had characterized the plan as proper on the grounds that it would help empower the parents of Britain's schoolchildren. A 1992 White Paper articulated this philosophy by stating that "parents know best the needs of their children—certainly better than most educational theorists or administrators, better even than our mostly excellent teachers" (Hughes et al., 1994, p. 12). But this statement is at odds with the ERA's move toward the development of curricular standards and of assessments—both in a tightly centralized framework that provided scant leeway for parental input. It seems possible to explain the government's claims about the natural aptitudes and rights of parents in more ulterior terms, namely as an attempt to mobilize Britain's citizens by instilling and encouraging impressions that schools had been unresponsive.

The theory underlying the ERA has deeper flaws, however. Chubb and Moe (1992) have pointed rather optimistically to the initiative as an example of the merits of decentralization: "[Schools] must be substantially free from bureaucratic control. . . . [The reformers'] call has consistently been for less bureaucracy and more autonomy" (pp. 7–8). Other observers, however, have pointed out the contradictions between localizing key choice and governance aspects of the system while nationalizing other vital elements of the system such as curriculum and assessment. Thus, a potent criticism of England's ERA from the standpoint of its theoretical tidiness is that the overall plan seems to invest halfheartedly in the market philosophy. Contrary to market principles, a school's capacity to adjust in order to provide a superior product is hamstrung because the content of virtually the entire course of study is centrally determined and is by mandate identical in all schools. "The proffered freedom of choice is illusory," because, although there is the prospect for choice, what variety of real choices does the reform nurture? "Parents are free to choose which institution will slavishly teach the Secretary of State's curriculum to their children" (Hughes et al., 1994, pp. 10–11). Some critics, such as Carl (1994), therefore, have asserted that the reform did not "roll back the state" as promised, but instead merely "reconstituted it at different levels" (p. 297).

Further criticisms of the theory underlying the ERA go to the relationship of the reform's measures to its promised outcomes. Possible flaws of human capital tenets in general surround the question of whether systemic educational improvement is related to improved occupational potential at the individual level (Fägerlind & Saha, 1989). The most meaningful factors for assessing accomplishment of that aim might be the equitability of educational financing and distribution; yet in the light of criticism that England's reformed schools are potentially elitist, the ERA's policies for educational reform fall short.

In addition to this basic problem, however, the reform initiative's causal claims are weak. For all the disruption the reform caused in institutional and human terms, the ERA begets the reconstitution and disruption of school oversight and governance but does not seem to eliminate any specifically identified problem:

> The education system has been broken up and many new forms of governmental structure created on the basis of evidence that education needs to improve—not on the basis of evidence that the particular aspects of the system to be challenged are the cause of the problem or evidence that changes will improve outcomes. (Cordingley & Kogan, 1993, p. 115)

This underscores the main theoretical weakness of the ERA. The reform responds to abstract concerns—and to the resulting political pressures—related to school reform. But there was no diagnosis of the education system's specific ailments, and no specific suggestion that the remedies prescribed were therefore well suited. Although it is true that the policy solutions undertaken fit the prevailing political ideologies, the British government did not in general undertake the more difficult work of matching solutions with certain problems. Their complaints differ, but even critics who are more affectionate to the ERA, such as Chubb and Moe (1992), conclude that British reformers failed to directly attack underlying causes of ineffective schooling. The case of the ERA tends to confirm the observation that, as a society's consensus broadens, that consensus also becomes shallower (Clabaugh & Rozycki, 1990). Although there was widespread support for educational improvement in the abstract, linkages between specific deficiencies and pointed policy remedies are difficult to locate when studying the British reform precisely because mobilizing support for anything specific would likely have been difficult or impossible.

Policy Effectiveness of the ERA. Those investigating the 1988 ERA (Chitty, 1989; Graham, 1993; Lawton, 1993) have emphasized the political nature of the process. Such observers asserted, for instance, that the notion of parental choice was a thinly veiled effort on the part of the ruling British Conservative Party to enlist the support of the English citizenry. Parental choice was not "a reflection of grass roots demands. . . . Populism served as political rhetoric designed to legitimate policies that were decided on other grounds" (Carl, 1994, p. 297). From that perspective, the broad appeal of choice in the abstract enabled popular support for changes that, in the end, furthered the interests of business and industry sectors and of other groups sympathetic to conservative ideologies. Some proponents of the reform, in fact, were quite frank. According to McAdams (1993), one leading Conservative politician remarked that "it was time, once again, to educate people to know their place in society" (p. 157).

Opponents of the 1988 reform program, meanwhile, objected to the plan's affront to the comprehensive school concept. They claimed that the initiatives of parental choice and grant-maintained schools contradicted the notion that the government should fund each school in ways that more systematically promoted equal education for students from all social classes. Also, England's problem of serving its minority populations continues to grow (see for instance, Connolly & Troyna, 1998); some claim that the reform plan raises the possibility that the emerging school system could be more segregated and that the schools could lag behind in terms of other worthwhile social ends. Indeed, these suspicions seem well founded, given the comments of one ERA supporter, who stated that "if parental choice leads to racially segregated schools, then so be it" (Hughes et al., 1994, p. 79). Teachers, for their part, have objected to the national curriculum because of its emphasis on factual learning and—not the least—because they feel little ownership for the material, since professionals had little hand in devising much of the new approach.

The cost of the ERA has been considerable, and the ERA's expense draws the policy's propriety into some question (Chitty, 1989). The country incurred major expenses in developing and implementing its standard curriculum and national tests, and constant adjustments of both of these elements contributed to further expense (Hughes et al., 1994). Another concern is that the curriculum is inflexible with respect to its use by the teachers. Teachers are expected to adhere to instructional directives—both large and small—and this has impeded them from applying professional judgment—a strong sign of disruptions to teacher authority that resulted in the name of choice and accountability. Successful teaching in many contexts requires such flexibility—for instance, in unexpected situations and in responding instructionally to children having varying needs and ability levels. An additional objection to the reform plan is that it promotes unwise use of other resources. Popular schools are crowded, for instance, while less popular schools go underutilized.

Finally, the rate at which schools were obliged to adopt the ERA reform package has been difficult for all concerned. Even parents indicated their awareness that the reformed system affords teachers insufficient time and resources to do their jobs properly (Hughes et al., 1994). Because of the revisions to the plan that have continued since its inception, critics complain that the system has been subject to "constant disjointed and incomplete experimentation. New practices have not had time to settle down before they have been replaced by yet further attempts to cause change" (Cordingley & Kogan, 1993, p. 114). These adjustments, moreover, were not the product of the advice of educators, a circumstance that points again to the constriction of teacher authority within the reformed system. Finally, there is little evidence that the reforms have had proper evaluation, aside from those that extend from nationalized student assessments.

Empirical Validity and the ERA. The 1988 ERA has generated considerable national and international discussion. Some participants in this discourse have been chiefly sympathetic to the idea of introducing greater competition among schools (e.g., Chubb & Moe, 1992, and to a lesser degree McAdams, 1993), while some are generally opposed to this principle (see Feintuck, 1994). The comments of others seem to come from a more neutral vantage (see Cordingley & Kogan, 1993; Hughes et al., 1994, for instance). The most germane findings based on empirical research revolve around the level of popular support for the reform, the general effects of choice and competition, the degree to which the initiative has increased accountability, and the perceived equity and fairness of the reformed schools.

Regarding English society's acceptance for the new system, McAdams (1993) referred to the results of polls and surveys to conclude that there was a relatively high level of support among both parents and teachers just after the reform was put in place. The national curriculum in particular—evidently because it appeals to the "English concept of 'entitlement'" (McAdams, 1993, p. 151)—enjoyed widespread acceptance. But others refuted these general conclusions. Hughes et al. (1994) used detailed anecdotal information to conclude that parents themselves had mixed feelings about the new system. Some specific objections revolved around the perception that schools and the curriculum in England are vulnerable to political manipulation. There is, therefore, a degree of cynicism among parents about the new system, not to mention the political machinery that conceived it. More recent observations about the discourse surrounding school choice (Poulson, 1998) have pointed out that parents progressed in the degree to which they identified themselves as consumers and schooling as a product. It seems possible that "reiteration of particular statements or metaphors [i.e., schooling as product] . . . may lead to the assumption of such attitudes or beliefs by those who previously had not done so" (p. 420).

Hughes et al. (1994) also argued that there was little evidence to suggest that policy makers could validly continue to justify the ERA on the grounds that the reform supplies what parents had wanted. Anecdotal evidence underscores parents' frustration with the inaccessibility of the reformed curriculum, in spite of other more optimistic assessments (McAdams, 1993). Further, it is noteworthy that substantial research conducted prior to 1988 suggests that parents care more about considerations such as their children's happiness, school location, and extracurricular offerings than they do about instructional excellence in the abstract (Hughes et al. 1994). This is ironic, given the presumptions under which the ERA was developed. In 1991, the government responded to parental requests for additional information, ensuring that parents would receive an annual report identifying their schools' standing on a number of counts. But Feintuck (1994) maintained that the information these reports held responded to only a limited set of factors that are mostly sympathetic to the market-sensitive measures and not to the parents' broader interests.

Turning to accountability within the reformed system, Feintuck (1994) claimed that there is little evidence of progress in that realm. The author points to examples that demonstrate how, in the absence of external governance clout from the weakened LEAs, head teachers and governing boards can now actually exercise more power, subject to less public scrutiny, than was true under the traditional system. McAdams (1993) noted that very few schools elected to pursue grant-maintained status (i.e., chosen to petition for independent status with direct government funding), and he concluded that this reflects deference to political rather than educational imperatives—contrary to the original predictions of the ERA's proponents. Further, Feintuck (1994) added that the results from the national assessments offer little evidence of educational improvement in the first place. Therefore, claims as to improved accountability at the classroom level are tenuous at best.

Finally, even early research following the ERA's inception suggested that there was some empirical justification for the apprehensions voiced about the system's potential to provide equitable opportunity. There was some evidence that schools were selecting preferred students using backdoor methods, for instance (Hughes et al., 1994). Certain popular institutions were able to choose students and families, contrary to the plan's declared intention, and some researchers claimed that parental choice appeared to be a largely tokenistic "means for legitimizing a change" (Feintuck, 1994, p. 132). Even where effectively exercised, school choice in Britain was "likely to be utilized only by those relatively advantaged in the distribution of resources, serving to entrench hierarchy within the state school system" (Feintuck, 1994, p. 132). At an administrative level, moreover, evidence suggested that within the reformed system there was an increased potential for "power to be exercised in an essentially corporatist and hidden manner" (Feintuck, 1994, p. 130). Thus, although Chubb and Moe (1992) had argued that greater equity would only be possible under a more competitive system, evidence from the ERA suggested that it remained possible, if not likely, that instead of leveling opportunity for the country's youths, the ERA might have worked in the opposite direction.

Conclusions Regarding the ERA

The parallels between the British and the American situations are obvious. In the United States, there are—as in England—vehement calls for educational change. Critics encouraging such change often identify educational reform as a key to national economic progress. The differences between the two situations are considerable, however. Because of its parliamentary form of government, for instance, England has enacted and implemented its reform far more rapidly than would be possible in the U.S. political arena. Because U.S. constituencies have greater access in the lawmaking process, that is, it is doubtful that such a complete set of changes could even be possible in the United States. Both supporters and detractors of the ERA agree that the British model has severe limitations in terms of its potential to demonstrate that choice and competition can drive successful educational change. The British plan, after all, is self-contradictory—nurturing competition in some cases and undermining it in others. Although the English experience provides little conclusive evidence about the merits of a more competitive system, the comments of England's parents and teachers indicated that there is more to school and learning than the original proponents of the ERA had acknowledged (Poulson, 1998). For a comparison of sociopolitical factors shaping education in England and Germany, see the Points of Convergence box (Figure 5.2).

FIGURE 5.2

Points of Convergence

ENGLAND	Sociopolitical factors and educational consequences	GERMANY
Aspect: In spite of its identity as a progressive democracy, England has retained strong links to its aristocratic past—the British monarchy being an overt symbol of the continuing appeal and power of that past. But other means by which elitism is preserved are more covert.		**Aspect:** In the wake of World War I, the Treaty of Versailles induced enormous war reparations on the Germans. The unrealistically high penalties contributed to a near complete loss of confidence in the German economy and hyperinflation so pronounced that during the early 1920s, a U.S. dollar was worth several trillion Marks.
Response: English "public schools," launched in the mid-19th century, were actually set up as privately endowed schools that were instituted as a charity of sorts providing education for poorer members of society. The wealthier members of English society, meanwhile, normally were educated by private arrangements with tutors.	How have unique sociopolitical factors shaped education?	**Response:** Adolf Hitler rose to power by appealing effectively to the Germans' collective sense of resentment.
Consequence: The emergence and growth of a middle class during the Industrial Revolution brought concurrent demand for a form of secondary school that might exclude the working classes. The public schools were reformed to provide an alternative that would exclude the poor for whom those schools had been created (Hobsbawm, 1999).		**Consequence:** Hitler's propaganda machine had many outlets. Among them were the schools, which became one of Hitler's most important mouthpieces (Wegner, in press). In the contemporary period, the German school system reflects safeguards against manipulation such as their relative decentralization at the *Land* level.

EDUCATION AND NEW CHALLENGES IN POST-REUNIFICATION GERMANY

The case of England's ERA depicts a situation in which change came as a result of popular processes and in which policy was produced under the more regular condition of legislated change. No such popular input or normal policy formulation process existed in the case of German school reforms following reunification. Instead, the former German Democratic Republic's (GDR) integration into the Federal Republic of Germany (FRG) resulted in the almost instant dissolution of and overturning of long-held East German patterns of social commitment (Mintrop, 1996; Pritchard, 1999). The social disruption that Germany has encountered since the fall of the Berlin Wall—as extraordinary as that might have seemed in 1989—is exemplary of a more widespread pattern of disintegration and reintegration in the global environment.

But the case of German reunification is relevant for reasons that transcend the peculiarities associated with it. Analyzing the German reunification provides insights into the challenges related to the acceleration of societal change in general. Disintegration of entire countries has occurred not only in the sphere of the former Soviet Union. Tensions in countries such as Yugoslavia and Indonesia exemplify a spirit of nationalism that is growing worldwide. Meanwhile, forces of integration and mass migration are bringing peoples together under unfamiliar governments. It is, therefore, important to develop a better understanding of the educational challenges associated with the kinds of radical change that this global environment begets. How are teachers and school structures recognizing and responding to emerging expectations as they enter uncharted social and political waters?

East Germany was by nearly any measure authoritarian in its control of education. The East German state—and the communist *Sozialistische Einheitspartei Deutschlands* (SED, or "Socialist Unity Party") as arbiter of the functions and ideals of the state—directed the country's teaching and learning with a level of control that matched its manipulation of the economy. This degree of centralization distinguished the school system of the former GDR in ways that make comparison with other nations' education systems difficult.

However, schools are instruments by which any country—not solely the most authoritarian—will actively and purposefully pursue futures the society deems desirable. As such, a country's schools will inescapably mirror the values that a society pursues. Education, in short, is regularly both a cause and an effect of its societal environment. With this in mind, one should be cautious about viewing the former GDR as entirely unique on account of its centralized control of teachers, schools, and the content of instruction. The case of the GDR provides insights into the nature of centralization at a time when nations such as England and the United States are moving toward more centralized educational practices in terms of curricular standardization. Significantly, the former GDR has moved in the opposite direction as it has merged with the FRG.

The East German case invites two levels of comparison. On one level, the revamping of the old East German system has required such complete adoption of the West German system that a country-to-country comparison is appropriate. On a second level, the case calls for examination of change across time within a single country. Our discussion of East German unification, therefore, starts by reviewing the division of Germany in the wake of World War II, by describing the nature of the reunification that commenced in 1990, and by describing schooling in the FRG and the former GDR, and making comparisons between the two countries. This sets the stage for subsequent focus on the former GDR's ongoing period of transition—a discussion that applies constructs from Frank's (1972) analytical framework introduced previously in this chapter and that enables more pointed comments about how the former East Germany is responding to its education reform challenge.

Two Germanies: Historical and Ideological Perspectives

Germany was divided following World War II as a result of ideological differences among the Allies. The Soviet Union and the Western Allies—most prominently the United States, France, and Britain—had been united during battle by the common task of defeating the German National Socialist (Nazi) regime. But East–West divisions had long been obvious.

The Soviet Union, a product of the 1917 Russian Revolution, embraced the socialist tenets of Marxism; the Western Allies adhered to capitalism. This ideological divide was embodied in the eventual emergence in 1949 of the GDR in the Soviet occupation zone and the FRG in the three zones of the Western Allies.

In significant ways, educational development in postwar Germany was more coherent in the Soviet zone than was true in Western Germany, partly because the East had a single overseer rather than three. Further, the Soviet state had itself assumed a strong and directive role in maintaining its own affairs. After a period of denazification—a goal that the Western Allies also pursued in their own zones—the Soviets sought in their German zone to establish political institutions that resembled Soviet ideologies. This is not surprising: Within the zones of the Western Allies as well, the three Western Allies each sought to cultivate practices that harmonized with their own political interests and cultural predispositions. For example, in significant ways, West Germans learned during their postwar transition to cope with a decentralized federalist form of governance that reflected the Western pattern and that prevails there today. The former East, in contrast, because of its virtual absorption into the West through unification, is faced with huge transition.

The Context of Reform: Schooling in the Former East Germany. In their analysis of the roles of school in the former GDR, Weiler, Mintrop, and Fuhrmann (1996) identify three overarching functions of the country's school system: Schools and education in the GDR aimed to guarantee society's economic development, to induce the breaking down of class structures and establish a classless society, and to ensure allegiance to the ideals of the communist SED party and the active engagement of East German citizens in securing the party's objectives (p. 13).

In terms of spurring economic development, the GDR's polytechnical upper school was the country's major instrument for furthering industrial vitality. The schools, 10-year institutions that students attended from age 6 to 16 years of age, were by 1964 the near universal mode of education for East German youths (Fishman & Martin, 1987). Following this 10-year stage, additional education in noncompulsory settings most often consisted of two additional years of specialized vocational education in trade schools (*Berufschulen*), though additional postsecondary education for less than 10% of East German youths occurred in the *Erweitereoberschule* (*EOS*)—the "extended upper school." The *EOS* provided the major route of entrance into the universities (Pritchard, 1999).

The polytechnical idea, according to Hearnden (1974), became the overarching principle under which the GDR unified the tandem aims of academic and vocational education. From a socialist perspective, these aims had been corruptly dualized in West Germany in ways that limited the students' versatility and that consequently stifled progress toward a more enlightened collectivist society. The polytechnical model also embodied the principle of a classless society because, unlike the ability-differentiated traditional school system that existed in the East before World War II, all students attended the polytechnical school together. Polytechnical education included substantial emphasis on science—an emphasis that tended to increase as students moved to higher grades. By the seventh grade level, around a third of a student's typical instructional week was devoted to math and science (Pritchard, 1999). In comparison, students spent around a quarter of their time on language instruction, consisting of required study of Russian and work in an additional language.

In spite of the polytechnical schools' emphasis on science, according to Hearnden (1974), the purposes of the school were deeper: Polytechnical education was "not any special subject of instruction" but, rather, "must penetrate all subjects," linking them with "practical activity, especially with manual skills" (Hearnden, 1974, p. 123). Thus, the polytechnical schools were intended to produce well-rounded and versatile citizens, who, through exposure to instruction designed to make ties between learning and socially productive work, were dedicated to the goal of becoming contributing members of the proletariat. In the Marxist conception, their contributions in the workforce would create an "unprecedented expansion of productivity" (Hearnden, 1974, p. 285) that would render class distinctions meaningless.

The East German government pursued its youths' allegiance to communist ideals in a number of ways. A focus in civics classes, for instance, was on inculcating collectivist values in students. Symbolic confirmations of students' readiness for constructive contribution came in the context of a ceremony known as *Jugendweihe* (literally, "youth dedication/sanctification"). Membership in the *Pfadfinder* (Young Pioneers, or "scouts") or in the Free German Youth organization was necessary in order to be reasonably secure in their prospects for advancement within the socialist culture (Führ, 1992, p. 8). Premilitary training had a place in the curriculum (Führ, 1992, p. 8). And, significantly, teachers had a prominent role in monitoring student activities—noting progress toward outcomes that were ideologically favorable and interceding sometimes heavy-handedly when students behaved unfavorably.

Although the former GDR's unitary 10-year polytechnical school was intended to strengthen the working class orientation and preparation of the GDR's youths, the system's working class ideology had its limits. Rooted in Marxist doctrine, it had been "historically defined and [was] probably outdated by the time it was so rigorously applied"; therefore, it "inevitably clashed with the advanced technological society of the 1970s and 1980s" (Hahn, 1998, p. 152). Thus, the former GDR's curricular challenge with respect to science education is not to simply introduce a specialty for which few instructors had specific up-to-date expertise—a large enough challenge in itself. Instead, the new *Länder*—that is, the "states" or "provinces" of the former GDR now joining the FRG—are faced with the more difficult work of reframing how citizens conceive of the uses of scientific and technological knowledge. As the 21st century approached, an education geared for traditional industrial productivity was arguably becoming outdated. But these were precisely the emphases of "polytechnical science" in the image of East Germany's Leninist ideology. The information age dawning at that time called for high-tech education and required considerably more specialization and instructional differentiation. These emphases simply did not fit well in a proletarian orientation toward productivity.

The opportunity for parents to participate in the education of their children was limited. For instance, there was little parental and student input regarding placements in further education after a student's compulsory attendance in the 10-year polytechnical schools concluded. Until postsecondary levels, little choice existed in the first place, because the polytechnical school was the only option for the vast majority of youths. In the relatively few cases in which divergences did occur at the postsecondary level, state-specified goals were the prevailing criteria by which postsecondary slots were allocated. The other major factors related to placement into advanced educational settings were educational achievement at lower school levels together with evidence of political and ideological leanings sympathetic to socialism.

The two-year, postsecondary *EOS* was controversial because its admissions were selective, and the institution, therefore, embodied an elitist divergence from the uniformity the polytechnical school system was supposed to overcome (Pritchard, 1999). And indeed, these exceptional institutions were innately elitist and specialized—founded in order to provide for the education of an advanced leadership corps. Controversy surrounding the *EOS* pertained to the charge that the children of those in the inner circle communist party were achieving disproportional access to the specialized schools. Both these criticisms exemplify contradictions in the East German educational system—contradictions that, according to Hahn (1998), led to disillusionment and withdrawal among German youths and contributed to a general impatience for change that boiled over by 1989.

The Prevailing System in the FRG and Comparisons with the Former GDR. In West Germany, substantial authority resides with each *Land* ("province" or "state"). This is significant in light of German reunification because the GDR, upon its dissolution, has had to accept the West German system quite entirely. Education is arguably the most pronounced and consequential sphere of influence that the FRG's various *Länder* enjoy.

In the FRG, government officials recognize the central role that education plays as a shaper of culture; this is reflected in the formal identities of the *Land*-level agencies in charge of educational oversight: *Kultusministeria* (ministries of culture). This, again, diverges significantly from the East German pattern of centralized educational directive. Although there is some federal-level framework in the FRG for articulating an overarching educational direction, this comes most prominently in the form of the *Kultusministerkonferenz* (Standing Conference of the [*Land*-level] Ministers of Culture). Thus, even this federal direction is itself supposed to be shaped through the bottom-up compromises among representatives of the various *Länder* rather than through rigid mandates emanating from an autonomous federal agency. Observers such as Stevenson and Nerison-Low (1999) have therefore described issuances of German national educational standards as "suggestions" (p. 48) that the individual *Länder* have the prerogative to shape. Further, teachers in the FRG exercise considerable latitude in shaping the lessons they deliver in their classrooms. This suggests a form of teacher expert authority that contrasts sharply with the sometimes less democratically sensitive and more coercive forms of authority exercised by teachers in the former GDR.

Turning to the roles of parent and students in the FRG, the West German basic law (the FRG's surrogate constitiution drafted following World War II), pursues the notion that "every citizen [has] the right to develop his or her personality freely by choosing the education and profession he or she wants" (Appelt 1990, p. 13). Thus, Germany appears at some level to formalize parental and student input, and this was in any case not a feature of education in the former East. Yet, there is a striking absence of unanimity in impressions regarding the extent to which student choice does in fact prevail in the West (Fossum, 1996). A 1988 publication of the German government emphasized the West German education system's goal of responding to each student's "abilities and interests" (cited in Donohue, Copa, & Pease, 1992, p. M-12). The differences between these two

German policy statements—one highlighting equality of opportunity, and the other, sensitivity to differing abilities and interests—epitomizes the equality-versus-ability tension that both East and West Germany have sought to resolve, each in its own way. In spite of some ambiguity as to whether West German parents and schoolchildren have genuine choice among the types of schools they attend, teachers in the West traditionally have had a prominent role in advising parents on matters of student placement within one of the various educational tracks or emphases the system features. This would suggest a significant degree of professional clout and prerogative for the teachers.

The FRG adheres to the principle of equality of opportunity, manifested partly through the country's regulations on compulsory attendance. Full-time schooling is required of students between the ages of 6 and 16 years, and part-time schooling at minimum for students through age 18 years. This requirement is comparable, then, to the schooling expectations of the former GDR. A particularly striking aspect of the FRG's education system—one that to many international observers is anti-egalitarian—is its three-part secondary school structure. Beginning at about age 10, students leave their homogenous primary-level groupings to continue their schooling in the *Hauptschule*, the *Realschule*, or the *Gymnasium* (McAdams, 1993). The *Hauptschule*, according to official descriptions, constitutes "a shorter and less difficult way towards completion of compulsory full-time attendance at school" (Organization of Economic Cooperation and Development, 1972, p. 59). The student body of the *Gymnasium*, in contrast, generally consists of people bound for the university, and students in the *Realschule* constitute a middle group that pursues various educational and career options (Appelt, 1990).

Thus, officials from German federal and provincial governments (i.e., those of the *Länder*) confirm the relative status accorded to the German *Gymnasium* in an educational policy summary presented to the Organization of Economic Cooperation and Development (1972): "[T]he social prestige associated with schooling at a *Gymnasium*" accounts for "many children being sent by their parents" to those schools (p. 59). Perry (1991) wrote that a student in the German system can always "move up or down the ladder" (p. 46)—a depiction that invites challenging questions about precisely what parent would choose to send their child "down the ladder" to a certain education alternative. Nonetheless, Perry's comment also implies that some choice of school prevails in Germany.

To understand modern-day Germany's situation, one must understand its historical philosophical underpinnings. In harmony with a philosophy of "new humanism"—of which Wilhelm von Humboldt was a leading exemplar—19th-century Germany relegated the vocational aspects of education (Oelkers, 1999). (For a biographical sketch of German philosopher Wilhelm von Humboldt, see pp. 167–168.) At that time, most schools concentrated on general education components and diminished their vocational learning endeavors because institutional recognition depended on it (Nübler, 1991). This foreshadowed continuing tensions in the unified Germany and elsewhere about the relative status of academic educational aims versus applied learning. It is worth stressing that, although the former East Germany and West Germany shared much of the same history, the GDR had instituted different answers to questions about how to balance academic and applied educational emphases. The founding of the East German polytechnical school, namely, affirmed the importance of applied knowledge and work-oriented instruction.

Wilhelm von Humboldt (1767–1835)

Wilhelm von Humboldt and his brother Alexander were among a circle of intellectuals who helped shape a new Europe in the aftermath of the French Revolution. Although the chief interests of the brothers diverged to a high degree, the contributions each made were monumental. The intellectual preoccupations of the younger, Alexander (born in 1769), were primarily in the natural sciences and resulted in discovery of climatic phenomena, observations about acoustic and sonic principles, early compilation of a natural history of Latin America (among many destinations in Alexander's extensive travels), and a host of additional scientific contributions of enduring importance. The interests of the elder brother Wilhelm were, by his own accounts, in the inner life rather than the world outside (Hohendorf, 1993). And Wilhelm's most enduring accomplishments stemmed from his stewardship and transformation of Prussia's educational system (Hohendorf, 1993).

Himself an exemplar of broad German philological study, Wilhelm was an accomplished scholar of linguistics, classics, and history. Wilhelm and his brother were born into the privileged world of the European nobility. Their father, Alexander Georg von Humboldt, had been a gentleman-in-waiting in the court of Friedrich II and is represented in historical descriptions as a "'great friend to other men'...'sociable and a benefactor'" and as a "'man of understanding and good taste'" (see Hohendorf, 1993, p. 665). The boys' zeal for intellectual development owes much to their father's encouragement, and given the testimonials regarding his nature and disposition, it is not surprising that their father's untimely death in 1779 weighed heavily on them, particularly Wilhelm.

Among a number of people contributing most directly to Wilhelm's and his brother's intellectual development, Johann Heirich Campe, who was later associated with the intellectual circle of figures known as the German philanthropic school, served as a tutor in the Humboldt residence first in Potsdam then in Tegel (both near Berlin). And it was Campe who later invited Wilhelm to accompany him on a trip to postrevolutionary Paris—a city animated by widespread political and social experimentation and discourse (Miniter, 1991). This trip made a large impact on Humboldt's political thinking and his theories of education. In particular, Humboldt was critical of a prevailing view in French society that force could be a necessary and justified instrument in reform. In Humboldt's view, force was detrimental to self-development, natural social evolution, and innovative thinking, and rewarded only those who conformed to imposition (Miniter, 1991). These beliefs had great bearing on Humboldt's conviction that education should as much as possible be free from outside interference. Education, he felt, would be most effective when latitude was left to the instructor and students emulate their teachers (Hohendorf, 1993).

Among the many other influential people in Wilhelm's life, Christian Kunth, another tutor, was particularly well organized as an instructor, sensitive to the abilities of Wilhelm and Alexander, and responsive to their intellectual and emotional needs—acting as a surrogate father of sorts for a time upon the death of Alexander Georg. But other influential relationships were cultivated by Humboldt himself, in line with his conviction that learning was best pursued "through a series of free associations" (Miniter, 1991, p. 58). Wilhelm and Alexander, for instance, took advantage of their proximity to Berlin, attending lectures and participating regularly in salon discussions hosted by Henriette Heinz, the wife of a prominent Jewish physician in Berlin. These interactions contributed to Wilhelm's emancipatory and progressive views of both women and Jews (Hohendorf, 1993). Other noteworthy friendships that Wilhelm developed were those with Goethe and Schiller, the foremost German literary figures of the era.

(continued)

(continued)

Humboldt's pervasive impact on education was well out of proportion with both the relatively short 16 months he spent formally in charge of Prussia's education office and the fact that this official service occurred in a single German region (Hahn, 1998). Humboldt ran his education office in a style that is described as decidedly collegial (Hohendorf, 1993) on the one hand, yet possessed of the organizational efficiency and precision of a Prussian general on the other (Miniter, 1991). Wilhelm's additional public service included stints in diplomatic posts in Vienna, London, and Rome, although letters to his wife, Karoline, convey his feeling that foreign service was considerably less important than the work of guiding domestic educational reform (Hohendorf, 1993). Among Wilhelm von Humboldt's most enduring accomplishments was his vision of the vital university, which stressed academic freedom and was incarnated with his founding of the University of Berlin in 1810 (Tenbrock, 1979). The Humboldtian model of the university, with academic freedom as its core value, was at the heart of a broad set of German influences imported into the United States in the mid-19th century. These influences revolutionized the conception and mission of America's higher education institutions, leading to Johns Hopkins University's establishment as America's first "pure" university, Harvard's transformation from liberal arts college to university, and contemporary American universities' enduring emphasis on graduate education (Brubacher & Rudy, 1997). Humboldt's view of elementary education was that it should offer an identical footing for all children, regardless of class or ability. And with regard to secondary-level education, the *Gymnasium* that Wilhelm envisioned and instituted emphasized broad humanistic education and is a model that has retained its influence in Germany and beyond (Kerbo & Strasser, 2000; Raff, 1988).

In 1791, Humboldt wrote, "'The primary law of reality is, educate yourself, and only the second, influence others by what you are'" (cited in Miniter, 1991, p. 59). Here, Humboldt captured in a few words the essence of his lifelong commitments. He worked to ensure individual freedoms and to instill in people the values of responsibility and self-reliance in the belief that attending to the development of the individual was the best way to safeguard society's prosperity (Tenbrock, 1979).

Eastern Reintegration in the West German Mold. German unification in 1990, as Pritchard (1999) has pointed out, was far from a "marriage of equals" (p. 17). Aligning the education systems of the former East and West German states has been a matter of assimilation—East into West—and not one of synthesizing a new whole out of equal components. In the realm of schools and education, as elsewhere in the former GDR, East German society has been substantially forced to adopt West German structures, institutional and classroom practices, and curricular emphases.

Among the most consequential causes for the FRG's domination in the unification process was the East German government's loss of political legitimacy as momentum toward reunification grew (Pritchard, 1999). East Germans' sense of difference had long been acute for various reasons, including the arbitrary nature of Germany's initial division following World War II and East Germany's sheer proximity to the West and Western influences—most conspicuous in the case of Berlin as a West German enclave of sorts within East German borders. By the late 1980s, when Soviet leader Mikhail Gorbachev introduced policies favoring greater self-determination among Eastern European states, support in East Germany for the SED-led regime had severely eroded. As discussions on the potential reunification of Germany progressed, no East German figure or institution possessed the political credibility necessary to counterbalance the FRG's voice.

Time was a second major factor that contributed to East Germany's absorption by the FRG. Nobody had predicted the speed with which the former GDR dissolved and with which negotiations regarding potential unification progressed (Pritchard, 1999). When Hungary opened its Austrian frontier, providing an exit route for East Germans—which reform-minded Soviet leader Gorbachev chose not to stanch—the flow of East Germans crossing into the West reached a rate of about 2,000 people each day. Pritchard (1999) has therefore maintained that "the threat of wholesale destabilization" (p. 11) forced West German Chancellor Helmut Kohl to move rapidly toward formalizing some process for unification lest a state of virtual chaos in the East thwart the chance for unification altogether. By this account, Kohl seized the only readily available framework for unification—namely the FRG's "basic law," which in any case contained provisions enabling possible reunification.

Pritchard (1999) has depicted East Germany's veritable absorption into the West as necessary in spite of its unfairness:

> The Easterners had hoped to bring more of their own values and outlook into the integrated framework than turned out in practice to be the case. The speed of the unification . . . mitigated against gentle handling of East German identity. . . . Broadly speaking, for understandable reasons the East Germans were given the framework that the West thought they ought to have, and this applied in the sphere of education, as elsewhere. (p. 14)

Fair or not, then, the onus for adjustment and accommodation rested on the former East Germans. And teachers from the former GDR continue to adjust to West German structures, institutional and classroom practices, and curricular imperatives that were stipulated by sudden membership in a vastly different social, political, and economic order. The need for a sharply new pattern of educator responsibility and obligation has arisen.

Pritchard's comments regarding East Germany's rapid entry into West Germany capture a sense of ambiguity surrounding the former East Germans' work of reintegration. On one hand, the East Germans' sense of disillusionment with their own country, although not universal (Hahn, 1998), had become widespread prior to the fall of the wall (Pritchard, 1999). Even though external factors were important, East Germans' own impatience for change and their eventual withdrawal of support for the ruling regime constituted a major factor in the momentum toward reunification with the West. To that extent, then, with reunification, the East Germans earned something they had awaited and generally supported.

On the other hand, observers like Hahn (1998) have maintained that it is simplistic to interpret East Germans' rejection of the GDR's leadership and official ideologies as a complete condemnation of all aspects of the ideals that the GDR had pursued. Regarding education in particular, the East Germans had succeeded in important ways in responding to the common set of challenges and legacies with which West Germany has also grappled. The East, with its comprehensive 10-year polytechnical upper school, for example, had confronted the issue of educational elitism that traditional German three-tiered secondary structures tended to reinforce. Quandaries about linking theory and practice are fundamental philosophical issues that continue to challenge all educators, and the East German schools embodied response to this universal problem that was coherent by almost any measure. By stressing students' productive potential, the East German education system injected practicality and a sense of the importance of applying knowledge, and had achieved this orientation toward the relevancy of knowledge within an inherited educational tradition that had tended to exalt academic and theoretical knowledge. Further, the East responded effectively to differences among students, again outside the framework of a formally tracked system.

In addition to the spiritual ambiguity that Pritchard's (1999) observation has captured, a sense of ambivalence confronts the citizens of the new *Länder* pertaining to the degree of the challenge surrounding integration itself. Given the new courses that neighboring countries are charting, is the former GDR better or worse off having the FRG to lean on? In one sense, among the countries in the sphere of the former Soviet Union, East Germany has been advantaged because of the help it gets from the FRG in the form of official financial and social support. The special relationship between the two Germanies, however, has in other ways been all the more difficult because it has substantially amounted to an imposition of "foreign" values and institutions.

Germans in both the former East and the former West refer to the East German uprising and the rejection of the sitting regime as the *Wende* (the "turning"). It is critical to understand that, from the perspective of most former East Germans in particular, the *Wende* did not correspond to the fall of the wall or even to the moment of unification itself. Instead, the *Wende* refers to the collective change of heart in the East that initiated momentum toward those more tangible results (Pritchard, 1999). In that light, it is easier to see that the imposition of a system that is solely West German in character has truly constituted an interruption for the people of the former GDR of a more homegrown social and education overhaul that had been underway. In short, the clamor for change that commenced in 1989 was "characterized by a search for a new as yet unknown democratic socialism," but it was "upstaged by . . . transition to a known model" (Mintrop, 1996, p. 359). In a sense, then, circumstances that unfolded prevented the citizens of the former East from attaining a change for which they had taken enormous risks in advocating. As a result, East German emotions about reunification are generally ambiguous at the least and often tinged with feelings of loss (Pritchard, 1999).

Critiquing Educational Reforms of German Reintegration

What might Frank's (1972) critical constructs of *theoretical adequacy, policy effectiveness,* and *empirical validity* yield when applied to the German case? Turning first to the matter of *theoretical adequacy*, it might be generous to describe the German educational reform as theory driven in the conventional sense. One would expect a union of two parts to produce a distinct new whole. Yet there has been no such synthesis of the school systems of the two Germanies. No legal impetus has compelled the West to adopt elements of the Eastern model that had existed prior to the *Wende*. The East has, in contrast, been confronted with the mandate of absorbing most of what it has inherited from the West. Much criticism regarding the policy effectiveness of this situation, therefore, revolves around the propriety of imposing a relatively raw and unadjusted set of regulations and expectations. It has become axiomatic in the field of comparative education that it is irresponsible to transplant, wholesale, the educational systems and practices of one culture into the schools of another. Yet, because of immense cultural differences that grew out of more than 40 years of political and ideological divergence between the two Germanies, such a transplanting is to a substantial degree exactly what has been attempted.

To be sure, it is not absolutely true that the East has been unable to shape its schools at least partially in the image of the schools of the former GDR. Advocating "greater legal latitude" (p. 7) in order to allow the new *Länder* to "gain an identity of their own" (p. 7), Führ (1992) admonished former West Germans to allow people of the East to become accustomed to "implementing their own educational policy" (p. 7). In this way, the so-called "New *Länder*" will be able to gain its own identity. The FRG's basic law extends to the individual *Länder* the prerogative of controlling education and in shaping school structures.

A turn toward *Land*-level autonomy and away from rigid uniformity and national-level centralization is most evident in the differences among the New *Länder* in the ways they have adapted the tracked secondary school structure described earlier (Führ, 1992). To illustrate, in the *Land* of Brandenburg, which leans toward viewpoints sympathetic to socialism, secondary structures that have emerged put into place an elite *Gymnasium* and a somewhat less elite institution known as the *Regelschule* while doing away with the low status *Hauptshule*. Brandenburg, like left-leaning Western *Länder*, maintains a robust comprehensive school system that hearkens at least to some extent back to the unified polytechnical school of the GDR, which drew virtually all East German students together for pursuit of the same curriculum. These examples of East German adaptation demonstrate that there has not been a complete *tabula rasa*. Meanwhile, right-leaning Thuringia has endorsed and adopted three-tier secondary school structures that are most like the traditional model promoted especially in conservative Western *Länder* such as the Rheinland-Palitanate (Führ, 1992, 1997).

In terms of *empirical validity*, research on postunification German education reform has been limited because East Germany was a closed society. It has, therefore, been difficult to create with confidence an accurate baseline profile of the pre-reform education system. Further, the speed with which the former GDR evaporated and with which its constituent parts were absorbed into the FRG has also had the effect of limiting attempts to profile the East in order to track the reform's impact. In addition, the reform effort—given its immensity and complexity—continues. Accordingly, some of the most fruitful and interesting research has used case study approaches and has focused often on the attitudes of teachers, parents, and students in the GDR. Mintrop (1999), for example, has gathered the perspectives of teachers regarding their responses to specific elements of the new system, such as the tracked structure and the new Western content. Neather (2000) used similar approaches in documenting that a mélange of anticipation and disappointment continues to characterize the everyday experiences of many of the former GDR teachers. In general, this research has suggested that the policy of reform has assumed a sink-or-swim mentality in prescribing change.

In terms of *policy effectiveness*, the reform effort implemented in the former East has been insensitive to certain aspects that might have been better accommodated through a more purposeful policy effort (Phillips, 2000). Again, timing—the imperative of deploying some strategy quickly—mediated against that sort of purposefulness (Pritchard, 1999). Some, however, question the extent to which there was volition in the West to consider a more accommodative policy as an alternative to the policy that was substantially imposed (Phillips, 2000). A barrage of challenges dealing with staffing issues surround the reform effort. As of 1997, there were in the classrooms of the New *Länder* about 160,000 teachers whose training preceded the dissolution of the former GDR (Führ, 1997). About 29,000 teachers lost their jobs, particularly in specialties such as citizenship. But subjects like history and politics were also deemed particularly susceptible to "ideological contamination." For the East Germans, this marks a second mass purging of teachers, since, in the years following World War II, the occupying powers in both the Soviet zone and the Western zones of Germany undertook denazification as a major goal. As in the wake of reunification, educational reform and realignment in the postwar era constituted in large part the removal of teachers whose connections, activities, and classroom foci were deemed suspect.

Different specialties fell from grace for less ideological reasons. Because Russian was the dominant second language prior to reintegration, for instance, teachers of Russian had been in steady demand. Major retraining initiatives implemented after 1990 focused on producing more teachers of English and French, which, with unification, gained instant cache as preferred second languages (Führ, 1997; Pritchard, 1999). Evidence of the prevalence of English as the favored second language in the FRG is profuse. Universities in Germany sometimes offer degree programs using English as the language of instruction, in some cases allowing dissertations to be prepared in English. Documents pertaining to earned degrees can, on the request of students, be issued in English. This is evidence, too, of a heightening degree of internationalization in Germany. Accordingly, one focus of the immense retraining effort that has occurred in the New *Länder* has been on teaching Russian teachers how to teach English (Pritchard, 1999).

Other challenges associated with building an ample and capable teaching force have revolved around the unfamiliar tasks associated with adapting to the tracked, differentiated secondary structure. This leads to pronounced problems relating to sheer numbers: Where once a single polytechnical school existed, there is now a set of more particularly conceived secondary schools. In Brandenburg, for instance, to pursue an example provided previously, a community must provide a *Gymnasium*, a *Regelschule*, and a comprehensive school at the secondary level (Führ, 1992). Because there are significant overlaps in the curricula that each of these schools offer, there has been considerable strain in finding qualified staff to cover all the resulting needs. Yet the curricular overlaps are not complete among these different forms of schools, nor are the instructional approaches that distinguish one sort of institution from the next. There is, therefore, an issue of specialization and particular preparation that has made the personnel issues harder to resolve.

Exacerbating the general personnel problem is the translation of credentials earned in the pre-unification East. Pritchard (1999), for instance, has noted that some of the highest qualifications available under the GDR's educational system are presently not deemed acceptable by the standards of the FRG. And a further confounding problem relates to the unpredicted decline in the birthrate in the New *Länder*. Any hard-won stability in overcoming staffing problems related to the teacher shortages could be precarious—ultimately threatened by the specter of teacher surpluses as the flow of children into and through the pipeline diminishes. Although these policy quandaries continue to require attention, many of the pressing issues are, in fairness, a function more of the unique circumstances surrounding this unusual reform context than they are attributable to poor policy conception. For a comparison of geophysical and economic factors influencing education in England and Germany, see the Points of Convergence box (Figure 5.3).

FIGURE 5.3

Points of Convergence

ENGLAND	Geography and educational consequences	GERMANY
Aspect: England is part of an island nation—an attribute that has influenced the country's history, politics, and development for millennia. This national trait has helped shape policies and behaviors that, while by no means isolationist or withdrawn, remain cautious and protective. The issue of European integration is complicated to navigate on account of this in part. **Response:** The United Kingdom, although a supportive and engaged member of the European Union (EU), has opted out of full participation in the structures of monetary union, for instance. **Consequence:** Education is a topic of special interest in European Union nations because of issues such as transferability and recognition of credentials among EU members. Like Germany and the other members of the EU, the United Kingdom's citizens and government are trying to reconcile the competing interests of retaining national autonomy while reaping the fullest possible benefit from the economic participation and security in the EU. To what extent should schools pursue their traditional roles of building and reflecting national identity? In what ways should schools support and reinforce a sense of citizenship within a collective European society? The United Kingdom's position epitomizes this sense of ambiguity, providing a case in point of how a balance might be achieved in negotiating this dual identity.	Geography and educational consequences How have geophysical realities influenced education?	**Aspect:** Precedents for German national identity date at least to Charlemagne, first Holy Roman Emperor of the German Nations, crowned 800 AD. But Germany was a shifting patchwork of principalities until the early 20th century. Nationalism culminated during the Nazi regime, at which time education was centrally controlled. **Response:** Following World War II, Allied forces oversaw the creation of 16 *Länder*—11 in the West and 5 in the East. These *Länder* (i.e., "provinces" or "states") were devised partially with older historical identity in mind, and considerable power was vested in each of the *Länder* in order to subdue nationalism and enable Allied oversight and management. **Consequence:** The locus of governance in Germany's education system remains at the *Land* level. Due to differences in political sensibilities, tradition, and other regional influences, the German educational system is characterized by significant variation among the *Länder* in terms of the instructional calendar, age-grade assignments, basic policies, and school structures, especially at the secondary level.

ETHICS AND THE ENGLISH AND GERMAN REFORMS

In addition to Frank's (1972) framework of a system for considering education reforms, the construct *ethical merit* (Paige, 1995) is especially appropriate in such a critique when the reform emanates primarily outside the environment reformed. This has certainly been true of the former GDR's adoption of the FRG's educational practices. In important respects, England's ERA, which was politically motivated and centrally conceived, was a reform introduced to the country's schools and not developed within them. Several ethical concerns emerge from each case and yield some comparisons between England and Germany. Also, this commentary on ethical considerations of the reforms allows several summary observations about the tension between authority and accountability.

Proponents of England's ERA were unabashed about the plan's heavy reliance on market forces as the key to the policy's potential success. Those supporters dismissed objections about extending the market philosophy to the realm of education on the grounds that such resistance was merely partisan contention. The implications of such a strong reliance on market dynamics are, however, severe. In a pure market, the theory goes, competitors for a certain clientele will range from those who are very successful to those that are forced from the arena because of their inability to provide a product that their potential clients value. In short, there are winners and losers: Markets embrace a zero-sum scenario to this extent. And this prompts the question of how the ERA measured up to the task of fairly educating all of England's children—one of its declared goals—in a system that seems to pivot on sorting and differentiating between good schools and lesser schools. If at least some spirit of egalitarianism is valuable in progressive democracies, then quality must be judged at least partially in terms of a school system's consistency. There are disparities implicit in a system in which quality is, instead, gauged in terms of relative strength or comparative excellence—as is the supreme assumption of the pure market or of any other competition-based system. Is it ethical for the government to endorse a system that will arguably produce and sustain lower-quality institutions side by side with high-quality institutions? In general, then, it seems questionable that the 1988 reform plan could encourage the kind of equitable access it heralded.

This tension between elitism and egalitarianism invites some comparison with Germany's reform experience. True, the circumstances surrounding Germany's school reforms differ widely from England's in terms of root causes. However, a marked difference between the schools of the GDR and those of the West revolves around the ways each system responded structurally to imperatives of equality of educational experience, on the one hand, or ability differentiation, on the other. In the GDR, the 10-year polytechnical school had embodied the former ideal, yet the polytechnical model received little or no serious attention as a plausible basic institution. Arguably, "[w]ith the political imperatives of its curricular provision removed, it could still have provided an educationally defensible model" (Phillips, 2000, p. 9) during the inception of Germany's reforms. Such a model—called the "comprehensive high school"—exists, after all, in the United States (Donohue, Copa, & Pease, 1992). And because of years of debate in West Germany about the fairness of the system of three tracked secondary institutions, the *Gesamtschule* (meaning literally the "collected school" but more universally translated simply as "comprehensive school") emerged as an alternative and had grown in favor, particularly in the northern *Länder* long efore reunification. By abandoning any consideration of the similarities between the polytechnicals and the *Gesamtschule*, the West's implicit statement to the teachers and the citizens of the former East was "that institutionalized equality of treatment of the pupil population was not acceptable" (Phillips, 2000, p. 9). Though answers do not come easily, societies must question their tolerance for structural inequalities. Arguably, more such questioning could have enriched the results of both the English and the German reforms.

Regarding the authority and accountability tension, the ethical ramifications of the ERA as implemented are particularly considerable in terms of the brand of accountability it envisions. Authentic "public" choice presumes the whole society's participation and mutual accountability (Feintuck, 1994). However, because it mandates nationalized curriculum, the ERA reduces parental participation to the mere choice of schools. "Except for those in the privileged sectors of fee-paying schools," one commentator observed, "freedom of choice is to be dramatically curtailed for schools, teachers, parents, and pupils" (Hughes et al., 1994, p. 10). A kindred source of ethical concern regarding the ERA is the extent to which the policy fails to address the individual interests and potential of British students. Parents questioned about the ERA expressed their concern that anything not recognized as "central" within the national curriculum would be "swept under the carpet" (Hughes et al., 1994, p. 132), and the reform plan's reliance on a set program of instruction, critics contended, discarded the individualized attention that British schoolchildren had received under the traditional system (McAdams, 1993). Parents also feared that the prescribed curriculum in tandem with the nationalized assessments would produce schools that emphasize fact-centered rote learning. "I hope it doesn't get parrot fashion," said one British mother. "[Children] need basics but to develop in their own way" (Hughes et al., 1994, p. 130).

Germany's reform plan, in contrast, did not overtly promote parental input in the same way that England's government did in its press for market-driven choice measures. But like the ERA, the German educational reform reflects some clashing purposes with regard to the vision of participation and engagement it should presumably reinforce. Most importantly, the reforms are a product of large-scale democratization and should therefore support the creation of a more pluralistic and participatory future. But, on the contrary, the German reform mandate has been conspicuously top-down and authoritarian. Given the network of obligation that Burgess (1992) attributed to functional democratic societies, the vision of accountability upon which the German reform policies are forged seems simplistic and ill-suited to the occasion. The same is even more true of the ERA.

Among the ERA's most serious ethical shortcomings involves the reform's treatment of teachers. Torrance (1993) objected to the practical impossibility of teaching the amount of material that the government dictates. Democracy itself has moral underpinnings based on consent of the governed. It relies, therefore, on broad participation in decisions. Though this participation can be arduous, its inclusiveness is supposed to produce a more durable course of action because of the sense of investment it nurtures among the governed. Some feel the British government's mandated curriculum under the ERA exploits the historically low status of the country's teachers. In this light, a more grievous shortcoming of the ERA is its deprofessionalizing effects on teaching (Pimm & Selinger, 1995). British teachers, Feintuck (1994) has asserted, have long been underpaid and undervalued—like their American counterparts—and have therefore derived the greatest share of their satisfaction from their professional prerogative in the classroom. The ERA process, however, was typified by political maneuvering rather than by dialogue, and the voices of professional educators were conspicuous in their absence (Hughes et al., 1994). The product is a curriculum for which the concerned teachers feel little ownership and within which they feel little instructional leeway (McAdams, 1993).

As to the German case, one ethical concern, as Mintrop (1996) has noted, is related to the sense of overload that teachers have about their new circumstances. East German teachers had been accustomed to considerable formal authority over their students, but the generally laudable freedoms they now enjoy paradoxically leave teachers feeling more powerless. This, Mintrop (1999) has concluded, is because teachers in the New *Länder* have not had time to replace the authority they once held as custodians of the state—a teacher role that had been clear in the former GDR. Their challenge is to supplant that lost authority with a new genre of authority based on professional expertise. But this has been hampered for many, because of the dominant continuing view that teaching in the GDR had consisted purely of ideological indoctrination. Teachers from the former GDR very often encounter the disqualification of their pedagogical skills and merits (Streitweiser, 2000). Nor are teachers able to make the claims to authority of other stakeholders, most notably students and their parents: "Teachers . . . are distressed by what the state does to them and what they cannot do to students and parents anymore—and what the latter two groups can now do to them" (Mintrop, 1996, p. 276).

Paradoxically, the teachers in the former East are in some pronounced respects in greater control—in terms, for instance, of professional duties such as curriculum selection and lesson planning. Yet, familiar as they are with receiving well-defined curricular direction from their government, the former GDR's teachers feel abandoned to some extent. Mintrop (1996) has noted teachers' tendency to recoil from some professional responsibilities, to avoid processing the implications of their past and present circumstances, and to be unable to seize control of the new authority available to them. Some have cautioned that, under a "parentocracy" (Hughes et al., 1994, p. 12), the wealth and wishes of parents are more important than the effort and ability of the students. In addition, parental interests do not always coincide with the best interests of students (Feintuck, 1994). In England, the ERA also does not account for this fact.

Former United States president Ronald Reagan once reportedly commented that "'choice works, and it works with a vengeance'" (Hughes et al., 1994, p. 79). This remark has negative implications for the ethics underlying choice reforms. In particular, the prevailing rhetoric about choice seems, for all its bluster, to overlook lessons about the relationship between authority and accountability in education. A "culture of surveillance" (Poulson, 1998, p. 431) seems to propel the typical accountability-based school reform, as in the case of the British ERA. Not surprisingly, teachers in Germany and England alike conveyed little enthusiasm for their circumstances, which they had little role in shaping. And the case of England in particular suggests that authentic accountability connotes a commitment to fulfill obligations even when nobody is watching and not compliance with procedures that one fulfills *because* someone is watching. Balance between authority and accountability is paramount. "Teacher power is an absolute precondition for teacher accountability" (Clabaugh, 2001, p. 62). What is at stake if no such balance exists? Teachers, likely, will withdraw from their work by burning out or by cynically accepting the narrowed and deprofessionalized world offered to them. One exasperated American educator complains about developments in the United States that are quite comparable to the British case, noting that teachers are now given "a number that tells [them] clearly the curriculum is, quite simply, the tests. Predictably educators are screaming. . . . But maybe we should shut up and listen. [The governor] has done something we've needed for a long time: he has defined our job for us. . . . We could [say], 'The governor has spoken . . . and we will obey. We will raise the test scores. That is our job. You raise the children. That's yours" (Carpenter, 2000, p. 14).

This chapter has addressed the issue of educator accountability and authority in the context of England and Germany. The next chapter explores the differing orientations to teacher professionalism and their subsequent impacts on teacher autonomy and professional development for Japanese and American educators.

Sustaining Reflection

- Think of examples in your own country of equalized instruction, whereby steps are taken to ensure that all participants have the same experiences and treatments. Think of examples of differentiated instruction. What are the implications of these contrasting circumstances in terms of teacher roles and accountability?

- List several determinate and several indeterminate teaching tasks you have observed recently.

- A British office circulated a statement that read, "Parents know best the needs of their children—certainly better than most educational theorists or administrators, better even than our mostly excellent teachers" (Hughes et al., 1994, p. 12). Do you agree or disagree with this perspective? What can you conclude about the vision of authority behind this statement?

References

Albornoz, O. (1991). Autonomy and accountability in higher education. *Prospects [Paris], 21*(2), 204–213.

Appelt, D. (1990). *Education in Bavaria* (D. Appelt and A. Nix, Trans.). Geiselhöring, Germany: Druckerei Klaus Fischer.

Brubacher, J. S., & Rudy, W. (1997). *Higher education in transition* (4th ed.). New Brunswick, NJ: Transaction.

Burgess, T. (1992). Accountability with confidence. In T. Burgess (Ed.), *Accountability in schools* (pp. 3–14). Essex, UK: Longman.

Carl, J. (1994). Parental choice as national policy in England and the U.S. *Comparative Education Review, 38*(3), 294–322.

Carpenter, W. (2000). The other side of dedication. *Educational Horizons, 79*(1), 13–15.

Chitty, C. (1989). *Towards a new education system: The victory of the new right?* Sussex, UK: The Falmer Press.

Chubb, J. E., & Moe, T. M. (1992). *A lesson in school reform from Great Britain*. Washington, DC: Brookings Institution.

Clabaugh, G. T. (2001). The other side of dedication. *Educational Horizons, 79*(2), 60–62.

Clabaugh, G. T., & Rozycki, E. G. (1990). *Understanding schools: The foundations of education*. New York: Harper Row.

Connolly, P., & Troyna, B. (Eds.). (1998). *Researching racism in education: Politics, theory, and practice*. Buckingham, UK: Open University Press.

Cordingley, P., & Kogan, M. (1993). *In support of education: Governing the reformed system*. London, UK: Jessica Kingsley Publishers.

Donohue, T. R., Copa, G. H., & Pease, V. H. (1992). The comprehensive high school: An international perspective. In G. H. Copa and V. H. Pease (Eds.), *New designs for the comprehensive high school: Volume II, working papers* (pp. M-1–M-56). Berkeley, CA: National Center for Research in Vocational Education.

Education Reform Act of 1988. (1988). London, UK: HMSO.

Education Reform in Britain. (1989). London, UK: DES.

Fägerlind, I., & Saha, L. J. (1989). *Education and national development* (2nd ed.). Oxford, UK: Pergamon.

Feintuck, M. (1994). *Accountability and school change*. Buckingham, UK: Open University Press.

Fishman, S., & Martin L. (1987). *Estranged twins*. New York, NY: Praeger.

Fossum, P. R. (1996). Implementing school-to-work reform policy: Three case studies in youth apprenticeship. *Dissertation Abstracts International, 57*, 11A (University Microfilms No. 9711407).

Frank, A. G. (1972). Sociology of development and underdevelopment of sociology. In J. D. Cockroft et al. (Eds.), *Dependence and underdevelopment: Latin America's political economy* (pp. 321–397). Garden City, NY: Anchor.

Führ, C. (1992). *On the education system of the five new Länder of the Federal Republic of Germany*. Bonn, Germany: Internationes.

Führ, C. (1997). *The German education system since 1945: Outlines and problems*. Bonn, Germany: Internationes.

Gorard, S. (2000). For England, see Wales. In D. Phillips (Ed.), *The education systems of the United Kingdom* (pp. 29–44). Oxford, UK: Symposium.

Graham, D. (1993). The first three national curricula and the millennium. *Educational Review, 45*(2), 119–124.

Hahn, H.-J. (1998). *Education and society in Germany*. Oxford, UK: Berg.

Hearnden, A. (1974). *Education and the two Germanies*. Oxford, UK: Basil Blackwell.

Hobsbawm, E. J. (1999). *Industry and empire: From 1750 to the present day*. London, UK: Weidenfeld and Hicholson.

Hohendorf, G. (1993). Wilhelm von Humboldt: 1767–1835. *Prospects: The Quarterly Review of Comparative Education, 23*(3–4), 665–676.

Hughes, M., Wikeley, F., & Nash, T. (1994). *Parents and their children's schools*. Oxford, UK: Blackwell.

Kerbo, H. R., & Strasser, H. (2000). *Modern Germany*. Boston, MA: McGraw-Hill.

Lawton, D. (1993). Political parties, ideology, and the national curriculum. *Educational Review, 45*(2), 111–118.

Macpherson, R. J. S. (Ed.) (1998). *The politics of accountability: Educative and international perspectives*. The 1997 Yearbook of the Politics of Education Association. Thousand Oaks, CA: Corwin.

McAdams, R. P. (1993). *Lessons from abroad: How other countries educate their children*. Lancaster, PA: Technomic.

McLean, M. (1993). The politics of curriculum in European perspective. *Educational Review, 45*(2), 125–135.

Miller, H. D. R. & Ginsburg, M. B. (1991). Restructuring education and the state in England. In M. B. Ginsburg (Ed.), *Understanding educational reform in global context* (pp. 49–75). New York, NY: Garland.

Miniter, R. (1991). Wilhelm von Humboldt: German classical liberal. *The Freeman, 41*(2), 57–63.

Mintrop, H. (1996). Teachers and changing authority patterns in Eastern German schools. *Comparative Education Review, 40*(4), 358–376.

Mintrop, H. (1999). Changing core beliefs and practices through systemic reform: The case of Germany after the fall of socialism. *Educational Evaluation and Policy Analysis, 21*(3), 271–296.

Neather, E. J. (2000). Change and continuity in education after the *Wende*. In D. Phillips (Ed.), *Education in Germany since unification* (pp. 13–36). Oxford, UK: Symposium.

Nübler, I. (1991). *Limits to change in training systems: The case of Germany*. Geneva: International Labor Office. (ERIC Document Reproduction Service No. 337661)

Oelkers, J. (1999). The origin of the concept of "Allgemeinbildung" in eighteenth century Germany. *Studies in Philosophy and Education, 18*(1–2), 25–41.

Organization for Economic Cooperation and Development. (1972). *Educational policy and planning: Germany*. Paris, France: OECD.

Ouston, J., Fidler, B., & Earley, P. (1998). The educational accountability of schools in England and Wales. In R. J. S. Macpherson (Ed.), *The politics of accountability: Educative and international perspectives* (pp. 107–119). The 1997 Yearbook of the Politics of Education Association. Thousand Oaks, CA: Corwin.

Paige, R. M. (1995). *Criteria for assessing school reform and innovation*. Unpublished instructional document, University of Minnesota, Minneapolis.

Perry, R. L. (1991). The German apprenticeship system: Everybody's talking about it, but is it the right model for America? *Vocational Education Journal, 66*(5), 30–31.

Phillips, D. (2000). The legacy of unification. In D. Phillips (Ed.), *Education in Germany since unification* (pp. 7–12). Oxford, UK: Symposium.

Pimm, D., & Selinger, M. (1995). The commodification of teaching: Teacher education in England. In M. F. Wideen & P. P. Grimmett (Eds.), *Changing times in teacher education: Restructuring or reconceptualization?* (pp. 47–66). Washington, DC: Falmer.

Pincoffs, E. L. (1973). Educational accountability. *Studies in Philosophy and Education, 8*(2), 131–145.

Poulson, L. (1998). Accountability, teacher professionalism, and education reform in England. *Teacher Development, 2*(3), 419–432.

Pritchard, R. M. O. (1999). *Reconstructing education: East German schools and universities after unification*. New York, NY: Berghahn Books.

Raff, D. (1988). *A history of Germany: From the medieval empire to the present*. Hamburg, Germany: Berg.

Raffe, D. (2000). Investigating the education systems of the United Kingdom. In D. Phillips (Ed.), *The education systems of the United Kingdom* (pp. 9–28). Oxford, UK: Symposium.

Simey, M. (1985). *Government by consent: The principles and practice of accountability in local government*. London, UK: Bedford Square Press.

Stevenson, H. W. (1998). Guarding teachers' time: Other countries do. We should, too. *Education Week, 18*(3), 32.

Stevenson, H. W., & Nerison-Low, R. (1999). *To sum it up: Case studies of education in Germany, Japan, and the United States*. Washington, DC: U.S. Department of Education, Office of Educational Research and Improvement, National Institute on Student Achievement, Curriculum, and Assessment.

Streitweiser, B. T. (2000). Memory and judgment: How East German schools and teachers have been regarded in the post-unification decade. In D. Phillips (Ed.), *Education in Germany since unification* (pp. 57–80). Oxford, UK: Symposium.

Strike, K. (1990). The ethics of educational evaluation. In J. Millman, & L. Darling-Hammond (Eds.), *The new handbook of teacher evaluation* (pp. 356–373). Newbury Park, CA: Sage.

Tenbrock, R.-H. (1979). *A history of Germany* [trans. P. J. Dine]. Munich, Germany: Max Hueber.

Torrance, H. (1993). Combining measurement driven instruction with authentic assessment. *Educational Evaluation and Policy Analysis, 15*(1), 81–90.

Wegner, G.P. (in press). *Anti-semitism and schooling unde the Third Reich*. New York, NY: RoutledgeFalmer.

Weiler, H. N., Mintrop, H., & Fuhrman, E. (1996). *Educational change and social transformation: Teachers, schools, and universities in eastern Germany*. London, UK: Falmer.

Willis, P. (1977). *Learning to labour: How working class kids get working class jobs*. New York, NY: Columbia University Press.

Chapter 6

Teacher Professionalism

Focusing Questions

- What is professionalism? How do cultural values affect teacher professionalism?

- How do teachers' views of the public and private spheres influence their work and roles? What responsibilities do teachers have to the public? When are the public's demands an infringement on teachers' professionalism?

- What is the appropriate balance between state control and teacher autonomy in educational decision making?

- How do the socializing practices in the teaching profession foster or limit teachers' professional growth and development?

INTRODUCTION

Recent reports of Asian student achievement have caused soul searching among non-Asian societies regarding the quality of their professional educators. Yet any consideration of teacher quality must begin with exploration into the nature of professionalism or risk sidestepping an important topic. Arguably, *professionalism* describes the relationship between a given society and a certain set of workers. Teacher professionalism is reflected when a society vests authority in teachers, who accept responsibility for rendering particular expertise and service. Teacher professionalism, however, involves more than teaching subjects or implementing instructional methods and activities. Teacher professionalism speaks to the deeper understanding that teachers possess about how classrooms and schools are structured, why they are structured in particular ways, and how teaching and learning might be structured differently to better meet the needs of students and societies.

According to Delpit (1995), "'We all interpret behaviors, information, and situations through our own cultural lenses; these lenses operate involuntarily, below the level of conscious awareness, making it seem that our own view is simply 'the way it is'" (cited in Darling-Hammond, 2000, p. 151). Comparative inquiry into teaching—examining how people in other places orchestrate teaching and learning—provides a way for teachers to become more familiar with their own perspectives and biases. Thus, comparative perspective taking is a mechanism for enlarging teachers' professional understanding. Because looking outward enables professionals to consider their own educational practices (Stevenson, 1998), such comparative inquiry can lead to informed schooling practice.

In this chapter we explore teacher professionalism in terms of factors that can reinforce or hinder teachers' professional legitimacy and consider the complex relationship between teacher authority and responsibility. Toward this end, we draw on the political and sociocultural dimensions to ascertain their impact on both teacher professionalism and the teaching–learning process in Japan and the United States.

EXPLORATION INTO THE NATURE OF TEACHER PROFESSIONALISM

The terms *professionalization* and *professionalism* are often used interchangeably. Like Ornstein and Levine (1997), we associate **professionalization** with entry requirements, licensing practices, national certification for teachers, and the like, whereas **professionalism** refers to the particular expertise, authority, and autonomy of teachers "to determine their work conditions and their effectiveness as teachers" (p. 40). Herbst (1989) has reinforced this definition by concluding that professionalism entails not only the teacher's obligation to educate the young, but a recognition by others—within and outside the profession—of the teacher's right to decide his or her tasks in the classroom.

Teaching, like other professions, embodies "a set of shared norms, values, taken-for-granted assumptions and a sense of mission that frame the patterns of the members' work activities" (Okano & Tsuchiya, 1999, p. 172). Although the characteristics that distinguish professionals from nonprofessionals have been discussed elsewhere by various scholars (Ornstein & Levine, 1997; Ryan & Cooper, 1998; Soder, 1986), a **professional** is commonly understood as one who renders a public service that requires the use of particular intellectual skills that are developed through a period of specialized training. In exchange for assuming responsibility for the decisions made and actions executed, the professional is afforded autonomy and authority to render that service. Thus, "a teacher's autonomy," as Ryan and Cooper (1998) have asserted, "is accompanied by a responsibility to teach effectively" (p. 512).

Claims For and Against Teaching as a Profession

Because education is viewed as important to personal fulfillment and societal development, two arguments have been levied to claim teaching as a profession. First, teachers are those persons officially assigned responsibility for educating the young so that they can participate in their culture; hence, the teacher has an important role in equipping students with skills that will enable them to think, reason, and manipulate ideas (Ryan & Cooper, 1998). Second, this responsibility to educate the young entails a degree of personal control over what is to be taught, how it will be taught, and in what sequence and at what rate. In reference to the United States, there are several areas in which teaching does not measure up to other professions, such as law and medicine. Ornstein and Levine (1997) have identified these areas in terms of knowledge, control and autonomy, and prestige. Specifically, they argue that teaching lacks a defined body of knowledge, as well as high status; moreover, teachers lack control and autonomy in deciding what is best for students' learning.

Ryan and Cooper (1998) have identified several reasons why the claim for teaching as a profession in the United States is problematic. First, the authors state that children have many teachers and that their learning takes place outside, as well as inside, school. For example, children learn from communication technologies, media, neighbors, peers, and family members. Second, Ryan and Cooper have asserted that teachers experience numerous constraints on their autonomy. To illustrate, teachers' decision making is controlled by local boards of education or, increasingly, by state and even federally mandated educational policies. Moreover, teachers often teach curriculum that they do not choose or that was developed by individuals who are not teachers. Third, in the United States, teachers are only minimally involved in professional organizations and activities, and they are often relatively low paid when compared with their counterparts in several other industrialized countries.

Orientations to Teacher Professionalism

Hoyle (1980) has contributed significantly to the discussion on professionalism by posing two orientations of teacher professionalism: *restricted* and *extended professionality*. According to Hoyle, *restricted professionality* describes a teacher who is primarily concerned with the day-to-day aspects of teaching, operates in an autonomous manner in the classroom, and views good teaching as being about the delivery of subject content. In contrast, *extended professionality*, for Hoyle, describes a teacher who sees his or her responsibility extend beyond the classroom to include collaboration with other colleagues in joint decision making and in evaluating quality teaching. "Such a person emphasizes professional cooperation and desires considerable involvement in activities at the school level" (van den Berg & Ros, 1999, p. 885).

The work of Hargreaves and Goodson (1996) has furthered the discussion by not casting professionalism as a choice between disparate dichotomies. They identify professionalism as classical, flexible, practical, extended, and complex, providing deeper insights about how teachers view their work and roles. *Classical professionalism*, according to Hargreaves and Goodson, refers to teachers' attempts to use models from the medical and legal professions to claim teaching as a profession. The authors have argued that this is an inappropriate comparison because different knowledge bases and exclusivity are attached to these professions. As Hargreaves and Goodson have explained, teachers' attempts "to model themselves too closely upon the classical professionals, may well have led them to embark upon a road of attempted professionalisation rather than of professionalism" (cited in Wright & Bottery, 1997, p. 250).

Flexible professionalism, as identified by Hargreaves and Goodson (1996), refers to the practical expertise of teachers that emerges from the day-to-day realities in their classrooms and communities, as opposed to practical and technical expertise grounded in scientific inquiry. A problem with this view of professionalism is that it may reinforce a narrow view of teaching—one connected to local communities—as opposed to the view that teaching is but one part of larger influences affecting education. As Wright and Bottery (1997) have explained, centralized, technically driven reforms focused on accountability could create an environment in which teachers are "not required to think too much or too deeply about the larger, social, moral and political issues, which a richer conception of professionalism would commit them to" (p. 251). This preoccupation with technical competencies, as opposed to broader issues of a social and moral kind, could contribute to depoliticized teaching and result in attempts by those outside the profession to direct and control the thinking of teachers.

Practical professionalism refers to teachers' practical knowledge and the judgments they hold about their work and roles (Hargreaves & Goodson, 1996). In this view, reflection is seen as central to teachers' expertise; however, attention to teachers' craft knowledge, to the exclusion of other knowledge bases, "may actually redirect teachers' work away from broader moral and social projects and commitments" (Hargreaves & Goodson, 1996, p. 13). The danger in this scenario, according to the authors, is that teachers are susceptible to concentrating on the more narrow aspects of their work, such as pedagogical strategies and technical skills, rather than exercising judgment on larger issues, such as curricular concerns.

Extended professionalism, for Hargreaves and Goodson (1996), emphasizes teachers' work as collaborators on whole-school policies, as found in Hoyle's (1980) concept of extended professionality. The caveat in this conception of professionalism is that, although teachers might be engaged in joint decision making at the school level, they might only be reacting to decisions about curriculum and schooling being made from those wielding power that is above and beyond the school. As Hargreaves and Goodson (1996) have explained, "extended professionalism often does turn into a kind of *distended professionalism*, where teachers are stretched so far by their new responsibilities they almost tear apart with the workload and strain" (p. 17).

Finally, *complex professionalism* describes the increasing degrees of complexity that characterize teachers' tasks; consequently, the teaching profession should be evaluated on the basis of "the complexity of the work tasks that comprise them" (Hargreaves & Goodson, 1996, p. 18). The authors have identified that the rationale behind this approach is based on globalization; for citizens to function in an increasingly complex environment, they also must have a complex set of cooperative learning, problem-solving, and thinking skills. Teachers, therefore, must be equipped with these skills in order to teach them effectively to their students. Hargreaves and Goodson (1996) have reasoned "that work complexity may be a vital key to improving teacher professionalism. It, rather than scientific claims to esoteric knowledge and specialized technologies, constitutes the strongest case for prolonging the period of professional preparation" (p. 18).

What is certain is that we cannot consider teacher professionalism "from a place that stands outside the social, political, and cultural dilemmas always facing teacher education" (Barnard, Muthwa-Kuehn, & Grimmett, 1997, p. 894). In other words, the authors suggest that teachers' work and roles are situated and embedded in multiple contexts. Yet, "teachers, like their own teachers before them, are gripped by the 'problem of familiarity.' They have spent many years as students in the work context" (Barnard et al., 1997, p. 901). Comparative perspective taking, therefore, provides a way for teachers and aspiring teachers to broaden their view and to see teacher professionalism from another cultural perspective in order to counteract the problem of familiarity. This provides a mechanism for reappraising in a new light the interrelated factors that reinforce or hinder teacher professionalism. We now turn toward an examination of these factors, or signals of legitimacy.

SIGNALS OF LEGITIMACY: FACTORS THAT REINFORCE TEACHER PROFESSIONALISM

There are a number of interrelated factors that signal the degree to which a profession is viewed as legitimate by society. Citizens surrender their children to the state based on the rationale that such surrender is for the public good. Children are entrusted to educational workers who assume an in *loco parentis* role in the schools; that is, teachers are expected to keep children from harm and provide them with the knowledge, skills, and dispositions valued by society. Teachers are called on, therefore, to provide a certain kind of expertise and service to society. Over time, the society either values or devalues the particular expertise and service provided by its educational workers. This public valuing of schooling is linked to a legitimation of the teaching profession, as evidenced by the deference and respect accorded to teachers by members of the powerful social classes (Soder, 1986). In effect, teacher knowledge and responsibility "must be coupled with cultural authority—authority gained through external legitimacy" (p. 26). Factors such as social contract and societal support, public valuing of education, and teachers' prestige and status signal the degree to which teaching is viewed as a legitimate profession by a society.

Social Contract and Societal Support

In Japan, the notion of education as a social contract with mutual obligation is reinforced through societal expectations and cultural respect for learning (LeTendre, 1999a). "Japanese teachers enjoy support for and take direction from an intricate social web of citizens, families, and public and private agencies" (Sato & McLaughlin, 1992, p. 366). Families place a great deal of importance on education, and children grow up with the message that education is valuable (Lewis, 1998). The high social value attached to education has been a prominent historical feature of Japanese society. Since the 19th century, the Japanese public has held book learning and literacy in high regard (Sato & McLaughlin, 1992). Research by Ladd (1995) has shown that the rates of divorce, single parenthood, and poverty in Japan are low when compared with the United States, creating an integrated network of support that encourages positive attitudes among Japanese students toward school and reinforces cultural values such as cooperation and hard work (cited in Linn, Lewis, Tsuchida, & Songer, 2000). Although Japanese teachers spend much of their time honoring obligations to students, parents, and communities, there is a strong obligation on the part of these constituencies to also assume responsibility for educating the young (Sato & McLaughlin, 1992).

This broad network of support from various segments in Japanese society differs from the way education is sometimes viewed in the United States. Herbst (1989), for instance, has argued that low esteem for many American teachers stems from the educational environment itself, as teachers conduct their work in isolation and lack a tightly woven network of colleagues, families, and communities. Although American society has needed teachers, it has rarely offered support to public school educators, much less rewarded them for their efforts. As Herbst has explained, American "society wants teachers to be present when needed, but it does not appreciate hearing them remonstrate about conditions in their schools. Like their students, teachers are to be seen in school, but they are not to raise their voices" (p. 3). The relative exclusion of teachers' voices, when combined with excessive paperwork, prescribed curricula, "and accountability systems that equate learning with factory production," may not foster environments that "sustain excellent teaching" (Lewis, 1998, p. 190). The social importance attached to education differs between Japan and American society, and this is reflected in the way the public in each nation values the schooling enterprise.

Public Valuing of Education

The sociocultural context of teaching and teachers differs in Japan and the United States in relation to the goals and purposes each country ascribes to schooling (Sato & McLaughlin, 1992). In the United States "public school teachers have always been," according to Herbst (1989), "at the beck and call of the public" (p. 3). American schools have been held to the almost impossible standard of being pivotal to the solution of a myriad of social ills, and the pressure that results makes it increasingly difficult for teachers to be viewed by the public as professionals who are doing "their job" effectively. It is interesting that curriculum focused on character development and citizenship education is often viewed with suspicion, even though there have been urgent calls for schools to address social problems, such as violence, crime, and high dropout rates.

Since the beginning of modernization in the 19th century, Japanese teachers "have been viewed as agents of character development and nation-building" (Shimahara, 1998b, p. 247). Although criticisms have been levied more recently by Japanese parents concerned about bullying and school violence, there is an expectation in Japan that educators are to teach morality and cultural sensitivity in school, for these aspects are safely ensconced in Japanese culture and fundamental to Japanese schooling (Shimahara, 1998b). Lewis (1998) has suggested, like Shimahara, that it might be easier for Japanese teachers—who operate in a culture characterized by respect for authority and recognition of professional expertise—to concentrate on the social and emotional needs of children. This is different when compared with American teachers, who are immersed in a culture that is often critical of its public schools. Learning, for both students and teachers, "requires the emotional safety needed to take risks and to recognize and learn from mistakes. When high status and professional treatment are lacking, so too may be the safety to learn" (Lewis, 1998, p. 190).

The nested cultural values of community, connectedness, commitment, and care, as generally manifested in Japanese schools and society, complement cultural values and school learning processes (Sato, 1993). These layers of safety, identified as "the four C's," are similar to the psychological needs of autonomy, belonging, and competence suggested by U.S. researchers as prerequisites for students to develop attachments to their American schooling experience (Lewis, 1998). In the U.S. context, this suggests that schooling must "become an actual—as opposed to a merely rhetorical—priority of the society. This [sic] priority would have to be deeply felt, and felt across social classes" (Soder, 1986, p. 32). Social cohesion, a prominent cultural value in Japanese society, generally supports teachers' roles and work; this value, in turn, legitimates teacher authority and reinforces education as valuable. For a comparison of how demographic attributes of the population affect education in Japan and the United States, see the Points of Convergence box (Figure 6.1).

FIGURE 6.1

Points of Convergence

JAPAN	Demography and educational consequences	UNITED STATES
Aspect: Of the 126,771,662 people in Japan, 99.4% are Japanese and 0.6% are Korean (*World Factbook*, 2001). Japanese citizens experience a high quality of life, with none below the poverty line. The average life expectancy is 77.62 years for males and 84.15 years for females (*World Factbook*, 2001). Long-term concerns include the aging Japanese population and the crowding of habitable land, since most people live on only 13% of land space due to Japan's rugged and mountainous terrain (Ginsburg, 2000).		**Aspect:** The United States has a population of 278,058,881, composed of 83.5% white, 12.4% black, 3.3% Asian, and 0.8% American Indian (*World Factbook*, 2001). (Hispanic is not listed because the U.S. Census Bureau considers Hispanic to mean a person of Latin American descent living in the U.S. who can be of any race or ethnic group.) Almost 12.7% of U.S. citizens live below the poverty line. The average life expectancy is 74.37 years for males and 80.05 years for females (*World Factbook*, 2001). Long-term challenges for the United States include the rising medical costs of an aging population and stagnating family incomes in lower economic groups (*World Factbook*, 2001).
Response: When considering the usual indices, such as infant mortality, malnutrition, child abuse, family stability, parental drug abuse, and poverty, "Japanese children are extraordinarily fortunate, even compared with children in other advanced industrialized nations" (Boocock, 1987, cited in Lewis, 1998, p. 185).	How have attributes of the population affected education?	**Response:** As cited in the *World Factbook* (2001), almost all household income gains since 1975 have gone to the top 20% of American households. Another social concern is that the United States, among other nations, is a major consumer of illicit drugs, such as cocaine, heroin, and methamphetamines.
Consequence: Japanese teachers rely on familial support. Almost 100% of students 6–15 years of age and 96% of those 16-18 years of age attend school regularly (Okano & Tsuchiya, 1999). Having had their basic needs for food, shelter, and adult provision met, most Japanese students come to school ready to learn.		**Consequence:** American teachers are increasingly being asked to teach children from families who do not always meet children's basic need for food, shelter, stability, and adult attention (Lewis, 1998).

CHINA

RUSSIA

Hokkaido

● Sapporo

Occupied by the
Soviet Union in 1945,
administered by RUSSIA,
claimed by JAPAN.

NORTH
KOREA

*Sea of
Japan*

● Akita

● Sendai

SOUTH
KOREA

*Korea
Strait*

Kobe

TOKYO

Nagoya

Fukuoka ●
Kitakyushu

Osaka

SHIKOKU

*East
China
Sea*

KYUSHU

*North
Pacific
Ocean*

*Philippine
Sea*

OKINAWA

| 0 | 200 | 100 km |
| 0 | 200 | 400 mi |

Japan

*Source: The World Factbook. (2001). Japan. Washington, DC: The Central Intelligence Agency, U.S. Government.
http://www.odci.gov/cia/publications/factbook/geos/ja.html*

Prestige and Status

Teacher status is reinforced when a society sees the attributes, value, and efficiency of the
teacher's role. Prestige for the teaching role emerges from the public's view of the complexity of the work involved. According to Ornstein and Levine (1997), this complexity is
evidenced in teachers' application of scientific principles to identify problems and make
conclusions, their proficiency in speaking, reading, and writing, and their ability to work
with a variety of people, including children, youth, peers, administrators, and parents.
Whereas in the U.S. there is a substantial mismatch between the societal valuing of teach-

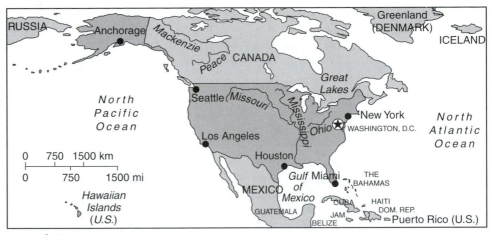

United States

Source: *The World Factbook. (2001). United States. Washington. DC: The Central Intelligence Agency, U.S. Government.http://www.odci.gov/cia/publications/factbook/geos/us.html*

ing and the importance of the profession, in Japan a more integrated network of support for and public valuing of education creates the conditions for teaching to be accorded a high status profession. Moreover, the high status of Japanese teachers is not dependent on their having received an advanced degree (Hawley & Hawley, 1997). Rather, Japanese teachers' salaries are based on professional longevity and their salaries increase in relation to that of other public workers.

"**Status discrepancy**," as defined by Soder (1986), "is a measure of the relationship between perceived self-value (and the implications of that self value) and perceived valuing by others" (p. 14). In the United States, teaching is an example of high status discrepancy because teachers view their work as important but feel they do not receive the status they deserve (Soder, 1986). Soder has argued that American teachers lack the clearly defined "cultural prescriptions" (p. 15) that characterize teaching in Japan. It is ironic that American teachers have experienced "exceptionally low prestige in a land that claimed universal education" (Robert Wiebe, cited in Soder, 1986, p. 6).

As a result of the high status and prestige accorded teacher professionals in Japan, obtaining a teaching position is a competitive endeavor. Kawakami (1997) found that the number of qualified applicants for primary school positions in 1994 "was 4.8 times the number of available positions. The equivalent figures for middle schools and high schools were 8.0 and 7.2 times respectively" (cited in Okano & Tsuchiya, 1999, p. 147). Although high school teachers and university instructors in Japan receive higher salaries than primary and middle school teachers, all teachers receive an annual salary increase of approximately $600–$1,000 (U.S. dollars); this system of reward is an incentive for teachers to remain in the profession for a long time (Okano & Tsuchiya, 1999). In the United States, some have expressed their concerns regarding the remuneration that American teachers have received, commenting on "why it has been that men and women to whom people entrust those who are dearest to them have nonetheless been granted scant respect and rewards for their labors" (Herbst, 1989, p. 3–4). An investigation of the relationship between authority and responsibility in the next section provides clues as to why status discrepancy exists for American teachers compared with the high prestige and status enjoyed by Japanese teachers.

THE AUTHORITY–RESPONSIBILITY RELATIONSHIP

An examination of the relationship between authority and responsibility serves to illuminate how teacher professionalism can be "supported or constricted within a given organization setting and cultural background" (LeTendre, 1999a, p. 43). Factors such as authority over knowledge construction and professional development, as well as the degree of autonomy and the intensification of teacher labor, shape teachers' status, work, and roles. Okano and Tsuchiya (1999) have asserted that teachers are endowed with specific responsibilities. To begin with, teachers are expected to ensure the rights of children to receive an education. Toward that end, teachers assume responsibility for delivering curricula and using teaching methods that are developmentally appropriate for children in a safe environment that encourages their growth (Okano & Tsuchiya, 1999). Parents entrust their children to teachers who hold authority to guide and direct learning processes. The expectation on the part of the public is that students are receiving the right "kind of education and culture" selected by teachers (Okano & Tsuchiya, 1999, p. 155). Moreover, teachers, as members of a profession, are responsible for maintaining an autonomous educational environment.

A combination of factors such as reciprocity, trust, and mutual obligation create what Star (1982, p. 80) has called "legitimate complexity," which is considered the real source of a profession's authority, power, and prestige (cited in Soder, 1986, p. 28). Thus, teachers hold the responsibility of "mediating the on-going relationship between parents, children, and the state" (Soder, 1986, pp. 45–46). Two areas that contribute to teacher professionalism—authority over knowledge construction and control and autonomy over educational processes—must be balanced with responsibility in the execution of teaching. The degree to which a balance exists between authority and responsibility is associated with the degree to which the public values the work of teachers and views them as professionals. We first discuss the authority side of the authority–responsibility relationship, in terms of teachers' authority over knowledge construction and their control and autonomy over educational processes.

Authority Over Knowledge Construction

Okano and Tsuchiya (1999) have asserted that, on one level, teacher professionals possess an academic understanding of child development, which they apply to decisions about what methods will foster students' cognitive growth. This represents the technical side of teaching—where scientific knowledge and procedures are applied to classroom practices. On another level, teachers draw upon the wisdom "acquired through first-hand attempts to resolve day-to-day issues while interacting with the children in [their] charge" (Okano & Tsuchiya, 1999, p. 158). This constitutes the practical capacity of teachers, also known as craft knowledge. Grimmett and MacKinnon (1992) have defined **craft knowledge** as the "sensible, experientially grounded know-how constructed by teachers to deal with evolving events in the classroom" (cited in Shimahara, 1998a, p. 452). Rather than viewing scientific knowledge (i.e., theories and techniques) as the only epistemology to guide teaching practice, craft knowledge in Japan is considered the kind of knowledge that teachers develop in response to practical demands for making teaching effective and for addressing classroom problems. Practical capacity, according to Okano and Tsuchiya (1999), is based on Japanese teachers' efforts to understand children's feelings, develop students' joy and pride in learning, and foster community and parental support in children's education. However, the effectiveness of teachers' practical capacity has been debated by the Japanese public and parents who sometimes blame teachers for problems, such as incidences of truancy, violence, or bullying in schools (Okano & Tsuchiya, 1999).

Although there are differences of opinion about how effective teachers are in applying both technical rationality and practical capacity in their classrooms, there is consensus among Japanese educators and the public that teaching is a combination of science and artistry. Professional development in Japan reinforces this notion. Through collegial conversation, peer interaction, and teacher reflection on classroom experiences, the image of teaching is socially constructed. That is, the group helps articulate the role of the teacher as well as the particular values and beliefs associated with the teaching profession. In this way, Japanese teachers become constructors of knowledge, as opposed to technicians who only implement predetermined and prescribed instructional strategies.

In the United States, Whitson and Stanley (1996) have asserted the importance of teachers' practical capacities by advocating what they term "the practical social competence approach" (p. 332). The authors define **practical social competence** as "nothing less than the full competence required for human praxis" (p. 321)—that is, the reflective and decision making abilities people need to function effectively in their private and public lives. Premised on the belief that individuals "can become more or less competent to make" complex judgments about personal and societal well-being (p. 326), Whitson and Stanley (1996) have contended that practical social competence is necessary to help citizens make informed decisions in their daily lives.

To help develop practical social competence, Whitson and Stanley have advocated the development of what Mills (1959) has called the "sociological imagination." According to this analysis, people who possess a sociological imagination understand: (1) their personal affairs in relation to larger historical forces and social processes that enhance or constrain individual opportunity; (2) how larger phenomena affect their daily practices; and (3) what actions might improve life at both personal and societal levels. Teachers, therefore, have an important role to play in providing an education in which students are encouraged to apply reflective thought and pose solutions to social problems. Exposure to the social science disciplines that examine "social causes, consequences, and relationships" (Whitson & Stanley, 1996, p. 330) can help foster practical social competence in teachers. Thus, practical social competence can be considered an important attribute of teacher professionalism and necessary in teacher education.

Darling-Hammond (2000) has argued that a professional is "one who learns from teaching rather than one who has finished learning how to teach" (p. 170). An important role of teacher education, therefore, is to develop in teachers the ability to examine, in a sensitive, systematic way, the processes of teaching and learning. For Darling-Hammond, this approach to the production of teacher knowledge is much like that sought by educational philosopher John Dewey (1859–1952), who aimed "to empower teachers with greater understanding of complex situations rather than to control them with simplistic formulas or cookie-cutter routines for teaching" (cited in Darling-Hammond, 2000, p. 170). Dewey (1937) asserted that if teachers inquired into the problems they experienced in the actual practice of teaching, then that knowledge could serve as a foundation for making professional judgments (cited in Darling-Hammond, 2000). Teachers, engaged in a process of inquiry with their peers, "become sensitive to variation and more aware of what works for what purposes in what situations" (Darling-Hammond, 2000, p. 170). Drawing on research conducted by Ashton, Crocker, and Olijnik (1986), Darling-Hammond has argued that teachers who possess more knowledge of the processes of teaching and learning, as opposed to more subject expertise, are more effective in the classroom. It is the combination of knowledge complexity and cultural demand for that knowledge that results in what can be considered legitimate work (Soder, 1986). For a brief biographical sketch of educator Linda Darling-Hammond, see the Personality Box.

Authority Evidenced in Professional Autonomy

In addition to authority over the process of knowledge construction, professional competence can also be measured by the degree of control and autonomy teachers have over deciding their work duties and roles. The kind of autonomy teachers have over educational processes and their work environments are linked to issues of professional control versus lay control and teacher input versus external input. If teaching is to be considered a profession, then teacher professionals are the ones who possess the ability and qualifications to make judgments about their work duties; laypersons, however, can limit teachers' autonomy and control of education by not giving teachers freedom to employ their particular competencies with students in the way they see fit (Ornstein & Levine, 1997). The degree of teacher autonomy can also be judged in terms of how much input teachers have in curricular decisions, such as textbook selection and the kinds of methods employed to teach students subject matter and key concepts that students can later apply in their own work and lives. When primarily those outside the teaching profession initiate school reforms, it is indicative of the kind and degree of autonomy teachers possess.

Opportunities for professional growth and teacher involvement in their own development are also signs of teacher professionalism and autonomy. According to Shimahara (1998a), the model of professional development in Japan was a result of both teacher initiative and governmental policy. Shimahara has suggested that the professional development teachers receive after initial teacher preparation is a key factor in the ability of Japanese teachers "to maintain and promote professional standards" (p. 453). In-service education, organized and conducted by Japanese teachers themselves, receives greater attention than in other nations where teachers seek graduate education for professional development and advancement. As Okano and Tsuchiya (1999) have revealed, the maintenance of teacher autonomy in Japan is a result of teachers actively engaged in shaping school policies and providing feedback to the school administration. In the United States, it has been suggested that the body of knowledge that teachers must know is ill defined, and the content in teacher education courses varies within and between states (Ornstein & Levine, 1997). Ornstein and Levine (1997) have argued that most Americans view teachers

Linda Darling-Hammond

A leading authority on school restructuring and reform, Linda Darling-Hammond contends that the best way to improve schools is to invest in teacher training. In a report issued by the National Commission on Teaching and America's Future, Darling-Hammond stated that the United States must give serious attention to the way it prepares, recruits, supports, and rewards its teachers. The report concluded that the educational standards in the United States could not be raised without an investment in teacher knowledge. Darling-Hammond defines teacher knowledge as the ability of teachers to examine, in a sensitive, systematic way, the processes of teaching and learning. Thus, Darling-Hammond (2000) advocates professional development programs aimed at teacher inquiry into the problems teachers experience during actual teaching practice.

After receiving her doctorate in urban education from Temple University in 1978, Darling-Hammond assumed a professorship at Teachers College, Columbia University from 1989 to 1998, while also serving as codirector for the National Center for Restructuring Education, Schools, and Teaching. From 1993 to 1998, she was the William F. Russell Professor in the Foundations of Education at Columbia University. In her award-winning book, titled *The Right to Learn: A Blueprint for Creating Schools that Work* (1997), Darling-Hammond has discussed how top-down bureaucratic attempts to improve teaching are unlikely to succeed because effective teaching is not routine but unpredictable, and students are not passive recipients of information but active learners.

Currently, Linda Darling-Hammond is Charles E. Ducommun Professor of Teaching and Teacher Education, a distinguished professorship that she has held at Stanford University since 1998. She also serves as faculty sponsor of the Stanford Teacher Education Program. As a member of the International Advisory Council, along with a host of other leadership positions on national advisory boards, commissions, and task forces dedicated to improving teacher effectiveness and preparedness, Darling-Hammond is often consulted for her views on the status of teacher education in the United States. Her current research is focused on the areas of education policy and practice, including teacher training and education, school reform, authentic assessment, and professional development schools.

In a chapter titled, "Performance-Based Assessment and Educational Equity" (1999), Darling-Hammond asserted that, due to the lack of investment in American teacher education and professional development, the "capacity for a more complex, student-centered approach to teaching is not prevalent throughout the current teaching force" (p. 390). Inadequate salaries and working conditions contribute to a lack of qualified teachers in America's poorest school districts, with minority and low-income students taught by the least experienced teachers (Darling-Hammond, 1991, 1999; Oakes, 1990). Thus, Darling-Hammond has argued that teacher quality is the most important factor in helping to create equitable educational opportunities in America's urban schools.

Drawing on comparative educational research, Darling-Hammond found that, unlike the examination systems in other nations, state control over the design, administration, and evaluation of externally driven tests in the United States occurs without the involvement of teachers (cited in Norman, 2000). This has led Darling-Hammond to conclude that school–community partnerships, as emphasized in high-achieving countries, would help create a better accountability and assessment process in the United States—one built on "'common understandings about what constitutes good work and how to achieve it'" (Darling-Hammond, cited in Norman, 2000, p. 2).

as public servants who are accountable to school officials, parents, and the public at large. "Thus, in many situations, teachers can be told what to do by parents and other citizens, principals, superintendents, and school board members, even when these directives go against the teachers' professional judgments" (Ornstein & Levine, 1997, p. 38).

This leaves one to wonder, "What responsibilities do teachers have to the public?" and "When are the public's demands an infringement on professional respect and autonomy?" The responsibility side of the authority–responsibility relationship, in terms of teachers' roles and responsibilities and intensification of teacher labor, is examined in the next section.

Teachers' Roles and Responsibilities

There are approximately 1.1 million primary and secondary teachers in Japan and about 3 million teachers in the United States. In both places, they assume a variety of commitments. The roles and responsibilities of Japanese and American teachers are shaped by their particular historical, cultural, and social contexts. In ancient times, teaching in Japan was considered a sacred profession, as teachers were commissioned to serve the emperor. Under the Meiji Empire, teachers were viewed as part of the state bureaucracy and charged with the task of socializing youth with patriotic views and support of the existing emperor (Okano & Tsuchiya, 1999). Post-World War II legislation, however, brought with it a fundamentally different conception of teachers as a result of "changes to the right-and-obligation relationship between citizens and the state regarding education" (Okano & Tsuchiya, 1999, p. 143). As Okano and Tsuchiya have discussed, the Allied Occupation required changes in Japanese education, demanding that teachers with militaristic and nationalistic sentiments be expelled from schools. Others left voluntarily, "feeling responsible for the fact that education had been an ideological force to mobilise the innocent young into the war" (p. 143). Still others continued teaching, determined to use schooling as a vehicle for peace and democracy; interestingly, this purpose of schooling was seen by some teachers to be "independent of politics" (p. 143).

To ascertain the differences in professional context that surround teachers' work and roles, Sato and McLaughlin (1992) conducted a comparative study between the University of Tokyo and Stanford University. The researchers administered two surveys, one developed by Japanese researchers and the other by American researchers, to elementary and secondary schoolteachers. The Japanese survey assessed teachers' goals, time usage, roles and responsibilities, and professional development activities. The American survey assessed organizational conditions, professional climate, teacher–student relations, and external support. The findings revealed that Japanese teachers experienced a longer workweek, spending almost 20 hours more per week at school compared with their American counterparts.

Moreover, Sato and McLaughlin (1992) found that the role of teachers in Japan is conceived of in broad terms, as Japanese teachers assume a wider variety of school duties, share more responsibility in the school's administration and planning, and fulfill a significant number of nonacademic duties. For example, a duty of Japanese teachers is to account for students' use of vacation time, personal hygiene and habits, and behavior on and off campus. The findings showed that Japanese teachers may more often than their American counterpart sacrifice personal weekend and vacation time in order to fulfill their teaching responsibilities; moreover, Japanese teachers participate in more professional development activities, both in and outside of schools, compared with American teachers. Although Japanese teachers spend more hours at school, they "do not teach all day, as do American teachers" (Sato & McLaughlin, 1992, p. 365). For example, the researchers found that only 60% of Japanese teachers' time is devoted to classroom teaching; the rest is spent in extracurricular duties and school responsibilities. Sato and McLaughlin (1992) also found that almost one third of American teachers in the study held other jobs, and many of these jobs were not education-related.

Some of the most interesting findings from this study focused on the ways in which Japanese and American teachers rate the leadership of administrators. The study revealed that Japanese teachers report stronger and better-defined collegial relations with their peers and administrators at the school level. Japanese teachers "also have a greater belief that their professional efficacy derives from their own efforts and abilities" (Sato & McLaughlin, 1992, p. 360). Compared with their Japanese counterparts, American teachers reported that they encounter more discipline problems and disruptions to student learning; moreover, Sato and McLaughlin found that American teachers expressed greater concern about their effectiveness with students compared with the Japanese teachers. The findings from this study suggest that Japanese teachers experience greater empowerment in their workplace than do American teachers, as evidenced by opportunities to exert influence on whole-school policies and to collaborate with peers. Sato and McLaughlin (1992) reinforced the argument put forward by Herbst in 1989 regarding the elusive professionalism of teachers in the United States:

> Judged by the sociologists' criteria—professional or graduate training comparable to that of lawyers or physicians; professional autonomy in the workplace; professional guidance through a code of ethics; performance evaluation by peers; immediate responsibility toward clients and ultimate accountability to society—administrators and specialists, not the teachers, are seen as the professionals in public education. (p. 8)

For a comparison of sociopolitical factors shaping education in Japan and the United States, see the Points of Convergence box (Figure 6.2).

Intensification of Teacher Labor

Studies by numerous scholars (Okano & Tsuchiya, 1999; Shimahara & Sakai, 1995) have concluded that the professional roles and duties of Japanese teachers are more extensive than those of American teachers. This broadened view of teaching is reflected in a concept central to traditional Japanese pedagogy. *Kizuna*, a term that describes the intimate relationship that teachers build with their students, is premised on a classroom climate in which empathy, trust, inclusion, and character building are highly prized (Okano & Tsuchiya, 1999). According to Okano and Tsuchiya (1999), teacher authority in the Japanese context emerges from teachers' interaction with students rather than teachers demanding respect from their students. Whereas beginning American teachers are warned to not be friends with their students, Okano and Tsuchiya (1999) have found that beginning teachers in Japan "are encouraged to 'mingle with students without disguise and pretence' in order to develop *kizuna*, as this "will eventually confer authority to the teacher" (p. 173).

Because Japanese teachers' roles include a broad array of responsibilities, ranging from teaching and administrative duties to parental communication and counseling tasks (Sato & McLaughlin, 1992), the workload for teachers is intense, alternating between six-

FIGURE 6.2

Points of Convergence

JAPAN		UNITED STATES
Aspect: Founded more than 2,000 years ago, Japan is the oldest monarchy in the world. As a constitutional monarchy with a parliamentary government, Japan's emperor serves as a symbol of national unity, while politicians, bureaucrats, and business executives wield actual power (*World Factbook*, 2001). **Response:** In ancient times, teaching was considered a sacred profession, with teachers commissioned by the emperor to socialize youth with patriotic views and support of the empire. Post–World War II legislation, however, resulted in a rights-and-obligations relationship among teachers, citizens, and the state. **Consequence:** Although Japan's educational administration is decentralized, with local educational boards assuming responsibility for the budget, curriculum, teacher appointments, and school supervision, the Ministry of Education, in practice, "keeps a tight rein on curriculum and other aspects of primary and secondary instruction" (*The New Encyclopedia Britannica*, 1997).	**Sociopolitical factors and educational consequences** How have unique sociopolitical factors shaped education?	**Aspect:** After breaking with Great Britain in 1776 and adopting its Constitution in 1789, the United States became the first modern democracy in the world (*World Factbook*, 2001). As a federal republic with a strong democratic tradition, the primary political parties are the Democratic Party and the Republican Party, with other groups and parties vying for the public's attention. **Response:** Education in the United States is characterized by an extremely decentralized system, and the federal government has no general mandate for the control or provision of public education (Valverde, 1995). Thus, elementary and secondary education is primarily the responsibility of the 50 states and the District of Columbia. **Consequence:** Curriculum policy is under the purview of each state and often each local school district or individual school. Although some states exercise more control over teaching content than other states, there has been significant movement in the United States over the past several years toward the widespread use of competency tests to measure student achievement. This use of testing will become even more universal with the enactment of federal provisions linking some federal funding to the use of tests.

and five-day work weeks. "While [Japanese] students have a forty-day summer vacation, a fourteen-day winter vacation and another fourteen days of spring vacation, their teachers often work during these periods" (Okano & Tsuchiya, 1999, p. 151). On a daily basis, primary teachers spend approximately 26.5 hours per week teaching, and additional time is given to the supervision of lunch, recess, and school cleaning (cited in Okano & Tsuchiya, 1999). Middle school and high school teachers spend 19.7 and 16.8 hours (cited in Okano & Tsuchiya, 1999), respectively, in classroom teaching; their remaining time is dedicated to the supervision of extracurricular activities, giving counseling sessions, and providing additional lessons to prepare students for entrance examinations so that they can increase their chances for access to high-level schools (cited in Okano & Tsuchiya, 1999). "Since teaching is considered a full-time occupation, teacher salaries reflect 12 months of work, and teachers are forbidden to do any other paid work, even on their own time" (Sato & McLaughlin, 1992, p. 362).

Because an individual's relations with other people are central to self-identity in Japanese society, teachers endure numerous inconveniences as educational workers (Sato, 1993). While Japanese "cultural values of collegiality and the desirability of consensus about decisions to be made support the assumption that professional development should be provided by peers and should take place among teachers" (Hawley & Hawley, 1997, p. 238), responsibility for professional development lends itself to an intensification of teacher labor. Although Japan experiences a more integrated network of support among community members, parents, the school, and its educational workers, making "the profession of teaching . . . a socially acceptable one" comes at a great cost for the teachers, who endure numerous hardships for the public good (Miller 1953, cited in Soder, 1986, p. 11). Japanese teachers find that they are involved increasingly in school management and disciplinary guidance because of more frequent incidences of deviant student behavior (Shimahara, 1998a).

Just as Japanese teachers assume a myriad of responsibilities, Japanese students are also accountable to teachers, and school serves as "the primary organization of their lives" (Sato & McLaughlin, 1992, p. 363). Students submit their daily schedules to their teachers, who review them for an appropriate balance of work, study, and play. Moreover, students, parents, and teachers are all accountable for students' misbehavior outside of school. As Sato and McLaughlin have explained, when misbehavior does occur outside school, the witnesses report it to the school as opposed to the family. "In cases of stealing, teachers, principals, and parents must all apologize in person to the store owners" (p. 363). Hence, while socially defined cultural and professional norms regulate teachers' behaviors, roles, and responsibilities, so, too, do these norms regulate the personal and school lives of students (Sato & McLaughlin, 1992).

An identifiable, socially understood educational philosophical core, combined with consistent educational expectations for students and the acceptance of a great deal of responsibility by teachers, contributes to the maintenance of Japanese society's confidence in its education professionals. In this way, teachers in Japan have been able to strike a balance between authority and responsibility, but not without much work and sacrifice. We now turn to a deeper examination of the philosophical context—that provides a common foundation for Japanese schooling.

BASIC EDUCATION AND HOLISTIC DEVELOPMENT

What constitutes basic education in Japan and the United States differs significantly, providing insights into what counts in schools and what is believed about child development. Holistic development is considered basic education in Japanese schools and is reflected in the roles and responsibilities of teachers. Physical education, art, and music are emphasized as much as academics, with attention given—especially at the elementary level—to students' social and ethical development. Teachers orchestrate learning in ways that foster Japanese children's sense of belonging and enable them to contribute to their school in meaningful ways. For example, Linn et al., (2000) have found that leadership roles are rotated so that all students are provided opportunities to assume authority in the classroom. Moreover, characteristics such as persistence, responsibility, and respect are considered essential goals of education, with instruction organized to foster students' needs to belong and contribute (Linn et al., 2000). This balance of social, emotional, ethical, physical, aesthetic, and intellectual development in Japanese schools is often referred to as whole person education (Cummings, 1980; Lewis, 1995; Linn et al., 2000; Okano & Tsuchiya, 1999; Sato, 1991). Through a process of active participation and character building, the Japanese elementary curriculum fosters "students' attachment to school and their disposition to take on the school's values as their own" (Lewis, 1995, cited in Linn et al., 2000, p. 8).

The development of *ningen* (human beings) is at the core of Japanese educational philosophy; this concept is well supported and articulated by teachers and Japanese society as a whole. *Ningen* "transcends basic skills and academic achievement" and "assumes a holistic conception of students' growth and learning" (Sato & McLaughlin, 1992, p. 361). This constitutes a major difference between Asian and Western views of education: Asian educators take a more phenomenological view of teaching and learning, and Western educators view learning as being "rooted in scientism" (p. 361). By *phenomenological*, we refer to the subjective experiences and perceptions of individuals and the meanings they give to their experiences (Mertens, 1998). A teacher assuming a phenomenological stance might ask, "What is the participant's experience like?" (Mertens, 1998, p. 169). The goal is to understand the learning experience from the viewpoint of the student. This necessitates that the teacher become integrally involved in the learning endeavor with his or her students. Rather than providing students with answers, Japanese elementary teachers devote a great deal of time to activities designed to foster student socialization. Because human relations skills are viewed as an essential quality of an educated person, teachers "place high priority on developing students' interpersonal competencies and promoting a sense of social cohesion and collective responsibility among students" (Sato & McLaughlin, 1992, pp. 360–361).

Particular features of Japanese schools support the development of *ningen* and peer relationships. Although classes average about 30 students each, the *han* (a group of four children) creates a family-like unit in which students participate together in activities throughout the school day (Linn et al., 2000). In these groups, peer teaching and peer supervision are encouraged. Ethnographic research studies—based on observations in elementary classrooms (Easley & Easley, 1983; Lewis, 1995; Peak, 1991)—have revealed that by fourth grade "Japanese children have had massive exposure to a social and ethical curriculum emphasizing responsibility, collaboration, kindness, and so forth" (Linn et al., 2000, p. 8). In addition to ethnographic research "designed to describe and analyze practices and beliefs of cultures and communities" (Mertens, 1998, p. 165), survey findings from comparative education research (Beaton, Martin, Mullis, Gonzalez, Smith, & Kelly, 1996; Hamilton, Blumenfeld, Akoh, & Miura, 1989a, 1989b; Schmidt, Raizen, Britton, Bianchi, & Wolfe, 1997) suggest that, by the time Japanese students reach fifth grade, they "have internalized school rules more strongly than have American students, and that American students are more likely than Japanese students to cite external reasons to learn—such as grades or adult expectations" (Linn et al., 2000, p. 8). In addition to the *han*, the 240-day school year in Japan, compared with the 180-day school year in the U.S., provides time for both academic studies and nonacademic activities (Sato & McLaughlin, 1992).

Prevailing Japanese and American views about ability and intelligence also differ. Singleton (1989) has argued that Japanese conceptions of cognition and learning are premised on principles of incrementalism. Incrementalism is defined "as a pattern of slow learning" (Hare, 1996; Singleton, 1989) by which students gain confidence through the completion of repetitive tasks that enable them to eventually complete more intricate tasks and engage in higher-order learning (cited in LeTendre, 1999b, pp. 11–12). Motivation figures largely in Japanese students' being able to improve their skills and abilities over time. With persistence (*gambaru*) and hard work based on effort (*doryoku*) and endurance (*gaman suru*) in academic subjects, it is believed that Japanese students themselves have the opportunity to change their ability levels (LeTendre, 1999b).

This more fluid view of intelligence, as suggested by LeTendre (1999b), provides a rationale as to why ability grouping is not used with primary students, why entrance examinations (beginning in the upper elementary grades), and why a standardized curriculum is considered beneficial. Because most students believe that their basic abilities can be raised through individual motivation and study, Japanese teachers do not rely on external rewards to motivate students. In contrast, American students believe that the most important factor in student achievement is the competency of their teacher (Hawley & Hawley, 1997). Drawing on the work of Kliebard (1987), Lewis (1998) has suggested that intellectual growth in Japanese schools is not fostered through student competition; rather, school activities and lessons are attuned to children's individual and social development, thereby enabling Japan to escape "the pendulum swing between social development and academic rigor that has blemished American educational history" (p. 192).

TEACHING AND LEARNING IN JAPANESE ELEMENTARY CLASSROOMS

Research studies about teaching and learning in Japan have centered predominately on the student-centered nature of Japanese pre- and elementary schools and the examination-driven feature of Japanese secondary education. While an extensive literature documents the child-centered focus in Japanese elementary classrooms (Hendry, 1986; LeTendre, 1999b; Lewis, 1995; Tobin, Wu, & Davidson, 1989; Tsuchida & Lewis, 1996; Peak, 1989; White, 1987), researchers have tended to discuss the behaviors of Japanese children in terms of pedagogical practices and perspectives. Rarely have their discussions been extended to a philosophical dialogue about Japanese education. Although it is accurate for scholars to identify Japanese early elementary education as student-centered, this often sidesteps inquiry into more philosophical and societal conceptions of teaching and learning in Japan. Examining Japanese elementary classrooms not only provides insights about teachers' and students' roles but reveals the attention being given to the development of students' democratic values and characteristics. Science and mathematics instruction at the elementary level provides a case in point of how teachers strive to create democratic classroom environments that foster students' intellectual, social, and ethical orientations.

What makes this examination of Japanese elementary instruction so intriguing is that students' academic achievement in math and science is soaring at the same time that their learning is being orchestrated in a democratic manner. In the United States, democratic education is most often the responsibility of social studies teachers, who strive to teach democratic values overtly through the social studies curriculum. The development of democratic characteristics are usually talked about, and democratic education is usually treated in isolation from other subjects, such as math and science, which are seen to be more concrete and culturally neutral. Due to this propensity to view science and math as universal and civic education as culture specific, Americans have been more inclined to value the international reports on students' academic achievement in math and science and to view these subjects as indispensable for technological progress and economic growth. In light of international comparisons from The Third International Math and Science Study (TIMSS), which have shown American students falling behind their Japanese counterparts between the fourth and eighth grades, a consideration of how Japanese teachers have orchestrated democratic learning in their math and science instruction might hold possibilities for strengthening both democratic education and student achievement in math and science in the United States.

Research on democratic citizenship education from a Western context has focused on a number of characteristics that, when combined, help establish democratic-oriented atmospheres for student learning. These include active participation, avoidance of textbook dominated instruction, reflective thinking, discussion, student decision making and problem solving, individual responsibility, recognition of human dignity, and relevance (concepts adapted from Kubow, 1996, and Radz, 1983). (See Table 6.1.) Although these characteristics emerge from an exploration of Western-based educational literature, it is striking to see how dominant these democratic tendencies are in Japanese elementary classrooms. Although simplistic conclusions are discouraged, one can gain a better understanding of how Japan's educational philosophy of holistic development is enacted and consider the relationships among educational values, classroom practices, and student outcomes. This, in turn, could illuminate the combination of factors that might influence

---

Table 6.1 Democratic Classroom Characteristics

- Active participation
- Avoidance of textbook dominated instruction
- Reflective thinking
- Discussion
- Student decision making and problem solving
- Individual responsibility
- Recognition of human dignity
- Relevance

Concepts adapted from Kubow, 1996 and Radz, 1983.

democratic instruction and subject-specific instruction in other schools situated in different cultural contexts.

Linn et al. (2000) observed 10 science lessons at five schools throughout Tokyo, interviewed classroom teachers and principals, and used video- and audiotape, in addition to field notes, to identify an activity structure supported by the Japanese educational system at large. Science activity structures were defined as "what students do, individually or in groups, as they learn science—for example, experiments, data sharing, discussion of findings, [and] assessments" (p. 4). The researchers found that science instruction in Japan followed an eightfold pattern. First, teachers connected the science lesson to their students' interests and background knowledge through questioning techniques or activities. Second, teachers elicited students' opinions about scientific principles to be studied that day. Third, students generated hypotheses about their proposed scientific study. Fourth, students conducted investigations to test their hypotheses by methods that were often designed by students individually or in large or small groups. Fifth, students shared the results of their investigations with peers. Sixth, students analyzed information as the teacher summarized or organized the students' results. Seventh, students reflected upon the hypotheses in light of the findings obtained. And, eighth, teachers connected the findings to upcoming lessons by encouraging students to think about what is of interest to them in order to plan their next investigations. The authors concluded that the eightfold activity pattern constituted a process of inquiry that was and could be continually manifested in science instruction (Linn et al., 2000).

It is interesting to note that each of the characteristics considered important, at least to Western researchers, in order for teachers to develop democratic classrooms can be evidenced in the Japanese elementary science classrooms observed by Linn et al. (2000). Although the eightfold activity pattern considered best practice in Japan might be a result of these schools being attached to Japanese national universities and therefore more apparent than in other locations, it is worthwhile to consider further the relationship between Japan's high academic achievement in math and science and the democratic tendencies, as identified by Kubow (1996) and Radz (1983), exhibited in Japanese elementary classrooms. These democratic characteristics might hold possibilities for improving math and science instruction in the United States. Thus, each democratic characteristic is addressed with this potential in mind.

Active Participation. Active participation is a common feature of Japanese elementary instruction. Okano and Tsuchiya (1999), citing the work of Sato (1988), stated that more than 60% of Japanese classroom teachers direct their instruction to their less-academically able students, whereas American teachers target instruction to those that are considered above average. In the Tokyo study, Linn et al. (2000) have suggested that the success of Japanese teachers in eliciting students' background knowledge and experiences might be due to social and cultural expectations that all students participate in learning. Others, such as Tsuchida and Lewis (1996), have argued that student willingness to contribute ideas is more a culturally prescribed obligatory act than an independent choice for students in Japan. Whether or not it is right for teachers to expect universal student participation, active participation does help students to internalize knowledge and make it their own. Toward that end, Japanese teachers use a number of strategies to elicit student response.

These include "walking up and down rows," representing students' ideas with magnets on a blackboard that displays each student's name, posting the work of every student on the bulletin board, and encouraging students "to publicly debate and 'vote' on their predictions about an experiment" (Linn et al., 2000, p. 11). In addition to active student participation, instruction in Japanese elementary schools is not dominated by material in textbooks.

Avoidance of Textbook Dominated Instruction. Japanese education is shaped by both its national curriculum and the ways in which teachers interpret how students can best learn the curriculum. Findings from the TIMSS have revealed that the Japanese curriculum is more focused and in-depth compared with the breadth of topics that U.S. students are exposed to during a given school year. Guided by this philosophy of "depth rather than breadth," Japanese educators teach fewer topics and devote more time to a selected number of them when compared with curricula in other nations (Linn et al., 2000, p. 9). This philosophy of "less is more" is reflected in the national curriculum itself, which consists of "one slim volume of general goals for elementary education, [titled] *The Course of Study for Elementary Schools*, and an additional slim guide for each subject area" (p. 9). Linn et al. found that of the 105 lessons (45 minutes each) over a given school year Japanese fourth graders are exposed to 12 lessons on "dissolving" and fifth graders to 12 lessons on "levers." Moreover, the science textbooks that eighth-grade Japanese students use focus on eight topics, whereas more than 65 topics are represented in American eighth-grade textbooks (Schmidt et al., 1997, cited in Linn et al., 2000). Although Japan's national curriculum stipulates the topics to be covered at each grade level, it seems that the instruction, at least in math and science, is not bound or limited by the textbook. Rather, learning is dominated by reflective inquiry that is supported by teacher- and peer-initiated questioning.

Reflective Thinking. Science instruction in Japan is animated by vibrant discussions in which students explore questions of interest to themselves and others. Higher-order thinking is evidenced in science classrooms as students relate concepts learned from past course work to current topics, foster understanding by asking challenging questions, and build on the ideas of their peers (Linn et al., 2000). Observations of Japanese and U.S. mathematics classrooms (Stigler & Hiebert, 1997) have emphasized differences between Japanese and American teachers' work environments: American teachers encountered frequent disruptions due to school-wide announcements and student pull-out programs, whereas Japanese classrooms experienced infrequent interruptions. As explained by Linn et al. (2000), these uninterrupted lessons might "reflect beliefs about the importance of deep 'sticky-probing' or students' thinking (Hess & Azuma, 1991) and lesson coherence (Stigler, Fernandez & Yoshida, 1996)" and might "*create* the conditions for these to occur" (p. 9). Uninterrupted lessons—with clear learning expectations—create a degree of predictability for students who are then able to monitor their time in science class in order to complete investigations and write lab reports (Tsuchida & Lewis, 1996, cited in Linn et al., 2000). Thus, reflective thinking and meaning making through hands-on activities constitute a significant part of teaching and learning in Japanese science and mathematics classrooms. The larger system features of Japanese schools, such as fewer interruptions during instruction, provide a more consistent and stable environment that allows students to focus on and complete the integrated steps of an inquiry-oriented learning process. Reflective thinking is also supported by vibrant student discussion.

Discussion. Opportunities to voice ideas and opinions and to inquire about concepts and curricular content with their peers and teacher seem to be a natural part of Japanese elementary classrooms. Linn et al.'s (2000) study revealed that a commonly shared foundation of practice underlies elementary science instruction, with students engaged regularly in verbal, as opposed to only written, information exchange by way of presentations and discussions. Small-group discussions, as Linn et al. observed, were "lively and students expected others to justify their views" (p. 10):

> In one group that we observed, two girls and two boys discussed how to investigate whether any oxygen or carbon dioxide was left in a closed jar after the candle in the jar burned out. The two girls argued that the burning of the candle in the jar had produced carbon dioxide. The two boys . . . argued that the carbon dioxide was originally contained in the air before the candle went out. The girls tried to win the boys over to their view by reminding them how humans inhale oxygen and exhale carbon dioxide. In the midst of this heated discussion, the teacher said to the group: "You should not be arguing so much about what you believe at this time; instead, write down how you can investigate what you're arguing about." (p. 10)

When students are free to express their views and listen to their peers, their own views are challenged, modified, or strengthened. Such dialogue also fosters greater awareness about and reflection on complex scientific topics. Peer discussions provide students with a "collection of perspectives" from which to better understand what they are learning while also sharpening communication skills (Kubow, 1996). The investigation of the other sides of arguments or issues put forward by peers creates an enriched learning context—that is, what is chosen for investigation emerges from discussion among all students as opposed to only one student or the teacher. It is interesting that discussion—a common feature of democratic classrooms—might be dependent on the ways in which teachers themselves conceptualize their subjects as well as what is supported by the educational establishment. For example, in Japan, teachers conceive of "science as being 'about' students' ideas (a concept strongly supported by Japan's *Course of Study*), rather than only about students experimenting on ideas offered by the teacher" (Linn et al., 2000, p. 11). Equating science with students' ideas necessitates that the teacher create an atmosphere of comfortability between self and students and between students and students to foster participation in discussions and activities. However, the degree to which elementary classrooms become forums in which Japanese students are free to wrestle with conflicting beliefs about science (e.g., worldviews, the relationship between human beings and the environment), as opposed to observations and experiments tested by the scientific method, is an area that requires further research.

An infrastructure for reflective discussion is created more often in Japanese classrooms than in American ones (Tsuchida, 1993; Tsuchida & Lewis, 1996). Japanese teachers encourage their students to agree or disagree with peers and strive to create atmospheres in which all ideas are welcomed (Linn et al., 2000) rather than dismissed or demeaned. Moreover, the making and sharing of mistakes is a common feature in Japanese elementary schools (Lewis, 1995; Stevenson & Stigler, 1992) where teachers employ a "sticky-probe" approach to learning that encourages students to uncover inconsistencies in arguments put forward and to avoid artificial consensus (Hess and Azuma, 1991, cited in Linn et al., 2000, p. 11). This slow-paced, in-depth approach differs from instruction in the

United States, where quick response is more valued and a relatively small number of students contribute regularly to class discussions. Hence, those in American classrooms who are quick to respond are usually rewarded (with participation and effort points), whereas those who are slower to respond remain silent. This practice of providing less "wait-time" for students to contemplate and wrestle with issues and concepts discourages the formation of reflective student responses. It also fosters artificial class consensus, with a small number of students participating and the rest feeling reluctant to voice opinions for fear of peer disapproval or not having the "right" answer for the teacher.

Research (Battistich, Solomon, & Delucchi, 1993; Cohen, 1984; Linn & Burbules, 1993) has shown that academic and social benefits of small group or cooperative learning are dependent upon the quality of students' interaction within those groups. If students experience inclusion and peer respect, then an increased use of small-group learning contributes to "increases in academic outcomes and prosocial outcomes" (Linn et al., 2000, p. 11). If, however, "group interaction is disrespectful and inequitable, greater use of groups is actually associated with reduced academic and prosocial outcomes" (p. 11). Although some have argued for the frequent practice of cooperative learning and the benefits of collaboration, negotiation (Johnson & Johnson, 1994), and the transference of democratic behavior to other learning situations (Bickmore, 1993), research in Japanese elementary classrooms illustrates the importance of the social quality that is manifested in small-group learning. Alleman and Rosaen (1991)—upon an extensive review of educational literature (Eisenberg, 1982; Honig, 1982; Leming, 1981; Radke-Yarrow, Zahn-Waxler, & Chapman, 1983)—have substantiated that prosocial behavior, defined as "encouraging actions intended to aid or benefit another person or group without the anticipation of external rewards" and the opportunity to practice prosocial behavior increases "the correlation between judgment and action" (p. 129). The linking of judgment with action is necessary for students to make informed decisions and solve complex problems individually and as groups of concerned citizens.

Student Decision Making and Problem Solving. Creative problem solving and reasoning among students are prominent features of mathematics classrooms in Japanese elementary schools (Lee, Graham, & Stevenson, 1996; Stigler, Fernandez, & Yoshida, 1996; Tobin, Wu, & Davidson, 1989). The opportunity for all students, regardless of their socioeconomic backgrounds, to be exposed to higher-order learning, such as decision making and problem solving, is a significant feature of Japanese education. In the United States, concern has surfaced as to which students are exposed to higher-order thought processes in public schools. The differing degrees to which American students are exposed to and participate in reflective thinking, decision making, and problem solving activities are often attributable to socioeconomic and cultural factors. Although a study conducted by Sato (1991) found subtle differences in how curricula was presented to Japanese students of diverse socioeconomic backgrounds, Sato and McLaughlin (1992) found that "the presentation of material in Japanese elementary classrooms appears to be highly consistent across a wide-range of schools" (cited in LeTendre, 1999b, pp. 10–11). Thus, "Japanese teachers appear to provide equal access in terms of students' opportunity to learn" (p. 10). This conclusion seems to be reinforced by the consistency of the eightfold activity structure across Japanese elementary science classrooms observed by Linn et al. (2000).

A study by Schempp, Chefferes, and Zaichkowsky (1983) revealed that American children whose teachers encouraged them to share in classroom decision making felt more positive about themselves than those in classrooms where decisions were made exclusively by the teacher" (cited in Alleman & Rosaen, 1991, p. 127). Observations by Linn et al. (2000) have shown that teachers in Japanese elementary schools provide a structure in which students can frame their discussions and arrive at reasons for their particular positions. "The mark of the good citizen," stated Engle (1960), "is the quality of decisions which he [she] reaches on public and private matters of social concern" (p. 118). And decisions cannot be made and problems cannot be solved until all students are provided opportunities to engage in higher order thinking and activities in their formal school settings (Kubow, 1996). Although teachers have obligations to provide such activities, students themselves must assume responsibility for engaging in the learning process.

Individual Responsibility. The ability of Japanese students to manage themselves in responsible ways is an indication of the extent to which they have internalized a set of study and learning skills early in their schooling. Linn et al. (2000) observed that during science instruction Japanese students displayed care in handling dangerous materials when conducting experiments and were responsible for cleaning up any spills—all without teacher supervision to monitor classroom behavior. Students also possessed the requisite study skills to aid their academic learning, for example Linn and her colleagues consistently witnessed students taking notes, managing their own transitions between class activities, and remembering to bring necessary materials to class. To illustrate, the researchers found that students automatically recorded information and glued instructional handouts distributed by the teacher in their notebooks. "Teachers did not use rewards, punishments, or threats; they appeared to rely on the commitment and skills developed by students in the course of earlier schooling" (p. 10).

Throughout the school day and even within 45-minute instructional periods, it seems that Japanese students are provided opportunities to assume a variety of roles—such as leader, teacher, group member, and researcher—as they engage in whole-group, small-group, and individualized learning activities. A central principle in constructing democratic learning environments, Cunat (1996) has argued, is that each "student must have equitable access to educational rewards and benefits, including resources, information, and materials for learning" (p. 133). This appears to be the case in Japanese elementary classrooms where a learning community is created "that recognizes and validates the individuality and responsibility of each participant" (Linn et al., 2000, p. 130). Such an environment reinforces students' feelings of dignity and self-worth.

Recognition of Human Dignity. It is commonmly assumed that recognition of the human dignity of each individual learner be modeled by the teacher and observed by every class member. The ways in which teaching and learning occurred in the Japanese elementary classrooms revealed opportunities for the expression of student opinions and ideas. A learning community was created in which peers interacted with each other and built on others' ideas to further their conceptual understanding and to even direct the course of their science learning. Students were engaged in multiple forms of participation (as researchers, leaders, and group members) as well as in reflective questioning and higher-order thinking. Moreover, the knowledge the Japanese students brought with them to the science classroom helped direct the course of investigations and discussions. The valuing of students' backgrounds, viewing them as capable learners, and setting high expectations for universal student participation in an atmosphere that is respectful and lively are all signs that the human dignity of students is an important consideration in Japanese elementary education. The type of instruction that occurred in the elementary science classrooms was premised on the notion of making science learning relevant and interesting to students.

Relevance. The eightfold activity pattern observed during Japanese science instruction seemed to provide teachers with concrete methods for tying learning to students' interests and questions. In this way, students were able to see the relevance of their own learning, as they determined what questions were of interest to pursue. Hands-on investigations and experimentation followed class discussion and small-group planning. As Linn et al. (2000) reported, "students moved easily through these structures; they willingly reasoned about observed phenomena and transferred findings from one lesson to another" (p. 5). The activity structures were also congruent with the Japanese conception of holistic development. Learning in Japanese science classrooms attended to not only students' intellectual development, but also to their social, emotional, and physical needs. In fact, it seems that the democratic-oriented classrooms provided an avenue for scientific learning to occur.

This foregoing examination of Linn et al.'s (2000) study of Japanese elementary science instruction is consistent with longitudinal, qualitative studies that have shown that elementary teachers across Japan do not emphasize rote learning or treat students as empty receptacles or blank slates; rather, teachers facilitate learning that is student centered and experiential in practice. Students are active participants in the solving of math and science problems, because they question their own and others' hypotheses and apply knowledge in new ways (LeTendre, 1999b). By applying the democratic characteristics framework to classroom instruction, the educational dialogue moves from recognition of student-centered practices as the basic modes of instructional delivery and student association in Japanese elementary classrooms to recognition that such arrangements are illustrative of the particular philosophical and social conceptions of teaching and learning held by some Japanese educators. Thus, the entire classroom enterprise seems to offer a lesson in democratic education.

Interesting questions remain about how the creation of democratic-oriented classroom environments might contribute to students' academic achievement, as opposed to deterring from it, and how some teachers come to view such teaching–learning arrangements as best practice. In Japan, the professional development of teachers is a contributing factor in fostering democratic education at the elementary level and its being linked to best teaching practice.

TEACHER PROFESSIONAL DEVELOPMENT IN JAPAN

Shimahara (1998a) has identified six interrelated domains that influence teachers' work and professional growth: learning from senior colleagues, a supportive environment, critical events, networking with teachers from other schools, assumption of roles, and in- and out-of-school in-service education programs. Each of these domains is featured in teacher education in Japan. High levels of collegial collaboration and interdependence among teachers—both novices and veterans—are derived, in part, from the cultural and structural features of Japanese schools (Sato & McLaughlin, 1992). In order to consider how the underlying professional environment supports Japanese teaching and learning at the elementary level, this section focuses on a number of aspects. Key features of teacher development in Japan that contribute to a professional growth environment include peer support and collaboration, teacher transfer, and openness to observation and critique. These features support teachers' commitments to professional growth and consistency in teaching practice and illustrate the ways Japanese teachers are socialized into the particular norms, values, and behaviors of their profession.

Peer Support and Collaboration

Collegial support and peer collaboration at the school level often characterizes the professional development of Japanese teachers. According to Shimahara (1998a), in-service education and professional development in Japan are guided by at least three assumptions: (1) teaching is inherently a cooperative process and is, therefore, improved through collaboration; (2) collegial planning is an essential part of teaching; and (3) "peer participation characterized by the active engagement of teachers in a variety of school activities is an indispensable element of teaching and schooling" (Shimahara, 1998, p. 455).

Kenkyuu jugyou is a term that describes this routine collaboration in which teachers plan lessons and reflect on the presentation of those lessons with their peers (Lewis & Tsuchida, 1997; Shimahara & Sakai, 1995; Stigler & Hiebert, 1997). This process of reflection and critique enables teachers to "develop, hone, and spread" activity structures that they see as essential to student-centered learning (Linn et al. 2000, p. 12). "In these research lessons, teachers jointly plan (often for months) how to improve some aspect of curriculum or practice, invite the entire faculty to observe and record the lesson, and then discuss it" (Lewis & Tsuchida, 1997, cited in Linn et al., 2000, p. 9). Thus, the research lessons provide a forum for the discussion of teaching practice, such as how more participatory instructional strategies like student problem solving and decision making might be effectively implemented in their classrooms. Linn et al. also discovered that the limited number of topics to be covered in Japan's national curriculum provides the time needed for teachers to choose student-centered approaches and provides a basis for teacher collaboration. These opportunities for collegial exchange help develop teachers' "sense of belonging to a professional community" (Sato & McLaughlin, 1992, p. 364).

Peer collaboration and exchange of ideas is also supported by the physical arrangement in Japanese schools. Teachers' desks—much like their students' work arrangements—are placed in a common faculty room, with the goal of building "family" cohesion and fostering regular collegial contact (Sato & McLaughlin, 1992, p. 363). In addition to close physical proximity, Shimahara and Sakai (1995) have argued that "an ethos of equality in status among teachers" (Okano & Tsuchiya, 1999, p. 174) helps to build interdependence among peers. A professional code of conduct exists for all teachers, regardless of age and experience, in that "no teacher tells another teacher what to do to his or her face, unless of course requested by the teacher himself or herself" (Shimahara & Sakai 1995, cited in Okano & Tsuchiya, 1999, p. 174).

This scenario depicting teacher professional development in Japan contrasts with the professional environment for many American teachers. A recent U.S. Department of

Education report prepared by Adelman (1998), titled *Trying to Beat the Clock*, compared the lives of American and Japanese teachers; American teachers reported the need for more preparation time, more collegial interaction, and more support, feedback, and constructive criticism to improve their teaching practice. Isolationism seemed to characterize teaching for a host of American teachers, who once they begin teaching, have few formal opportunities to share with colleagues or exchange lesson plans and teaching techniques to refine practice (Stevenson, 1998). The physical arrangement in many U.S. schools is cited as a reason for the limited collegial exchange. With desks often located in their own classrooms, some American teachers "complain of the lack of common space where they can come together routinely, by grade level or department, to confer about students, practice, and problems" (Sato & McLaughlin, 1992, p. 364). However, as Sato and McLaughlin have argued, collegiality is defined differently by Japanese and American teachers who hold differing expectations for the kind, degree, and frequency of collegial contact and exchange of teaching practice.

Teacher Transfer

A notable feature of teaching in Japan is that teachers do not remain in the same school in which they begin their professional careers. Rather, three years for the novice teacher and five years for other teachers are typical time periods spent at any one school (Sato et al., 1991, cited in Okano & Tsuchiya, 1999). In 1994, Shimizu found that 16.5% of Japanese teachers were transferred to another school. Many teachers view these transfers as positive experiences, enabling them to adjust to new environments, to ascertain their teaching strengths and weaknesses, and to "find their own identities" (Okano & Tsuchiya, 1999, pp. 147–148). A study by Sato et al. (1991) showed that 50% of teachers viewed transfers as favorable to their professional development. Like teachers, administrators also change schools every three to four years, thereby placing all educators in new situations and exposing them to new students and colleagues. This, in turn, widens their network of professional peers and contacts (Sato & McLaughlin, 1992).

Openness to Observation and Critique

Professional growth activities are a central aspect of the professional lives of Japanese teachers, who view their involvement in these activities as necessary for instructional improvement. The twofold purpose of professional development activities is to enhance "individual competence" and foster "group identity" (Sato & McLaughlin, 1992, p. 362). Teachers in Japan tend to initiate voluntary study groups to critically review and evaluate one another's lesson plans, materials, and instructional activities and will often spend time after school and over holiday breaks engaged in the exchange of classroom practice. Whereas "professional norms of privacy constrain the open examination of practice" (Sato & McLaughlin, 1992, p. 364) in the United States, peer observation and critique are common practices among Japanese teachers. "Student work—drawings, cassette tapes of singing, videotapes of classroom activity or of physical education—forms the basis for study group meetings" (Sato & McLaughlin, 1992, p. 362). This openness is due to a general belief that "shared, public lessons" serve "as a catalyst for improvement" (Linn et al., 2000, p. 12) and that improvement occurs from the grassroots level, as teachers reflect on their own classroom practice with their peers.

School leadership, like professional development, is viewed differently in Japan and the United States. The strong collegial network among Japanese teachers contributes to a sense of empowerment, and many believe they have more influence over school policy matters and receive more support from their peers than do teachers in the United States (Lewis, 1998). Drawing upon the work of Ito (1994), Okano and Tsuchiya (1999) have argued that American and Japanese teachers hold differing beliefs about the position and power of the principalship in their respective countries:

> American teachers believe that the principal's leadership strongly affects the school's educational policies. Japanese teachers, on the other hand, rate the influence of ordinary teachers much higher than the principal's leadership in forming school policies; [*sic*] and believe that what is expected of principals is not to exercise strong leadership but to create cooperative consensus amongst all teachers. (p. 175)

Whereas American educational administrators often draw upon their own subject area expertise to initiate instructional improvement, principals in Japan serve more as facilitators of teacher collaboration (Linn et al., 2000). Japanese administrators are confident that "through discussion and trial of actual lessons" (Linn et al., p. 12), teachers will be able to improve their own and one another's instruction. Although Japanese elementary teachers are responsible for teaching all subject areas, they view themselves as experts in one subject "which they pursue as the main focus of their own professional development and their leadership within the school" (p. 9). In comparison, American teachers spend relatively limited time on professional growth activities, yet "consistently suggest that one of the biggest constraints on the rate and success of education reform is their lack of time for professional activities other than the direct instruction of students" (Stevenson, 1998, p. 32). This point underscores a structural factor of U.S. schools in that teaching schedules are often rigid and compact, leaving teachers little time for the exchange of teaching practice. Moreover, many American teachers draw distinct boundaries between the public and private spheres, which might also account for the lower levels of involvement of American teachers in professional development activities and professional organizations (Sato & McLaughlin, 1992).

Commitment to Professional Growth

Commitment to professional growth can be evidenced in the in-service programs and professional behaviors exhibited by Japanese teachers. There are two kinds of in-service education in Japan. One type consists of voluntary groups that meet on a continual basis within individual schools. Some of the voluntary meetings are planned by the teachers themselves and some by professional teacher organizations. The second type consists of workshops that are conducted monthly and yearly by local and administrative bodies. Interestingly, the context of in-service education for teachers differs from the training provided to other public employees in Japan. Whereas the training offered general public employees is aimed at the improvement of worker efficiency, the in-service education for teachers "is legally guaranteed as an important component of their professional tasks" (Okano & Tsuchiya, 1999, p. 149).

Thus, there is a public expectation in Japan that teachers must "constantly improve their professional knowledge in order to assist children's development"; however, it is recognized that teachers must "have the freedom and independence to select the education that they consider to be the most appropriate to their own teaching" (Okano & Tsuchiya, 1999, p. 149). In Japan, teachers are expected to assume responsibilities for their own improvement. The voluntary study groups are organized outside teachers' regular workday. At these meetings, "teachers, like students, work together in cooperative groups, have interdependent work assignments, and have rotating duties that all must perform" (Sato & McLaughlin, 1992, p. 364). Studies on teachers' perceptions of in-service education, such as that done by Shimahara & Sakai (1995), have shown that the most effective approach to enhancing individual professional teaching competence is the regular, informal sharing of experience with colleagues and that this approach "has the most significant impact on their teaching, in comparison with other forms of in-service training programs" (Okano & Tsuchiya, 1999, p. 174).

In addition to assuming responsibilities for in-service education, teachers also engage in knowledge production. Sato and McLaughlin (1992) found that "journal articles by teachers about their educational research outnumber by a third those of university educational researchers in Japan" (p. 363). Okano and Tsuchiya (1999) concur that more professional journals are written by and for classroom teachers than by and for academics in higher education institutions.

Consistency in Teaching Practice

Taken together, peer collaboration, teacher transfer, openness to observation and critique, and a commitment to professional growth seem to contribute to consistency in teaching practice in Japan. "While Japanese teachers ultimately choose the instructional approaches they will use in the classroom, shared research lessons may offer opportunities for teachers to collectively build and refine not just instructional techniques, but also norms about what is good instruction" (Linn et al. 2000, p. 11). The voluntary in-service meetings and informal sharing with colleagues provide Japanese teachers with opportunities "to reaffirm purpose, to resolve problems, and to set goals" (Sato & McLaughlin, 1992, p. 363). This model of teacher learning provides an avenue for teachers to gain "personal experience with the type of instruction they are trying to build in their classrooms" (Linn et al., 2000, p. 12). Moreover, because research lessons are subject to peer observation, Linn et al. contend that there is increased pressure on teachers to improve their practice. A shared curriculum, with a manageable number of topics, also enables Japanese teachers to focus their discussion during in-service training on "the strategies, purposes, and fine points of teaching a unit" (p. 12). Overall, professional development might contribute to a less diffuse conception of good teaching practice across Japan (Rohlen, 1995, cited in Hawley & Hawley, 1997). But, while less variation might result regarding what constitutes good teaching practice, this reduced variation might also suggest strong socializing tendencies within the teaching profession in Japan.

Socialization

According to Sato and McLaughlin (1992), "norms established within the teaching profession combine with social expectations to further differentiate the roles and responsibilities of Japanese teachers from those of their American counterparts" (p. 362). The culture of teaching in Japan influences the ways teachers organize their professional activities

(Okano & Tsuchiya, 1999). Although particular features such as peer collaboration, teacher transfer, and consistency of practice are viewed as catalysts for effective instruction, Okano and Tsuchiya argue that some Japanese educators consider these same features hindrances:

> The all-inclusive nature of teaching can be a source of burn-out; strong interdependence among teachers can act as an unnecessary pressure for conforming to group norms; [and] an individual teacher's failure to form a rapport with colleagues may result in not only an uncomfortable work environment but also a denial of valuable opportunities for professional development. (p. 175)

In other words, what might be considered the strengths of professional development in Japan or elsewhere can also be considered its weaknesses, thereby hindering the development of individual competence and teacher professionalism. For example, less variation in teaching practice, as cited in the previous section, might lend itself to consistency in how the Japanese curriculum is delivered and may well contribute to the public's confidence that students are gaining the skills that they themselves learned. Less variation in teaching practice, however, might also mean teacher resistance to improving curriculum and instruction. This resistance to new ideas and approaches could limit the ability of teachers to teach students the necessary knowledge and skills to function successfully in an ever-changing world and could contribute to the public's mistrust of schools.

Thus, it is important to examine how socialization serves to foster or hinder professional growth and instructional improvement. American researchers Engle and Ochoa (1988) have defined socialization as "the process of learning the existing customs, traditions, rules and practices of a society" (pp. 29–30). In this traditional definition, socialization is viewed as being rooted in the past and assumes a more static view of culture. It also assumes that an openness to new ways of thinking about education or the expression of dissenting viewpoints will be sequestered by those who favor the status quo in the teaching profession. That is to say that critical reflection about the existing socializing practices manifested in a culture, whether it be Japanese, American, or other, can conflict "with the tendency of culture to reproduce itself with all its rigidities, inconsistencies, and inequities" (p. 14). This line of thinking has led Engle and Ochoa to reason that a process of countersocialization—defined as independent thinking and social criticism—is needed. However, the notion of countersocialization may seem threatening to some teachers, administrators, parents, and community members precisely because it elevates criticism of a status quo to which these members of a society may be wedded.

A problem that could be found in a system in which group consensus dictates best practice, such as Japan, is that those teachers who do not agree with particular instructional methods, educational philosophies, or teaching responsibilities might be marginalized or isolated by their peers. Or they might feel uncomfortable questioning and critiquing others honestly, if their opinion is in opposition to the majority's views. Applying Engle and Ochoa's concept of socialization practices to the teaching profession, it could be said that socialization preserves what is considered standard teaching practice, whereas countersocialization ensures that standard practice is critically examined so that teaching and learning might be improved. The problem with this conceptualization is that the individual teacher is left to strike an appropriate balance between "the group" (socialization) and "the individual" (countersocialization). In other words, the teacher must balance independent, analytical inquiry with the cultural norms and social rules of the teaching profession.

More recently, this socialization–countersocialization dichotomy has been thoughtfully challenged by Whitson and Stanley (1996) who view socialization as *both* the learning of established societal practices, values, and norms *and* the learning of skills to critically think about, challenge, and change those norms if necessary. Drawing upon the sociological tradition, these authors define socialization "as the development in individuals of the competence afforded as members of their society" (Whitson & Stanley, 1996, p. 330). To explicate this, the authors draw an analogy to the maturation of a scientist to underscore how shortsighted it is to assume that countersocialization can somehow be separated from socialization. The analogy can be extended to the teaching profession as well:

> We do not think that the socialization of young scientists [young teachers] is limited to training in the replication of past findings or conventional procedures. Fresh thinking and the challenging of established paradigms are not regarded as antiscientific, and thus requiring some kind of "countersocialization" opposed to their socialization as members of their disciplines. No more should we describe as "countersocializing" those educational experiences in which students [and teachers] acquire the abilities to challenge social norms or policies; for these abilities also are not antisocial, but are essential aspects of the educated democratic mind. (p. 331)

Thus, Whitson and Stanley find it problematic to "combine reflective inquiry with countersocialization" (p. 316) when an important part of education's socializing role is to foster in students and teachers the "habits of mind" to naturally recognize what they are being taught as well as to think about and question what they are learning. This revised conceptualization of socialization has an important role to play in teachers' professional development and in the transformation of societies. Reflective inquiry, critique, and action are indispensable elements of education. These skills are necessary competencies for educators to possess so that they, in turn, are able to teach them to their students (Kubow, 1996).

Gutmann (1987) has reminded educators and policy makers who would seek to limit critique and action in schools that "the distinctive virtue of a democratic society [is] that it authorizes citizens to influence how their society reproduces itself" (p. 15). This applies to teacher education as well. Professional development has an important role to play in encouraging teacher critique and action as well as developing group unity (Kubow, 1996). But as Cunat (1996) has stated, it might be favorable to change "systems when they are at odds with the values and ideals that must undergird a democratic and socially just way of life" (p. 129). As Dewey (1937) recognized almost 50 years ago, "it is not whether the schools shall or shall not influence the course of future social life, but in what direction they shall do so and how" (p. 236, cited in Whitson & Stanley, 1996, p. 319).

Socialization, understood as teachers and students in all societies learning both the norms of their society and possessing the reflective skills to critique those norms, is a way to re-envision teacher professionalism as being about teachers engaged in the process of creating environments that help develop democratic citizens. A lesson produced from the mutual viewing of Japanese and American professional development is effectively summarized by Darling-Hammond (2000):

As teachers look beyond their own actions to appreciate the understandings and experiences of their students, and evaluate these in light of their self-developed knowledge of individual learners and their professional knowledge of factors influencing development and learning, they grow wiser about the many ways in which learning and teaching interact. (p. 171)

Arguably, teacher autonomy is an integral part of socializing teachers into the teaching profession. Autonomy enables teachers to voice the support they need to educate the young, to use their expertise and practical competence to shape school content and procedures, and to exercise social and political latitude in order to direct the course of learning and instruction. In the next section, we examine teacher autonomy in the Japanese context and employ a political–analytical framework to further investigate teacher professionalism.

TEACHER AUTONOMY IN JAPAN

Teacher autonomy, understood as the ability of teachers to make informed judgments and decisions that affect their work and roles and that of their students, is an important characteristic of teacher professionalism. Teachers—those responsible for the formal education of a society's youth—make numerous decisions on a daily basis about what to teach, how to teach, and in what ways content and instruction should be modified to accommodate new educational research. In this way, "the nature of education" is "autonomous" (Okano & Tsuchiya, 1999, p. 155). However, the degree to which teachers experience autonomy in their work environments is subject to the ways in which government, at its various levels, assumes responsibility for formal education.

Thomas (1983) has contributed to a deeper understanding of the relationship between the state and education by posing a framework for the examination of political–educational symbiotic exchanges. Defining **symbiotic** as the degree to which politics and education influence the fate of each other, Thomas has argued that education socializes youth to support decision making and power patterns advocated by those in power, thereby legitimating a country's existing political system. Schools, through human resource production and the sorting and selecting of youths, provide society with the kinds and amounts of workers needed, thereby contributing to the stability and longevity of the existing political organization and enabling some to enjoy a favored position in terms of the amount and kind of education they receive (Thomas, 1983). Extending his argument further, Thomas has stated that education systems play a social assessment and interpretive role. That is, education can stimulate youths to engage in critical social analysis; however, the degree to which teachers and students engage in this social evaluator role can be limited by the state, which might label them as "true patriots," "the nation's social conscience," or "subversives" (Thomas, 1983). Education systems, therefore, according to Thomas, influence the political realm through their social control and social change functions, with some schools serving more as followers and reflectors of the existing social order than as sources of reform.

In ascertaining the effect of political groups on education, Thomas has suggested that education is influenced by politics in at least three ways, including (1) the support provided to schools, (2) the content and procedures allowed in schools, and (3) the latitude of social and political action permitted the people who inhabit schools. Each of these concepts has been placed in the form of a question to aid in the thoughtful examination of educational issues. (See Table 6.2.) Although the symbiotic linking of politics and education has been applied to 10 different societies in a volume edited by Thomas (1983), we shift this political-educational analysis to the particular issue of teacher professionalism—a discrete aspect of education in any modern or modernizing society. The next section illustrates an application of the concepts of support, content and procedures, and latitude of social and political action to teacher professionalism in Japan. This framework, however, is not limited to an examination of teacher professionalism, as one could also apply it to other issues to help understand how the complex relationship between politics and education affects any given issue.

Support

Support refers generally to the state's provision of necessary resources (e.g., school supplies, facilities, salaries), but when applied to teacher professionalism can be understood as public and state confidence in the work that teachers perform accompanied by limited political intervention in educational affairs. Although the state has assumed responsibility for formal education in Japan since 1872 (Shimahara, 1998b), teachers have experienced changes in their relationship with the state. In general, teaching has moved from being viewed as "a holy order dedicated to the state" (p. 460) to one of public service. Teachers have come to view themselves as "public servants" whose standards are regulated by "the state" (p. 460). This transition in teacher identity has implications for the kind and degree of autonomy that teachers view as necessary in carrying out their professional roles and responsibilities. According to Fujita and Wong (1997), "professionalism as an ideological icon was extensively used by the Japan Teachers' Union in the 1960s to struggle for greater control over education" (p. 6, cited in Shimahara, 1998b, p. 460). Interviews with Japanese teachers have led Shimahara to conclude that "professionalism in teaching is

---

Table 6.2   **Framework to Examine the Relationship Between Politics and Education**
Political Influence on Education
Political groups affect education in the following ways:
1. Support   How much support does the education system (e.g., teachers) receive from political groups?
2. Content and procedures   What is taught, by what methods, and how is it assessed?
3. Latitude of social and political action   To what extent should school staff (and students) be allowed to engage in whatever social and political behavior they choose?
Based on the work of R. Murray Thomas, 1983.

hardly understood by grass-roots teachers as the pursuit of professional excellence by self-regulated standards . . . [thus] teacher development is constrained by the lack of professionalism" p. 460).

Content and Procedures

Intrusions on teacher autonomy are evidenced by the state's control of Japanese teacher education and school curriculum. "The nature of the teachers' rights that Japanese educationalists and teachers consider fundamental"—such as autonomy—varies from teacher to teacher and "influences the ways in which teachers see themselves and experience schooling" (Okano & Tsuchiya, 1999, p. 154). However, on a large scale, the struggle between teacher unions and the state for the control of education is well known in Japan. An example of this struggle is found in the tight control the state has kept on teacher education. Viewing teachers as "agents of national development and students' development of character, morality, and cultural sensitivity" (Shimahara, 1998b, p. 257), the state legitimized its involvement in teacher education on the basis of the assumption that education plays an important role in the industralization of a nation and the development of citizenship characteristics that support national progress.

In 1989, teacher in-service education in Japan experienced a major change when the Ministry of Education (a state apparatus) required recently employed, public elementary teachers to complete a one-year internship (*shoninsha kenshu*) designed to foster "teachers' practical competence, *shishitsu*" (Shimahara & Sakai, 1992, cited in Shimahara, 1998b, p. 249). *Shishitsu,* according to Shimahara and Sakai (1992) "is a Japanese concept connoting a broad gamut of skills, knowledge, and orientation to handle classroom management, teaching, lesson plans, student guidance, moral education, extracurricular activities, home relations, and teacher committee work" (cited in Shimahara, 1998b, p. 249). The goal of the government-sponsored internship program was to develop in teachers an educational mission premised on "an awareness of purpose in teaching and a broad social and cultural perspective" (Shimahara, 1998b, p. 249). According to Shimahara (1988b), the program consists of three elements: in-house, in-service education through mentor supervision; 20 workshops and lectures created and delivered by local education centers; and approximately 10 days of summer workshops and retreats.

Although teachers had little influence over the internship being legislated, they did have considerable control over how the program would be implemented (Shimahara, 1998b). Hargreaves (1980) has emphasized that teachers have an important role to play in executing educational reforms, even if they are top-down, because the "reforms must pass through 'the teachers' culture as a medium'" and "they are frequently shaped and transformed in that passage" (Shimahara, 1998a, p. 249). Shimahara (1998a) has argued that mutually influencing interactions exist between "two spheres of practice" (p. 255): the official sphere (the state) and the unofficial sphere (the culture of teaching). According to Shimahara, government-sponsored in-service education, teaching regulations, and national curriculum constitute the official sphere of practice, whereas "the culture of teaching"—defined as teachers' "shared interests, commitments, and strategies to cope with external pressures" (p. 255–256)—represents the unofficial sphere of practice. It is in the unofficial sphere, as Shimahara has reasoned, that "teachers exercise an appreciable degree of independence and freedom" (p. 255). According to the work of Hargreaves (1980) and Shimahara (1998a), the teacher is placed at the center of the process; it is his or her task to interpret and respond to the two spheres of practice whose actions influence each other. (See Figure 6.3.)

Arguably, the internship program in Japan placed greater demands on teachers' time, thereby intensifying teacher labor. For example, not only did the newly employed Japanese elementary teachers have to immediately assume responsibility for their professional development, but their supervisors were obligated to provide practical experience and training (Okano & Tsuchiya, 1999). Thus, successful implementation of the internship program was based on the commitment and participation of a host of educators, including mentors, other classroom teachers, and school administrators (Shimahara, 1998b). However, cooperation among the classroom teachers might be one of the most important factors in effective implementation of the official reform, as classroom teachers especially "influence the occupation socialization of beginning teachers" (p. 249). If teachers see that their teaching culture is being threatened, they will often find ways to modify or subvert "official" reforms.

As early as 1982, The Study Commission of Teacher Education, sponsored by the Japan Pedagogical Association, reported concern about decreasing levels of teacher autonomy and academic freedom as the result of imposed, official in-service education that imposed more regulations and greater uniformity upon educators (Shimahara, 1998b). More recent critique has been raised by the Japanese Teacher Union (JTU) that the

FIGURE 6.3

Teachers as Conduit or Medium of Two Spheres of Practice Whose Actions Influence Each Other

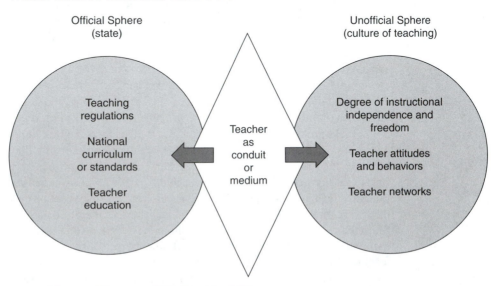

Official Sphere
(state)

Unofficial Sphere
(culture of teaching)

Teaching regulations

National curriculum or standards

Teacher education

Teacher as conduit or medium

Degree of instructional independence and freedom

Teacher attitudes and behaviors

Teacher networks

Note: Modification of Hargreaves, 1980; Shimahara, 1998a.

Ministry of Education's (*Monbusho*) internship program subjected teachers to a centralized authority that could make advancement to school administrative positions dependent on how well teachers performed in *kenshu,* government-regulated in-service training (Shimahara, 1998b). Further, the union reasoned that school leadership would be subjected to increasing state control. The JTU insisted that teacher autonomy was protected by the Fundamental Law of Education and that Japanese "teachers' right to organize their in-service education [was] inherent in the concept of teacher autonomy" (Shimahara, 1998b, pp. 252–253). Exercising their right to initiate their own teacher education, Japanese teachers developed a form of voluntary in-service with the goal of promoting effective teaching practices. According to Shimahara (1991), "almost every school has an in-house study group that organizes study activities, such as curriculum development, demonstration classes, observation and discussion of teaching" (cited in Shimahara, 1998b, pp. 254–255). Although the state capitalized on the convergence of two phenomena—the public's sentiment to improve teacher quality and the union's declining power base (Shimahara 1992, cited in Shimahara, 1998b), Japanese teachers embarked on their own program of in-service education, which has largely promoted consistency of practice and has socialized its classroom teachers to this particular form of professional development.

There are other ways in which Japanese teachers have tried to strike a balance between state control and teacher autonomy, such as teachers' efforts to exert influence on the national curriculum. Although some have argued that classroom activities must be in line with the *Monbusho* guidelines, Sato and McLaughlin (1992) have found that "Japanese teachers respond to centrally determined objectives by choosing the materials, events, and opportunities appropriate to their students, their locale, and their school" (p. 361). The authors contend that Japan's centralized "education system actually requires more planning, curriculum development, instructional decision making, and professional choices at the local level and engenders more diversity at the classroom level than does the apparently less controlled American system" (p. 361). A possible explanation for this is that U.S. textbooks, supplemental materials, and curriculum manuals "specify the details of the content of classrooms to a greater extent in the U.S. than in Japan" (p. 361). This creates pressure on American teachers to construct original materials as opposed to thinking about how "skilled interpretations of standard curricula" might be provided (Lewis, 1998, p. 187). Lewis has argued that a state-controlled curriculum in Japan ensures that schoolchildren across the country receive the same content and that teachers have the same set of lessons across subject areas. Consequently, Japanese teachers spend less time deciding what is important to teach and more time planning how children might explore a concept or topic in depth (Lewis, 1998).

Lewis (1998) found that, whereas American teachers spend a great deal of time deciding what concepts are important to teach and sorting through texts filled with vocabulary lists and application problems, Japanese teachers focus their attention on how to make the curriculum meaningful to their students. Moreover, Lewis has found that the teacher's manual in Japan often provides information on the kinds of "thinking children are likely to bring to the problem, [thus] supporting teachers' treatment of children as active, thoughtful participants whose ideas should help drive the lessons" (p. 187). The author has suggested that elementary education in the United States lacks an informed "process for defining what is important to teach children and bringing this to bear on the taught curriculum"

(p. 189). Despite debate by American education professional organizations about what is most important to teach in their respective subject areas, Lewis contends that these deliberations have had minimal effect on "the de facto curriculum" (p. 189) that is largely determined by commercial texts and standardized tests. From this standpoint, reasoned Lewis, "there is already a national curriculum in the United States"—but, on account of the exclusion of practitioners in its development, "not one that lays out, thoughtfully and frugally, the knowledge, thinking, and attitudes central to children's development" (p. 189).

In relation to how content is taught, Stevenson and Stigler (1992) have found that Americans and Japanese place different values on performance and innovation and that these differing perceptions affect definitions of teacher effectiveness.

> In America, teachers are judged to be successful when they are innovative, inventive, and original. Skilled presentation of a standard lesson is not sufficient and may even be disparaged as indicating a lack of innovative talent. It is as if American teachers were expected to write their own play or create their own concerto day after day then perform it with expertise and finesse. These two models, the skilled performer and the innovator, have very different value in the East and West. It is hard for us in the West to appreciate that innovation does not require that the presentation be totally new, but can come from thoughtful additions, new interpretations, and skillful modifications. (pp. 167–168, cited in Lewis, 1998, pp. 187–188)

Interestingly, Eastern observers have also recognized creativity to be a strength of Western education, and a number of Asian governments (Japan, Hong Kong, Malaysia, Singapore, South Korea) have been looking globally to find ways to pursue creative innovation in addition to academic rigor. Although early elementary social studies and language instruction in Japan is centered on involving students in creative learning activities—such as opportunities "to map the neighborhood and study the local sewer system" (Lewis, 1998, p. 189)—activities and texts falling outside the national curriculum guidelines must be stated on lesson plans and submitted to the principal for approval. As students progress through their schooling years, language instruction, like other subject areas, becomes more focused on memorization and factual recall as opposed to thoughtful discussions about "the important ideas raised by a work of literature," for instance (p. 189). Although rarely used in the early grades, standardized testing becomes an increasingly prominent feature of Japanese schooling as students grow older. Ironically, as the United States embarks on increased standardized testing in its quest to raise academic achievement scores, some Asian countries are presently reexamining their educational policies and standardized testing practices for ways to cultivate students' independent thinking (*Newsweek*, 1999). Lewis (1998) has provided an insightful, comparative commentary on teacher autonomy and externally imposed assessment measures:

> That standardized testing can be the enemy of good teaching is hardly a new point, but it is one that needs to be emphasized in comparing Japanese and American schools. Although some researchers have argued that entrance examinations positively influence Japanese educational achievement, exactly the opposite case can also be made: that elementary achievement is high because Japanese teachers are free from the pressure to teach to standardized tests. Japanese teachers are simultaneously supported by clear national objectives that emphasize social, ethical, and intellectual development and free to teach for understanding rather than drill students for test performance. (p. 191)

Latitude of Social and Political Action

A major area of contention between the state and Japanese teachers revolves around the degree of latitude teachers are allowed in schools and society. The state places strict regulations on its teachers and prohibits them from engaging in political activities such as forming and participating in political organizations, seeking votes, and using documents to support candidates in an election format (Okano & Tsuchiya, 1999). Political involvement can also be detrimental to Japanese teachers seeking promotion and advancement. To obtain recommendations from their principals, teachers must leave their union activities behind (Okano & Tsuchiya, 1999). Okano and Tsuchiya (1999) contend that these restrictions on teachers' civil rights are in direct violation of international standards put forth in "Advice on Teachers' Status," a document issued by UNESCO and the International Labor Organization. The authors argue that "teachers' civil rights are fundamental human rights, which are indispensable in the conduct of their professional duties for all (not just a particular group or individual), and in the cultivation of the political knowledge needed by all citizens" (p. 157).

The state's curbing of Japanese teachers' civic involvement has implications for teaching practice as well. As Okano and Tsuchiya (1999) have articulated, "teachers actively make their own sense of a system that imposes constraints on, and governs, their professional lives" (p. 191). The debate about teacher autonomy in Japan centers on "the degree to which Japanese teachers are civil servants, obligated to follow the scripted guidelines and mandates imposed by the national government, and the degree to which they are professionals with latitude to exercise their wisdom and professional judgment" (Sato & McLaughlin, 1992, p. 361). In comparison, the pressures that American teachers face in a decentralized system of education and a legalistic society include increasing standardization in student assessment, as well as legal concerns about liability and insurance that often limit the educational opportunities (e.g., field trips and events) that teachers are able to plan for children. Commenting on the U.S. situation, Herbst (1998) has argued that although teacher unions have struggled to improve working conditions and teachers' salaries, they "have been slow to address the status of teachers as autonomous professionals" (Herbst, 1989, p. 7).

An area that may warrant further examination in Japan and the United States is the degree of latitude teachers have to critique the existing guidelines for education that restrict their teaching practices. For example, if the development of students' political knowledge is an important characteristic of citizenship in each country, then teachers must be allowed to engage in political behavior themselves and stimulate critical questioning about societal concerns in their classrooms. In the case of Japan, it is ironic that teachers are viewed as "civil servants" but prohibited from exercising their civil rights. As Okano and Tsuchiya (1999) have claimed, "one cannot expect teachers to ensure children's rights, when they themselves do not enjoy what they consider to be their own freedoms and rights" (p. 156).

In the United States, although individual rights sometimes override the need for individuals to assume their civic responsibilities, a key factor affecting political knowledge is the degree to which teachers feel comfortable discussing controversial social issues with their students. In a longitudinal study of political attitudes, Ehman (1980) found that controversial issues, range of student viewpoints during class discussion, and student attitudes related "directly and positively to measures of both political confidence and political interest" (cited in Harwood, 1992, p. 70). However, Patrick and Hoge (1991), citing research by Hahn (1988), have found that "overuse of controversy and one-sided teaching about issues in . . . authoritarian classrooms [sic] can produce negative effects, such as passivity, disinterest, and civic intolerance" (p. 433). Moreover, some schools in both countries "maintain strict rules in the name of anti-delinquency measures and improving students' academic performance, without questioning whether this might contradict the underlying assumption of respect for children's rights" (Okano & Tsuchiya, 1999, p. 155).

Overall, teachers in Japan and the United States do have some autonomy to conduct their professional responsibilities despite state policies (Okano & Tsuchiya, 1999). However, the degree to which the state is open to criticism from teachers about the existing guidelines for education—and the degree to which teachers can voice their concerns about the state's control over what to teach, how to teach, and how to assess student learning—are areas that remain less clear. Any further inquiry into these areas must take into consideration a country's social, political, and cultural conditions that shape schools and the degree of autonomy permitted the teachers and students who inhabit those schools.

TEACHER PROFESSIONALISM IN THE UNITED STATES

Although teachers in any country need to be able to argue from their own definitions of professionalism in light of their particular work contexts, comparative inquiry into the issue of professionalism helps to bring particular factors to the foreground for deeper inquiry into teacher professionalism debates at home. Because "compulsory schooling . . . carries with it immense moral obligations . . . [it] provides the legitimate basis for restructuring teacher professionalism [sic] rhetoric" (Soder, 1986, p. 43). In this section, we draw on the eight democratic characteristics previously used to interpret the teaching–learning context in Japanese elementary science classrooms to examine teacher professionalism in the United States. Casting the characteristics as philosophical commitments to a more democratic oriented teacher professionalism, these suggestions provide some starting points for reflective dialogue. The following philosophical commitments are meant to be suggestive rather than prescriptive:

- Teacher professionals are active participants in their own professional development.
- Teacher professionals avoid textbook dominated instruction.
- Teacher professionals are reflective thinkers.
- Teacher professionals engage in discussion.
- Teacher professionals are decision makers and problem solvers.
- Teacher professionals assume individual responsibility.
- Teacher professionals recognize and foster human dignity.
- Teacher professionals determine what is relevant in education.

Teacher Professionals are Active Participants in Their Own Professional Development. One way teachers in the United States might reflect on their professional work is by constructing and participating in their own professional development programs.

Herbst (1989) has argued that teacher professionalism is "most crucially tested" and demonstrated as teachers engage in "collegial relations among themselves" because these relationships "rest on the certainty of shared aims and mutual respect" (pp. 6–7). Herbst's argument is a call for what Ryan and Cooper (1998) have termed "self-determination," in which teachers voice their ideas about what should be taught, how it should be taught, and who should teach it. In the United States, there is an increasing recognition of the importance of teachers' beliefs, values, and experiences as implementers of school reform (Linn et al., 2000). For example, the recent "No Child Left Behind" legislation by the George W. Bush administration places teacher accountability front and center, giving heightened attention to the work of teachers and schools. A thoughtful, critical discussion of this legislation could be a starting point for teacher dialogue in professional development programs.

Although union policies usually dictate the number of in-service hours required for teachers, most professional development programs in the United States consist of one or two-day workshops offered at schools or universities (Ornstein & Levine, 1997). This leaves relatively little time for teachers to engage in a more thorough analysis of their teaching concerns, much less to seek solutions to them. Although some might argue that American teachers have been relatively unwilling to teach lessons in front of their peers for purposes of self-reflection and peer critique, what can be gained from examining Japanese professional development is that Japanese teachers' willingness to be more vulnerable in front of their peers has provided the opportunity for professional growth and improved instruction.

Another area that deserves considerable attention is the way professional development is orchestrated in the United States. It is often the case that an external expert, arranged by administrators as opposed to teachers, comes to the school to offer professional development training sessions. Teachers might then tend to infer that they are not considered "the real experts" and may, just as that detrimentally, conclude that the information imparted under this mode of professional development is disconnected from their work "in the trenches." As a result, these sessions are treated with suspicion rather than as opportunities for growth as intended. A possible way to enhance teacher professionalism is to encourage teacher involvement in deciding their own professional development programs, such as choosing the topics that are of most interest to them and addressing those topics through peer-critiqued lessons and discussions. These possible strategies for professional development embrace the assumption that an environment characterized by sharing teacher expertise and reflecting on professional practice is more conducive to professional growth than win–lose evaluations. This kind of teacher professionalism would include opportunities for teachers to individually assess their effectiveness, while creating more collegial arrangements to help them meet students' learning needs and to increase the competence they feel about their work.

Teacher Professionals Avoid Textbook Dominated Instruction. Research from the TIMSS has revealed that breadth, as opposed to depth, is characteristic of most U.S. textbooks. Popkewitz (1994) has noted the scripted nature of teachers' textbook manuals that even suggest where teachers should stand and what they should say, thereby limiting teacher creativity, decision making, and professional latitude. Textbooks do not play such a prominent role in education in Japan as they do in the United States. The compounding problem is that most American textbook publishers are concentrated in relatively few states, bringing regional biases to the texts and giving little attention to multiple views. Moreover, the predominance of textbook instruction and prepackaged materials in the United States lends itself to test assessments of students' learning. As Lewis (1998) has concluded, "tests play nowhere near the role in Japanese elementary schooling that they do in the United States, where school funding, real estate prices, and legal sanctions may all hinge on standardized test scores" (pp. 190–191). To counteract this tendency toward textbooks and standardized testing, American teachers have sought out a variety of resources and materials and continue to search for more authentic assessment measures, such as portfolios that might include writing samples, lab reports, and musical scores produced by students over the course of their schooling careers. Increasingly, teachers see the need for curricula that foster both teacher and student creativity and learning. This concern, as we have seen, parallels Japanese efforts.

Teacher Professionals are Reflective Thinkers. In the United States, scholars such as Zeichner (1999) have given a great deal of attention to developing the notion of teachers as reflective thinkers and practitioners. Reflection, however, must entail an examination of the ways in which the United States structures schooling and include consideration of the larger ecological influences on education (those factors external to schools that affect the way society views schooling). Thus, reflection must include opportunities for teachers to think about their own classroom practices and to craft lessons and acquire techniques to effectively present information. But, as Stevenson (1998) has suggested, time alone will not improve teacher professionalism; individual reflection must be accompanied by discursive interaction among American teachers.

Barnard et al. (1997) posed a question that captures the spirit of inquiry advocated for professional growth: "What kind of experiences need to be created in a teacher education program to help teachers see with new lenses?" (p. 902). Cross-national reflection on schools and teaching might help teachers acquire knowledge about their own practices, while also helping teachers to ask and answer the tougher questions about what they stand for and what responsibilities they are willing to assume. As Barnard et al. have stated, "central to what we see is what we are looking for and where we are looking. Any search is thus constrained by the questions we pose" (p. 893). Yet questions must be posed to foster professional growth and to improve teaching practice.

Teacher Professionals Engage in Discussion. In the United States, discourse about education and educational reform seems to be occurring increasingly at the state and federal levels; meanwhile, teachers' voices at the local levels are often marginalized from the larger discourse. The absence or occasional participation of teachers in the larger educational debate is receiving some attention, as prominent teacher educators such as Cochran-Smith (2000) call for teachers to contribute their knowledge and views on education to the larger political arena. Cochran-Smith has argued that the political landscape is shaped by voices external to the teaching profession that emphasize subject matter and on-the-job experience. In her view, this emphasis dismisses those courses in schools of education that address the knowledge base of teaching and learning. Although teacher education programs, both preservice and in-service, must give attention to the development of teachers' political voices especially, the fact that little time is given for American teachers, especially at the local level, to share their concerns with colleagues does not necessarily position them in ways that will ensure that their voices will be heard and educational expertise considered in the national debates surrounding teacher professionalism and school reform.

Teacher Professionals are Decision Makers and Problem Solvers. Another concern in the United States is that teachers who are outstanding at their work "cannot reach positions of highest prestige, responsibility, and reward in the classroom"; rather, "to advance professionally they must leave the classroom for the administrator's or specialist's office" (Herbst, 1989, p. 7). Therefore, conversations focused solely on teacher praxis and improvement dismiss the larger structural and organizational features in the United States that limit teachers from decision making and leadership arenas. It might be useful, then, to examine the "boundaries of teaching" and "the power relations within it" and how these boundaries and power relations affect teacher professionalism (Barnard et al., 1997, p. 903). Thus, Barnard et al. have argued that attention be given to the notion of "critically reframing perplexing difficulties and dilemmas in teaching in a manner that engages thought and compels conversation" in order that "teachers might both envision and realize possibilities" (p. 903).

Mawhinney (1998) has argued that other proposals that focus on the technology of teaching—those more discrete aspects of the teachers' work centered on techniques to increase students' basic skills and efficient methods for enhancing fast-paced student outcomes—dismiss concerns for higher-level thinking for students and the larger issue of professionalism for teachers. Yet such discussions are central to an understanding of "professionalism [that] promotes teaching as an exercise in professional discretion, autonomy, collegiality, and leadership" (Mawhinney, 1998, p. 41).

Teacher Professionals Assume Individual Responsibility. For a major transformation of the teaching profession to come about in the United States, changes must take place "within the teaching profession and within the larger societal context" (Soder, 1986, p. 29). As Soder has explained, "schooling would have to become an actual—as opposed to a merely rhetorical—priority of the society. The priority would have to be deeply felt, and felt across social classes" (p. 32). Thus, individual responsibility for education must be assumed by a variety of stakeholders, namely parents, administrators, community members, and students, as well as teachers. For example, administrators can accord professional status and respect to American teachers by structuring schooling in ways that provide fewer interruptions during their lessons. Students might assume more responsibility for their academic progress and performance.

However, any strategy for improving educational outcomes must include families and the larger society, who play crucial roles in preparing children for learning and in sustaining their commitment to schooling. Lewis (1998) has found that American teachers, in contrast to their Japanese counterparts, are increasingly being asked to teach "children whose families—poor, alienated, or stressed—do not always meet children's basic need for food, shelter, and adult attention" (p. 185). According to the "the usual indices—infant mortality, malnutrition, child abuse, family stability, parental drug abuse, poverty—Japanese children are extraordinarily fortunate, even compared with children in other advanced industrialized nations" (Boocock, 1987, cited in Lewis, 1998, p. 185). Moreover,

Japanese teachers cater to a student population that regularly attends school, with attendance rates of almost 100 percent for children 6–15 years of age and 96 percent for children 16–18 years of age (Okano & Tsuchiya, 1999).

American teachers may consider pursuing certain actions in order to encourage families to assume responsibilities for children and for children to feel more attached to their schooling. Epstein (1995, cited in Mawhinney, 1998) has suggested six kinds of school–community involvement. First, teachers can support student learning by visiting children's homes and developing strategies between children and their parents for improving home conditions for student learning. Second, teachers can foster communication between the home and school regarding school programs and student progress. Third, teachers can organize parental volunteers to support teaching and learning. Fourth, teachers can extend students' learning after school hours with creative projects and homework. Fifth, teachers can include parents in educational decision making. And, sixth, teachers can collaborate with community members to gather resources that can strengthen student learning.

These suggestions for enhancing the school–community relationship have implications for the current culture of teaching in the United States. The study by Sato (1993) showed that American teachers often draw distinct boundaries between public and private spheres. This separation of public (school) and private (home) domains is culturally consistent with American society. Although Japanese teachers, in general, experience monetary reward, high status, and public support, their responsibilities for students' behaviors and actions extend beyond the school. Although American teachers are less likely than their Japanese counterparts to experience more tangible rewards and public support, they benefit more privately, in terms of their own personal time after their teaching day has ended. In sum, where American teachers obtain personal benefits, Japanese teachers obtain public benefits, especially in terms of high status, prestige, and societal support. Paradoxically perhaps, Japanese teachers, by assuming a great deal of responsibility for students' academic, emotional, and social well-being, have established their professionalism and have, arguably, experienced some power in being able to define what counts as quality in their own field. For a comparison of geophysical and economic factors influencing education in Japan and the United States, see the Points of Convergence box (Figure 6.4).

Teacher Professionals Recognize and Foster Human Dignity. The attention teachers give to fostering classroom and school environments that recognize human dignity help develop students' attachment to school. If children's personal and social development is of central importance in a society, like Japan, "where most children are well cared-for economically and socially," shouldn't holistic student development "demand even more [attention] in the United States?" (Lewis, 1998, p. 192). Although both American and Japanese educators believe in the importance of teacher–student interactions beyond the classroom, "only in Japan is this extra-classroom function an integral part of teachers' duties" (Sato & McLaughlin, 1992, p. 365). Lewis's (1998) study also revealed that American students come to school more mistrustful of adults compared with Japanese children. That is to say that "conflict with adults and punishment are much more common experiences in the lives of young American children" (Lewis, 1998, pp. 185–186) than

FIGURE 6.4

Points of Convergence

JAPAN	Geography and educational consequences	UNITED STATES
Aspect: Located in Eastern Asia, Japan is an island chain situated between the North Pacific Ocean and the Sea of Japan, with the Korean Peninsula to the east. Japan has the largest fishing fleets in the world, accounting for 15% of the global catch (*World Factbook*, 2001). Slightly smaller in size than the state of California (U.S.), Japan is mostly mountainous.	**Geography and educational consequences**	**Aspect:** After Russia and Canada, the United States is the world's third largest country. The United States is bordered by the North Pacific and Atlantic Oceans, Canada, and Mexico. The U.S. economy, considered the largest and most technologically powerful in the world, is based on a market system in which businesses and private individuals have decision-making power and the government buys its goods and services (*World Factbook*, 2001).
Response: Industry, therefore, is the most important sector of the Japanese economy. A strong work ethic, government–industry cooperation, and small defense spending make Japan the second most technologically powerful economy in the world after the United States and the third largest economy after the United States and China (*World Factbook*, 2001).	How have geophysical realities influenced education?	**Response:** Enjoying greater flexibility than their counterparts in Western Europe and Japan, U.S. businesses can "expand plant capital, lay off surplus workers, and develop new products" (*World Factbook*, 2001). Although their advantage has narrowed since World War II, American firms are at the forefront in computers and medical, military, and aerospace equipment (*World Factbook*, 2001).
Consequence: Japan's modern education system is key to its emergence as a highly industrialized nation. Where a student attends school determines social status and future financial success; consequently, students work hard to pass competitive entrance exams to qualify for the best high schools and universities (*The New Encyclopedia Britannica*, 1997).		**Consequence:** Rapid technological advances have resulted in a "two-tier labor market," in which Americans at the bottom lack the education and skills of those at the top, with increasing numbers unable to obtain pay raises, health insurance coverage, and other social benefits (*World Factbook*, 2001).

Japanese children. Hence, the time American teachers give to building stable, close, and caring relationships with their students provides an alternative to the disruptions and difficulties they might experience outside school (Lewis, 1998).

Teacher Professionals Determine What is Relevant in Education. Cochran-Smith (2000) has contended that teacher education in the United States is characterized by differing positions, with "no clear consensus about what teachers need to know, who should provide education for teachers, how teachers should be certified and licensed, and what role university-based teacher preparation should play in school improvement" (p. 163). In

Cochran-Smith's estimation, this fragmentation contributes to a public judgment that teachers do not have a sense of the knowledge that students should know or a sense of how education might better meet students' and society's needs. It could be argued that there is little in the American educational context that demonstrates to the public at large what constitutes the "practical capacity of teachers," a term coined by Okano and Tsuchiya (1999, p. 142). In considering Linn et als., (2000) study of science activity structures within Japanese elementary classrooms, it is reasonable to conclude that democratic oriented classrooms might contribute to students' academic achievement in science. As the researchers found, the success of the science activity structures seemed to depend on the social and ethical dimensions that had been cultivated within Japanese schooling at large. These dimensions were evidenced by the ways in which students assumed responsibility for directing their own learning and expressing their ideas in front of their peers and teachers.

A way to restructure the teacher professionalism dialogue in the United States, then, might be to claim that it takes particular expertise and knowledge of democratic teaching and learning processes to orchestrate the complexity among social, ethical, intellectual, and emotional dimensions within classrooms and schools in order to promote academic achievement. Consequently, not just anyone can manage this complexity and channel it in ways that foster student learning. Rather, only teachers practiced in how to create and sustain democratic learning environments and those who are familiar with a democratic philosophy of education can perform teaching tasks. At the very least, this strategy of claiming teacher professionalism based on these eight democratic philosophical commitments might provide the American public with a clearer understanding of what teachers do and why they, according to Soder (1986), "accept the sacred trust of mediating the ongoing relationship between parents, children, and the state" (pp. 45–46).

Comparative perspective taking on the issue of teacher professionalism has revealed that "what *is* central [to Japanese education] is a set of values deeply consonant with widely held American values" (Lewis, 1998, p. 181). As products of "the histories, economies, and cultures of the societies in which they exist," teaching and teacher education are political, socially constructed, and value laden (Cochran-Smith, 2000, p. 165). An examination of these complex dimensions provides a more nuanced view of professionalism and helps to disentangle the "'relationships of authority and autonomy between those who provide and those who demand the services'" (Wirt, 1980, p. 66, cited in Mawhinney, 1998, p. 45). Thus, cultural considerations deepen understanding of the dilemmas faced by educators at home and abroad.

In the next section, Part III, the reader is encouraged to apply frameworks to analyze complex educational issues. Chapter 7 briefly summarizes the frameworks used for comparative examinations (Part II of the text) and then applies the frameworks to issues in more domestic and localized contexts.

Sustaining Reflection

- Assess teacher professionalism, schools, and classrooms based on one or more of the eight democratic characteristics identified in the chapter. You might want to construct a five-point scale (1 = least prevalent; 5 = most prevalent) for each characteristic to aid in your assessment.

- Based on your assessment, what democratic characteristics are prominently featured in your teacher programs? Schools? Classrooms? Which characteristics need more development?

- How might one or more of the eight democratic characteristics be fostered in your teacher programs? Schools? Classrooms? Create an action plan.

References

Adelman, N. E. (1998) *Trying to beat the clock [microfilm]: Uses of teacher professional time in three countries.* Washington, DC: U.S. Department of Education, Office of Policy and Planning; Educational Research Improvement, Educational Resources Information Center.

Alleman, J. E., & Rosaen, C. L. (1991). The cognitive, social emotional, and moral development characteristics of students: Basis for elementary and middle school social studies. In J. P. Shaver (Ed.), *Handbook of research on social studies teaching and learning: A project of the National Council for the Social Studies* (pp. 121–133). New York, NY: Macmillan.

Ashton, P. A., Crocker, L., & Olijnik, S. (1986). *Does teacher education make a difference? A literature review and planning study.* Gainesville, FL: Institute on Student Assessment, Florida Department of Education.

Barnard, K., Muthwa-Kuehn, T., & Grimmett, P. P. (1997). Getting the questions right: Reforming teacher education in America. *Teaching and Teacher Education, 13*(8), 893–904.

Battistich, V., Solomon, D., & Delucchi, K. (1993). Interaction processes and student outcomes in cooperative learning groups. *Elementary School Journal, 94*, 19–32.

Beaton, A. E., Martin, M. O., Mullis, I. V. S., Gonzalez, E. J., Smith, T. A., & Kelly, D. L. (1996). *Science achievement in the middle school years: IEA's Third International Mathematics and Science Study (TIMSS).* Chestnut Hill, MA: Center for the Study of Testing, Evaluation, and Educational Policy. Boston, MA: Boston College.

Bickmore, K. (1993). Learning inclusion/inclusion in learning: Citizenship education for a pluralistic society. *Theory and Research in Social Education, 21*, 341–384.

Boocock, S. S. (1987). *Changing definitions of childhood crosscultural comparisons.* Jerusalem, Israel: National Council of Jewish Women, Research Institute for Innovation in Education, Hebrew University of Jerusalem.

Cochran-Smith, M. (2000, May/June). Editorial: Teacher education at the turn of the century. *Journal of Teacher Education, 51*(3), 163–165.

Cohen, E. G. (1984). Talking and working together: Status, interaction, and learning. In P. L. Peterson, L. C. Wilkinson, & M. Hallinan (Eds.), *The social context of instruction: Group organization and group processes* (pp. 171–187). New York, NY: Academic Press.

Cummings, W. (1980). *Education and equality in Japan.* Princeton, NJ: Princeton University Press.

Cunat, M. (1996). Vision, vitality, and values: Advocating the democratic classroom. In L. E. Beyer (Ed.), *Creating democratic classrooms: The struggle to integrate theory and practice* (pp. 127–149). New York, NY: Teachers College Press.

Darling-Hammond, L. (1991). The implications of testing policy for quality and equality. *Phi Delta Kappan, 73*, 220–225.

Darling-Hammond, L. (1997). *The right to learn: A blueprint for creating schools that work.* San Francisco, CA: Jossey-Bass.

Darling-Hammond, L. (1999). Performance based assessment and educational equity. In A. C. Ornstein & L. S. Behar-Horenstein (Eds.), *Contemporary issues in curriculum* (2nd ed., pp. 382–402). Boston, MA: Allyn & Bacon.

Darling-Hammond, L. (2000). How teacher education matters. *Journal of Teacher Education, 51*(3), 166–173.

Delpit, L. (1995). I just want to be myself: Discovering what students bring to school "in their blood." In W. Ayers (Ed.), *To become a teacher: Making a difference in children's lives* (pp. 34–48). New York, NY: Teachers College Press.

Dewey, J. (1937). Education and social change. *The Social Frontier, 3*(26), 235–238.

Easley, J., & Easley, E. (1983). Kitamaeno School as an environment in which children study mathematics themselves. *Journal of Science Education in Japan, 7*, 39–48.

Ehman, L. H. (1980). Change in high school students' political attitudes as a function of social studies classroom climate. *American Educational Research Journal, 17*(2), 253–265.

Eisenberg, N. (1982). The development of reasoning regarding prosocial behavior. In N. Eisenberg (Ed.), *The development of prosocial behavior* (pp. 219–246). New York, NY: Academic Press.

Engle, S. H. (1960). Decision making. In W.C. Parker (Ed.), *Educating the democratic mind* (pp. 117–125). Albany, NY: State University of New York Press.

Engle, S. H., & Ochoa, A. S. (1988). *Education for democratic citizenship: Decision making in the social studies.* New York, NY: Teachers College Press.

Epstein, J. L. (1995). School/family/community partnerships: Caring for the children we share. *Phi Delta Kappan, 76*, 701–712.

Fujita, H., & Wong, S. (1997, May). *Teacher professionalism and the culture of teaching in Japan: The challenge and irony of educational reform and social change.* Paper presented at the sixth Norwegian National Conference in Educational Research, Oslo, Norway.

Ginsburg, N. S. (2000). Japan: Land and economy. In *The Encyclopedia Americana* (Vol. 15, pp. 739–740). Danbury, CT: Grolier Incorporated.

Grimmet, P. P., & MacKinnon, A. M. (1992). Craft knowledge and the education of teachers. In G. Grant (Ed.), *Review of educational research* (Vol. 18, pp. 385–456). Washington, DC: American Educational Research Association.

Gutmann, A. (1987). *Democratic education.* Princeton, NJ: Princeton University Press.

Hahn, C. L. (1988). *The effects of the school, media, and family on the civic values and behaviors of youth.* Paper presented for the International

Conference on the Development of Civic Responsibility Among Youth, University of Urbino, Italy. (ERIC Document Reproduction Service No. ED 314 291)

Hamilton, V. L., Blumenfeld, P. C., Akoh, H., & Miura, K. (1989a). Citizenship and scholarship in Japanese and American fifth grades. *American Educational Research Journal, 26*, 44–72.

Hamilton, V. L., Blumenfeld, P. C., Akoh, H., & Miura, K. (1989b). Japanese and American children's reasons for the things they do in school. *American Educational Research Journal, 26*, 545–571.

Hare, T. (1996). Try, try again: Training in Noh drama. In T. Rohlen & G. LeTendre (Eds.), *Teaching and learning in Japan* (pp. 323–344). New York, NY: Cambridge University Press.

Hargreaves, A., & Goodson, I. (1996). Teachers' professional lives: Aspirations and actualities. In I. Goodson & A. Hargreaves (Eds.), *Teachers' professional lives* (pp. 1–27). London, UK: Falmer Press.

Hargreaves, D. (1980). The occupational culture of teachers. In P. Woods (Ed.), *Teachers strategies: Explorations in the sociology of the school* (pp. 125–148). London, UK: Croom Helm.

Harwood, A. M. (1992). Classroom climate and civic education in secondary social studies research: Antecedents and findings. *Theory and Research in Social Education, 20*, 47–86.

Hawley, C. A., & Hawley, W. D. (1997). The role of universities in the education of Japanese teachers: A distant perspective. *Peabody Journal of Education, 72*(1), 233–244.

Hendry, J. (1986). *Becoming Japanese: The world of the preschool child.* Manchester, UK: Manchester University Press.

Herbst, J. (1989). *And sadly teach: Teacher education and professionalization in American culture.* Madison, WI: The University of Wisconsin Press.

Hess, R. D., & Azuma, H. (1991). Cultural support for schooling: Contrasts between Japan and the United States. *Educational Researcher, 20*, 2–8, 12.

Honig, A. S. (1982). Research in review: Prosocial development in children. *Young Children, 37*, 51–62.

Hoyle, E. (1980). Professionalization and deprofessionalization in education. In E. Hoyle & J. Megarry (Eds.), *World yearbook of education* (pp. 42–54). London, UK: Kogan Page.

Itō, Y. (1994). Kyōshi bunka gakkō bunka no nichibei hikaku. In T. Indgaki & Y. Kudomi (Eds.), *Nihon no Kyōshi Bunka* (pp. 140–156). Tokyo, Japan: Tokyo Daigaku Suppankai.

Johnson, D., & Johnson, R. (1994). *Joining together: Group theory and group skills*. Boston, MA: Allyn & Bacon.

Kawakami, H. (1997). *Rusu nikki: Kawakami Hajime Fujin gokugai no kiroku*. Tokyo, Japan: Iwanami Shoten.

Kliebard, H. M. (1987). *The struggle for the American curriculum, 1893–1958*. New York, NY: Routledge & Kegan Paul.

Kubow, P. K. (1996). Reconceptualizing citizenship education for the twenty-first century: A study of postbaccalaureate social studies students from Canada, England, and the United States. *Dissertation Abstracts International, 57*, 11A (University Microfilms, No. 9711423).

Kubow, P. K. (1999, December). Preparing future secondary teachers for citizenship educator roles: A possible direction for preservice education in the new century. *Asia-Pacific Journal of Teacher Education & Development, 2*(2), 53–64.

Ladd, E. (1995). Japan and America: Two different nations draw closer. *The Public Perspective: A Roper Center Review of Public Opinion and Polling, 6*(5), 18–36.

Lee, S. Y., Graham, T., & Stevenson, H. (1996). Teachers and teaching: Elementary schools in Japan and the United States. In T. Rohlen & G. LeTendre (Eds.), *Teaching and learning in Japan* (pp. 157–189). New York, NY: Cambridge University Press.

Leming, J. (1981). On the limits of rational moral education. *Theory and Research in Social Education, 9*(1), 7–34.

LeTendre, G. K. (1999, March). The problem of Japan: Qualitative studies and international educational comparisons. *Educational Researcher, 28*(2), 38–45.

LeTendre, G. K. (1999b). International achievement studies and myths of Japan. In G. K. LeTendre (Ed.), *Competitor or ally?: Japan's role in American educational debates* (pp. 3–24). New York, NY: Falmer Press, a member of Taylor & Francis Group.

Lewis, C. (1995). *Educating hearts and minds: Reflections on Japanese preschool and elementary education*. New York, NY: Cambridge University Press.

Lewis, C. C. (1998). What is a successful school? In E. R. Beauchamp (Ed.), *Dimensions of contemporary Japan: A collection of essays* (pp. 168–194). New York, NY: Garland.

Lewis, C., & Tsuchida, I. (1997). Planned educational change in Japan: The case of elementary science instruction. *Journal of Educational Policy, 12*(5), 313–331.

Linn, M. C., & Burbules, N. C. (1993). Construction of knowledge and group learning. In K. Tobin (Ed.), *The practice of constructivism in science education* (pp. 91–119). Washington, DC: American Association for the Advancement of Science.

Linn, M. C., Lewis, C., Tsuchida, I., & Songer, N. B. (2000). Beyond fourth-grade science: Why do U.S. and Japanese students diverge? *Educational Researcher, 29*(3), 4–14.

Mawhinney, H. B. (1998). Schools wars or school transformation: Professionalizing teaching and involving communities. *Peabody Journal of Education, 73*(1), 36–55.

Mertens, D. M. (1998). *Research methods in education and psychology: Integrating diversity with quantitative and qualitative approaches*. Thousand Oaks, CA: Sage.

Miller, T. (1953). *Annual Report of the NEA/National Commission on Teacher Education and Professional Standards*. Washington, DC: National Education Association.

Mills, C. W. (1959). *The sociological imagination*. New York, NY: Oxford University Press.

The New Encyclopedia Britannica. (1997). London, UK: Europa.

Newsweek: The International Newsmagazine. (1999, September 6). Education. Now, please think: As Americans embrace testing, Asians pursue creativity, 37–47.

Norman, M. (2000). Linda Darling-Hammond: Teach the children well. *Converge*. Retrieved July 2001 at *http://www.convergemag.com/Publications/CNVGNov00/darling/index.shtm*.

Oakes, J. (1990). *Multiplying inequalities: The effects of race, social class, and tracking on opportunities to learn mathematics and science.* Santa Monica, CA: RAND.

Okano, K., & Tsuchiya, M. (Eds.) (1999). *Education in contemporary Japan: Inequality and diversity.* Cambridge, UK: Cambridge University Press.

Ornstein, A. C., & Levine, D. U. (1997). *Foundations of education (6ᵗʰ ed.).* Boston, MA: Houghton Mifflin.

Patrick, J. J., & Hoge, J. D. (1991). Teaching government, civics, and law. In J. P. Shaver (Ed.), *Handbook of research on social studies teaching and learning: A project of the National Council for the Social Studies* (pp. 427–436). New York, NY: Macmillan.

Peak, L. (1989). Learning to become part of the group: The Japanese child's transition to preschool life. *Journal of Japanese Studies, 15*(1), 93–124.

Peak, L. (1991). *Learning to go to school in Japan.* Berkeley, CA and Los Angeles, CA: University of California Press.

Popkewitz, T. S. (1994). Professionalization in teaching and teacher education: Some notes on its history, ideology, and potential. *Teaching and Teacher Education, 10*(1), 1–14.

Radke-Yarrow, M., Zahn-Waxler, C., & Chapman, M. (1983). Children's prosocial dispositions and behavior. In P. Mussen (Ed.), *Handbook of child psychology: Vol. IV. Socialization, personality, and social development* (pp. 469–545). New York, NY: John Wiley.

Radz, M. A. (1983). The school society: Practical suggestions for promoting a democratic school climate. In M. A. Hepburn (Ed.), *Democratic education in schools and classrooms* (pp. 67–87). Washington, DC: National Council for the Social Studies.

Rohlen, T. P. (1995). Differences that make a difference: Explaining Japan's success. *Educational Policy, 9,* 103–128.

Ryan, K., & Cooper, J. M. (1998). *Those who can, teach* (8ᵗʰ ed.). Boston, MA: Houghton Mifflin.

Sato, N. (1991). *Ethnography of Japanese elementary schools: Quest for equality.* Unpublished doctoral dissertation, Stanford University, Palo Alto, CA.

Sato, N. (1993). Teaching and learning in Japanese elementary schools: A context for understanding. *Peabody Journal of Education, 68*(4), 111–153.

Sato, N., & McLaughlin, M. W. (1992). Context matters: Teaching in Japan and in the United States. *Phi Delta Kappan, 73*(5), 359–366.

Satō, S. (1988). Gendai no gakkō to tōkō kyohi. In S. Jinbo & K. Yamazaki (Eds.), *Gakkō ni Ikenai Kodomotachi: Gendai no esupuri 1988/5* (pp. 24–35). Tokyo, Japan: Shi bundō.

Satō, Z. et al. (1991) Kyōin no jinji gyōsei ni Kansuru Kenkyu. *Nihon Kyoiku Gyōsei Gakkai Nenpō, 17,* 149–162.

Schempp, P. G., Cheffers, J., & Zaichkowsky, L. (1983). Influence of decision-making on attitudes, creativity, motor skills and self concept in elementary children. *Research Quarterly for Exercise and Sport, 54,* 183–189.

Schmidt, W. H., Raizen, S. A., Britton, E. D., Bianchi, L. J., & Wolfe, R. G. (1997). *Many visions, many aims: A cross-national investigation of curricular intentions in school science.* London, UK: Kluwer Academic Publishers.

Shimahara, N. (1991). Teacher education in Japan. In E. Beauchamp (Ed.), *Windows on Japanese education* (pp. 259–280). Westport, CT: Greenwood Press.

Shimahara, N. (1992). Overview of Japanese education: Policy, structure, and current issues. In R. Leestma & H. J. Walberg (Eds.), *Japanese educational productivity* (pp. 7–33). Ann Arbor, MI: Center for Japanese Studies, the University of Michigan.

Shimahara, N. K. (1998a). The Japanese model of professional development: Teaching as craft. *Teaching and Teacher Education, 14*(5), 451–462.

Shimahara, N. K. (1998b). Teacher education reform in Japan: Ideological and control issues. In E. R. Beauchamp (Ed.), *Dimensions of contemporary Japan: A collection of essays* (pp. 247–263). New York, NY: Garland.

Shimahara, N., & Sakai, A. (1992). Teacher internship and the culture of teaching in Japan. *British Journal of Sociology of Education, 12*(2), 147–162.

Shimahara, N., & Sakai, A. (1995). *Learning to teach in two cultures: Japan and the United States.* New York, NY: Garland.

Shimizu, C. (1994). OL Kara mita kaisha. In K. Uchihasi, H. Okumura, & M. Sakata (Eds.), *Shūshoku Shūsha no Kōzō* (pp. 115–134). Tokyo, Japan: Iwanami Shoten.

Singleton, J. (1989). *Gambaru*: A Japanese cultural theory of learning. In J. Shields (Ed.), *Japanese schooling* (pp. 8–15). Pittsburgh, PA: Pennsylvania State University Press.

Soder, R. (1986, June). *Professionalizing the profession: Notes on the future of teaching*. Center for Educational Renewal, Occasional Paper Number 4. Seattle, WA: University of Washington.

Starr, P. (1982). *The social trasformation of American Medicine*. New York, NY: Basic Books.

Stevenson, H. W. (1998, Sept. 16). Guarding teachers' time: Other countries do. We should, too. *Education Week, 18*(2), 32.

Stevenson, H. W., & Stigler, J. W. (1992). *The learning gap: Why our schools are failing and what we can learn from Japanese and Chinese education*. New York, NY: Summit Books.

Stigler, J. W., Fernandez, C., & Yoshida, M. (1996). Cultures of mathematics instruction in Japanese and American elementary classrooms. In T. Rohlen & G. LeTendre (Eds.), *Teaching and learning in Japan* (pp. 213–247). New York, NY: Cambridge University Press.

Stigler, J. W., & Hiebert, J. (1997). Understanding and improving classroom mathematics instruction: An overview of the TIMSS video study. *Phi Delta Kappan, 79*(1), 14–21.

The Third International Mathematics and Science Study (TIMSS). (1995). Retrieved June 2001 at http://nces.ed.gov/timss.

Thomas, R. M. (1983). The symbiotic linking of politics and education. In R. M. Thomas (Ed.), *Politics and education* (pp. 1–30). Oxford, UK: Pergamon.

Tobin, J., Wu, D. Y., & Davidson, D. H. (1989). *Preschools in three cultures: Japan, China and the United States*. New Haven, CT: Yale University Press.

Tsuchida, I. (1993). *Teachers' motivational and instructional strategies: A study of fourth grade U.S. and Japanese classrooms*. Unpublished doctoral dissertation, University of California, Berkeley.

Tsuchida, I., & Lewis, C. (1996). Responsibility and learning: Some preliminary hypotheses about Japanese elementary classrooms. In T. Rohlen & G. LeTendre (Eds.), *Teaching and learning in Japan* (pp. 190–212). New York, NY: Cambridge University Press.

Valverde, G.A. (1995). United States. In T. N. Postlethwaite (Ed.), *International encyclopedia of national systems of education* (pp. 1033–1041). Oxford, UK: Elsevier Science Ltd.

van den Berg, R., & Ros, A. (1999). The permanent importance of the subjective reality of teachers during educational innovation: A concerns-based approach. *American Educational Research Journal, 36*(4), 879–906.

White, M. (1987). *The Japanese educational challenge*. New York, NY: Kodansha.

Whitson, J. A., & Stanley, W. B. (1996). "Re-minding" education for democracy. In W.C. Parker (Ed.), *Educating the democratic mind* (pp. 309–336). Albany, NY: State University of New York Press.

Wiebe, R. (1967). *The search for order, 1877–1920*. New York, NY: Hill & Wang.

Wirt, F. (1980). Professionalism and political conflict: A developmental model. *Journal of Public Policy, 1*, 61–93.

The World Factbook. (2001). Washington, DC: The Central Intelligence Agency. The U.S. Government. Retrieved February 2002 at http://www.cia.gov/cia/publications/factbook/index.html.

Wright, N., & Bottery, M. (1997). Perceptions of professionalism by the mentors of student teachers. *Journal of Education for Teaching, 23*(3), 235–252.

Zeichner, K. (1999). The new scholarship in teacher education. *Educational Researcher, 28*(9), 4–15.

Interpreting Educational Issues: Comparison and the Use of Analytic Frameworks

Part III consists of two chapters (chapters 7–8) that help the reader apply frameworks to analyze issues, both domestic and international, and also to summarize the advantages of comparative perspective taking for educators.

- **Chapter 7: Applying Frameworks to Analyze Educational Issues**
  In this chapter we suggest how the frameworks used to examine selected issues comparatively in Part II of the text can also be effective in helping educators consider issues in domestic and localized contexts.

- **Chapter 8: The Value of Comparative Education**
  In this chapter we summarize the benefits of comparative perspective taking for practitioners and an issues orientation for the field of comparative education.

Chapter 7

Applying Frameworks to Analyze Educational Issues

Focusing Questions

- In what ways do educators address the complexity in their work environments?

- How might analytic frameworks be useful in more familiar, localized contexts? International contexts?

- What other dilemmas in education might be better understood by critically applying analytic frameworks?

INTRODUCTION

Our purpose in placing the analytic frameworks used in Part II together in this chapter is twofold: (1) to demonstrate the applicability of these frameworks to other educational issues and (2) to demonstrate their usefulness in considering issues in domestic and localized contexts, as well as international ones. Frameworks are freestanding devices that can be applied to issues in order to analyze the complex factors, influences, and motivations affecting education. Thus, frameworks can help educators to deal with the complex interplay of forces affecting education and to ask questions to help foster deeper reflection on education.

Frameworks necessarily limit reflective inquiry to a select number of items for analysis, thereby privileging some information and factors over others and allowing some insights to be gained while excluding from view other factors that might influence the interpretation of the issue. Thus, although frameworks provide a way to address education's complexity, it is important to recognize that a myriad of factors still lie outside the purview of any one framework. One benefit of using analytic frameworks is to help educators become more comfortable managing the ambiguity and complexity inherent in the educational landscape. Another benefit is that frameworks encourage a spirit of exploration and a structure for momentarily suspending judgment on an issue in order to aid in the critical investigation of that issue, whether domestic or international.

FOUR ANALYTIC FRAMEWORKS

Four frameworks were used to analyze the different educational issues in Part II: (1) Hofstede's cross-cultural framework provided a psychosociological critique of the purposes of schooling; (2) Harvey's framework enabled a policy critique of educational equality and access; (3) Frank's framework, derived from education theory, was employed to examine the relationship between educator accountability and responsibility; and (4) Thomas's political framework was applied in a critique of teacher professionalism. Because each framework originates from a particular discipline with its own standards and rules for analysis, each framework privileges some factors over others in its explanation of a certain educational phenomenon. By bringing some information to the foreground and relegating other factors to the fringes, frameworks enable the reader to view a selected educational issue in a deeper way.

Our intention in this chapter is to discuss briefly each framework without exhaustively reviewing the country-specific details covered in earlier chapters. The goal is to encourage the ongoing use of frameworks in the study of education. As analytical tools, frameworks enable readers to systematize their own thinking about education in familiar, as well as unfamiliar, geographical, political, economic, and sociocultural contexts.

Hofstede's Framework

Hofstede's (1980) model is composed of four dimensions: *power distance, uncertainty avoidance, social principledness*, and *locus of control*. Power distance refers to the degree to which citizens tolerate social inequalities. *Power distance* can be described as a situation in which those with less power accept the power imbalances and view them as a normal part of society (Hofstede, 1980, cited in Friederichs, 1991). Hofstede's second dimension, *uncertainty avoidance*, is the degree to which a cultural group becomes nervous about unpredictable and complex situations and tries to avoid them through the maintenance of strict behavior codes and faith in absolute truths (cited in Friederichs, 1991). *Social principledness*, the third dimension elaborated on by Bond (1986), is associated with a strong inclination on the part of a culture to acquiesce, without question, to authority, thereby accepting the society's conventional values and norms. The fourth dimension, *locus of control*, refers to "a set of generalized beliefs or expectancies about how positive and negative reinforcements are obtained" (Friederichs, 1991, p. 203). Internality is the belief that one receives rewards and avoids punishments through his or her own skills, efforts, and personal responsibility, and externality is the belief that positive outcomes depend on outside circumstances, such as luck, chance, and the actions of powerful others (Friederichs, 1991).

Together, these dimensions provide a psychosociological framework for the critique of education. In this framework, the concept of power becomes a major factor in helping to interpret not only the individual–society relationship, but the education–society relationship as well. *Power*, defined by Shiraev and Levy (2001) as "the capacity or ability of an individual to exercise control and/or authority" (p. 318), can be manifested formally and informally. Formal power is exerted through official laws and institutional rules, whereas informal power refers to the ability of an individual or group to influence others without official sanction (Shiraev & Levy, 2001).

Because power creates differences between individuals and nations in terms of wealth, prestige, and opportunity, Hofstede (1980) has argued that human inequality is an inevitable result. The general population's toleration of social inequalities, or *power distance*, occurs because an elite group is able to convince those with less power that their situation is a result of their own inadequacies. Individuals, consequently, come to accept that there are particular roles to be filled in society and that the high status roles are filled by individuals who have the prerequisite knowledge and skills.

Whereas Hofstede (1980) concluded that wealthier countries are more likely to have citizens with more individualistic intentions and attitudes, Friederichs (1991) postulated that it is a society's exposure to Western values and culture that results in the society's reluctance to challenge existing power imbalances. Hence, from a critical perspective, market-oriented economic principles and capitalistic motivations are linked to widening gaps in wealth, power, and prestige experienced by people within and among nations. This indictment of capitalism, however, has been criticized because individualistic and elitist tendencies can be found in socialistic societies as well.

Although the model has its limitations, the four dimensions provide insightful critique as one moves from the cultural dichotomies premised on a country's work-oriented values, proposed by Hofstede (1980), to an analysis of education and society. Working from Hofstede's dimensions and their accompanying definitions, a framework has been created and questions generated that can be applied to a wide number of educational issues (see Table 7.1). The framework provides a structure for examining how ideology and social privilege are embedded in a country's school content and practices.

Harvey and Knight's Framework

Calls for greater accountability in a climate of shrinking budgets typify the elementary, secondary, and postsecondary education environment. With an eye on generating a more fitting educational policy for the 21st century, Harvey and Knight (1996) have noted that educational improvement is characterized by conflicting forces, such as pressures to cut educational costs against the concern that such cost cutting might erode the quality of education. Focusing their policy critique primarily on higher education, the authors have contended that while it seems essential to employ standards for judging existing educational programs and for monitoring their improvement, there is no concurrence about what vision of quality a set of educational standards might pursue. From this perspective, then, the goals of education will consequently remain impossible to achieve.

Different visions of educational quality connote different means for assessing quality and for monitoring improvement. Harvey and Knight (1996) have noted five particular notions of quality, identifying key aspects about them as well as some important tensions among them. *Exceptionality* refers to the more traditional view whereby quality is seen as distinctive and exceeding a set of germane standards that are, by definition, "unattainable by most people" (Harvey & Knight, 1996, p. 2). Rooted in the notion of exclusivity, this view's crucial implication is that a good many schools will not attain educational quality.

Table 7.1   Hofstede's Dimensions, as Expanded by Bond (1986) and Friederichs (1991), Applied to Education

Power Distance	Uncertainty Avoidance	Social Principledness	Locus of Control
Citizens' toleration of social inequalities	*Discomfort with unknowns*	*Acquiescing to authority and accepting conventional norms*	*Beliefs about the degree to which an individual controls outcomes*
What equalities and inequalities surround the relationships that are central to the issue?	What possible uncertainties surround the issue?	What norms seem especially pertinent regarding the issue?	What actors have some hand in influencing the issue?
What are the overt and implicit (hidden) functions of the educational process at hand?	To what extent is there a tendency to limit the aims of schooling for purposes of assessment?	How are students, teachers, and others encouraged or discouraged from questioning authority and critiquing conventional norms?	What risks and benefits accrue to individuals who perceive that they influence outcomes?
What kinds of knowledge are validated in the curriculum? Who is exposed to high status and low status knowledge?	To what degree are controversial topics addressed?	What images about race, ethnicity, class, and gender are presented in textbooks and other educational materials?	To what degree do teachers, students, and others see their roles as significant in the educational process?
How are students selected and stratified for learning?	Who deals with complex and ambiguous topics? And to what extent can these topics be left unresolved?	How does the classroom environment reinforce authority and reflect conformity?	To what degree does the school distribute rewards and punishments in unequal ways based on students' perceived abilities and backgrounds?
What messages do students receive regarding their future roles in society?	What messages do students receive about their ability and willingness to wrestle with complexity?	What messages are students given about questioning and changing prevailing conditions in society?	What messages do students receive about their abilities to influence the direction of society?

In contrast to exceptionality, some view quality as being defined by achieving *consistency*. This perspective exalts the importance of processes through its focus on producing a predictable defect-free result, in doing so as a matter of routine, and in reaching this goal on the first attempt as much as possible. This view of quality is well suited to the production of known outputs or to the execution of defined and relatively stable and predictable tasks. Moreover, there are additional tensions associated with the consistency view of quality that arise when the product of a service is intangible. Intangible results certainly typify education in part: Society's members expect schools, for instance, to reinforce in students several less-than-precise skills, such as the ability to think critically and to possess a general resourcefulness suited to a future whose shape is itself unclear. Pointedly, therefore, Harvey and Knight (1996) have emphasized that quality as consistency "does not fit well with the idea of discovery learning" (p. 4).

Whereas the view of quality in terms of consistency is particularly focused on the refinement of processes, a third notion of quality, *fitness for purpose*, emphasizes the end point more completely by considering how a process or service suits specific aims. To illustrate, educational accreditation processes often incorporate judgments about an institution's adherence to a self-declared mission or framework. By definition, naturally, this situation raises questions about whether "standard" is intended to imply adherence to and conformity with expectations defined externally. Harvey and Knight (1996) have contended, however, that "standard" sometimes signifies uniqueness. American commitment to the ideal of "local control," for instance, rests on the widely held belief that schools should reflect needs and values particular to the surrounding community and that they should therefore be unique rather than "standard" in the sense of conforming. Even if one concedes, as one must, that schools' purposes are certainly not defined solely internally, fundamental ambiguities remain. If quality is to be judged in terms of the customers' rather than the schools' stated purposes, who, after all, is the customer? The students? Their parents? The business community? Or perhaps even the government on whose behalf schools serve as executors of policy? Education is, in short, a participatory process that creates roles that are far more nebulous than judgments of quality strictly in fitness for purpose terms would allow.

A notion of quality that is particularly prominent with respect to schools involves *value for money*. Bound up in this view of quality is the idea that educational effectiveness must be maintained but with much greater efficiency (Harvey & Knight, 1996). Evidence of *returns on investment*—a pivotal concept from this perspective—might include increased competency with respect to upward career mobility. Concerns regarding the use of this view of quality in educational contexts include the possibility that gains in efficient provision of educational services will come at the cost of improvement. In the United States, Barber (1993) has pointed to a certain hypocrisy underlying such claims, noting that money is how Americans demonstrate their dedication to a problem. This focus on monetary inputs could distract from educational processes and outcomes, aspects that other conceptions of educational quality promote.

A major intention of Harvey and Knight's (1996) analysis is to argue that, due to the unique nature of education, a *transformative* view of quality is necessary. The most consequential benefits for students, according to the transformation perspective, derive from the enhancement of their skills and from their empowerment through participation in self-evaluation and instructional evaluation as well. The greater latitude for students to choose electives, design instruction, and create knowledge of relevance stands as a challenge to instructor authority as the judges of students' work and curriculum design.

Harvey's framework of different conceptions of quality helps undo the notion that a pat set of educational standards can be identified, for each of the five contrasting perspectives of quality promotes an alternative normative vision of the key imperatives of education. A pronounced advantage of considering competing definitions of quality is that such an exercise demonstrates that trying to measure educational success is far from being a clear-cut enterprise (see Table 7.2).

Frank's Framework

Frank (1972) has provided a set of criteria for critiquing policy theory and, in employing these criteria to challenge the effectiveness of certain theories of development, has demonstrated their usefulness. Frank's framework of critical criteria consists of three elements: *policy effectiveness, theoretical adequacy,* and *empirical validity. Policy effectiveness* refers to the feasibility of a policy or program. The support of government

---

Table 7.2   Harvey and Knight's Definitions of Quality Applied to Education

Exceptionality

Quality is seen as distinctive and exceeding a set of standards.

–To what degree does rhetoric on the issue include or imply superlatives or comparisons?
–At whose expense do such comparisons come? Who are the "less-than-exceptional" schools, students, teachers, and so on?

Consistency

Quality viewed in terms of processes and producing predictable results.

–To what degree does discussion emphasize process over outcomes?
–What educational experiences might be undermined by emphasis on routines, repeatability, precision, and so on?

Fitness for Purpose

Quality determined in relation to how a process or service suits specific aims.

–What educational endpoints or purposes are declared or implied? By whom?
–What unstated purposes could be forgotten or ignored?

Value for Money

Quality viewed as being maintained with greater efficiency.

–To what degree does the issue involve emphasis on costs associated with a program? If so, what factors help account for or explain this emphasis? To what extent are costs paramount or essential?
–What other imperatives could compete unfavorably with emphases on cost?

Transformation

Quality viewed in terms of change.

–To what extent does the issue emphasize empowerment of students or others?
–Does increased latitude for one party result in decreased latitude for others? If so, is this fair?

or an educational bureaucracy or establishment might or might not be crucial to the viability of a proposal for educational change, and those who form proposals should be sensitive to the relative importance of this kind of support. Similarly, groups having less formal legitimacy, but nonetheless consequential political voice, such as parents, the business community, and the like, may influence the success or demise of a program. In addition, a policy must be financially feasible: Costs associated with new curricular materials, with improvements to the educational infrastructure, and with the training of teachers are a few common concerns. Finally, any program for change requires time to implement, and the policy in question should purposefully incorporate enough time for its own success.

Theoretical adequacy entails considering the evidence for a compelling linkage between the targeted or desired outcomes and the strategies the proposal envisions for accomplishing them. If a proposal for change is to be successful, the theory supporting it should account for factors that, although tangential, could contribute in important ways to achieving intended outcomes.

Analyzing a policy's *empirical validity* involves examining the evidence that pairs a program's assertions with its strategies. In contrast to policy effectiveness, empirical validity involves assessing a policy in terms of past efforts to which the plan in question might be likened. A plan should embody some effort to incorporate differences or responses between proposed strategies and similar plans that might have preceded it. To the extent that differences between past similar efforts and present policy are absent, evidence of the success of the associated elements of the policy is in order.

A limitation of Frank's framework for assessing models of educational change is that it fails to account for ethical considerations, or *ethical merit* (Paige, 1995). Quite apart from analyses of effectiveness, theory, and validity, a program of change should articulate and adhere to ethical principles. This is especially necessary in education because of the intensely social nature of the enterprise, and all the more so because of the vulnerability of the young people implicated. Assessments of a policy's effectiveness, of the conceptual adequacy of the supporting theory, and of the merit of its empirical foundation must therefore be augmented with judgments as to the general spirit of openness with which the policy is introduced. Assessing the degree to which roles and responsibilities are clear, for instance, is a matter that should receive more scrutiny than Frank's model demands. Similarly, the positions and background—and even the biases and proclivities—of those championing the proposal should be considered for their transparency.

Guba (1984) has emphasized the degree to which teachers are not only instruments of policy but agents of the policy-making process. His claim is that one's conception of policy "determines the kinds of policy questions that are asked, the kinds of policy relevant data that are collected, the sources of the data that are tapped, the methodology that is used, and, finally, the policy products that emerge" (p. 63). The ability to assess an educational program or proposal for change is a crucial skill for policy makers. This must include teachers themselves, because they have a central role in the business of interpreting circumstances, making decisions that affect the allocation of resources, adapting plans for action to suit emerging realities, and other activities that occupy the core of policy making (see Table 7.3).

Table 7.3 Frank's Framework for Critiquing Educational Policy and Reform			
Policy Effectiveness	**Theoretical Adequacy**	**Empirical Validity**	**Ethical Merit**
Feasibility of the policy or program	*Linkage between desired outcomes and strategies employed*	*Efforts to incorporate differences between past and present plans*	*Plans adherence to ethical principles*
–How do sources and degrees of support and dissent affect action on an issue or proposal? –What monetary and other costs are associated? –What are the possible consequences of various options related to the issue?	–What reasoning and justifications are associated with the issue? –Are rationales reasonably well contextualized with respect to background, current pressing needs, and so on? –What effects might more tangential factors have?	–Are interpretations of circumstances consistent among stakeholders? –What signs or specific changes related to an issue might be relevant? Will these be broadly recognized? –What are the strengths and limits of these means of judging?	–Do proposals related to an issue's resolution acknowledge the variety of demands upon affected parties? –Are roles and responsibilities openly discussed? –Are values and biases acknowledged?

Thomas's Framework

Thomas's (1983) examination of the political influence on schooling contributes to a deeper understanding of the relationship between the state and education. Thomas has used the term *symbiotics* to represent the notion that politics and education simultaneously influence the fate of each other. Viewing education through a political lens, Thomas has suggested that education is influenced by politics in at least three ways: (1) the *support* provided to schools, (2) the *content and procedures* allowed in schools, and (3) the *latitude of social and political action* permitted the people who inhabit schools.

Applying the Thomas framework to the issue of teacher professionalism, one can examine teacher autonomy in relation to the state's control (or lack thereof) of teacher education and school curriculum through the kinds of resources provided, the kind of ideologies of citizenship and society promulgated, and the degree of latitude on the part of educational workers (both teachers and students) to engage in a social critique of the state. Just as the state affects educational processes, education influences the political realm in a number of ways. Thomas has identified education's impact on politics in terms of political socialization or citizenship training, political legitimation, human resource production, sorting and selecting of youths, social assessment and interpretation, social control, and stimulation of social change.

According to Thomas (1983), the education system in any given country plays an important role in socializing youth to support decision making advocated by those in power. In this way, schools play a role in legitimating a country's existing political system. Moreover, through human resource production and the sorting and selecting of youths, schools provide society with the specific kinds and numbers of workers needed, thereby contributing to the stability and longevity of existing political arrangements and enabling some individuals to enjoy a favored position in terms of the amount and kind of education they receive (Thomas, 1983). In relation to the social assessment and interpretive role of education, Thomas has argued that schooling can stimulate youths to analyze their society critically; however, the degree to which teachers and students engage in social critique can be limited by the state, which can label them as patriotic citizens, the conscience of the nation, or dissidents (Thomas, 1983). Thus, education systems, according to Thomas, influence the political realm through their social control functions, whereas schools, in turn, can serve as either reflectors of the existing social order or agents of social change.

Like the preceding frameworks, Thomas's political model privileges the concepts of power, control, and influence. The term *politics*—defined as the "efforts exerted by groups to promote their beliefs or welfare in relation to other groups" (Thomas, 1983, p. 2)—refers

Table 7.4   Thomas's Framework for Examining Political Influences on Education

Support	Content and Procedures	Latitude of Social and Political Action
How much support does the education system (e.g., teachers) receive from political groups?	What is taught, by what methods, and how is it assessed?	To what extent should school staff (and students) be allowed to engage in whatever social and political behavior they choose?
To what extent do authorities provide the necessary resources (i.e., supplies, facilities, professional incentives) to aid student learning?	To what extent do the textbook and prepackaged education materials dominate instruction?	To what extent do teacher professionals engage in discussions about the educational issue at hand?
To what extent do teachers assume individual responsibility for student learning?	To what extent do teachers determine what is relevant in education? What about education is left for others to determine?	To what degree are teachers encouraged or discouraged to engage in reflective inquiry?
In what ways do various stakeholders exert influence over the education process? To what degree is there political intervention in educational affairs?	To what extent are students evaluated on academic outcomes? Social outcomes? To what extent do teachers attend to human factors?	To what extent are teachers educational decision makers and problem solvers?
To what degree is there public confidence in the work that teachers do? State confidence?	What assumptions about education and society are manifested in content, pedagogy, and assessment measures?	To what extent do teachers design their own professional development programs?

to one group's exercise of power over another group(s). In schools, the exercise of power might take the form of educators seeking to control their own professional affairs by maintaining autonomy over their work. For the state, this might involve expecting teachers to assume greater responsibility for student performance through demonstrable outcomes. The degree to which education is said to be "politicized" is dependent upon "the extent to which groups outside the education system are able to direct or control the conduct of education" (Thomas, 1983, p. 7).

Although a political critique helps to define problems in education and causes one to question the extent to which education can be viewed as a benevolent influence, a preoccupation with power and influence precludes the fact that education can enhance opportunities for individuals and stimulate economic growth. Schooling, therefore, does provide some students with the opportunity to achieve their ambitions and to realize their potential. Although education could be viewed as "a rather minor component in a multiple intervention process" (Thomas, 1983, p. 23) to help people obtain their goals, it cannot be denied that it is a factor in enabling citizens to gain skills that can enhance their quality of life.

Despite the framework's limitations, a political critique helps one to recognize the diverse motivations of various actors and to reinforce the notion that education is enveloped in an environment characterized by conflicting values and limited resources. Such critique enables one to consider the symbiotic political–educational exchanges in societies (see Table 7.4).

BRIDGING THE FRAMEWORKS TO OTHER DILEMMAS IN EDUCATION

The preceding chapters apply analytical frameworks as a means of lending method to comparing issues cross-nationally. Educators and other actors must grapple with the values and assumptions underlying these issues, with their multiple views and controversies, in order to see where educators' and others' commitments lie. Considering the various forces (i.e., historical, social, cultural, political, and economic) affecting a given issue can foster a deeper understanding of that issue. Frameworks enable systematic investigation and are also useful for analyzing educational issues in more familiar and localized contexts. Toward that end, we draw on the concept of *power distance* from Hofstede's model and the concept of *support* from Thomas's model to explore the controversy surrounding homework, an issue of particular relevancy in the United States.

SCENARIO 1: THE HOMEWORK DILEMMA

Consider the relationship between parents and teachers with regard to the homework dilemma in the United States. In recent sustained discussions on homework at one American middle school, some parents asserted themselves in an effort to reduce the amounts of homework for their children. Their arguments revolved around concerns that the homework loads were too heavy, requiring children to spend considerable after-school time in assignment completion and not accommodating of students' additional commitments. To examine this issue, we draw on one dimension in Hofstede's model, namely *power distance* (see Table 7.5).

To examine the issue further, we draw on an element from Thomas's political–educational framework, the concept of *support*, and apply it to the U.S. homework dilemma (see Table 7.6).

In addition to the country-specific analysis conducted with the concepts of power distance and support, international comparison yields a noteworthy contrast to the U.S. homework dilemma. In Germany, *Klassenarbeit*, literally "class work," is the term for an assignment that

Table 7.5 Hofstede's Power Distance Concept and the Homework Dilemma	
Power Distance	**Citizens' Toleration of Social Inequalities**
What equalities and inequalities surround the relationships that are central to the issue?	Some scholars (e.g., Kralovec & Buell, 2000) argue that homework could exacerbate existing social inequities because families in the United States with higher incomes are more apt to have time at home to monitor and otherwise assist their children in completing homework. A further claim is that better-educated parents are naturally better equipped to help their children succeed. Thus, too much emphasis on out-of-school work reinforces inequities along educational and occupational lines and further divides people by socioeconomic class distinctions.
What are the overt and implicit functions of the educational process at hand?	Compared with other countries, the U.S. school day runs longer, partly because the school functions as a day-care provider. Thus, parents in dual-income families might express the view that they are too busy or too tired to supervise children's homework. Ironically, schools enable dual careers and dual incomes in the first place, further transferring to schools responsibilities that parents previously assumed.
What kinds of knowledge are validated in the curriculum? Who is exposed to high status and low status knowledge?	There seems to be impatience with, if not contempt for, homework assignments that are more open-ended and require student attention and parental supervision over a longer period of time. For instance, projects or exploratory assignments might be greeted with parental disapproval, despite their agreement in the abstract regarding the value of skills these longer-term assignments might reinforce (e.g., lifelong learning, resourcefulness).
How are students selected and stratified for learning?	Children reflect different needs in terms of the time it takes for them to complete homework tasks. Teachers, responding to these innate student differences, adjust requirements from student to student. These adjustments to meet differing paces of learning result in students' exposure to differentiated curriculum and instruction. This aspect of stratified learning illustrates pressure on teachers to comply with parental input, thereby constricting the professional prerogative of teachers.
What messages do students receive regarding their future roles in society?	Pressure to reduce homework loads could send negative signals to students about the importance of schooling in the United States. Because more emphasis is placed on student completion of work during classroom hours, the onus of educational success is transferred from students to teachers. The claim is that, by assigning too much homework, teachers do not accommodate students' other commitments, signaling that school is but one of many activities to prioritize.

Table 7.6 Thomas's Support Concept and the Homework Dilemma	
Support	**The Degree of Support that Political Groups Provide to Schools**
To what extent do authorities provide the necessary resources (i.e., supplies, facilities, professional incentives) to aid student learning?	One striking aspect regarding the overall issue of homework in the United States involved parental concerns about the weight of their children's backpacks. One middle school's in-house survey effort, for instance, suggested that backpack weights considerably exceeded physician-recommended thresholds. A remedy proposed was that schools furnish an extra set of books, one for home use and one for school use.
To what extent do teachers assume individual responsibility for student learning?	Parents questioned whether teachers were coordinating their assignments with each other. From parental perspectives, more than one teacher might assign a major project to be completed at or around the same date. The suggestion was that teachers spread out their assignments over a longer period of time to better facilitate time for enhanced student learning.
In what ways do various stakeholders exert influence over the education process? To what degree is there political intervention in educational affairs?	Parental demands to reduce homework in the United States seem to contradict their demands for more accountability. One implication is that students need to spend extra time on task—that is, out-of-school time, because in-class time is not plentiful enough to foster the desired levels of academic success.
To what degree is there public confidence in the work that teachers do? State confidence?	There was considerable parental approval of the quality of in-class methods underlying homework assignments. In other words, parents did not feel that their children lacked the tools necessary to perform and complete homework; rather it was a matter of sheer quantity of homework that bothered U.S. parents.

ultimately could become homework. Although this terminology would at its literal level imply that such schoolwork is to be done in schools or classrooms, exactly the opposite is true: The social expectation in Germany is that class work is something that naturally extends into the home. Somewhat ironically, in contrast, the long standing existence of the term "homework" in the United States suggests some cultural acceptance for the inevitability of out-of-school class work. Instead, the current discourse on homework tends to reject the necessity for out-of-school work, and the case points to the politicization of the issue at local levels.

Thus, in addition to illuminating issues in country-specific or more localized contexts, frameworks can also be applied to educational issues in more comparative, cross-national settings. In the next section, we use Harvey's quality definitions to consider the differences between Germany and the United States in relation to high-stakes standardized testing.

SCENARIO 2: THE STANDARDIZED TESTING DILEMMA

Although public calls for school standards are intended to increase certainty about U.S. educational goals, a problem encountered is the relative impossibility of standardizing all that schools are normally expected to do. For example, the focus on discrete subjects on high-stakes standardized tests could be considered out-of-step with the more diffuse curricular demands of the instructional day and week (e.g., special programs to respond to perceived social needs, such as peer mediation and conflict resolution) and other important noneducation functions, such as health screenings, other subject areas (e.g., music, art, physical education), and social events that most would see as appropriate (e.g., school assemblies). In other words, goals that are purported to be valuable but are less concrete (e.g., critical thinking, lifelong learning) are not as easily subject to evaluation through economical methods such as standardized testing.

An application of Harvey's alternative definitions of quality in relation to education reveals that some countries, like Germany, have methods other than tests that serve to sort and select students. In Germany, students, at about eleven years of age, enter one of three separate schools based on a combination of assessment measures, such as teacher recommendations, parental input, and students' academic performance over their previous schooling years. Students determined to be exceptional generally enter the *Gymnasium* for college preparatory coursework. Using a rationale that adopts a *fitness for purpose* outlook, it is possible to interpret the three-tiered system in positive terms: Each tier—*Gymnasium*, the *Realschule*, and the *Hauptschule*—offers a form of education that, in its own way, specializes instruction with an eye on optimizing students' readiness for certain vocational niches. However, the German *Gesammtschule* (comprehensive school) has emerged as an alternative. Many Germans, particularly among working classes in the northern provinces, believe the *Gesammtschule* embodies a more egalitarian approach to educating children and alleviates the high stakes nature of student placement into the traditional three-tier system.

In the United States, momentous decisions are increasingly based on standardized assessments. *High-stakes testing* refers not to any unified method or purpose but, rather, to the increasing use of educational assessments as qualifications for a number of consequential decisions, including student college admissions, eligibility for scholarships and other honors, teacher retention and remuneration, and so forth. Although the U.S. educational establishment has cautioned the broader public about the limits of overemphasizing standardized tests for such decisions, proponents of the so-called accountability movement see such assessments as necessary and appropriate. Recall that in previous chapters we indicate that the designation *exceptional* is meaningless without some comparison and, ultimately, sorting. High-stakes tests are seen as an instrument of this sorting impetus. In the United States, there is increasing pressure to use student performances on standardized tests in a larger pool of data by which schools themselves are rated. These performances are further abstracted to compare communities themselves. Realtors, for instance, might tout locations as desirable or less desirable based on such data. This case, then, demonstrates at least some overlap between *value for money* and *exceptionality* imperatives: For the sake of holding schools and teachers accountable to taxpayers, sorting of schools, communities, and children is generally tolerated as acceptable or even desirable.

Harvey and Knight's (1996) definitions of quality framework gives rise to a number of questions with which the issue of student sorting, in general, and high-stakes testing, in particular, might be analyzed. Consider the following:

- For what end is testing argued to be necessary? What parties are supposed to be most directly affected? What additional parties are affected and in what ways?
- Is the purpose of the tests to identify "best" and "worst" performers? If so, what are the proposed consequences of this sorting? If not, is sorting nonetheless a by-product of the process?
- Are costs to society (e.g., private taxpayers, corporate taxpayers) overtly or tacitly implicated in discourse surrounding the issue? If so, by what measure are costs assessed as reasonable or unreasonable?
- What educational purposes or end points are served by the status quo? To what parties are these educational results described as lacking? On what grounds?

In the next section, we explore the issue of moral education in American and Japanese contexts.

SCENARIO 3: THE MORAL EDUCATION DILEMMA

Moral education has constituted one approach to citizenship education in the United States. Moral education in Western societies has emerged out of three philosophical traditions—mechanism, romanticism, and dialecticism. Although each vision of moral education emphasizes a different understanding of the learner and the learning process, each defines—whether explicitly or implicitly—what constitutes appropriate behavior and right from wrong (Scharf, 1978). From a Western perspective, a mechanistic view of education, as advocated by Locke, emphasizes students' conformity to defined social rules, with good and bad behavior rewarded accordingly. Diametrically opposed to mechanism, Rousseau advocated a more romantic view of moral education, one focused on protecting children from unnecessary coercion and authority so that they might be relieved of societal pressures to develop into free moral beings (Scharf, 1978). Unlike the mechanistic and romantic conceptions of moral education, advocates of dialecticism—such as Socrates and Plato and contemporary theorists such as Piaget and Kohlberg—view education as a progression toward an ultimate truth achieved only through dialectical inquiry (Scharf, 1978). Although stage theories of moral development have their merits, it has been argued that moral reasoning must also be accompanied by changes in ethical behavior.

The increase in social ills such as violence, crime, and terrorism in the United States have prompted public outcry for schools to pay greater attention to students' moral development. This soul-searching for how moral education might be accomplished in schools has led some U.S. educators to consider how educators in other countries address character and ethical development in students. In Japan, for instance, "basic education" entails attention to not only academics but to social and moral aspects as well. It has been found that Japanese teachers tend to orchestrate learning in ways that help foster children's sense of belonging and enable children to contribute to their school in meaningful ways.

Characteristics such as persistence, responsibility, and respect are considered essential educational aims in Japan. *Ningen*, meaning "human beings," is a Japanese term that describes an educational philosophy of holistic development, whereby students' moral learning is nurtured in a school environment where human relations are considered an essential quality of the educated person. By the fourth grade, Japanese children have been exposed to schooling practices designed to develop cooperation, kindness, and responsibility (Linn, Lewis, Tsuchida, & Songer, 2000). In comparison, U.S. educational history is characterized by a "pendulum swing between social development and academic rigor" (Lewis, 1998, p. 192). Hence, moral education does not receive the consistent attention in U.S. classrooms that it does in Japan.

CONCLUSION

Analytic frameworks can help foster deeper reflection on educational dilemmas in country-specific contexts, as well as cross-national ones. Because the educational and social concerns of one nation are increasingly the concerns of other nations, the ability to view educational issues through a comparative lens will not only enlarge one's thinking about the issues, but also enable one to ask questions of education in other societies to gain insight about educational practice in one's own local context. Through the process of comparative perspective taking, analytic framework application, and educational issues examination, practitioners can learn from others in order to deepen their understandings of education–society relationships.

In the final chapter, we summarize the benefits of comparative perspective taking for practitioners and an issues orientation for the field of comparative education.

Sustaining Reflection

- Using two elements of Frank's framework, *policy effectiveness* and *theoretical adequacy*, continue to explore the issue of moral education.

- For *policy effectiveness*, consider the following: How do sources and degrees of support and dissent affect action on the issue of including moral aspects in school? What groups approve and disapprove of moral education in schools? Why? What monetary and other costs are associated with incorporating moral education in school? What kind of curricular content is used to teach moral education? Does it involve the school purchasing prepackaged educational materials? Whose interests are served and whose views are purported through such materials? Who absorbs the costs of these educational materials?

- For *theoretical adequacy*, consider the following: What reasoning and justifications are associated with the issue? What is the rationale for schools assuming responsibility for students' moral development? How does one define moral education in increasingly pluralistic societies? How should the school balance moral, ethical, and social development with other purposes of education, such as physical, aesthetic, and intellectual aims? What effects might more tangential factors have, such as the hidden curriculum? Is there a danger in inculcating students with particular ways of thinking about morality and cultivating specific behaviors?

References

Barber, B. (1993). America skips school: Why we talk so much about education and do so little. *Harper's, 287*(1722), 39–46.

Bond, M. H. (Ed.) (1986). *The psychology of the Chinese people.* Hong Kong, China: Oxford University Press.

Frank, A. G. (1972). Sociology of development and underdevelopment of sociology. In J. D. Cockcroft, A. G. Frank, & D. L. Johnson (Eds.) *Dependence and underdevelopment: Latin America's political economy* (pp. 321–397). Garden City, NY: Anchor.

Friederichs, J. O. (1991). Whose responsibility? The impact of imminent sociopolitical change on Hong Kong education. *International Review of Education, 37*(2), 193–209.

Guba, E. (1984). The effect of definitions of "policy" on the nature and outcomes of policy analysis. *Educational Leadership 42*(2), 63–70.

Harvey, L., & Knight, P. (1996). *Transforming higher education.* Buckingham, UK: Society for Research into Higher Education and Open University Press.

Hofstede, G. (1980, 1984). *Culture's consequences: International differences in work-related values.* Beverly Hills, CA: Sage.

Kralovec, E., & Buell, J. (2000). *The end of homework: How homework disrupts families, overburdens children, and disrupts learning.* Boston, MA: Beacon Press.

Lewis, C. C. (1998). What is a successful school? In E. R. Beauchamp (Ed.), *Dimensions of contemporary Japan: A collection of essays* (pp. 168–194). New York, NY: Garland.

Linn, M. C., Lewis, C., Tsuchida, I., & Songer, N. B. (2000, April). Beyond fourth-grade science: Why do U.S. and Japanese students diverge? *Educational Researcher, 29*(3), 4–14.

Paige, R. M. (1995). *Criteria for assessing educational reform and innovation.* Unpublished document, University of Minnesota, Department of Educational Policy and Administration.

Scharf, P. (1978). *Moral education.* Davis, CA: Responsible Action.

Shiraev, E., & Levy, D. (2001). *Introduction to cross-cultural psychology: Critical thinking and contemporary applications.* Boston, MA: Allyn & Bacon.

Thomas, R. M. (1983). The symbiotic linking of politics and education. In R. M. Thomas (Ed.), *Politics and education* (pp. 1–30). Oxford, UK: Pergamon.

Chapter 8

The Value of Comparative Education

There is a growing sense that the educational concerns of one nation are the concerns of other nations as well. Thus, in this book we have departed from the more traditional comparisons of educational systems and have used an issues orientation, exploring the aims and outcomes of schooling, educational access and opportunity, education authority and responsibility, and teacher professionalism. These issues are at the center of public scrutiny and debate. They generate considerable controversy and involve people in a variety of places and contexts. As Noll (1999) has contended, "the struggle to find the most appropriate answers to these questions now involves, as in the past, an interplay of societal aims, educational purposes, and individual intentions" (p. xv). This book—like the field of comparative education in general—alerts its users to enduring social questions as it introduces and discusses some of the ways in which these questions inform fundamental relationships between schools and their respective societies. *Issues* are matters over which informed and well-intentioned people disagree. They are points of conflict, controversy, and differences in values. Accepting the value-laden nature of educational issues requires mental nimbleness and the ability to suspend judgment so that multiple perspectives can contribute to a deeper understanding and genuine learning.

In a second departure from the mainstream, in the text we have also reflected a conviction that comparative education is beneficial and necessary not only for scholars and policy makers—the more traditional participants in the field—but for education's practitioners as well. As Gutek (1993) has reminded, teachers function simultaneously in two dimensions in their work: First, as citizens of particular nation–states, they foster students' national identity; and second, as citizens of a global society, they recognize that possibilities for human growth and threats to human survival transcend national boundaries. Teachers must therefore learn to look outward to other cultural contexts—to the practices of their counterparts in classrooms throughout the world and to the ways schools fill their roles in their respective societies. Comparative education, therefore, offers systematic exposure to these international settings.

A third facet of the book is to encourage a spirit of exploration in the field of comparative education—one for which figures such as Horace Mann have set precedent.

But this exploratory stance has not generally been extended to or encouraged in educational practitioners. Joining company with Stake (1978), an expert on educational assessment and evaluation, we observe that people intrinsically pursue the general by looking at the specific. People, that is, make sense out of the new circumstances they encounter by comparing these particulars to a universe that includes their own frames of reference. We have named the process of performing cross-cultural investigation and then deriving insights from these investigations the skill of *comparative perspective taking*.

Precisely because people naturally pursue comparisons and because these comparisons are often speculative, this book has lent discipline to the process of comparative exploration by encouraging and demonstrating use of frameworks for analysis. Systematic critique and reflection must accompany the general attitude of curiosity, interest, and inquiry regarding things foreign. Comparative investigations, whether speculative and exploratory or driven by more specific purposes, require framing and boundary. Analytic frameworks of the sort employed in this text offer method and direction to comparative investigations. True comparative perspective taking blends human curiosity with a system and method.

TENSIONS EXPLORED, LESSONS GAINED

The Latin terms for tension are *tensio* and *tensus* and emphasize the notion of forces and combinations of forces that create resistance. Educational issues are replete with tension. Schools are arenas in which tensions—combinations of forces—are at play. Understanding and coping with these tensions requires critical skills. Authentic critical mental capacity includes the ability to understand the political underpinnings of societal circumstances and provides a means for envisioning alternatives to prevailing institutions and circumstances (Kaplan, 1991). Comparative education—through the kinds of critical thinking it can foster—is geared toward enrichment and improvement.

Expressed as questions, the issues undertaken in this book take the following form:

- What are the purposes of schooling?
- What is "equitable education" and who decides?
- What is the appropriate balance between educator authority and accountability?
- What factors reinforce or hinder teacher professionalism?

Like the answers that emerge from these questions, an innate feature of an issue is that responses or resolutions are multiple, and ambiguity is never fully resolved. Moreover, the issues themselves are not discrete but are overlapping in marked ways.

In considering the purposes of schooling, for instance, we have observed that there are indeed specific societal expectations of skills and bases of knowledge that schools are to reinforce and convey, but that members of a given society expect less defined forms of learning to be undertaken in their nations' schools as well. The tension between stated aims or intents of schooling versus its effects on students is evidenced in class divisions in Hong Kong and class and ethnic divisions in Israel.

The cases of Brazil and South Africa have illustrated another persistent tension embodied in competing notions of educational quality. Contrasting connotations of the term "elite"—often used in discussions about education—capture much of this tension. A person might at one moment favorably tout education in an Ivy League or a prep school, while in the next moment criticize differentiated instruction at within-school levels as inappropriately "elitist," snobbish, or intended for a privileged few. The notion that education is, in the vision of Horace Mann, a "great equalizer," may offer an appealing image to many educators. Yet the goal of promoting individuals' social mobility through education has competitive aspects at its core. In the vernacular of Harvey and Knight (1996), society's interest in educational "consistency" and equality is at least in part at odds with "exceptionality"—with differentiated instruction and with distinguishing the best educational performances and institutions, for instance. Simultaneous pressure toward both these goals implies compromises at all levels. Societies have different rules in resolving questions of educational access and opportunity, and these rules tend to reflect their justifications for differences in social status. While societies reach different conclusions about these questions, however, the questions themselves are fundamental.

Preceding discussion of the tension between authority and accountability reveals that a teacher's work is shaped by goals that are sometimes specific and at other times less tangible. Teaching itself consists of both determinate and indeterminate tasks. Although few reject the notion that students learn important lessons about both social interaction and traditional school subjects, social skills are not subject to testing and assessment. For teachers, the tension implicit in this situation is clear: Although all kinds of learning are important, other forces such as standardized testing and other mechanisms of accountability convey the opposite message—one stressing the supreme importance of learning in the discrete subject areas.

Focus on accountability and authority provides insights into the equivocal nature of the rhetoric surrounding much current educational reform. Discourse about school improvement, for instance, often focuses on the desirability of a high quality education for all, as is true in England. But this egalitarian claim is at odds with some of the very practices associated with accountability-based school improvement policies. Societies tend, as prior discussion has shown, to compare schools in order to interpret relative performance and quality. This leads inevitably to distinctions between better and lesser schools—distinctions that rhetoric elsewhere indicates should be resisted. Schools often face ridicule and scrutiny when they move to limit or curtail their sorting practices in deference to expectations that education be equalized.

Discussion within the preceding chapters has also shown the tension between academic and vocational purposes of school is also persistent, and that this theme cuts across societies, as evidenced in the Israel and Hong Kong discussion, The academic vocational debate was also addressed within the German context. The former East Germany's devotion to equalized polytechnical education was widespread but ultimately undermined by its need for some means of preparing a cadre of political leaders—specialized work for which the polytechnical school was ill suited. "Social mobility," an often-heralded goal of education, prompts the question, ultimately, of who is to perform society's work with respect to tasks we encourage our children to "rise above" by applying themselves in school. Meanwhile, the traditional West German system of differentiated secondary level instruction features an institutionalized system of tracking that starts in the fifth and sixth grade.

Moreover, as teachers struggle for professional autonomy over their own work roles and responsibilities, their work continues to be the subject of public scrutiny and value judgments. Tensions also exist in relation to what is considered the appropriate balance between centralization and decentralization in education, in terms of who determines schooling aims, curricular content, and instruction. Democratic tendencies exhibited in some Japanese elementary classrooms, for instance, seem to conflict with the restricted opportunities of Japanese educators to engage in political and social action themselves. Yet, Japan's continuing prominence in mathematics and science achievement gives pause to policy makers and others in the United States who seek answers to improve academic achievement in their own educational settings. Answers to these questions have implications for how teacher professionalism is understood in various country contexts.

FINAL WORDS

Comparisons challenge us to expand our understanding beyond our own localized perspectives. Comparative perspective taking on educational issues enables us to recognize that any given issue transcends national boundaries and that every nation wrestles with the contradictions within and between its societal ideals and its educational realities.

In value-laden human contexts, social forces such as nationalism, pluralism, and societal needs greatly affect the kind of knowledge that is valued and the kinds of pedagogy and learning that schools promote. Further, these social forces coalesce to shape practitioners' work roles and responsibilities and to influence others' perceptions of schools and of teaching and learning processes. As educators navigate the confusing array of philosophies, viewpoints, practices, and alternatives, they encounter dilemmas.

Preceding discussion has explained that dialectics is a way of accounting for change from one state of affairs to another. Underneath any significant change is an opposition or conflict. Contradictions are not strictly battles between opposing sides, but they emerge in particular contexts. Further, among the laws of dialectics is the notion that although change is in a sense a negation of what is changed, the nature of change as a process depends on the thing ultimately changed. In this light, change is a process of development characterized as a progression rather than as sheer difference between one state and the next. The study of issues embraces the view of education as a process because of the ultimately irresolvable nature of issues and of the contradictions and compromises implicit in any proposed solution.

In commenting on the relatively low use of controversy in classrooms, Johnson and Johnson (1992) have observed that teachers are reluctant to spark disagreements despite the fact that, as Thomas Jefferson noted, "difference of opinion leads to inquiry" (p. 1:3). As our review of issues within their international contexts has suggested, the problems and questions confronting other societies and their educators are familiar to most members of the global community of educators.

Comparative education contributes to theory building about education–society relations. It has long contributed to the application of research for purposes of improved practice. But it has a significant role to play in the preparation of more insightful educators and, so, in the nurturing of more thoughtful classrooms. As Epstein (1983) has written, comparative education has practical usefulness, because it helps educators decide what issues are of primary importance and identify factors that are germane to educators' own efforts to improve the educational experiences of students. Comparative education can foster international understanding, individual growth, national development, and global cooperation. Due to such benefits of comparative education, it is our hope that practitioners be encouraged to view education from multiple perspectives, thereby contributing to educational reform and progress.

References

Burbules, N. C., & Berk, R. (1999). Critical thinking and critical pedagogy: Relations, differences, and limits. In T. S. Popkewitz, & L. Felder (Eds.), *Critical theories in education: Changing terrains of knowledge and politics* (pp. 45–65). New York, NY: Routledge.

Epstein, E. (1983). Currents left and right: Ideology in comparative education. *Comparative Education Review, 27*(1), 3–29.

Gutek, G. L. (1993). *American education in a global society: Internationalizing teacher education.* New York, NY: Longman.

Johnson, D. W., & Johnson, R. T. (1992). *Creative controversy: Intellectual challenge in the classroom.* Edina, MN: Interaction Book Company.

Kaplan, L. D. (1991). Teaching intellectual autonomy: The failure of the critical thinking movement. *Educational Theory, 41*(4), 361–370.

Noll, J. W. (Ed.) (1999). *Taking sides: Clashing views on controversial educational issues* (10th ed.). Guilford, CT: Dushkin/McGraw-Hill.

Stake, R. E. (1978). The case study method in social inquiry. *Educational Researcher, 6*(7), 5–8.

Glossary

Note: Citations that appear within glossary definitions are listed in the chapter where the term first appears.

accountability   in general, the norm at the center of a relationship of obligation. In traditional usage, being accountable connotes trust in that people obligated will adhere to expectations without special monitoring by parties to whom they are accountable. In the education discourse of some countries, however, accountability has a more specific meaning, referring to the desired outcome of strengthened scrutiny and surveillance—a perceived remedy for weak teaching and school governance. Unlike the traditional use of the term, accountability in this sense implies strict oversight and a general lack of trust.

alienation, estrangement   from the Marxist perspective, alienation or estrangement is a consequence of peoples' increased concentration on the process of work and their concurrent distancing from the social context of that work. Increased specialization, especially under capitalism, reduced peoples' sense of purpose by undermining their ability to identify themselves with an end product of value to the others in society. Estrangement or alienation also reinforces a sense of powerlessness, numbing alienated workers as to their exploited condition and therefore mediating against their desire to change or improve conditions for themselves, let alone to press society ahead toward the attainment of social justice.

apartheid   a policy of racial separation associated with South Africa's recent past; the term is probably best understood in terms of its most literal translation, "aparthood." In that light, we see apartheid as an embodiment of formalized discrimination, in which a state of separation is maintained as a matter of policy.

authority   generally, a rationale or belief that power is legitimately asserted. Just as sociologists have defined many different types of power, several distinctions have been articulated differentiating among various types of authority. For teachers, expert authority might be particularly important because of its basis in recognized expertise such as knowledge or ability.

center, decenter, recenter   having two important meanings in comparative education theory; in poststructuralism, first, constructs or elements at the center are those accepted by society as mainstream; decentering is the intellectual exercise of exposing or of making implicit hierarchies explicit, and recentering is a matter of reversing such explicit hierarchies in a conscious effort to challenge the superior/inferior relationships that the center dictates (e.g., the distinction of developed/underdeveloped, see *dichotomy*). The goal of this work of explicating and reversing linguistic and conceptual hierarchies is to propagate new interpretations of "mainstream," or, less radically, to promote new understandings of an entity formerly relegated to an inferior position or role. But most vital in the postmodernist schema, these understandings of the essence of such a formerly marginalized entity should be in its own terms rather than in terms of a dominating other entity. *Center,* in its second connotation, stemming from dependency theory, is synonymous with the term *core* (see *core/periphery*). The fact that there are two meanings of *center* helps to explain partial affinities between dependency theory and poststructuralist/postmodernist thought, to clarify differing frames of reference of contemporary theoretical discourse, and even to account for some muddled argumentation.

centralizing   centralization (also see *decentralization*) generally refers to the level of the major locus of school governance. A very centralized school system would be one in which a single office or ministry made a set of decisions to which all schools were then required to adhere. Levels of centralization differ greatly from country to country. For instance, the United States is generally perceived to have the least centralized governance, and Japan is among the most centralized of the industrialized nations. See *decentralizing* for additional relevant information.

charter school   in the United States, a school that is publicly funded like traditional schools, but, unlike the traditional school structure, is not under the oversight of a local school district. Charter schools are sometimes called "public school academies," particularly by supporters. The term is a reminder that definitions of *public school* differ from culture to culture. In Germany, for instance, parochial schools are publicly funded, rendering that construct imperfect as a test of an institution's status as public.

choice   a theory or general set of strategies bound by the common claim that school choice introduces the prospect of "winning" or "losing" students and that this introduces competition among schools. Competition, in turn, is seen by some as a force for positive innovation, responsiveness, and maintenance of quality.

colonialism   having various manifestations, classical colonialism features overt nation-to-nation control or domination, whereas neocolonialism consists of the more covert but still deliberate policies by which industrialized nations maintain domination over less developed countries. Internal colonialism, meanwhile, is the domination within the borders of a country of one group by another (Kelly and Altbach, 1978).

comparative education   draws on multiple disciplines (e.g., sociology, political science, psychology, anthropology) to examine education in developed and developing countries.

comparison   a process of studying two or more things to see how they are alike or different—gives attention to certain aspects through the copresence of the other (Eckstein, 1983).

core/periphery   an adaptation in dependency theory of Marxist tenets, core countries are those that occupy positions of advantage relative to the peripheral countries. Dependency theory describes the world's countries as a single society with class structures among nations accounting for underdevelopment and exploitation. Dependency theory's core and periphery correlate to the bourgeoisie and proletariat classes in classical Marxism.

correspondence   a neo-Marxist construct used to critique circumstances in schools in the United States and elsewhere in the capitalist economies of the industrialized West. *Correspondence* refers to the presence in schools of elements that correspond to counterparts in the world of work. Schools exhibit structures and practices, such as their hierarchic organization of authority (with principals in charge of teachers, and teachers, in turn, in charge of students), that have a purpose in preparing more compliant workers.

craft knowledge   a term that refers to the wisdom that teachers develop through firsthand experience and from which they use to address daily issues that arise as they interact and work with students. Both craft knowledge and scientific knowledge (i.e., theories and techniques) guide teaching practice.

critical perspective   considered a primary purpose of the foundations of education, a critical perspective refers to student development of the ability to question the contradictions and inconsistencies of educational beliefs, policies, and practices.

cultural capital   a term, coined by French sociologist Pierre Bourdieu, is used to describe the kind of knowledge, learning styles, and language of the upper and middle classes. These attributes enable students from such socioeconomic backgrounds to experience success in school. Language, for example, is a form of cultural capital and functions to differentiate the treatment of schoolchildren.

cultural reproduction   a process by which class-based differences, cultural and linguistic practices, and politics are embedded in the school's formal curriculum.

culture   the transmission of shared values accomplished, in part, through the schooling of new members (i.e., children or members from other cultures) into the society's shared meanings.

curriculum   although traditionally defined as a student's formal course of study, curriculum has come to encompass the entirety of a student's school experience, whether those experiences are intentionally planned by educators or occur unintentionally.

decentralizing   a decentralized school system is one in which decisions are made independently by several generally more local agencies rather than in a single more central place. Degree of centralization can be fluid. For example, although the United States has perhaps the most decentralized school governance, there is movement in the direction of centralization both from local to state levels and state to the federal level (e.g., requirements mandated regarding testing, discussions about standardizing the curriculum). See *centralizing* for more information.

deconstruction   from literary criticism, a type of close reading aimed at identifying textual claims' hidden but fundamentally contradictory assumptions (see *text/narrative*). Less formally, because poststructuralists hold language to be a principal determinant of human perception, deconstruction is the wider effort in the social sciences to dismantle and question claims and their underlying purposes and presuppositions.

developing, developed, underdeveloped   a set of words often used to differentiate the relative economic status of various countries. Although useful for discussion, perhaps, a liability of this method of grouping is that it employs oversimplifications that can obscure the unique experiences of each culture in each category.

dialectics   systematic study of change in human conditions. Dialectic analysis normally likens social change to an argument or conversation among people explaining progress as negotiated movement from existing circumstance (thesis) through a reconciliation of this circumstance with an alternative (antithesis) toward the production of a new status quo (synthesis).

dichotomy, duality   a descriptive simplification of complex elements in terms of a pair that is argued to be exemplary of a key difference. Poststructuralist analysis often critiques dualities and dichotomies (see *deconstruction*), arguing that one element of such a linguistic pairing tends to exist within the pair only because of its dissimilarity with the other term rather than because of its own innate, essential, and unique qualities. Dualities are therefore particularly exemplary of the way language can produce inaccuracies in our observations of the world, shaping our perceptions and conceptions of objects and events we purport to observe and describe "objectively."

discipline   connotes dedication to a specified set of rules and standards. Any discipline's adherents dedicate themselves to techniques and procedures belonging to that discipline while implicitly or explicitly rejecting methods and techniques of other paths. Along with the rigorous adherence to discipline-specific inquiry comes a tendency to subordinate or dismiss other disciplinary perspectives and thereby limit understanding.

duality   see *dichotomy*.

egalitarian, egalitarianism   describing a spirit or mind-set that values equality in social endeavors. In the realm of schools, this spirit can manifest itself in concern that school funding be equalized or that the same curriculum be made available to everyone. Contrast *elite*.

elite, elitism   describing a mind-set that values or promotes differentiation in social endeavors and circumstances, particularly differentiations that result in privileges or other positive distinctions. Compare *egalitarian*.

endogenous   from biology, refers to something produced within an organism. Comparisons of ecosystems to organisms is embodied in the term.

equality   a norm referring to parity or sameness of conditions for all members of a society; the term often assumes the form of a slogan, which is an often-repeated term or phrase that is rarely defined in spite of its generally abstract nature. This and other slogans are rarely operationalized in political or popular discourse—that is, translated from the abstract into concrete policies and practices. See also *liberty, quality.*

estrangement   see *alienation.*

externalization   Circumstances of separation between the researcher and practitioner communities. Two general factors contribute to this separation or "externality." First, the distance between the researcher and the object of inquiry is presumed to promote levels of objectivity required by traditional empirical scientific inquiry; this is supposed to promote the rationality and impartiality of judgments about the significance of aspects observed. Second, researcher specialization in the study of research techniques makes the preoccupations of the researcher separate from or "external" to those of the practitioner.

field   draws upon a variety of disciplines to better understand the complexity of particular educational phenomena; as such, a field is larger than a discipline.

hegemony   the process by which dominant social groups construct a social consensus—a consensus that is based on the dominant groups' views and legitimated through positions in the media, government, churches, and schools that reinforce their power.

hidden curriculum   the implicit messages students receive about proper values and behaviors, such as punctuality, neatness, and appropriate interaction between teachers and students.

ideology   a systematized body of ideas; a process by which one social group exerts its own views and beliefs onto other social groups; in turn, the dominated groups come to understand and accept this distorted view as reality.

indoctrination   refers to educators' or others' intent to restrict information from students or to teach false content.

instrumentalization, instrumentalism   connotes movement toward attending in stepwise fashion to procedural concerns rather than to context-sensitive approaches. A concern with instrumentalism, some feel, is that effective behavior in complex human contexts requires human judgment, which in an instrumentalized world is discredited in favor of repeated and repeatable actions; instrumentalism is habitual or routine commitment to this breaking down of complex tasks into sets of procedures; instrumentalized human activity connotes close regulation or self-regulation.

interpretive perspective   considered a primary purpose of the foundations of education, interpretive perspective refers to concepts and theories derived from the humanities and social sciences to examine and explain educational phenomena by considering the diverse cultural, philosophical, and historical contexts that affect the meaning and interpretations of that phenomena.

latent functions   the unintended or unrecognized outcomes of schooling.

legitimate knowledge   the ideological dominance by powerful groups over less powerful groups in a society and the process by which these ideological messages are communicated through the educational curriculum and practices.

legitimate power   the ability of the dominant group to exert influence through a set of values that have been internalized by the dominated groups. In this way, power and authority are entrusted to the dominant group.

liberal   ambiguous as used in the intertwined contexts of politics and economic policy, liberal economic theories generally argue in favor of fair trade and, thus, against regulatory or managing roles for government; but these are tenets that are otherwise generally associated with a conservative or "right leaning" (rather than progressive or "leftist") political persuasion.

liberty   referring in this case to the notion of freedom, this term is typically used as a slogan—a term or phrase that is repeated often and assumed to be widely understood; slogans can be problematic because people can often decouple such terms from their concrete actions, failing to consider how their concrete policies or practices do or do not embody the slogans to which they subscribe in the abstract. Sometimes one slogan contradicts or disrupts another once operationalized or made concrete. One theorist, for instance, has claimed that, since people generally associate "liberty" with "democracy," they often come to assume that if people are simply left alone (i.e., "liberated"), democracy emerges naturally—a position he rejects in favor of a more proactive and participatory vision. See also *equality, quality.*

manifest functions   the intended purposes or aims of schooling often stated in government documents and school mission statements.

methodology   the kind of reasoning applied to scientific or philosophical inquiry.

mobilization of bias   a description of politics; groups or people are political whenever they assert their own narrow interests.

modernity, the modern problem   foundational to postmodern thought, the problem of modernity is typified by realizations that human explanations of the natural world are structures of society rather than of nature itself, that psychological wants and needs shape conceptions of "truth," and that absolute and conclusive verification of truth is ultimately impossible.

narrative   see *text.*

neocolonial   colonial-like exploitation even after a nation has achieved independence from a mother country; a deliberate process of domination by industrialized over less industrialized nations occurring through a variety of avenues, such as publishing centers, foreign aid, and technical assistance provided. See *colonialism* for other associated forms.

norm   broadly, a norm is both a sort of average of what currently exists as well as a projection of judgment as to what should exist. In social systems, too, norms can serve as both averages of typical social behaviors and expectations and as visions of what behaviors would be desirable. Some (e.g., Fukuyama, 1999) hold that societal agreement about norms and values tends to result in a larger pool of "cultural capital," making other forms of social interaction and progress easier.

normative perspective   considered a primary purpose of the foundations of education, normative perspective refers to the ability to examine and explain education in relation to differing value orientations and assumptions about schooling. Educational policy is examined in light of these differing value positions, and educators are encouraged to develop their own values about education.

otherness   from Foucault, the human experience or existence of those outside the cultural and social mainstream. Because the *other* is at once both defined by yet excluded from the cultural mainstream or center (see *center*), the experience of otherness is especially exemplary of the paradoxical and ambiguous nature of modernity (see *modernity/the modern problem*). Otherness is also emblematic of the problems that poststructuralists emphasize regarding the ways people create distinctions among themselves and preserve and reinforce these distinctions linguistically, often in order to create and nourish positions of power and relative advantage.

plus-sum   a win-win scenario, or one in which all those involved in an interaction benefit to some degree through their participation. The term is used broadly in the social sciences and is descriptive of the ideology underlying consensus perspectives such as modernization and human capital formation, which involve optimism regarding the beneficial nature—both within nations and across the globe—of economic development. The term derives from game theory, which was developed primarily in the mathematical subfield of probability and is now widely influential in areas such as economic forecasting. Contrast with *zero-sum.*

postmodernism   stemming from the modern problem (see *modernity/the modern problem*), postmodernism is therefore a spirit of "incredulity toward metanarratives," in the words of Lyotard, that is, of skepticism regarding the usefulness or even the plausibility of overarching theories. Postmodernists, arguing that truth is subjective, tend to critique dominant social structures and norms showing how they are based on general assumptions about natural order that cannot be verified, stressing the importance of perspective, and/or demonstrating the merits and equal validity of localized and context-laden alternative conceptions of social order.

poststructuralism   a generalization to the social and even the natural sciences of arguments in linguistics that the object(s) of scientific study are unobservable. Because of ways language shapes perceptions, the object of any scientific field (and not linguistics alone; see *structuralism*) are not absolute, certain, and objective, but instead are subject to perceptions imposed by observer viewpoint and amplified through observers' attempts to describe their observations.

practical social competence   the ability to make informed decisions in one's daily life. Such competence is developed through reflective thinking and can increase or decrease in a person and a society, as a whole, on the basis of the degree of exposure and practice citizens have in reflecting and acting prudently on issues at the personal and societal levels.

professional, professionalism, professionalization   commonly understood as one who renders a public service that requires the use of particular intellectual skills that are developed through a period of specialized training; professionalism is the particular expertise, authority, and autonomy of teachers to exert authority and direction in relation to their work and standards for effective teaching. Professionalization, in education, refers to a set of reforms and a body of discourse attending to the status of teaching and the ways this might be elevated through revisions to entry requirements, licensing practices, national certification for teachers, peer evaluations and mentoring, and a number of other strategies.

quality   like *liberty* and *equality,* this term is often used as a slogan in referring the discourse surrounding education to some high standard. Slogans are terms that are abstract but are often used in more specific realms. They are often useful in politicized discourse. Because slogans are both familiar and abstract, the "dirty work" of translating the abstract term into specific plans or policies might not be necessary at the level of discourse, even though such "dirty work" is ultimately unavoidable and brings to light contradictions with other values and disagreements about those specific plans of action. See also *liberty* and *equality* for more about the nature of slogans.

socialization   the process by which citizens learn the rules, traditions, practices, and customs of the society in which they reside; the ways a society passes its values and standards to the next generation.

social mobility   the ability of an individual to raise his or her socioeconomic standing during life; citizens' movement, either upward or downward, in relation to their social positions over the course of a lifetime or between subsequent generations.

status discrepancy   the difference between personal and societal perception as to the value of one's work. Teaching in the United States has been described as an example of pronounced status discrepancy, because teachers view their work as important but feel they do not receive the status from the public.

stratified curriculum curriculum that is ordered in a logical fashion, whereby students progress from simple to more complex materials and skills. Judgments are made about students' abilities to handle complex material and, as such, those identified as capable of complex mastery are exposed to higher order thinking and curriculum designed to meet their needs. Oftentimes, curriculum, stratified under the pretense of efficiency, actually serves to categorize students based on their socioeconomic backgrounds and to lower the expectations underachievers hold for themselves.

structuralism originally, linguistic theory emerging in the late 19th and early 20th century that focused on the relationship between sound (signifier) and concept (signified). Because this relationship is unobservable, early structuralists—most notably, Ferdinand Saussure—held the object of study in linguistics to be uniquely abstract, focusing on "representations of representations." Poststructuralists disagree with Saussure's claim that this characteristic of linguistics is in fact unique to linguistics.

symbiotic describes the process of distinct entities influencing the fate of each other.

symbolic action refers to the means by which the government, the educational system, or other entity expresses concern for school problems without actually providing the resources for problems to be solved or changes to occur.

teacher autonomy the opportunity afforded teachers to make their own judgments and decisions about their work and roles and that of their students.

temporal distancing tendencies for colonizing peoples to excuse themselves of responsibility for exploitive conditions in colonies on the grounds that more primitive moral rules apply in the less developed world due to societal immaturity (see Fabian, 1983).

text, narrative poststructuralists see language as the principal determinant of perception. Thus, texts are taken broadly to be human representations of "reality" that are intrinsically subjective. From the perspective of poststructuralism or postmodernism, pictures, then, or other observations of life are themselves texts or narratives and are only appropriately treated as subjective representations.

zero-sum a scenario in which gains made by some involved in an interaction come at the expense of others. The term is descriptive of Marxism's general conflict perspective, which, in comparative education, systematically questions who gains and who loses in programs of national development. The term derives from game theory. Contrast with *plus-sum*.

Author Index

Note: *f* indicates figure.

Subject Index